MAGIC & MADNESS

MAGIC & MADNESS

The Midwest Radio Phenomenon

James Laffey

This book is dedicated to the Midwest Radio 'family' of listeners. Thank you for inviting us into your homes since 1985.

Picture on previous page: a packed house in Midas Nightclub in Ballyhaunis on December 30, 1988, to mark the closure of the pirate Midwest Radio. *Picture: Michael Connaughton*

Design by Seán Lynch, Derrynagullaun, Knockmore

ISBN No.: 978-1-9998911-2-1

CONTENTS

FOREWORD

'The radio of the people'

By **Michael Hughes,** Chairperson, Midwest Radio

THE directors, management and staff of County Mayo Radio Ltd. (trading as Midwest Radio) are pleased to bring you this history of radio, local radio and Midwest Radio in particular. We sincerely thank you for your support over the last 30 years. We hope you will enjoy this history of Midwest Radio, which has been researched, compiled and edited by James Laffey.

On July 19, 1989, we published our challenging "ambition" that Midwest Radio would *"act as a binding force, to cement the local community and facilitate the social, economic and cultural development of the region for the future"*.

Now, 30 years later, we share our reflections with you on how we succeeded or failed to achieve our challenging ambition and to what extent we really are.... "The radio of the people".

Throughout the chapters of this book you will find several examples of local characters, stories, events, milestones, achievements, disappointments and developments, all of which have moulded Midwest Radio into what it is today – the top-rated local radio station in Ireland.

In our modern, internet-connected and smartphone-dominated world, it is easy to forget our local history and traditions. Local radio is one excellent method of capturing and communicating the essence of our communities' history, traditions, culture and values. As quoted within this book: *"Midwest wasn't just bringing radio to the people; it was bequeathing the rich cultural heritage of our forefathers to a new generation."*

We believe the successful development of Midwest Radio has been mainly attributable to the following:

- Listening, understanding and interacting with the needs and wishes of the listeners in our 'catchment area'. Our catchment area includes all of Co Mayo and listeners from parts of the surrounding counties.
- Serving the needs of listeners through constantly developing our broadcasting facilities, which include studios, transmission equipment and outside broadcast unit and, most importantly, our programme content and schedule.
- Promoting our service to advertisers locally, regionally and nationally by highlighting the exceptionally high listenership loyalty as independently certified by the JNLR (Joint National Listenership Research).
- Prudent financial management by always attempting to invest as much as required but avoiding the trap of unnecessary or unproductive spending.

We constantly try to have a deep understanding of the needs of our listeners, our shareholders, our advertisers, our staff and contracted programme presenters and, of course, the Broadcast Authority of Ireland (BAI), which regulates our industry. In theory, this sounds easy but, of course, in reality there are always challenges in balancing the multiple aspirations and needs of all the participants or stakeholders in Midwest Radio.

Our shareholders were very diverse and varied. The pre-licence Midwest Radio operators Paul Claffey and Chris Carroll successfully formed our consortium in 1989 comprising (in alphabetical order): Connaught Airport Ltd, *Connaught Telegraph* newspaper, Federation of Western Churches, NCF Co-Operative Society Ltd. (now trading as Aurivo) and the *Western People* newspaper.

Paul and Chris had already "tested the waters" during the affectionately known 'era of pirate radio', which I prefer to refer to as 'pre-licence' local radio operators (after all, if they really were pirates, they would neither have been charged nor would have paid government taxes). Paul and Chris had discovered many elements of the style of broadcasting that would be attractive and unique to the west of Ireland and would be practically impossible for a national broadcaster or other local station to compete against.

Pictured at the Ardilaun Hotel, Salthill, Co Galway, in March 1989 at the IRTC oral hearing for the Mayo broadcasting franchise were some members of the Midwest Radio board from left: Tom Courell, *Connaught Telegraph;* Michael Hughes, Chairperson; Terry Reilly, *Western People,* and Paul Claffey. Picture: Michael Connaughton

Connaught Regional Airport was at an early stage of development at that time and its board of directors decided to invest in the Midwest Radio group as a useful media for communicating in its primary catchment area.

The *Connaught Telegraph,* while a potential competitor to local radio, decided to participate in the new shareholder group of Midwest Radio.

The experience of the *Connaught Telegraph* provided an invaluable input to Midwest Radio in the areas of newsgathering and current affairs.

The *Western People* equally supported Midwest Radio in the areas of the newsgathering, sport and current affairs.

Despite the *Connaught Telegraph* and *Western People* being competitors – both between themselves and the fledgling Midwest Radio – their respective nominees to the board of directors ALWAYS communicated in an open, objective, positive and professional manner. Equally they fully respected their primary fiduciary responsibilities as directors of Midwest Radio.

The Federation of Western Churches invested in the Midwest consortium with a view to supporting our efforts in developing a radio service, which would succeed in winning, holding and serving our listenership and to do so with a spirit of excellence, truth and integrity – with a Christian ethos. Serving our listenership was indeed no small challenge – and it is still a big challenge today.

The station went on to develop respected religious programmes such as *Faith Alive.*

NCF Co-Op invested in the Midwest consortium as a support to a local communications network across much of the area of the west and northwest, where many of its shareholders, milk suppliers and customers lived. Here again the radio would go on to develop such informative programmes as *Farming Matters.*

With such a mixed group of shareholders and their respective differing objectives, it would, indeed, be easy to understand that many of our board meetings might be filled with conflict and 'hidden agendas'. However, the reality was that we almost always reached decisions though objective debate and consensus, rather than resorting to subjective argumentation and voting.

I wish to record our appreciation to all of our shareholders for their enduring patience for a financial return on their respective investments during the early years of Midwest Radio's operation and development. The board were at all times loyal to our agreed 'low-cost generic strategy', which enabled us to adequately invest in suitable programming and adequate broadcasting facilities, while needing limited borrowings. All of this enabled us to develop a solid and sustainable financial structure for Midwest Radio. Spending too much at the start-up stage of any business has proven to be a primary cause of business failure. So, our humble beginnings with our 'basic but functional' studios in a house at Abbey Street in Ballyhaunis were a deliberate part of our start-up strategy.

In 1989, Midwest Radio was the first radio station outside Dublin to go on air under the new licensing arrangements. So, there were no rules or precedents to follow, except for the broad requirements laid down by the Independent Radio and Television Commission (IRTC). Effectively, we had to make up the operating rules as we went along.

The principal sources of revenue which local radio has in Ireland are advertising and sponsorship. There are no government subsidies and many levies must be paid. Our advertisers and sponsors have provided us with the lifeblood of survival and growth. Whether they are local, regional or national advertisers, their loyalty to Midwest Radio needs to be constantly supported with evidence that their message reaches their target audience. We continue to maintain our 'pole position' by having independently certified listenership figures (from the JNLR), which now demonstrate that our listenership is greater than the combined listenership of all other radio broadcasters within our franchise area. Consequently, advertising and sponsorship on Midwest Radio continues to be good business practice for our advertisers and we constantly strive to keep it that way.

Our management, staff and contracted presenters, of course, continue to play a vital role in our progress. Whether we talk of our technical, administrative, programming or commercial/sales departments, our team successfully compete with the best and we constantly strive for excellence – tough as that may be. Programme management is a very complex and challenging task. Our aim is to reflect, listen, adapt and serve the changing needs of the vast majority of our listeners within our area. In this regard, it is sometimes necessary to make hard decisions relating to programme formats and presenters. Understandably, such decisions have occasionally caused upset to and conflict with passionate presenters.

However, that's the reality of striving for excellence and it is simply not possible to please all of the people all of the time. Such is the normal 'loneliness of leadership', when unpopular decisions must be made.

Indeed, we can have the most magnificent strategies and plans at director and management level BUT as the saying goes, "strategy without implementation is hallucination". So, our board of directors have a deep respect for the success that our management, staff and contract presenters have achieved through their creativity, flexibility and persistent hard work over the last 30 years. We are particularly indebted to our core of long-term staff that have been with us since the beginning and have been consistently committed, loyal, flexible and professional in the service they have provided.

The Broadcasting Authority of Ireland (BAI), formerly known as the IRTC, regulates our industry on behalf of the Department of Communications, Climate Action and Environment. The BAI sets the operating standards for local radio; it awards the local radio licences and oversees our compliance with its operating standards as specified in our licence. Consequently, it is vital for Midwest Radio to maintain effective communications with the BAI. We have enjoyed excellent collaboration with the management and staff of the BAI for the last 30 years.

Our greatest disappointment by far over this period was the loss of the local radio franchise by Northwest Radio when it came up for renewal in 2003. This issue is dealt with in some detail in the book so I will let readers make up their own minds about the unfortunate saga. However, the sense of bewilderment among the board at Midwest at the BAI's inexplicable decision was only compounded in 2004 when Northwest was voted Irish Local Radio Station of the Year.

Despite the huge disappointment at the loss of the Northwest franchise, our management and staff 'got over it', survived and still thrived. The following inspiring thought from the formidable "Stockdale Paradox" proved relevant:

"You must never confuse faith that you will prevail in the end, which you can never afford to lose,
with the discipline to confront the most brutal facts of your current reality, whatever they might be".

Admiral Jim B. (James Bond) Stockdale
23/12/1923-07/05/2005

It proved once again that the real test of management is not how we deal with success but rather how we recover from challenge and adversity.

For the future we expect the pace of change in our business to increase. In the words of Saint Cardinal John Henry Newman:

"To live is to change, and to be perfect is to have changed often."

Though we are far from perfect, we constantly work to develop our capacity and ability to change and adapt, while not forgetting our valued roots and our unique past. Our operating environment is changing particularly in the areas of social change, technological change, commercial change and legislative change. On the social side we see the influences of age profiling, consumer behaviour, local community challenges and opportunities. Technological changes are most evident in the areas of digital media, which is driving changes in listenership and advertising trends. On the commercial front we have changes driven by the consolidation in retailing and online shopping. Additionally, the economic recovery has been very slow to arrive in many parts of rural Ireland. Change on the legislative front is seen in the various developments of corporate governance, financial reporting, industrial relations, data protection, health and safety etc.

For the future we will continue to have a clear vision and strategy in order to maintain and develop our value to our listeners and viewers, advertisers, staff, contract presenters and shareholders.

I was born 'in the dark' in 1952 before the rural electrification scheme came to Knockdoe, Claregalway.

Having worked as a business manager and director in many companies, countries and continents, an enduring highlight of my life is my role as chairperson of the board of Midwest Radio for the last 30 years. The people with whom we work are outstanding, the challenges were – and continue to be – huge, the business is, of course, serious and the enjoyment and enrichment I have gained have been fantastic. The qualities of energy, creativity and commitment of many of the Midwest Radio team are 'world class'.

Whether working in Ireland, Spain, Great Britain, Sweden, China, Portugal or elsewhere in the world, I could always be assured that the periodic Midwest Radio issues, board meetings and AGMs would bring my feet back to earth and back to the wholesome challenges and positive, good-humoured and creative attitudes of life within the world of Midwest Radio.

I thank all of our directors (past and present), our company secretaries, management, staff, contract presenters and professional advisors for their excellent collaboration, teamwork, professionalism and support. They have been a classic example of a well-respected slogan of the co-operative movement, which reads: *Working Together Means Winning Together.*

We hope you enjoy reading our history of Midwest Radio's 'Magic & Madness' as much as we enjoyed making this history with you.

PROLOGUE

The cheques were a hoppin' and a leppin'

IT was well after closing time in Midas Nightclub in Ballyhaunis. Big Gene Stuart and the rest of the members of his band, The Homesteaders, had stashed their gear in the van and were enjoying a drink at the bar before they commenced the long trip back to their native Tyrone. There'd be the customary British Army checkpoints to negotiate at the border but at least dawn would be rising for the last leg of their journey into Dungannon.

The band members chatted uneasily amongst themselves as the nightclub proprietor morosely served the drinks. It hadn't been a good night and everyone knew it. The club's Sunday Country Nights were only running for a few weeks but already the venture had the gloomy air of a Hank Williams song about it; and the nightclub proprietor certainly looked like he was in the mood to uncork a whiskey bottle and listen to some Hank.

The band members had seen it all before. This was one of those wretched nights in the entertainment business when the optimism of early evening had given way to the deflation of early morning as the expected crowds failed to materialise. Stuart and the rest of his band were long enough on the road to know when a dancehall proprietor was down on his luck and the man serving the drinks certainly possessed the demeanour of someone who had enjoyed better nights.

The band members shifted awkwardly on their stools and threw each other a few knowing glances as they made small talk. It was a situation where a person was as well to just finish their drink quickly and hit the road because there was nothing to be said to a man who had just paid a band for playing to a half-empty dancehall. One thing was certain: it would be a surprise if they were performing in Midas Nightclub again because this place was unlikely to be open for much longer, and its owner had the forlorn look of a man at the very end of his tether.

Just a few months earlier it all seemed so different when Paul Claffey confidently told the *Western People* that Midas Restaurant and Nightclub was about to become the biggest entertainment venue in the West. The Castlerea man had been operating the revamped dancehall with limited success for the past few years but the conversion of part of the venue into a restaurant gave him new cause for optimism. The restaurant licence meant Midas was now able to serve alcohol to its patrons, a crucial advantage in an entertainment industry dominated by hotel-based nightclubs where patrons could purchase alcohol into the early hours of the morning. The days of the mineral bar were long gone and ghostly empty dancehalls like Pontoon were a testament to those changing trends; either you moved with the times or the times moved without you.

But Claffey had been slow to change. At the start of the decade, while still in his mid-twenties, Claffey was operating the Midnight Club in Ballaghaderreen. It was one of the most modern and innovative dancehalls west of the Shannon and the crowds were piling in to enjoy the music of everyone from Horslips to Big Tom. But already the disco craze that had taken root in New York and London in the late 1970s was sweeping into provincial Ireland, and nightclubs – with full bar facilities – were quickly supplanting the traditional dancehalls of the showband era.

"Because I didn't drink back then I underestimated the strength of a bar," he recalls. "I thought people would enjoy the dancing and the live music. I didn't realise the strength of the pint."

Within a matter of months, a business that was painstakingly fashioned over half a decade came crashing down around the ears of its perplexed promoter; to say he didn't see it coming would be an understatement but then change tends to catch the most surefooted of us off guard.

"Legislation was passed that hotels could get late-night exemptions for discos and in one fell swoop it killed the dancehalls. One minute I was booking all the big names in Irish music and the next I was closing the doors in Ballaghaderreen and a couple of other places that I was leasing in Castlerea and Gort. I went from driving a BMW when I was 23 to driving a Fiat 127! That change in the legislation literally wiped me out overnight – and a lot more like me. We became yesterday's men."

But Paul Claffey wasn't a quitter. He'd been earning his own living since leaving school at 14 and wasn't prepared to join Castlerea's ever-lengthening dole queue. Now in his mid-thirties and the father of two young children, emigration wasn't really an option either, so there was only one thing to do: rev up the engine on that oul Fiat 127 and get over the road to Ballyhaunis where the only dancehall from his once thriving entertainment empire remained open.

In the early summer of 1985, Paul relaunched the new-look Midas Nightclub complete with restaurant facilities for 300, a bar licence and late-night exemptions. The name alone said it all: the new nightclub's beleaguered owner was desperately searching for that Midas touch.

In those early weeks, Claffey tried everything to lure the public through the door, from Country Nights to Cabaret Nights to special deals offering reduced admission for those attending the adjacent Star Cinema. He even offered patrons the chance to win £300 by finding Midas' hidden crock of gold but the truth was that nobody in Midas needed to find a crock of gold more urgently than its owner. In an era of double-digit interest rates, the debt pile from Claffey's failed dancehalls was growing as big as that famous butter mountain over in Europe and the re-launched Midas Nightclub – far from easing the financial strain – was only adding to its owner's woes. By the time Gene Stuart and the Homesteaders arrived in Ballyhaunis on a dreary Sunday night in late July 1985, Paul Claffey was a man on the precipice of financial ruin.

"I was in bits," he recalls. "I was non-stop in court dealing with debt summonses. I had 18 cases against me and I was finding it impossible to keep the payments up on all of them because I was penniless – and I mean penniless.

"I had a wife and two children to support and no food on the table at home… literally no food on the table. The electricity was cut off in the house, it was that bad. The pressure was just unreal; it became so bad I almost lost my mind with financial worries."

The debt summonses continued to mount on the kitchen table in Castlerea throughout that miserable, wet summer of 1985 and Paul became increasingly desperate in his efforts to extricate himself from the financial quicksand into which he had fallen. The shock of seeing his business empire crumble within a matter of months was bad enough – it was like suddenly losing your job – but the worry of not being able to provide for his family was simply overwhelming. He struggled to sleep at night and spent every waking hour trying to think of new and increasingly desperate ways to earn a few quid.

"Just when I'd feel I might be getting my head above water the postman would deliver another bunch of court summonses. The pressure was immense and my mind was scrambled with worry and stress, absolutely scrambled. I was in a very bad place mentally and that is the truth.

"I don't know what I'd have done without my wife Maureen. Not only was she running a house with two young kids, but she was fantastic at dealing with banks and helping me to work my way through the various money problems at that time. She was an absolute rock of support during that really difficult period in my life when everything I had worked for since I was a teenager seemed to be disappearing before my eyes."

When he had finished serving the drinks to Gene Stuart and the rest of the band members, Claffey poured himself an orange juice and retired to the end of the bar, removing his trademark glasses to rub the weariness from his eyes. He hadn't slept in days and the prospect of another court appearance in the morning meant he wouldn't sleep that night either.

Chuck Owens, the Longford-born steel guitar player with Stuart's band, could see the nightclub proprietor wasn't his usual ebullient self and broke away from the rest of the group to have a quiet word with him. The two had known each other since the early 1970s when a teenage Claffey was serving his apprenticeship as a disc jockey, warming up crowds for the top Country artists in ballrooms across Connacht.

"Business isn't good, is it Paul?" Owens asked in his soft Midlands accent.

"It's not, Chuck, it's surely not," Claffey replied wearily. "In fact, it couldn't be worse. I'm going to get up tomorrow and there will be cheques jumpin' and hoppin' and leppin' all over the place. I just can't get the sort of crowds in here that I need to pay off my debts."

"You know what you need to do?" said Owens.

"What?"

"Start a radio station."

"But sure I did that before over in Castlerea and it was a disaster."

"I bet it was a disaster because you were playing the kind of music you wanted to hear, not the kind of music the people wanted to hear."

"But I had signal problems too…"

Owens put his hand in his pocket and took out a diary.

"Here," he said, scribbling a name and telephone number on a page and tearing it from the diary. "Ring this man above in Cavan. Gerry Reilly is his name. He'll get you a signal that will go around the whole county."

From the far end of the bar came the grinding screech of bar stools being pushed back as the other band members rose to leave. Chuck Owens put his diary back in his pocket and gave his host a gentle punch on the arm.

"I'm telling you Paul, a radio station will get you back on your feet in no time but it'll only work if you play the music the people want to hear."

Owens and the rest of the band said their farewells and walked off into the night. When they were gone, Paul Claffey set about tidying the bar and gathering up the night's takings, which would barely cover the bills from that evening let alone the crippling debts accrued over the last few years. As he walked briskly towards the front door with the bag containing the takings in his hand, a piece of paper fluttered gently from the bar onto the floor. Picking it up and moving towards the nearby bin, Claffey absent-mindedly glanced at the barely legible scrawl comprising a telephone number and the words: *Gerry Reilly, Cavan, MW transmitter…*

It was only then he remembered the earlier conversation with Chuck Owens. He stuck the piece of paper into his jacket pocket and headed out into the early dawn, the sound of birdsong breaking the stillness of another wet Monday morning in this never-ending washout of a summer.

"A radio station?" Claffey muttered to himself as he climbed into his battered Fiat 127, the engine struggling to catch fire. "Haven't I enough headaches to be going on with without opening a radio station and, anyway, where in the name of God would I get the money?"

Finally, at the third time of asking, the Fiat's engine chugged painfully into life and Claffey slipped the car into gear, hoping he had sufficient petrol in the tank to make it home.

"A radio station?" he muttered again as he reached The Square and turned the Fiat in the direction of Castlerea. "Sure I don't even have enough money to get the radio fixed in this bloody yoke."

And on Paul Claffey drove through the dawn, alone with his glum thoughts of bills and bills and more bills and cheques a jumpin' and a hoppin' and a leppin'.

PART I

CHAPTER ONE

The first broadcasters

PIRATE radio is older than the State itself. Indeed, the first radio broadcast from Ireland was during the iconic rebellion that became the catalyst for Ireland's War of Independence.

On the afternoon of Easter Monday 1916, a group of Irish Volunteers emerged from the recently occupied GPO in Dublin and made their way across Sackville Street (now O'Connell Street) to the Irish School of Wireless, located above Reis's Jewellers' shop. Radio had been banned under the Defence of the Realm Act, which came into effect at the start of World War I, but the school was still in use as a training centre for wireless operators.

The sortie across Sackville Street was as deliberate as the rebels' earlier decision to seize the General Post Office. Joseph Plunkett, one of the signatories of the Proclamation and a key strategist in the rebellion, was an enthusiastic advocate of wireless technology and believed it could be used to the rebels' advantage. Plunkett developed an ambitious plan to use radio to spread the word of the Irish rebellion across the world, even going so far as to establish a wireless unit within the Irish Volunteers. One of the members of that unit was Dubliner Fergus O'Kelly who led the mission on Easter Monday to take over the Irish School of Wireless.

"While in the GPO, I was called aside by Joseph Plunkett and instructed to take a few men and take possession of the Wireless School and to do everything possible to get the transmitting plant and receiving apparatus into working order..." O'Kelly later recalled.

When the rebels entered the building they discovered the British military had sealed the wireless room two years earlier but O'Kelly and his men were able to break the seals and gain access to their prospective 'radio studio'.

"Quite a lot of work had to be done to put it into working order," he recalled. "We went out on the roof and found that the aerial had been taken down, but the poles had been left lying in the valley of the roof. We immediately set about making a new aerial and setting the poles upright to carry it."

While one member of the group went off to source electrical wire from a shop on Trinity Street, O'Kelly sent word back to Plunkett in the GPO to dispatch another party of Volunteers to the nearby Dublin Bread Company factory to protect the men in the Wireless School from sniper fire. This was pirate broadcasting at its most treacherous.

"These [Volunteers] were of great help in keeping up constant sniping against enemy positions that were firing at us while we erected the aerial and made the necessary connections," O'Kelly recalled. "The heavy sniping eventually forced us to stop work on the roof until dark. The aerial was completed during the dark hours of Monday night."

One member of the group, David Burke, who was a trained Marconi operator, managed to get the spark transmitter connected, but the batteries for the receiver were long since dead so it was not possible to get in direct contact with any station or ship. However, O'Kelly reported back to the GPO that the transmitting apparatus was operational, prompting the commanding officer of the Dublin brigade, James Connolly, to hastily compose the first message for broadcast. Connolly dispatched it in the hands of a Volunteer who crossed Sackville Street under a shroud of darkness, hoping his furtive movements would not be detected by the British snipers already beginning to train their sights on the GPO. The unnamed Volunteer made it safely to the Wireless School and handed Connolly's message to David Burke who hurriedly punched it out in Morse code. The message read:

> *Irish Republic declared in Dublin today. Irish troops have captured city and are in full possession. Enemy cannot move in city. The whole country rising.*

They were not to know it but Burke and the other Volunteers in the Wireless School at 10-11 Sackville Street in Dublin were making the first ever radio broadcast from Ireland. Indeed, some have even claimed it was the first of its kind in the world; and in the true traditions of pirate radio, the broadcasters weren't even sure anyone was listening.

"It was not possible to get in direct touch with any station or ship but the message was sent out on the normal commercial wavelength in the hope that some ship would receive it and relay it as interesting news," recalled O'Kelly in a statement to the Bureau of Military History in 1950.

David Burke continued to punch out the same message at regular intervals throughout the night, hoping that if he sent it often enough some radio operator might eventually pick it up. In fact, Ireland's inaugural broadcast was picked up by radio operators in Wales, Bulgaria and Germany, as well as on several ships, and by Tuesday afternoon, the news of Ireland's political rebellion had gone global.

A new form of communication – radio transmission – was born on that April night in 1916 and the rebels of Easter Week had inadvertently become Ireland's first pirate broadcasters.

The year 1935 was significant in the history of radio broadcasting in Co Mayo. On the weekend of August 14 and 15, Knock Shrine hosted an estimated 20,000 pilgrims who travelled by bus, train, car and bike from all parts of Ireland, as well as a large contingent of visitors from England. Among them was a London nurse, Kathleen Flynn, who was said to have made a miraculous recovery from incurable spinal disease after visiting Knock as a youngster in 1925.

Radio Athlone, which had been founded a decade earlier as 2RN, broadcast a one-hour programme from Knock Shrine with commentary provided by District Justice Liam Coyne, who, along with wife Judy, was instrumental in establishing Knock as a major pilgrimage centre.

While it is impossible to be definitive on such matters, the radio programme from Knock Shrine on Sunday, August 15, 1935, appears to have been the first outdoor radio broadcast ever held in Co Mayo.

A few weeks later, the county was again dominating the airwaves of Radio Athlone when American-born pilot Felix Waitkus crash-landed in a field near Ballinrobe while attempting to fly non-stop from New York to Lithuania. Radio Athlone provided hourly weather updates to Waitkus as he made his transatlantic voyage, thus generating maximum publicity in Ireland for the daring expedition.

"For 18 hours he was flying blindly in fog and storm, his only communication with the outside world being the weather reports and gramophone concert broadcasts from the Athlone radio station," revealed the *Connaught Telegraph.* "The broadcasts were given in the first quarter of every hour, and were followed by a few minutes of light music for his entertainment. The machine landed as one of the reports was being sent out."

1935 was also significant in the history of radio broadcasting in Ireland because the country got its first pirate station that year. On April 6, The *Cork Examiner* carried a short report on the 'unsolved mystery' of Limerick's 'wireless nuisance'.

"The mysterious announcer can be heard at intervals, and as well as broadcasting his own views on topical events and commenting on political personages, he gives unwilling listeners the benefit of his vocal abilities in the form of popular songs," revealed the *Examiner.* "The annoyance caused by the station is distinctly perturbing to owners of sets."

The post office authorities sent a detection van to Limerick in an effort to locate the pirate broadcaster but almost a year later the station was still going strong with the *Irish Press* reporting that listeners in the city were treated to a "gramophone record programme" on the afternoon of February 24, 1936. By June, two female announcers had joined the pirate broadcaster, which was calling itself the 'Curraghrock Station', and the post office detection vans were still no closer to locating the law-breakers.

However, after several more broadcasts, members of the Civic Guards called to the home of sound engineer Jim O'Carroll who freely surrendered a radio transmitter and other broadcasting paraphernalia. O'Carroll was never prosecuted or named in the press but his achievement in becoming Ireland's first pirate broadcaster was long celebrated in his native Limerick where he was known for the rest of his life simply as 'The Pirate'.

The growing popularity of radio in the 1930s made it an attractive form of communication for hard-line political organisations wishing to gain publicity for their particular causes. But setting up a pirate radio station was easier said than done and the consequences of detection could be severe, especially if those involved were linked to a proscribed organisation such as the IRA.

In the spring of 1940, Mayo man Jack (Seán) McNeela was found guilty at the Special Criminal Court in Dublin of conspiracy to usurp the functions of government after he was found in possession of an unlicensed radio transmitter used to broadcast Republican propaganda. Ballycroy-born McNeela subsequently died on hunger strike in a Dublin hospital. He was aged just 22.

The summary trial and imprisonment of McNeela and five other members of the IRA's so-called radio broadcast staff served as a stark warning to anybody else who might be minded to establish a pirate radio station in Ireland for political motives. With war raging in Europe and a German invasion of Ireland a distinct possibility, de Valera and his government were in no mood to show leniency to young revolutionary broadcasters like McNeela even if they were merely replicating the tactics of the founding fathers of the Free State less than a quarter of a century earlier when they took over the Wireless School on Sackville Street.

By May 1945, when de Valera delivered his famous response on Radio Éireann to Churchill's criticism of Ireland's neutrality during World War II, the State broadcaster enjoyed an unassailable domestic monopoly in an ever-expanding radio landscape as more and more households acquired wireless sets. Two years later, an estimated one million people listened in awe as renowned GAA commentator Micheál O'Hehir delivered a typical *tour de force* from the Polo Grounds in New York where Kerry played Cavan in the only All-Ireland football final to be played outside Ireland.

By the late 1940s, there were approximately 300,000 licensed wireless sets in Ireland – and a fair few unlicensed sets too – but for all of radio's growing appeal, there was still an air of intrigue about this new form of communication, and some older folk remained thoroughly unconvinced of the reliability of the wireless, especially when it came to weather forecasting. Mayo-born businessman Joe

Kennedy, who became one of the most successful building contractors in the United Kingdom and has been no stranger to Midwest Radio over the years, fondly recalls Pat Flannery, a local character in his native Doocastle who was so suspicious of the wireless he insisted on checking each of the three sets in the village for the weather forecast.

"What's the oul wireless saying about the weather tomorrow," Flannery asked Battie Tivnan.

"Oh, it's saying it'll be bad tomorrow, Pat. Wind and rain as usual."

Not satisfied with that forecast, Flannery sauntered on to Curley's where he again got the same weather report: wind and rain for the next day.

Finally, the intrepid farmer called to Kennedy's pub, pulled up a stool at the bar and ordered a bottle of stout.

"Pat," he said to Joe Kennedy's father, "what's your wireless saying about the weather tomorrow."

"It's saying it'll be a mighty day," Pat Kennedy replied good-humouredly. "Dry with plenty of sunshine."

On hearing this latest optimistic forecast, Flannery sipped contentedly from his bottle of stout and declared loudly to the rest of the men at the bar: "Musha, doesn't it pay to buy the right sort of an article!"

Radio came to the East Mayo parish of Aghamore in 1941 when the family of future Midwest Radio presenter Séamus Duffy purchased the village's first wireless set. It created something of a 'sensation' – to use one of the favourite words of the era – and Séamus can still recall the queues of neighbours who would dutifully file through the front door on a Sunday evening to listen to *Céilí House* with Seán Ó Murchú on Radio Éireann.

There had been music in the Duffy household long before Séamus' parents, Pat (Sonny) and Agnes, saved up enough money to purchase a wireless set.

"My mother and father got married in America in 1929 and brought back a gramophone – His Master's Voice (HMV) – and a collection of Pye records. That's what I was reared on," he recalls.

"Every Sunday evening, with monotonous regularity, my mother would take down the gramophone and put in a record of Michael Coleman or Paddy Killoran or John McKenna or Jim Morrison, all of the great Irish musicians of the day who had made recordings in America."

The eldest in a family of four, Séamus was immersed in Irish traditional music while still in the cot; it became as natural as the air he breathed.

"My parents were very much into music but they were not musicians. My mother had an endless amount of songs, and although she wasn't the greatest singer, she was good enough for me to learn the melodies of the many Republican ballads she'd sing when we were children. Now my father was staunch Fine Gael but we'd have been regularly singing ballads like *Seán Corcoran* [an eponymous song in memory of an IRA volunteer and Kiltimagh native who was killed in a Black 'n' Tans' ambush at Crossard, near Tooreen, in 1921]."

Séamus was aged 11 when the family acquired a wireless set, opening up a whole new frontier in his burgeoning passion for traditional music. But the airwaves of Radio Éireann were not as rich in musical gold as the young Séamus had hoped: traditional music was mainly restricted to the half-hour *Céilí House* programme on Sunday night and 15-minute sponsored programmes on weekdays. In fact, a fair proportion of Radio Éireann's daily programming (which was restricted to just six hours) was given over to gramophone recordings of chamber and symphony music. Consequently, the wireless was not nearly as important in Séamus' musical formation in the 1940s as the ballads of his mother or the instrumentation of neighbours who regularly called to the Duffy home, which became known in Aghamore as a bastion for traditional Irish music and culture.

"Traditional music was always strong in the country but there was no organisation in those days," Séamus explains. "Comhaltas had yet to be formed and there was no local radio like Midwest to give traditional music, and especially local musicians, a forum on which they could display their talents to a wider audience. But the music was there in every parish in Ireland."

As a young schoolteacher in counties Longford and Leitrim in the early 1950s, Séamus came to fully appreciate the depth of musical talent – and the vast array of traditional styles – that existed in Ireland, local talent that lay undiscovered and often underappreciated. In those years, Séamus was something of a musical troubadour as he moved from student days in Garbally College in Galway and St Patrick's College in Dublin to working as príomhoide in small primary schools in Longford and Leitrim.

"I was soaking up all of the influences as I moved around the country," he recalls. "I was absorbing the music and the songs of these different parts of Ireland where I was studying and then teaching."

Séamus' decision to leave his native Aghamore hadn't been easy and there was an expectation at home after he left primary school at the age of 14 that he might stick around to assist his father on the family farm. The war was still raging in Europe and self-sufficiency was the buzzword in an Ireland that could no longer rely on its nearest neighbour for fuel and food security. In the summer of 1944, Séamus and his father had just finished digging a field of potatoes when the youngster stuck his fork in the ground and declared: "That's the last time I'll be digging spuds here."

"What's wrong with you?" his father asked.

"I'm going to college," came the reply.

Unbeknownst to his parents, Séamus had obtained a coveted scholarship to Garbally College in Co Galway where he joined several Ballyhaunis students who soon became firm friends; among them were George Delaney, Joe Greene, Joe Mulligan and Ed O'Kelly. By 1951, the Aghamore man was a student at St Patrick's teacher training college in Drumcondra in Dublin and was one of a few hundred Irish music enthusiasts to attend the inaugural Fleadh Cheoil na hÉireann in Mullingar. Comhaltas Ceoltóirí Éireann was established a few months later with the express aim of arresting the decline in traditional music, and one of its obvious early targets was Radio Éireann, which continued to provide only limited exposure to an integral part of Irish culture rooted in every town and village the length and breadth of the country.

But Radio Éireann faced its own financial struggles too. The early 1950s marked the beginning of a period of deep economic gloom in Ireland as wartime rations gave way to post-war recession. When Séamus Duffy was appointed *príomhoide* of a small primary school on the shores of Lough Gowna in north Longford in the autumn of 1952, there wasn't even sufficient money to purchase a proper lock for the front door.

"I used to have to put my bike up against the door to stop the wind from blowing it in," he recalls. "One day an inspector called and he couldn't get in!"

Understandably disillusioned with the poor teaching conditions, the young *príomhoide* took up a new post in a three-teacher school at Aughavas on the Leitrim-Cavan border. He was soon immersed in the local traditional music scene and was elected chairman of the Cavan branch of Comhaltas, while also becoming familiar with several of the personalities who were involved in the IRA's so-called 'Border Campaign' of that era.

On New Year's Day in 1957, two IRA volunteers – Seán South and Fergal O'Hanlon – suffered fatal injuries during a failed attack on an RUC station at Brookeborough in Co Fermanagh. Upon hearing the news that South had died from his injuries, the young *príomhoide* from Aghamore, who had been reared on songs like *Seán Corcoran,* returned to his room in digs on the Cavan-Leitrim border, sat down at his little bedside desk and began to write:

Sad are the homes around Garryowen
Since they lost their joy and pride
And the banshee cry links every vale
Around the Shannon side that city of the ancient walls,
The broken treaty stone, undying fame surrounds your name,
Seán South from Garryowen.

Séamus performed his rebel song at the Fleadh Cheoil in Dungarvan, Co Waterford, later that year but *Seán South* was never likely to feature on Radio Éireann, especially in an Ireland where Taoiseach Eamon de Valera, who had returned to office after a three-year stint in opposition, was preparing to introduce internment without trial for IRA suspects. The song might, however, have got a more sympathetic airing on a republican pirate radio station that commenced broadcasting in Dublin on Easter Week 1958. Describing itself as 'Irish Freedom Radio in Occupied Ireland', the station's presenters – three women and a man – delivered a series of short programmes during which the 1916 Proclamation was read and the Irish government's policy of internment condemned.

Radio detection vans were immediately dispatched from the GPO to track down this latest band of political pirates now assailing the nation with their Republican rhetoric. The rebel station was on 209 medium wave (MW), just 'next door' to Radio Luxembourg, the increasingly popular English-speaking music station that broadcast throughout Europe on 208MW. Teenagers who were rocking around the clock to Bill Haley and the Comets were probably more likely to choose Radio Luxembourg over a pirate station transmitting Republican propaganda but the Irish government wasn't taking any chances and the station was promptly closed down.

The radio detection vans had only been sporadically called into action by the Department of Posts and Telegraphs during the preceding decades but these crack units were about to become a whole lot busier as a new posse of broadcasting rebels prepared to take to the airwaves in the 1960s.

The age of the pop pirates was dawning.

CHAPTER TWO

What's This World A Comin' To

WHEN that historic first radio broadcast from Ireland was made on Easter Week 1916, the rebel party in the GPO included a larger-than-life Kerryman named Michael Joseph O'Rahilly, better known as The O'Rahilly.

A staunch nationalist and a key figure in the Irish Volunteer movement, O'Rahilly opposed the rebellion because he believed the British authorities would mercilessly quell the sort of open revolt planned by Pearse and Plunkett. The Kerryman spent much of that Easter weekend touring the country, informing Volunteer leaders they were not to mobilise their men for planned manoeuvres on Sunday morning.

But it was all in vain. When O'Rahilly returned to Dublin he learned that Pearse, Connolly, Plunkett and many other long-standing nationalist comrades were about to overrule their chief-of staff Eoin MacNeill and launch an armed insurrection on Easter Monday morning. There was only one thing for The O'Rahilly to do. He donned his immaculately-kept Volunteer uniform, bade farewell to his wife and children and set off in his distinctive De Dion-Bouton motorcar, famously declaring as he stepped from the vehicle at City Hall: "Well, I've helped to wind up the clock… I might as well hear it strike."

By the end of the week, the Kerryman was dead having volunteered to lead a party of men in a wildly courageous charge across Moore Street during the retreat from the GPO. As he lay bleeding to death in a doorway, The O'Rahilly penned a farewell letter to his wife Nannie and young sons, ending it with the immortal line: *It was a good fight anyhow.*

Almost half a century later, O'Rahilly's grandson Ronan was leading a revolution of his own against the British establishment but this time the rules of engagement were a little less deadly. In the spring of 1964, the *Evening Herald* reported that 23-year-old Ronan O'Rahilly had anchored a ship in the North Sea, nine miles off Harwich in Essex, and was preparing to launch a new pirate radio station called Radio Caroline.

The ship, a former passenger vessel, had been converted into a makeshift radio centre at O'Rahilly's parents' private port at Greenore in Carlingford Lough, Co Louth, and was registered under a Panamanian flag, which meant the British authorities could not board it as long as it remained outside their territorial waters.

Unlike the political propagandists of previous pirate radio incarnations, O'Rahilly and the rest of the Radio Caroline team intended to confine their broadcasts to popular music – along the lines of Radio Luxembourg – but the emergence of this new form of broadcasting was sufficiently revolutionary to raise the hackles of senior figures at Westminister who immediately demanded that the Postmaster General Anthony Wedgwood Benn 'ban them or jam them'. Wedgwood Benn, however, was powerless to take action against Radio Caroline because the ship was protected under traditional maritime laws and by the middle of 1964, O'Rahilly had a second pirate radio ship, also fitted out in Greenore, anchored off the Isle of Man.

Locating pirate radio stations on the high seas was not an entirely new phenomenon. Radio Veronica, a Dutch pirate station, had been broadcasting from the North Sea since 1961 while Radio Syd was located outside Swedish territorial waters and both were replicating the Radio Luxembourg template of delivering wall-to-wall popular music to a largely teenage audience.

O'Rahilly, who ran a London nightclub and managed several pop music artists including Georgie Fame, established Radio Caroline after the BBC and Radio Luxembourg refused to play Fame's latest record because it was recorded on O'Rahilly's small independent label and not one of the big labels like EMI, Decca or Pye.

The Irishman certainly had the last laugh: Radio Caroline's success was instant and unprecedented. Unlike previous pirate operators, O'Rahilly had sufficient wealth to be able to invest in powerful transmitters, and his two radio ships were soon broadcasting across the UK, Ireland and even into Western Europe. The news that a pirate pop music station was broadcasting from a ship off the east coast of England captured the rebellious spirit of the 1960s and soon Radio Caroline had supplanted Radio Luxembourg as the 'trendy' station of choice for music-loving teenagers in England and Ireland where the pirate's reception on the east coast was generally as good as that of Radio Éireann.

The European authorities moved quickly to outlaw the pirate broadcasters. In September 1964, 17 European nations adopted draft resolutions to ban pirate radio broadcasting on the grounds that the world's airwaves were becoming too crowded.

A meeting of the Council of Europe was told that in 1949 there were just 200 broadcasters using the world's entire radio airspace but now that number had jumped to a whopping 400 and stations were operating very close to each other, causing interference and overlapping. It was also claimed that some pirate stations were transmitting on shortwave frequencies, which were reserved for ships, police, ambulance and fire services, and it was only a matter of time before a tragedy occurred.

In Britain, where Radio Caroline was going from strength to strength, the message from MPs in Westminister to the Postmaster General was simple: 'Close it down now.'

But that was easier said than done. The offshore broadcasters were operating out of reach of the long arm of the law and as long as they stayed on the high seas they were immune from prosecution or even confiscation of equipment. And pirates were also appearing on land too, including in Ireland.

Radio Atlantis took to the airwaves on the south side of Dublin in late 1964, playing pop records for one hour each day. One of the three schoolboys who operated the station told the *Irish Press:* "We believe

Radio Éireann does not stay open long enough so we decided to start our own pop record programme for young listeners."

But when a spokesman for the Department of Posts and Telegraphs told the press that officials would not show any leniency to operators of pirate radio stations – be they schoolboys or altar boys – the promoters of Radio Atlantis decided it was time to quit while they were ahead.

"We learned that the fine for operating the station is a maximum of £300 or six months in jail, or both. That's why we decided to go off air," one of the boys ruefully told the *Irish Press* a week later.

But pirate radio stations were opening as quickly as they were closing. In January 1965, the *Irish Press* reported that another Dublin-based station, Radio Showband, had commenced transmitting across a 12-mile radius using equipment smuggled from Belfast. One of the promoters of the project told the *Press:* "There is nothing wrong in this. We are not cutting any other station. Anyway, a station like this is long overdue."

It was a fair point. Ireland was in the throes of the showband craze in early 1965 with artists like the Miami, The Freshmen, Joe Dolan, Dickie Rock and Larry Cunningham packing out dancehalls the length and breadth of the country.

It was estimated there were as many as 800 showbands in Ireland, including dozens in the West of Ireland, and the whole industry was said to employ several thousand young men and women. But Radio Éireann paid scant attention to this musical phenomenon with only one young disc jockey named Larry Gogan giving airplay to these hugely popular bands.

Radio Showband aimed to fill that void but its promoters were soon on the run after the Department of Posts and Telegraphs unleashed no fewer than three squads of post office engineers to track them down. The station, which had been broadcasting from a city centre location in Dublin, disappeared from the airwaves as quickly as it arrived and was never heard of again.

The Radio Showband experience was similar to a lot of the early pop pirates who tended to have the impact of a comet by burning brightly for a very short period. Young broadcasters might launch a small local pirate station with the ambitious aim of achieving national recognition but a knock on the door from post office engineers or a friendly word on the street from a garda in the know was often enough to make them run for the hills.

Initially, the authorities in Ireland took a fairly benign view of the pop pirates – for one thing, they were far less threatening to the security of the state then the political pirates who came before them – but as pressure mounted across Europe to take these illegal stations off the air, the Department of Posts and Telegraphs adopted a tougher stance.

In January 1966, two teenage boys from Clontarf in Dublin became the first pop pirates to be prosecuted in Ireland when they pleaded guilty at Dublin District Court to keeping a wireless transmitter without a licence. They were both fined the princely sum of one shilling each while the father of one of the boys was fined £1 for allowing his house to be used for the illegal station, known as Radio Romeo.

The boys' solicitor Herman Good, who was a friend of Ronan O'Rahilly and a director of Radio Caroline, told the court: "This was no Radio Caroline."

However, there was a lot of speculation that Ireland would, indeed, get its own Radio Caroline. In October 1966, a nightclub promoter in Waterford announced he was planning to establish a new pirate station on a boat off the coast of Dunmore that would broadcast 18 hours of pop music every day. The *Cork Examiner* reported that Radio Waterford would record its programmes in Waterford City before transporting the tapes by ferryboat to the seafaring station. The pirate was due to be launched on New Year's Day 1967 but that date came and went with radio silence from Dunmore and nothing more was heard of the project.

The truth was the tide had already started to go out on the first wave of pirate broadcasting. In early 1966, one of Radio Caroline's two ships ran aground off the Essex coast after dragging her anchor in heavy seas and although she was quickly refloated, the incident seemed a harbinger for the dark clouds gathering over the entire pirate radio industry. There were now four other major pop pirates in the UK – including the hugely successful Radio London – and the government had little choice but to take Draconian measures.

In the summer of 1966, legislation was brought before the House of Commons that prohibited British citizens or firms from working for pirate radio stations – whether it was directly as DJs or indirectly by purchasing advertising or even providing basic supplies such as food and mechanical repairs.

The Marine Broadcasting Act came into effect at midnight on August 14, 1967, and immediately all but one of Britain's offshore pirates acknowledged the jig was up and went off the air: the exception was Radio Caroline, which vowed to continue on with non-British DJs, foreign advertising and foreign supplies. Like his grandfather half a century earlier, O'Rahilly was making one last heroic charge against the British establishment.

But the Irishman's efforts were doomed. Radio Caroline continued to operate from its two ships in the North Sea until March 3, 1968, when they were simultaneously boarded and seized before the day's broadcasting was about to begin. A salvage company towed both ships to Amsterdam to secure unpaid bills arising from contracts with a Dutch tender company. O'Rahilly's pirate broadcasting revolution was at an end but – in the immortal words of his patriot grandfather – *it had been a good fight anyhow.*

As a youngster growing up in Castlerea, one of Paul Claffey's most prized possessions was his transistor radio, a compact, portable device that was a must-have item for every self-respecting teenager in the 1960s and 1970s.

The transistor radio changed the history of broadcasting, making it possible for pop music stations such as Radio Luxembourg and Radio Caroline to easily reach large audiences of young people.

Before the transistor, the experience of listening to the radio was, more often than not, a communal one as families and neighbours gathered around a single wireless set. The wireless itself was an unwieldy, immovable apparatus with its own special place in the home, usually the kitchen, and was – in the words of Séamus Duffy – "a problematic yoke to keep in tune".

"The first wireless we got had dry and wet batteries so my mother would have to go into Bertie Lynch's in Ballyhaunis every two weeks to get the wet battery recharged," Duffy recalls. "There was only one car in the parish so she'd bring the battery in on her bike.

"Now the battery was a big, heavy lump of a thing to be carrying on a bike and it was made of glass, so you wouldn't dare let it fall. We always had a second wet battery fully charged because we never wanted to miss Sunday night's *Céili House.*"

The transistor radio was as revolutionary for broadcasting as the smartphone was for computing half a century later; here was a handheld listening device that could be carried around the house, making it possible for teenagers to listen to their favourite pop tunes in the privacy of their bedrooms long into the night. Disc jockeys like Radio Luxembourg's Barry Alldis, who presented the weekly Top Twenty Show, became household names and even to this day many people can still recall Alldis' famous catchphrase: *Whether at home or on the highway, thanks for tuning my way.*

Like most music-mad youngsters in the late 1960s, Paul Claffey dreamed of one day following in the footsteps of men like Alldis or Radio Éireann's Larry Gogan but first he intended to create a business empire founded on packets of crisps and bottles of Fanta Orange. Claffey's initial foray into the world of entrepreneurship came at the tender age of nine when he fell upon an ingenious, foolproof way of becoming a millionaire by ten – or 11 at the very latest.

"There was a gang of us who'd be down in the swimming pool in Castlerea during the summer and we'd draw lots to see who would go up to Cleary's Shop to get the minerals and the crisps," he recalls. "I always drew the short straw because I had a bike. One day I thought to myself that if I bought a crate of Fanta I'd be able to sell the bottles to my friends and make a few bob."

Fired with enthusiasm, the young Claffey leapt on his bike and pedalled as fast as he could to Johnny Kearney's shop where the buses always stopped on their way to Knock Shrine. Throwing his bike against the front door, he burst inside:

"Mr Kearney, Mr Kearney will you sell me a crate of Fanta," the youngster shouted breathlessly.

"Slow down, slow down, young man. What do you want with a crate of Fanta?"

"I'm going to sell it up at the swimming pool."

"What's your name?"

"Paul Claffey…"

"Are you Gerry Claffey's young fella?"

"That's me."

Johnny Kearney was long enough on the road to recognise a promising business proposition – even if it was coming from the mouth of a nine-year-old in short pants.

"Right so, Mister Claffey, come with me," he said, pointing the youngster in the direction of the storeroom at the rear of his premises. Piled high from floor to ceiling were crates and crates of Fanta and Coca-Cola, enough minerals to salve the thirst of every child in Co Roscommon, let alone Castlerea.

"Now," said Kearney, placing a crate of Fanta Orange into the hands of his new business partner. "I'm going to sell you these at tuppence a bottle and you can sell them up at the swimming pool for whatever price you want. Come back to me with the money when you have this crate sold. Is that a deal?"

"It's a deal," the nine-year-old replied gravely before loading the crate onto the bars of his bicycle and setting off for the swimming pool. Ten minutes later he was back in Kearney's shop.

"What is it now?" asked the impatient shopkeeper.

"I need two more crates," declared the youngster as he triumphantly dumped a fistful of coins onto the dusty counter.

"Begad," said Kearney. "Are you sure you'll sell another two crates?"

"I will," said Castlerea's newest entrepreneur. "They're stone mad for Fanta above in that swimming pool."

"Right so, let's get you sorted then," said the clearly impressed Kearney. "Bring your bike around the back and we'll load her up."

An hour later, young Claffey was back in Kearney's yet again, shoveling fistfuls of coins from both pockets onto the counter. He had already made a tidy profit by selling each bottle at two and a ha'pence and was ready to gamble the lot on one final big sale for the day.

"I'll have three crates this time, Mr Kearney," he said.

"Ah sure you'll never sell that many. I'll give you one more and be on your way."

"No, I'll take the three. If I don't sell them today, I'll sell them tomorrow."

"Right so, it's your money."

The shopkeeper retired to the storeroom and emerged with three crates of Fanta, the muscles in his arms straining from the weight of the load.

"How in the name of God are you going to carry these?" he asked.

"Stick them up on the handlebars there, sure they'll be grand," Castlerea's newest entrepreneur confidently proclaimed as he impatiently played with the pedals on his bike, thinking that smart, up-and-coming businessmen like him hadn't the time to be talking to fussy old shopkeepers when there was good money to be made above at the swimming pool.

Once the crates were loaded, the youngster set off down the street with the three crates of Fanta perched precariously on the handlebars of the bike as it swayed dangerously from side to side. Johnny Kearney had barely returned to his usual berth behind the counter when he heard the unmistakable sound of breaking glass. He rushed outside to be greeted by a flood of the finest Fanta orange gushing down the street while Castlerea's newest entrepreneur lay in a crumpled heap on the ground, the tears flowing as fast as the Fanta. All three crates had tumbled off the bicycle, smashing every single bottle to smithereens.

The nine-year-old Paul Claffey had just learned his first important lesson in business: always know your limitations.

While Paul Claffey was cutting his teeth as an entrepreneur, the West of Ireland was getting its first radio station when a group of Irish-language enthusiasts established Saor Raidió Connemara, which made its first broadcast from a caravan in Carna, Co Galway, on the evening of Saturday, March 28, 1970. The station had a transmission range of 15 to 20 miles and was powered by a transmitter smuggled across the border from Derry where political activists had been broadcasting Free Radio Derry during the Civil Rights marches in 1969. The Connemara station's technical team included two Cork men, Martin

Dwyer and Michael Healy, the latter having established the short-lived pirate Radio Juliet in his native city some years earlier.

The day after the station launched, the *Irish Independent* published a front-page photograph of Martin Dwyer in the caravan in Carna, but the newspaper made sure to disguise the Cork man's identity by only showing him from behind, his pristine white Aran jumper appearing in sharp relief to the gloomy interior of the caravan-cum-radio studio.

Later that day, Dwyer rang home and spoke to his mother who had been kept blissfully ignorant of her son's pirate broadcasting exploits having been told he was going on a camping trip to Kerry with Michael Healy. But Mrs Dwyer was a keen reader of the *Irish Independent* and spotted the front-page photograph earlier that morning.

"Are you enjoying your time in Kerry?" she asked her son

"I am," said Martin. "We're having a mighty time."

"Don't give me that," said the mother. "I know you're above in Galway with that pirate station. Didn't I see you on the front of today's *Indo.*"

Martin tried valiantly to protest his innocence but Mrs Dwyer was having none of it.

"There's no way I wouldn't have recognised the Aran jumper you were wearing in that picture," she remarked. "Sure didn't I knit it for you myself!"

Years later, Dwyer ruefully recalled that he had been 'hoisted by his geansaí'.

Saor Raidió Connemara broadcast Irish news and music for six hours per day throughout the spring of 1970. A week after the station was launched, the *Connacht Tribune* reported that the new pirate was operated by the men and women of the Gaeltacht "when they come in from the fields after milking the cows". This was grassroots broadcasting in its most literal sense.

The amount of media coverage of Saor Raidió Connemara meant it came into the sights of the authorities very quickly. Soon the promoters were moving the station from one part of the Connemara Gaeltacht to another in an increasingly desperate effort to avoid the long arm of the law. The transmitter and studio equipment were usually transported on the back of a Honda 50 motorbike in the dead of night when only foxes and poitín makers stalked the byways of West Galway.

Saor Raidió Connemara enjoyed a fairly brief lifespan but the pirate broadcaster provided the impetus for the government to establish Raidió na Gaeltachta in 1972. Dwyer, Healy and the rest of the promoters of the Irish-language pirate also had the distinction of giving the West of Ireland its first proper radio station, but it was the end of the 1970s before local broadcasting really took off in Connacht and, even then, many of the western pirates struggled to attract a large audience due to transmission difficulties. A transmitter with a reach of 10 to 15 miles was fine in a city like Dublin or Cork but it wasn't much use in the sparsely populated rural landscape. However, that didn't stop radio enthusiasts outside the urban centres from trying to reach the masses and one of the most notable successes in the early 1970s was Radio 99, a Country and Western music station established in Co Monaghan in 1971.

Broadcasting on the former Radio Caroline frequency – 199 medium wave – Radio 99 had one of the best transmission systems of all the Irish pirates and was even said to be reaching listeners in England and Scotland. In August 1971, the *Sunday Independent* sent a reporter and photographer in search of the Monaghan-based pirates who were operating under the strictest cross-border secrecy.

It took a week of exhaustive enquiries on both sides of the Border before reporter Patsy McArdle eventually tracked down the pirates to Clones where an elderly lady in a local housing estate was accepting postal requests on their behalf. And it wasn't just a few requests either: Radio 99 was attracting hundreds of requests each week as more and more listeners tuned into the only station in Ireland offering non-stop Country and Western music.

The old lady wasn't giving much away other than confirming that she had agreed to accept the postal requests because she regularly listened to Radio 99 and really enjoyed it. But McArdle eventually met one of the promoters who took the intrepid reporter on an "after-midnight mystery trip" along the border to Radio 99's studio in a disused farmhouse where DJs JJ and Jim were spinning the discs. A photograph of Big Tom took pride of place on the studio wall alongside many other Irish Country and Western artists of the era who were by now all sending their records to Radio 99. The tongue-in-cheek theme tune for the evening broadcasts was Slim Whitman's *What's This World A Comin' To.*

Although it only broadcast for a few hours five nights per week, Radio 99 had built up a very loyal following in Clones and the surrounding north-east, prompting the chairman of the local urban council to tell McArdle: "Nearly everybody in the town tunes in and takes great pleasure in the programmes. If they are granted a licence it could be a great boost for the area."

But there was no prospect of the government granting radio licences to pirate DJs like JJ and Jim. Although they were filling a void in Radio Éireann's programming, the pirates were still law-breakers as far as the authorities were concerned. The Department of Posts and Telegraphs told the *Sunday Independent* the station was "under investigation" and would be closed down in due course. But in a dark era of lawlessness along the border, local desperadoes raided Radio 99's makeshift studio before the officials from the Department of Posts and Telegraphs in Dublin could even figure out where it was.

The cottage itself was actually located in a disused farmhouse in Co Fermanagh and JJ and Jim faced something of a dilemma when several members of a local Loyalist gang, who were clearly not fans of Country and Western music, paid them a visit in the dead of night. The Loyalists gave the pirates' a stark choice: either close down immediately or prepare to have a few bones broken and the studio thrashed. And, no, they didn't want to hear *A Boy Named Sue*...

JJ, Jim and their friend Ray, who was the technical wizard of the operation, wisely decided to pack up their equipment and beat a hasty retreat back across the border, thus ending the short but glorious reign of Radio 99.

They were not to know it but the promoters of Radio 99 blazed a trail for Ireland's local broadcasting industry, pioneering a unique – and, some might say, unfashionable – playlist that was completely different to Radio Éireann or the pop pirates. By playing non-stop Country and Western music – the music of the people, as it were – DJs JJ and Jim were tapping into a sense of community and 'Irishness' largely absent from pirate broadcasting up to then.

More than a decade later, Chuck Owens would tell Paul Claffey to "give the people the music they want to hear, not the music you want to hear". It was a winning formula that had its genesis in a tumbledown farmhouse on the Fermanagh-Monaghan border in the early 1970s.

When asked by the *Sunday Independent* why she was willing to run the risk of falling foul of the law by taking postal requests for Radio 99, the little old lady in the housing estate in Clones put it simply: "Because they play great stuff."

In essence, that was the recipe for a successful local radio station; just play what the people wanted and the rest would fall into place.

CHAPTER THREE

'Are you doing something illegal?'

BY the age of 10, Paul Claffey was running a tuck shop at the swimming pool during the summer holidays, selling up to 60 crates of minerals and a few boxes of crisps every week. He was wise enough to give the caretaker, Tom Doyle, a cut of the action while Coca-Cola was now supplying directly to him at bulk prices.

"I'd cut out the middle man, Johnny Kearney," he recalls, laughing. "The rep from Coca-Cola would come down from Dublin and I'd order 100 crates of Coca-Cola, 70 Fanta Orange and 30 Fanta Lemon. I'd then sell these over a period and make a nice bit of money out of it. I did that for four years; it was my first enterprise."

There was an entrepreneurial streak in Claffey's genes. When recession struck in the mid-1960s, Paul's mother, Eileen, started a bakery business from the family home at Patrick Street and quickly built up a loyal customer base. Some of Paul's earliest memories are of making delivery runs with his father, travelling around in the family's old Ford Cortina – registration number BDI 94 – as they sold fresh brown bread and penny buns to the local shops.

As he grew older, Paul became increasingly interested in the entertainment industry and he and two friends were soon spinning records at school discos, or 'hops' as they were called in those days. The boys were making nice money from the discos but the other two suddenly dropped out leaving Paul to continue alone. Soon he wasn't just playing records at discos but was also booking bands from as far away as Dublin for local events. The work came easy to him but there was one problem: he was still only 14.

"I was running a couple of one-off events with bands but I couldn't let on that I was a 14-year-old kid from the West," he recalls. "So when I was trying to persuade the bands to play at the events, I'd have to deepen the voice a bit to try and pass as someone older."

Among the bands Paul brought to Boyle in the late 1960s was a Dublin-based outfit called Orphanage whose lead singer – a gangly black teenager with an unruly Afro hairstyle – caused quite a stir, both on and off the stage. It was an era when Ireland was still a very mono-cultural society and provincial towns, in particular, were not places where one expected to meet people of different race or even nationality. The black frontman in Orphanage was all the more exotic because he spoke with a heavy Dublin accent.

"What are age you?" he asked Claffey.

"I'm 16," declared the 14-year-old impresario.

"You're a bit young to be promoter aren't you? What's your name?"

"Paul Claffey."

"I'm Philip Lynott. Nice to meet you."

A few years after that meeting, Phil Lynott and his new band Thin Lizzy were riding high in the British singles charts with a reworking of an old Irish classic *Whiskey in the Jar.* By then, Paul Claffey had left school and was touring the dancehalls of Connacht with his bag of records, acting as the warm-up man for the big musical acts of the day. He enjoyed a friendly rivalry with Manulla man PJ Hennelly, who managed Nan Monaghan and the Jets, the older man none too impressed that this whippersnapper was playing records instead of live music. But the times they were 'a changin' and Paul soon became a regular feature on festival programmes in towns and villages across Co Roscommon and east Mayo. As far back as 1971, 'Paul Claffey's Disco 80 Show' was being advertised in the *Western People* (on that occasion he was playing a Christmas gig at Tooreen Community Centre) and four years later, Claffey was promoting 'An Evening With Niall Tobin' at the Savoy Cinema in Galway City.

Paul readily admits he flitted from one project to another in the mid-1970s and wasn't afraid to take risks or try something different. As well as continuing with the disco roadshows, he ran his own entertainment company, Paul Claffey Promotions, and even managed the Marine Ballroom in Enniscrone for a few months in 1977.

A year later, Paul decided to start a radio station in Castlerea and asked his neighbour and friend John Waters, who knew a bit about current affairs, to take charge of the station's news content. He called the station 'Midwest Radio' and set up a studio in the shed at the bottom of his parents' garden.

"I hadn't a clue what I was at really," he recalls, laughing. "I mean, look at the name I gave the station... Midwest Radio! Sure Roscommon and Mayo aren't even in the mid-west – Limerick and Clare are! I was so clueless I didn't even know what part of the country I was broadcasting from!"

The first incarnation of Midwest Radio took to the airwaves on September 29, 1978, and its launch even managed to make the pages of the Dublin-based *Evening Herald.*

"Transmission tests have shown that the signals can be picked up within a radius of 25 miles," the *Herald* reported. "Booster stations are planned to encompass the whole county and the fringes of neighbouring counties, which will make Midwest Radio one of the most powerful pirate radio stations in the country."

It all sounded very promising but the new station was plagued with early problems. For one thing, the transmitter didn't do what it was supposed to do and there were regular transmission breakdowns, which were as frustrating for Paul as they were for his burgeoning listenership. There was also the small matter of the endless demands on his and John Waters' time as they tried to provide an entertaining and engaging schedule of music, news, views and even weather updates. The latter involved Waters sticking his head out the window of the shed every couple of hours, which was a fairly unscientific form of weather forecasting by any standards but one that proved uncannily accurate.

To add to the complications, the owner of the shed that was housing Midwest Radio, one Mrs Eileen Claffey, was none too impressed to learn that her son was in danger of becoming a fugitive from the law if he continued with this broadcasting nonsense.

"Are you doing something illegal here?" she asked Paul as he sat at the kitchen table one afternoon eating his dinner. "I was down the town this morning and someone told me that what you and young Waters are doing is illegal. Is that true?"

"No, not at all, Mam," said her son cheerfully. "Don't be fretting about it."

"Now listen here, buck," declared Eileen Claffey, waving a wooden baking spoon in her son's direction. "If there is any trouble around here, if the Guards come snooping around, I'm not getting involved."

When he had finished his dinner, Paul left the house and walked down the street to the nearest telephone box. He then rang the operator and asked to be put through to Gerry Claffey's on Patrick Street. His mother answered the telephone. She was about to become the first victim of a Paul Claffey surprise phone call.

"Hello, Mrs Claffey? Sgt Flannery here from the barracks."

There was a deathly silence. Finally, Mrs Claffey stuttered:

"Oh... yes... yes Sergeant.... what, em, can I do for you?"

"It's a rather serious matter," continued the 'Sergeant' in a suitably grave voice. "We have reason to believe that your son Paul is involved in some illegal activities with a radio station. Would you know anything about that?

There was an audible gasp before Eileen Claffey replied in a high-pitched tone:

"Oh *Sergeant,* I wouldn't know *anything* about that kind of thing. I have *no* idea what that lad is up to."

"Well Mrs Claffey, I'm just advising you that we could be down to search your premises at any moment."

Another nervy silence ensued, this one seeming to last forever until finally Eileen Claffey uttered a panicked response, the words tumbling over each other as she blurted them out:

"Sergeant, sergeant, I know nothing about this radio business at all, nothing whatsoever. You'll have to see himself; now thank you, thank you."

The telephone was slammed down before the prankster had time to reveal the true identity of 'Sergeant Flannery'. When he returned home a few minutes later, Paul found his mother standing at the front door in a state of great agitation.

"Quick, quick," she called out as her son sauntered casually up the street. "The Guards are on their way down here to raid the place.

I'll close the gate and head them off while you get all that stuff out of the shed!"

Sgt Flannery and the rest of the officers at Castlerea Garda Station never troubled Midwest Radio throughout its first short-lived existence in the autumn and winter of 1978. Paul made the decision to close the station in early 1979, telling the *Irish Independent* he hoped Midwest might be considered for a licence when the government eventually legalised local radio broadcasting in Ireland. But the truth was that Claffey had had his fill of pirate radio and instead wanted to concentrate on his promising dancehall business. The Midnight Club in Ballaghaderreen, which he had been leasing from the local parish committee, was enjoying great popularity and Paul believed he could replicate its success in other towns in Connacht.

Midwest Radio's small band of loyal listeners in Castlerea – mainly teenagers who enjoyed the station's non-stop diet of pop and rock music – briefly mourned its sudden passing but one local woman was delighted to finally see the back of it. Eileen Claffey could now return to her baking, safe in the knowledge she wouldn't have the long arm of the law knocking on her front door any time soon. The garden shed would be staying locked from now on.

Paul Claffey wasn't the only aspiring disc jockey in Castlerea in the mid-1970s. A teenager from Main Street was also making a name for himself on the disco scene and had secured a coveted residency in the local Don Arms Hotel where he was warming up the crowds for Country stars like Big Tom and Margo, as well as Irish pop acts such as Gina, Dale Haze and the Champions.

Music was Chris Carroll's lodestar from a young age and some of his earliest memories are of marching alongside the Castlerea Brass and Reed Band, trying to keep pace with his father Christy who was the band's trombone player. The Castlerea Brass and Reed Band provided the musical entertainment at countless events across Roscommon and further afield – from Corpus Christi processions to Connacht football finals – and the young Chris was only too happy to tag along with his father.

It was inevitable the son would want to emulate the father and Chris was soon playing drums before switching to the guitar in his teenage years. Christy Carroll was keen to encourage the youngster's passion for music but could never have imagined the long-term impact one simple gift would have on his son's life.

"Dad was a carpenter by trade and one day he was putting new windows in a shop in Tuam," Chris explains. "He saw a record player in the window and thought it would make a nice gift for me because he knew how much I liked music.

"I will never forget the evening he brought that record player home. In many ways, it changed my life forever and set me off on a path that eventually allowed me to turn a pastime into a career."

Chris was soon setting aside the money he earned each summer as a staff member of Tom Flynn's shop in Castlerea to build up a vast vinyl collection that was the envy of his peers. A rock music fan at heart, Chris snapped up the latest records from the likes of Rory Gallagher, Thin Lizzy and Pink Floyd, playing them endlessly as he strummed along on his guitar. In an era long before Internet downloads, school friends regularly called over to the Carroll home to sample one of Castlerea's finest collections of vinyl. But the notion that its owner might become a disc jockey never crossed anyone's mind, least of all the teenage Chris who, by his own admission, was a shy, introverted youngster.

Everything changed one evening in 1976 when two local lads, Paudge Mulvihill and Gerry Farrell, called to the Carroll home in a panic. The duo had organised a 'hop' only for the DJ to cancel at the last minute, leaving them with a packed hall and no music.

"We know you have a fair few albums, Chris," Farrell explained. "Is there any chance you'd loan them to us for the hop. We'll have them back to you in the morning."

Chris had no doubt the lads would return his records, but like any true vinyl aficionado he wasn't keen to let his precious collection out of his sight – even for a night.

"I knew if the records came back scratched I'd really kick myself for letting them out of my sight so I told the lads I'd go up to the disco and put the records on but I wouldn't be going anywhere near a microphone!"

Chris went to the 'hop' where he spun the discs for a couple of hours and when it was all over Paudge and Gerry paid him the princely sum of £5. It was a real Eureka moment for the teenage Chris Carroll. Up to then, he'd never really thought he could make money from his record collection but now a real business opportunity presented itself. A few weeks later, Chris hired his first piece of disco equipment and was soon providing the music for teenage discos and other functions around Castlerea.

Initially, Chris asked a friend to introduce the records and play the requests but when the friend failed to turn up one evening there was only one thing to do: step out from behind the turntable and into the limelight. It turned out to be easier than he had thought and soon the shackles of shyness were thrown off and Chris Carroll had become a fully-fledged disc jockey.

By now, Chris had completed his Leaving Certificate but had no real interest in attending college because – in his own words – "it was all music, music, music". Like most teenagers in the 1970s, he harboured ambitions of forming a rock band and touring the globe but for now the disc jockeying wasn't a bad substitute. And while he might have opted to end his formal education he had found a job in a place that could be best described as a university of life: Tom Flynn's in Castlerea, an archetypal provincial shop-cum-pub that sold everything from a needle to an anchor.

"The best way I can describe Tom is that he was like a second father to me," says Chris. "He gave me a loan to buy my first piece of disco equipment and I paid him back out of my weekly wages. His shop was – and is – an incredible place that sold everything – and I mean *everything*.

"I learned so much from Tom and I enjoyed every minute of the time I spent working in his shop. It was the university of life for me, and Tom was the greatest mentor I could ever have found apart from my parents. We travelled to lots of places together and it was from Tom I got my education in business, which obviously stood me in good stead for later in my career. The job in Flynn's also allowed me to do the DJ work at the weekend so it really was the perfect position for me at that particular time in my life."

By the late 1970s, Chris' DJ work was taking him all over the West of Ireland and the Castlerea man's shows were quickly earning a reputation for the diversity of the music and the elaborate sound and lighting system, which Chris kept updating at considerable financial cost.

"I always prided myself on having the most up-to-date record collection," he remarks. "Of course, if I had my way I'd have been playing Rory Gallagher and Thin Lizzy all night but I knew from working in Flynn's that the customer is always king so my target as a DJ was to always have every single in the Top 30."

It was a wildly ambitious target, especially for a rural disc jockey without ready access to the big record shops in Dublin.

"John Hunt's Record Shop in Castlerea had some of what I wanted but not all so I had to find a way of getting to Dublin on a fairly regular basis to get the latest records," Chris explains.

Heavey's Fruit Merchants in Castlerea sent a van to Dublin early every Monday morning to collect their weekly supplies from the fruit traders on Mary Street so Chris decided to hitch a lift with them.

"I'd get on Heavey's lorry at 6am every Monday and while they'd be collecting their fruit on Mary Street I'd be over in Golden Discs in Henry Street buying the latest hit singles."

As his record collection grew so too did the requests for Chris Carroll's DJ-ing services. Soon he was spinning the discs four or five nights each week and his impressive sound and lighting show was nearly as professional as one might expect to see at a rock concert.

A teenage pastime was gradually turning into a full-time career.

CHAPTER FOUR

The novel theory of showbands and sheep

BY closing Midwest Radio in early 1979, Paul Claffey was swimming against the popular tide. More and more pirate radio stations were opening across the country and the campaign to end RTÉ's monopoly appeared to be gaining an unstoppable momentum. In January 1978, the *Irish Press* confidently declared that "the arrival of commercial radio seems inevitable" after an estimated 1,000 teenagers marched in Dublin in support of pirate radio. The teenagers carried transistor radios – with Radio Dublin blaring out – as they brought traffic to a standstill.

But the national broadcaster was about to fight back. RTÉ Radio 2 took to the airwaves on May 31, 1979, with Larry Gogan introducing the first song, *Like Clockwork* by Bob Geldof's band The Boomtown Rats, who were then riding high in the British and Irish charts.

Gogan, Vincent Hanley and Jimmy Greeley transferred across from Radio 1 but the new station was largely staffed by former pirate DJs, men like Ronan Collins, Gerry Ryan and Dave Fanning. In many ways, RTÉ was paying the ultimate compliment to Ireland's illegal radio industry by employing some of its star men. The state broadcaster was determined to steal the pirates' teenage audience, which was estimated to be worth £1 million per annum in advertising revenue.

And it worked. By the end of 1979, pirate broadcasters all over the country had switched off their microphones for the last time, among them Radio Tralee, one of three pirates in Co Kerry to close within a short period. Its spokesperson summed up the sentiments of an entire industry when he told *The Kerryman:* "We just cannot afford to continue."

The golden age of Ireland's pop pirates appeared to be over. RTÉ Radio 2 had neatly turned the tables on its troublesome adversaries and the prospect of any future government issuing licences to the few surviving pirates – if there even were any – looked slim indeed.

As he counted the cash after another busy December night in Ballaghaderreen, Paul Claffey felt mightily relieved at having emerged financially unscathed from his brief dalliance with illegal broadcasting.

One thing was certain: the young promoter of the Midnight Club wouldn't be taking any more voyages on a leaking pirate ship. Closing the radio station to concentrate fully on his dancehall interests had been the best decision Paul Claffey had ever made, and the sparkling new BMW parked across the street was testament to his foresight. It would be crazy to go back into pirate radio, especially when there were so many opportunities to turn a pound in the dancehall business.

Before he turned out the lights in the Midnight Club on that December night in 1979, Paul Claffey took a quiet moment to survey this splendid, modern dancehall that only hours earlier resounded to the glorious beat of more than 400 happy punters who flocked from all over Co Roscommon and East Mayo. This was the culmination of everything he had worked for since those far-off days in Castlerea when he was ringing bands in Dublin trying to sound older than his 14 years. It had taken the best part of a decade – and there were a few false turns along the way – but Paul Claffey had finally arrived in the entertainment industry. He was now the proud promoter of one of the most successful music venues west of the Shannon.

Another man sailing into the 1980s on the crest of a wave was the Roscommon-born Country and Western singer Brendan Shine, whose song *Do You Want Your Oul Lobby Washed Down* had been the big hit single of the summer of 1979, spending four weeks at the top of the Irish singles charts. The song was Shine's 12th top ten hit in the 1970s and his fifth No 1, a remarkable achievement for a Country artist who had to constantly fight for his share of airplay on RTÉ Radio. Were it not for Larry Gogan and later Paschal Mooney, who were both willing to give homegrown artists a fair crack of the whip, Brendan's long-held ambition of cracking the Irish singles charts would have been nigh impossible.

Brendan, a native of Co Roscommon, had dreamed of having a hit single since the mid-1960s when he was a teenager playing the button accordion and singing with Ciaran Kelly's Céilí Band.

"The rest of the band and myself would be travelling home from gigs in the van and would tune into Radio Luxembourg because Radio Éireann went off the air at midnight," he recalls. "Luxembourg played a cross-section of music and I remember they'd play the likes of Joe Dolan and Larry Cunningham and the Mighty Avons."

Larry Cunningham's first single, *Tribute to Jim Reeves,* was released in January 1965 and reached No 9 in the Irish charts, while a year later the Longford man hit the coveted top spot with *Lovely Leitrim.*

"To hear guys that we knew from the Irish showband scene on Radio Luxembourg was incredible and it was a huge source of inspiration for me," says Brendan. "I started my own band in 1968 with Johnny Dawson and my younger brother Owen and we immediately began recording professionally."

Brendan and his five siblings came from a farming background but there was a rich vein of musical talent running through the family too. His father, Paddy, had played in the dancebands of the 1950s and Brendan first appeared on stage with his dad in the early 1960s, playing a diverse set that included the music of Glen Miller, Perry Como, Hank Williams, Buddy Holly and Elvis Presley.

"We were a two-piece outfit and we called ourselves Paddy Shine and his Two-Piece Orchestra... we were very cheeky!" recalls Brendan with a chuckle. "Dad played the sax and I was on accordion. I remember we played an open-air dance called The Maypole in Summerhill, which was a short distance from our home."

Home to the Shine family was a small farm in Kielty, a picturesque townland in South Roscommon, straddled between the rivers Shannon and Suck. The Shine homestead was adjacent to the local dancehall and Brendan played there regularly with his father while the dancers tripped the light fantastic under the ever-watchful gaze of the vigilant parish priest.

"The priest used to separate the couples that were dancing too closely and say 'Leave enough room for the Holy Spirit'!" he recalls.

Dances were not permitted during Lent so when Brendan left school to join Ciaran Kelly's Céilí Band on a full-time basis he quickly became accustomed to touring the UK in the spring, playing to packed-out venues in Irish emigrant cities like Liverpool, Leeds, Birmingham and London.

"We'd go across on the cattle boat from Dublin to Liverpool," he recalls. "We were on deck in the torrents of rain while the cattle were downstairs with a roof over their heads!

"It was quite adventurous but it was hard work too, playing six nights a week and going around different dancehalls in big cities like London. Landing there was quite a shock to the system for a young lad of 16 from a small village in the West of Ireland."

Music had resounded through the Shine farmhouse during Brendan's childhood years in the 1950s. He turned ten in 1957 when Billy Haley's *Rock Around The Clock* hit cinema screens in Ireland – a watershed for so many youngsters of the era – but Brendan's real love was the music of American Country artists like George Jones and Hank Williams, rarely played on Radio Éireann but regularly featured on Radio Luxembourg and the BBC World Service.

As he grew older, Brendan asked friends and neighbours who had emigrated to America to send home tapes of some of the great Country music radio stations. He was amazed to discover that a lot of these stations were playing Irish music, sometimes reinterpreted for an American audience but often as authentic and unvarnished as when the people who carried those tunes in their heads and hearts started out on their transatlantic voyages decades or maybe even a century earlier.

"A lot of my school pals emigrated to the States and they brought home tapes of some great Irish programmes broadcast in America. It was through those tapes that I heard for the first time the McNulty family from Kilteevan in my own county of Roscommon. They were absolutely massive in America from the early 1930s to the 1960s.

"I also heard the music of lots of Irish dance orchestras and other American performers who had been influenced by Irish music. Those tapes were a huge part of my musical education because I was soaking up influences that weren't available in Ireland at that time.

"This was long before the Internet and sourcing music was a real challenge so it was really exciting when I'd get one of these reel-to-reel tapes in the post. There could be four or five hours of music on it and I'd listen for days on end, picking up all kinds of songs that wouldn't have been widely known in Ireland."

Brendan released his first single, *Treat My Daughter Kindly,* with the Ciaran Kelly Céilí Band in 1967 but had to wait another three years for his first top ten hit, *A Bunch of Violets Blue,* which reached number six in 1970. A year later, Shine topped the charts with *O'Brien Has No Place To Go,* a song that had its roots in those emigrant tapes from across the Atlantic.

"*O'Brien* was an old music hall song that came from America," he explains. "Everything I have ever played I basically inherited from our forefathers and the hits I was recording in the 1970s came from listening and watching people I admired – whether it was in my own native area or through the tapes from America, which opened my ears to such a wide range of musical influences."

To reach number one was special, but to do it with a song rooted in the traditional canon he held so dear made it all the more memorable for Brendan Shine.

"I can still recall Larry Gogan announcing the number one on the radio that evening [Shine replaced Neil Diamond's *I Am, I Said* at the top of the charts]. Larry remarked that 'The bonfires will be burning in Kielty tonight'.

"Larry was a great man for the Irish artists. He was, first and foremost, a pop man but he always had great time for the fella who came up from the country."

Brendan scored a second number one in 1973 with *Where The Three Counties Meet,* a song penned by Co Longford man Patsy Farrell, and his third number one came with *Abbeyshrule* in 1974. But his momentum stalled later that year when his next single *(Turn Out The Lights) Love Me Tonight* only reached number 11 after Radio Éireann declined to play it regularly because of the song's "suggestive title". Brendan first heard Don Williams singing it on WHN, a big Country music station in New York in 1973.

Do You Want Your Oul Lobby Washed Down was Brendan's last number one. The problem for Country artists was that management in RTÉ had vowed to use its new, all-music radio station to supplant the pop pirates before these imposters claimed millions of pounds in precious advertising revenue. The decision had a devastating effect on Ireland's Country music industry.

By the summer of 1985, when Midwest Radio was established, an Irish Country and Western act hadn't reached the top of the charts since Foster and Allen scored with *A Bunch of Thyme* in the autumn of 1981. It wasn't that Irish people's musical tastes had suddenly changed; it was just that Irish artists were no longer getting the same airplay they previously enjoyed from the state broadcaster.

Ironically, in those halcyon days of the 1970s when the likes of Brendan Shine, Big Tom, Dickie Rock, Joe Dolan and Red Hurley were all scoring number one hits, there was a view in the Irish Country scene that Radio Éireann could do an awful lot more to promote indigenous music. But what happened in the early 1980s made the preceding decade seem like a golden age. Once RTÉ Radio 2 took to the airwaves in May 1979, Irish Country and Western music was effectively frozen out of the national broadcaster's playlist, apart from the occasional exposure offered by the likes of Larry Gogan and Paschal Mooney who continued to fly the flag for homegrown traditional artists such as Brendan Shine, Joe Dolan and Big Tom, all of whom still boasted enormous fan-bases. But there was little hope for an emerging artist who needed radio exposure to get noticed, especially in an era when dancehalls were closing all over the place.

RTÉ Radio's decision to give the cold shoulder to Irish Country music created a gap in the market that was eventually exploited by local radio stations. RTÉ's loss would ultimately be Midwest Radio's gain.

Paul Claffey roared into the 1980s in a sparkling BMW but it wasn't long before he was forced to reassess the naïve optimism that propelled him into the new decade. Ireland was on the cusp of a massive recession and the year was barely a week old when the then Taoiseach Charles Haughey delivered a televised address to the nation in which he revealed a dismal economic situation.

"I wish to talk to you this evening about the state of the nation's affairs," Haughey began, "and the picture I have to paint is not, unfortunately, a very cheerful one. The figures, which are just now becoming available to us, show one thing: as a community we are living away beyond our means."

Watching at home in Castlerea, Paul was initially unperturbed by Haughey's gloomy assessment of Ireland's economic affairs. The entertainment industry was robust and had survived plenty of short-term economic recessions over the past two decades; it would surely survive this one too.

The young dancehall promoter's early confidence seemed well founded. The crowds kept flocking to the Midnight Club and the venue enjoyed one of its biggest ever attendances in March 1980 when Irish band Horslips took to the stage. But storm clouds were beginning to gather. Ireland's dancehall promoters were about to be swept away by one of those inexorable tides of change that render those caught in their wake utterly powerless.

For almost half a century, Ireland's entertainment industry was governed by the Public Dancehalls Act of 1935, an archaic piece of legislation enacted by Éamon de Valera's Fianna Fáil government at the behest of the Catholic Church, which wanted to put an end to the tradition of all-night house dances. Under the act, all public dances must be licensed and the conditions of those licences were laid down in the local district court.

In the late 1960s, the singing pubs tested the 1935 legislation by bringing music, dancing and alcohol under the one roof for the first time but they did not impact on the dancehalls to any great extent. The big showbands continued to perform in large venues that could hold several thousand patrons while the singing pubs catered for smaller audiences and, therefore, lesser-known musical acts starting out in their careers.

But the emergence of the nightclub a decade later presented an altogether more formidable challenge for the dancehall proprietors. The nightclubs were a product of the discotheque scene, which took root in New York in the mid-1970s and soon blossomed across Europe. Discos differed from the old-style ballrooms in that patrons danced to the music of disc jockeys playing the hits of the day over a loudspeaker system accompanied by special effects such as strobe lighting. Crucially, in Ireland, discotheques also sold alcohol to patrons by taking advantage of a loophole in the 1935 legislation that allowed intoxicating liquor to be served up to 2am as long as it came with a freshly cooked meal.

Dancehalls were ill equipped to provide meals to their patrons – some of the older venues barely had proper toilet facilities – but hotels were ideally placed to capitalise on the increasing popularity of discotheques. In a matter of months, the entire entertainment industry was turned on its head and dancehall promoters like Paul Claffey saw their entire business model – one that had survived recessions, widespread emigration, shifting musical tastes and clerical interference – swept away in a tsunami of change. Brendan Shine, who was a part-owner of the Rose Club dancehall in Moate saw the transformation at close quarters.

"Joe Dolan was the biggest draw on the Irish circuit at that time and we had 2,200 in to see him one Saturday night. The next time he came there was only 800. Why… because a nightclub [Rockfords] had opened in Roscommon town.

"The day it launched they had a small plane flying over the town trailing a banner for this new nightclub. The people went in a different direction that night and they never came back to Moate. Inside of eight weeks there was a padlock on the door of the Rose Club because the crowds had dropped to 200 and it was no longer viable."

One of the most successful entrepreneurs in Galway in the 1960s was Con Hynes, a wool exporter from Portumna who also owned the Las Vegas Ballroom in Tuam and ran a thriving sideline business renting marquees for festivals throughout the West. Shine was friendly with Hynes and one day in the 1980s, while reminiscing on the glory years of the showband era, the Portumna man remarked:

"Brendan, do you know what was the key to the success of the showbands?"

"What?" said Shine.

"Sheep," came the reply.

"How to you figure that out?" asked a bemused Shine, struggling to figure out how his friend had managed to make a link between his two very different enterprises.

"Well, it's like this," explained Hynes. "If you put one sheep out a gap, 2,000 will follow."

Recalling the rapid demise of the Rose Club, Shine immediately grasped the logic of the Galway man's novel theory of showbands and sheep. People followed the crowd, it was as simple as that, and once the crowds started to drift towards the discotheques, the demise of the dancehalls was inevitable.

The 1980s promised so much for Paul Claffey but by the start of 1981, the business he scrupulously fashioned over the course of a decade was already on borrowed time. The lights would soon be going out at the Midnight Club.

CHAPTER FIVE

'I'm thinking of starting a radio station'

IN 1983, Brendan Shine entered the Irish charts with the song *Three Pubs in Bohola,* a catchy little ditty composed by a young journalist who worked for the *Connaught Telegraph* newspaper in Castlebar.

Michael Commins had been writing songs for almost a decade by the time *Three Pubs in Bohola* hit the charts, peaking at No 14. Indeed, the Claremorris man even enjoyed a number one hit with Susan McCann's rendition of his song, *Big Tom Is Still The King,* which spent two weeks at the top of the charts in the summer of 1977. By his own admission, *Three Pubs in Bohola* was "a bit of a novelty song" that might never have made it into the charts were it not for its dynamic debut at the annual fundraising concert in Claremorris for the Knock branch of the Irish Red Cross. The man singing the song that night was not Brendan Shine: it was, in fact, an inimitable Mayo GAA fan from Kiltimagh.

"The first man to perform *Three Pubs* on stage was the great John Regan, dressed in his leathers and just back from England," recalls Michael with a chuckle. "The Red Cross concerts were a big thing in the 1980s and there could be anything up to 1,400 people there. All the great bands of the era played at those concerts – Big Tom, The Champions, Gene Stuart and Brendan Shine. They were great nights."

Brendan Shine was backstage when the diminutive John Regan launched into the opening verse of the then unknown song. The Kielty hit-maker quickly noticed the audience's positive response.

"Jaysus that's going down awful well… what is it?" Shine asked Michael.

"It's a bit of a ditty I wrote, a bit of craic," the Claremorris man replied.

"Well, whatever it is, it's getting a good reaction!"

A few weeks later, Shine rang Michael to ask if he could record *Three Pubs in Bohola* and release it as a single. Commins readily agreed and the rest, as they say, is history. Although it failed to reach number one, *Three Pubs in Bohola* became one of Shine's best-loved songs and is today regarded as something of a Mayo anthem, a regular party piece for anyone with connections to the county.

"It amazes me how *Three Pubs* took on a life of its own," notes Michael. "It was a complete throw-away song and I never even expected it to be recorded let alone to be one of my best known songs."

Michael Commins' love of Country music can be traced back to a Friday night in February 1966 when Doc Carroll and the Royal Blues became the first band from the West of Ireland to make it to the top of the Irish charts after their song *Old Man Trouble* replaced Larry Cunningham's *Lovely Leitrim.*

"Home for me was Cloonmore, just over three miles from Kiltimagh but in the parish of Claremorris," recalls Michael. "Our neighbour Pake Hyland was in the house with us the night Doc Carroll and the Royal Blues went to number one.

"The Gill brothers, Frank and Vincent [members of the Royal Blues] came from the nearby village of Murneen, where I now reside. The previous week the Royal Blues had come into the top ten, which was a huge thing in a rural area like ours. So we were waiting all week for the top ten to see if they had made it to number one.

"I can still recall everyone gathered around the old electric wireless as Larry Gogan counted down the top ten and when he announced the number two we knew the Royal Blues must be at number one because they couldn't possibly have gone out of the charts altogether… and then next thing they were number one.

"We were so proud to think that a band from our local area had become the first from the West of Ireland to reach number one. In many ways, it brought national radio to a local level and it is something I can recall vividly to this day."

Growing up in the 1960s in a house without television, Radio Éireann provided the soundtrack to Michael Commins' formative years.

"Radio Éireann was the dominant force in our young lives," he recalls. "Nostalgia reigns supreme when I think of names and programmes like Paddy Crosbie and *The School Around the Corner,* Michael Dillon and the *Cattle Market Reports,* which my late father, Tom, would listen to religiously, Seán Ó Murchú and *Céilí House,* Din Joe and *Take The Floor,* and, of course, *The Waltons Programme* with Leo Maguire and those famous sign-off words every Saturday – 'If you feel like singing, do sing an Irish song.'"

Listening to the weekly top ten became a ritual for the young Michael Commins, and there were even a few occasions when he sneaked away from the hayfield on a summer's evening to hear Larry Gogan count down the latest Irish singles. Michael was drawn to Country music from an early age and was a big fan of the sponsored music programmes on Radio Éireann, which featured Irish singers like Larry Cunningham, Dickie Rock and, of course, Big Tom and the Mainliners from Co Monaghan, who scored their first top ten hit in January 1967 with *Gentle Mother.*

Michael became one of Big Tom's most devoted fans in the West of Ireland and the two eventually developed a close friendship that endured right up to the Castleblayney man's death in April 2018.

If Country music was an important part of Michael Commins' formative years, so too was the GAA, which came to life each summer through the mesmerising commentaries of the incomparable Micheál O'Hehir.

"Micheál O'Hehir took us on magical journeys that only radio can do," says Michael. "He was the voice of the GAA and sport in this country for so many years. To this day, something wells up deep inside when I hear an archive clip of the man who brought us to Croke Park and Thurles, Clones and Castlebar, Tuam and the deep south."

As a student at St Colman's College in Claremorris in the early 1970s, Michael's interest in radio extended beyond Radio Éireann and the self-confessed night owl soon became a late-night listener to the BBC stations, AFN (American Forces Network) and pirates such as the re-launched Caroline and North Sea.

"North Sea Radio broadcast off Hilversum in Holland and that's where I heard the great voice of Don Allen from Canada who later became a Country music presenter with Midlands Radio in Tullamore," he explains. "I was a big fan of North Sea Radio and even wrote to them a few times and got some letters back, which was a great thrill for a teenager in those days."

By the late 1970s, Michael was working as a bank official in Abbeyleix after spending a short period in Athlone where he developed a great friendship with Brendan Shine. Having dabbled in songwriting since his mid-teens, Michael got his first big break in 1975 when Pat Ely recorded one of his compositions, *The Western Counties,* for the B-side of the single *Any Tipperary Town*. Two years later, *Big Tom Is Still The King,* reached the top of the Irish charts, fulfilling a childhood dream for a young Mayo man who only a decade earlier had been sprinting through freshly-cut hayfields on a summer's evening in Cloonmore to catch Larry Gogan's top ten on the wireless.

Later in 1977, Michael achieved another long-held ambition when he participated in an RTÉ community radio broadcast to coincide with the Abbeyleix summer festival.

"Abbeyleix got a licence for the nine-day festival and the station operated from RTÉ's outside broadcast unit, which was able to cover a four to five-mile area," he recalls. "I brought in my bag of vinyl and broadcast a show."

Michael Commins was not to know it but he had just taken the first step in a broadcasting career that would eventually see him become one of the best-loved voices on local radio in Ireland.

The Midnight Club celebrated its fifth anniversary in September 1981 and Paul Claffey marked the occasion by taking out a full-page advertising feature in the *Western Journal,* the Ballina-based newspaper founded a few years earlier by former *Western People* editor Jim McGuire and legendary Charlestown-born journalist John Healy. Claffey's old friend from Castlerea, John Waters – now a freelance journalist with the *Western Journal* – used his burgeoning literary skills to extol the Midnight Club, describing it as "one of the best maintained and efficiently run ballrooms in the country". Referencing the widespread closure of rural dancehalls, Waters said the Midnight Club was one of the few "willing to face up to the challenge of the age [by] combining top quality entertainment with a high standard of comfort for its patrons".

Waters was not gilding the lily. A year earlier, the parish council had built an extension to house a soundproofed television lounge where patrons who didn't wish to dance could relax in comfort watching movies and enjoying tea, sandwiches, soft drinks and snacks. Having pioneered the concept of Friday night dancing in the West (up to then dances were usually held on Saturday and Sunday nights), Claffey was now running discos each Friday while continuing to book the likes of Joe Dolan and Big Tom for Saturday and Sunday nights. John Waters predicted a bright future for the venue:

"Gone are the days when the public are prepared to put up with draughty halls, low quality entertainment, poor lighting and an almost total lack of facilities. As long as places like the Midnight Club continue to supply their own special alternative to drink-orientated entertainment, such primitive conditions will exist only in the memory! Here's to the next five years!"

But the optimism was misplaced; even significant investment in modern facilities could not save dancehall promoters like Paul Claffey who simply could not compete with discos where alcohol was readily available into the early hours. Six months later, the *Western Journal* carried a front-page story in which reporter Anthony Hickey predicted that many of Mayo's ballrooms were "dancing out their last waltz".

"Already, halls in Westport, Swinford and Belcarra have faded into memory as the thirsty crowds quickstep it to alcohol-serving discos, cabarets and club socials with 1am exemptions. And now worried dancehall managers, fearing the worst for the remaining halls, have banded together to defend their interests."

The newspaper went on to explain that ten ballroom owners in counties Mayo and Roscommon had sought a meeting with local Garda Superintendents to see what could be done about curbing the exemptions. But already there was an air of resignation among the ballroom owners who realised they were simply out of step with the changing times. Having recently opened Swingers Nightclub in Ballyhaunis, Paul Claffey told the *Journal:*

"The exemptions are definitely giving the halls an awful hammering. There is no way we can compete against bar exemptions."

A lesser man might have cut his losses and ran but Claffey was an incorrigible optimist who refused to become despondent, even in the face of mounting evidence that the days of the dancehalls were over. Swingers in Ballyhaunis was barely up and running when he took over Cupid's in Castlerea and by 1983, Claffey was being linked to the Classic Ballroom in Gort, telling the *Tuam Herald* he planned to spend £15,000 on its refurbishment.

But it was money he didn't have. By now, the BMW had been traded in and replaced with a two-door Fiat 127, a car that was as banjaxed as the Irish economy. Debts taken out in the boom years of the 1970s were now subject to crippling interest rates of over 15 per cent and the banks were no longer willing to lend money to men like Claffey, thus making it virtually impossible to operate a business, especially one dependent on a ready supply of cash. How could he pay suppliers in advance or book advertisements in newspapers if he didn't have cash in hand?

It was a vicious circle. As the recession worsened, the credit lines dried up completely and businessmen like Paul Claffey needed to find new ways of making money if they were to stay afloat.

"There was nothing I didn't try at the time to make a few bob," he recalls. "I even went into the rag trade. I went to Germany and bought 2,000 feckin' jump suits and went around selling them door to door."

In late 1984, Claffey bowed to the inevitable and converted part of Swingers into a restaurant. He then applied to the local district court to register Swingers as a restaurant for the purposes of the Intoxicating Liquor Act of 1927, which would allow him to sell alcohol and apply for late-night exemptions like his rivals. He was desperate to get the licence for the busy Christmas period but Judge Bernard Brennan was in no mood to be hurried along, telling Paul he couldn't be "handing out restaurant certificates like parking tickets".

The legal process dragged on until the following summer when Paul finally launched the renamed Midas Restaurant and Nightclub with Big Tom and the Mainliners providing the entertainment on the opening night. But even the lure of a late-night bar failed to attract the crowds in sufficient numbers who, like the sheep in Brendan

Shine's analogy, had set off for a different gap altogether. Within a matter of weeks it was as good as over for Paul Claffey: he was stone cold broke.

"I remember Oliver Barry rang me and offered The Wolfe Tones but I had to turn them down because I had no money to stock the bar. I knew I'd have the people but what good was that if I couldn't stock the bar? I knew I was fecked then."

More than a week after Gene Stuart played Midas, Paul awoke early one morning to discover the postman had already delivered another batch of new bills, old bills and legal threats for oldest bills of all. A copy of that morning's *Irish Independent* was sitting on the kitchen table and he turned the pages absent-mindedly as he ate breakfast, his mind adrift in a fog of money problems, the kind of problems that could cause a man to lose his mind altogether.

The headlines in the *Irish Independent* weren't doing anything to improve his mood either. The jobless crisis was worsening with another 15,000 expected to join the dole queues in 1985, bringing the total number of unemployed in the country to a record 231,000. Interest rates were stuck at over 14 per cent while the government was planning to introduce a 12-month pay freeze in the public sector, which was expected to lead to industrial chaos.

Even the weather reflected the miserable mood in the country. Average rainfall for the summer was double the norm and Met Éireann could see no sign of a dry spell on the horizon. Despairing farmers were bracing themselves for the loss of €200m in crops and €50m in fodder while cattle prices had hit rock bottom as farmers tried to sell their stock ahead of an impending fodder crisis.

Paul closed the newspaper, gulped down the last of his tea and pulled on his jacket, which was still damp from the soaking he had received the night before after his car ran out of petrol a mile from home. Checking the pockets for any loose change, he pulled out a scrap of paper and five 10p coins, hoping against hope the paper might turn out to be hard currency. Imagine if it was a £20 note, he thought.

But it wasn't. Of course, it wasn't. Claffey gloomily unfolded the small sheet, which appeared to have been torn from a book, and spread it on the kitchen table, straining to read the now barely legible ink. It was probably another IOU.

He could make out a telephone number and the name Gerry Reilly but the rest was barely decipherable.

"Who the hell is Gerry Reilly?" he wondered out loud as he pulled the piece of paper towards him for closer inspection. The word at the end seemed to begin with *trans*...

And then it dawned on him. *Transmitter.*

Gerry Reilly, Cavan, MW transmitter. That was it.

This was the piece of paper Chuck Owens had given him more than a week earlier in Midas Nightclub. Maybe Owens was right, maybe the only way to get a crowd into Midas on a Saturday night was to start a radio station. At the very least, he should give this Gerry Reilly fella a call and see if he could do business with him, though how in the name of God he'd find the money to pay him was another matter entirely.

On that wet, dreary summer's morning in 1985, Paul Claffey's entire future hung on a scrap of damp paper and five 10p coins. He stepped out into the rain, pulled the jacket over his head and ran down the street to the telephone box, which was occupied, as it always seemed to be in those days. Sheltering under a doorway as the rain teemed down, Claffey glanced at the teenage girl in the booth who seemed to be settling down for a long conversation.

"I can't be waiting here half the bloody day while she's talking to her boyfriend," he muttered to himself. "To hell with this radio business anyway. Sure it's a daft idea."

But just as he was about to step back into the rain and make a dash for home, he saw the teenager put down the receiver and gently nudge the door open. Paul leapt forward, grabbed the door for the teenager and then slipped into the comfort of the booth. He carefully placed the five 10p coins above the keypad, pulled the piece of paper from his pocket and dialed the number, the receiver cradled on his shoulder. The call was answered so promptly Claffey almost missed his cue to drop the first 10p coin in the slot.

"Hello, hello, is this Gerry Reilly?"

"It is," came an unmistakable Cavan accent. "Who's this?"

"This is Paul Claffey here. I run Midas Nightclub in Ballyhaunis... in Co Mayo..."

"Oh, aye."

"I'm thinking of starting a radio station..."

CHAPTER SIX

A set of false teeth on the dresser

By the time Paul Claffey made his fateful call in the summer of 1985, Gerry Reilly had already established a full-time business installing and maintaining transmitters for pirate radio stations along the circuitous Irish border.

Still in his twenties, Cavan-born Reilly was doing things he now cheerfully admits were dangerous to the point of being potentially fatal. It was bad enough to be manufacturing transmitters carrying lethal levels of electrical current but to repeatedly cross the Irish border at the height of the Troubles with a van full of suspicious looking electronics equipment was a first cousin to madness.

"When you're young you don't realise how dangerous things are. I'd have to go to Clones to get to Donegal but that meant crossing the border three or four times on the way from Kilnaleck to Clones. The British Army brought me in a few times because they didn't know what the stuff was in my van. If it was now I wouldn't do it, no way."

But negotiating army checkpoints on notoriously dangerous border roads was actually the safest part of Gerry's day job back then.

"Looking back on it now, the transmitters were lethal things, carrying massive power – 2,500 to 3,000 volts and 20 amps of current – so there was always the potential for a tragedy. I had a friend who was electrocuted while working on a radio transmitter.

"I realise now how lucky I was to avoid serious injury or worse but I had great fun in those years too. The pirate radio days were magic."

Gerry traces his lifetime love of all things electronic to a local priest, Fr Pat Brady, who established a branch of Macra na Tuaithe in

Gerry's native Kilnaleck in the 1960s. Fr Brady encouraged the teenage members of the new club to undertake various initiatives and one of Gerry's projects was to make a crystal radio receiver, which he built from scratch, later winning national award for it.

Soon, Gerry and his school-friends were making amplifiers for their guitars before eventually graduating to loudspeakers. One day, they persuaded a local singer, Derek McCormack, later of the band Barleycorn, to give an impromptu performance outside Gerry's house.

"My house was up on a hill in the countryside so I stuck the speaker up on the roof and pointed down to the valley below. Derek started singing and sure people didn't know what was going on. They were coming out from their houses and looking up at the sky! That was my first broadcast."

Kilnaleck had once been a mining village but by the 1960s local employment was concentrated entirely on agriculture and some of Gerry's elderly neighbours were horrified at the electronic adventures of the local teenagers. One woman was even heard to say: "What's going to become of those fellas? They will never amount to anything because they have no interest in the land."

Gerry, however, was determined to make a career out of electronics. One morning, while stepping off the schoolbus in Kilnaleck, he spied a one-pound note on the ground near a local pub. He put it in his pocket and later that evening called into the shop opposite the pub and asked the lady-owner if anybody had called in about the missing pound. She suggested he put a notice in the local newspaper, *The Anglo Celt,* but after a few weeks the money was still unclaimed and Gerry decided it was high time he applied the age-old rule of finder's keepers.

"I used the money to buy a soldering iron," he recalls. "That was my first piece of equipment."

After a short stint at Bolton Street College in Dublin, Gerry took a job in a television store in Oldcastle in Co Meath where he remained for six months before getting a position closer to home in Bernie Master Vision in Cavan town. The shop, which specialised in radios and televisions, served a vast area along the border, taking in counties Cavan, Monaghan and Fermanagh.

"That's when I really got an interest in radio broadcasting," he explains. "What you got to remember is that it was very difficult to get involved in electronics back then. Nobody knew anything about it. There was no Internet so information was not as readily available as it is today. I remember going up to the library in Kevin Street College in Dublin for information."

Most of Gerry's work in those formative years involved fixing transistor radios and installing the odd black and white television. Most of the television sets were leased because people did not have enough money to purchase them outright.

Gerry built his first radio transmitter in 1978 but his big break came four years later when Dubliner Peter Gibney asked him to supply the transmitter for the newly established Cavan Community Radio (CCR). Building the transmitter was the easy part; getting sufficient power was another matter entirely.

However, Gerry was fortunate to be able to turn to a fellow Cavan man, Anthony Tully, whose firm, Anthony Tully Components (ATC), supplied him with everything he needed to build a radio transmitter, including valves imported from the Soviet Union at a cost of £25 each.

In 1984, Gerry built transmitters for three new radio stations in Co Donegal, where pirate broadcasting had really taken off, and within a year he and his brother Charlie were servicing a region stretching from the Inishowen peninsula in Donegal to Carlingford Lough in Co Louth. The Reillys were also moving further south after Breffni Radio, which had been founded in his native Kilnaleck, expanded into Co Longford where it was heard over a vast tract of the Midlands, thanks to the powerful medium wave (MW) transmitters Gerry built.

Breffni Radio was established in the spring of 1985 and its choice of music was unapologetically Country and Western, making it an heir to the tradition of older border pirate stations such as Radio 99. Paul Claffey admits he was impressed by Breffni's success when it expanded into the Midlands but had no fixed idea on the kind of pirate station he wanted to launch in the summer of 1985. He was merely trying to create a cost-effective promotional vehicle for his ailing nightclub, which wouldn't see out the year if he didn't do something drastic to revive it.

As soon as he put down the phone after speaking to Gerry Reilly, Paul knew he had encountered his first – and, possibly, fatal – obstacle in his quest to establish a radio station in Ballyhaunis: he was going to have to find £1,500 for a transmitter. And how, in the name of God, would someone on the brink of bankruptcy be able to stumble upon £1,500?

It was the only question on Paul's mind as he went to sleep that night. His conversation with Gerry Reilly had left him excited about the potential of pirate radio, the Cavan man having explained in some detail the success enjoyed by several of the border stations that seemed to be making good money out of their illegal ventures. But without start-up capital there was absolutely nothing Paul could do to get his radio project off the ground.

The following evening, Paul was driving through Castlerea when he spied Chris Carroll entering his house with a box of records under his arm. It was a Eureka moment. If anyone could assist in establishing a radio station it was the young DJ from Main Street in Castlerea who had invested in so much kit over the years his discos were like mini-rock concerts. The two men were archenemies in the local entertainment industry but Claffey needed the money so badly he was walling to forget past enmities, and hoped Chris would be of a similar mindset.

"Hey Chris," he shouted, opening the car door. "Have you a minute?"

The disc jockey wandered over and propped himself against the door. Paul launched into his best sales pitch.

"I'm thinking of starting a radio station over in Midas but I can't get the money for the transmitter. Do you think you could lay your hands on £1,500?"

Chris had the money but wanted to give Paul's proposal a little thought so he kicked for touch.

"Well," said Chris. "I know Tom Goodwin up in the bank. Maybe he'll give me a loan."

Paul didn't know it but he couldn't have found a more opportune time to put his proposition for a radio station to Chris.

"I gave up the job in Tom Flynn's in the early 1980s and was working as a DJ full time," Chris recalls. "Paul probably knew I was at a loose end so the timing was perfect from my perspective.

"I didn't know Paul particularly well but I was immediately attracted to the idea. But to be honest, that's all it was – an idea.

"Paul was really charged up and was hopping with enthusiasm. In my head, I knew it could work but I wondered how we would go about it, where we would set up shop and, most importantly, how much would it cost."

The two men talked for a little longer before saying their goodbyes and agreeing to meet again once Chris had sourced the start-up capital. As Chris walked back to his house, he heard Paul calling him again. He turned around to see his future business partner leaning out the door of the car, gesticulating furiously with his hands.

"Chris, you know when you go up to Tom for that loan?"

"Yeah?"

"Whatever you do don't tell him it's for a radio station… tell him it's for a feckin' car!"

And with that the Fiat 127 stuttered off into the dreary haze of yet another wet summer's evening, the driver's door struggling to stay closed.

Summer turned to autumn and Midas Nightclub stumbled from one mini-crisis to another. Paul kept juggling the bills while the court appearances became more frequent, creditors swooping for their share of the ever-diminishing asset pool before the inevitable bankruptcy.

With so much on his mind, Paul forgot all about the pirate radio project until one day in mid-September Chris Carroll hailed him down while driving through Castlerea.

"Hey Paul, I got that money," he shouted over to him.

"Money?" asked Paul quizzically. "What money?"

"The money for the radio station!"

"Oh Jesus, yeah. I'd forgot all about it."

Later that evening, Paul and Chris met in the ballroom of the local Casino to carry out an experiment. Using some of Chris' disco equipment, they set up a mini-radio studio and recorded several demo advertisements on a tape deck. Then they discussed the next stage in the project.

"Paul laid his cards on the table right away," recalls Chris. "He was in dire financial straits and had no money to invest. But he had a cloakroom in Midas Nightclub that would be ideal for a radio studio and assured me that a twin-deck record player, a couple of cassette machines and a microphone would get us up and running. The biggest cost would be the transmitter and I'd pay for that with my so-called car loan!

"To be honest, I knew it would take time to establish a listenership in order to sell advertising but in the meantime it was a great opportunity for Paul to promote Midas and for me to promote myself as a DJ."

Paul suggested they revive the name of his old pirate station, Midwest Radio, and the two discussed at length the type of music they'd play. Chris, who was still the resident DJ in the Don Arms Hotel in Castlerea, had a record collection that was mostly chart based but both agreed Country music would have to form some element of the playlist; they just weren't sure how much.

"To be honest, I thought we'd be a pop station in the main with a bit of Country," recalls Paul. "But I didn't want to make the mistakes I'd made the first time around in 1978 so I decided to do a little bit of research before we began broadcasting."

Like so much of the Midwest story, Claffey's market research proved fairly unconventional. A few days later, he went to the psychiatric hospital in Castlerea and stood outside, waiting for the nurses to finish their shift. When they started to emerge, Paul fell into conversation with them, asking what kind of music they'd like to hear on a local radio station.

"Big Tom," said one nurse. "He's still the king!"

"Philmonena Begley," remarked another.

"You'd have to play Susan McCann too," exclaimed a third.

"What about Joe Dolan? You can't leave him out."

"And Brendan Shine..."

It was another Eureka moment. Paul Claffey had accidentally fallen upon a winning radio formula.

"Sure no-one is playing that kind of music," he muttered to himself while driving home. "The nurses in Castlebar are the same as the nurses in Castlerea. This has to work."

Paul also knew that if he gave frequent airplay to the Country artists who were performing regularly in Midas he'd be able to attract more people to his nightclub. For as long as he'd been in the entertainment business, he'd heard complaints from Country artists and their managers about the lack of airplay they were getting on the national broadcaster.

"When I was booking the bands in the 1980s, if you came down the ladder at all people didn't know who the bands were," he explains.

Galway-band The Conquerors had been on the road for over a decade and were highly regarded among dancehall owners like Paul, but without regular airplay the band couldn't attract the sort of crowds they deserved. While thinking about the type of music he'd play on the new station, Paul recalled a conversation he and Willie Carty, the manager of The Conquerors, had had a few years earlier.

"You know The Conquerors are good," Claffey told Carty. "I know they're good but how do I convince the people out there they are good?"

"Well," said Carty, "We have a record out now and Larry Gogan is going to play it next Tuesday week at a quarter to two on the sponsored programme on RTÉ."

"For Jaysus sake, Willie, how many people who come to my dancehall on a Sunday night will be listening to Radio 2 at a quarter to two next Tuesday week!" replied a frustrated Claffey.

The conversation remained buried deep in Paul's mind until the day he spoke to the nurses outside the hospital in Castlerea.

"If I was playing a single from The Conquerors four times a day they'd be huge," he thought as he drove home.

Paul's impromptu survey of the musical tastes of Castlerea's nurses was one the smartest – and cheapest – pieces of market research in the history of local radio.

"Play the music the people want to hear," Chuck Owens had told Claffey a few months earlier. Well, the nurses of Castlerea had just made it abundantly clear what they wanted to hear and it wasn't chart-toppers like Michael Jackson or Prince or Madonna.

Later that evening, Chris called over to Midas and the two chatted in the cloakroom about the radio project. Chris was long enough in the entertainment business to know that a DJ had to put the musical interests of the audience ahead of his own.

"I had long since learned that I had to give the people what they wanted to dance to not what I wanted to listen to so I completely understood where Paul was coming from," he says.

It was agreed there and then: Midwest Radio would be primarily a Country music station with a sprinkling of pop from the 1960s and 1970s.

All that was needed now was to install the transmitter and then the pirates of Ballyhaunis were ready to set sail.

A few weeks later, Gerry Reilly met Paul in the Longford Arms and immediately warmed to the nightclub promoter's infectious enthusiasm and mischievous sense of humour.

"I knew I'd enjoy working with him and I have to say that he and Chris couldn't have been nicer to me. They were absolute gentlemen to work with."

But it wasn't all plain sailing. Gerry confesses to experiencing a few moments of doubt when he came to Ballyhaunis in mid-November to install the transmitter.

"I was waiting on the street outside Midas and the next thing Claffey arrives in this battered oul Fiat with the driver's door hanging off!" he recalls. "I said to myself 'Jaysus, there's something wrong here.' But he was great fun so I said 'To hell with it, I'll give it a chance'."

The two greeted each other and went into the nightclub's dressingroom where Chris had already set up the most basic of radio studios. Reilly explained that he intended to install a small transmitter in the studio and a larger one on a site outside the town.

"Will we be able to fit the transmitter in the studio?" Claffey asked.

"Ah yeah, sure it's only the size of a biscuit tin," explained Reilly.

"Mighty. What about the big transmitter?"

"Now that's a different story. Have you got a site for it."

"Well… yeah…" replied Claffey, a little uneasily. "There should be no problem there."

"What do you mean *should* be no problem?"

"Come on, I'll show you and see what you think."

Reilly climbed into his van and set off in pursuit of Claffey's Fiat, driving past the railway station and continuing for a couple of miles out the Castlerea Road. They eventually came to a halt outside a derelict cottage where Chris was waiting. Paul and Chris had hastily rented the property at Spadagh after realising they couldn't locate a large transmitter in the vicinity of Midas because it would interfere with the radio and television signals of householders in Ballyhaunis.

Gerry Reilly wasn't a faint-hearted man – he couldn't be if he was regularly negotiating border checkpoints with a van full of dodgy-looking electronics components – but he had a bad feeling from the moment he stepped into the musty, eerie cottage at Spadagh.

"I thought the bloody place was haunted," he recalls with a hearty laugh. "It was an oul house that nobody had lived in for donkey's years and it was pure creepy. I'll never forget there was a dresser in it and a set of false teeth sitting on the dresser. Jaysus, I didn't like the place at all."

After agreeing to locate the transmitter in the main room, the trio continued into the back garden where Reilly explained how he intended to erect a 100-foot mast.

"I'll do a four-way pole," he said, looking up at the beautiful apple trees that overshadowed the little garden. "But I'll need a good bit of clearance for the wires so you'll have to cut a load of branches."

"What?" Claffey and Carroll exclaimed in unison.

"Sure there's not enough room here at the moment. If the four-way pole isn't wide enough you won't get a good signal. I'll get the saw from the van."

When he returned, Reilly found the two pirates standing under an apple tree in animated discussion. Suddenly, Chris broke away, pulled off his jacket, threw it to the ground and started to march with purpose towards Paul.

"Jaysus," thought the baffled Gerry Reilly. "These lads are going to come to blows."

Instead, Paul positioned himself under the nearest apple tree, placing both hands together to give his business partner a leg up as Chris began to climb the tree with surprising alacrity for a townie. Soon he was seated precariously on a misshapen branch that looked none too sturdy.

"Right," he shouted down to Reilly. "Gimme that saw and let's get to work."

While Chris was above in the tree, furiously sawing branches like a man possessed, Paul was climbing over the garden wall into a nearby field where there was a large pile of wet clay. Minutes later he returned to the garden with a lump of clay in each hand and started to pass the stuff up to Chris who proceeded to painstakingly rub it on the edges of the freshly cut branches. Meanwhile, at the other end of the garden, an increasingly bemused Gerry Reilly scratched his head in wonderment at the surreal scene unfolding before his eyes.

"Obviously they didn't want the owner of the house to know they had cut down his trees so they put this stuff on the branches to cover their tracks," he recalls with a chuckle. "I definitely knew I was in Dodge City then! But sure it was great oul craic so I said I might as well stick around to see what would happen next!"

PART II

CHAPTER SEVEN

'This was my fight for survival'

MIDWEST Radio took to the airwaves on the morning of Monday, November 25, 1985, with Paul behind the mike. He hadn't planned it that way.

"I had no intention of being a presenter," he explains. "I didn't see myself as a radio presenter at all. I owned a nightclub, that was my day job, and I just saw the radio station as a way to promote Midas and get me out of the financial hole I was in."

But needs must. Paul and Chris hadn't the resources to hire professional presenters so they took on multiple roles themselves, agreeing an ambitious programming schedule that would see them take it in turns to play non-stop music from 10am to 7pm seven days a week.

"I went on at 10 in the morning and played Country and a small bit of pop," explains Paul, "then Chris came on from 1pm to 4pm and played music from the '60s and I came back on from 4pm to 7pm and broadcast pure Country."

The two men were committing to a very punishing workload, especially as they also intended to continue with their regular jobs, Paul as promoter of Midas Nightclub and Chris as a five-night-a-week DJ. Looking back on it now, they both wonder how they managed to do it all, especially as the odds seemed so heavily stacked against them at the beginning.

"We couldn't advertise the station because the papers weren't allowed take ads from pirates," explains Paul. "So all we could do was put a speaker outside the door of Midas and distribute flyers at dances around the area."

Paul and Chris worried they might end up broadcasting to an audience of just a few family members and friends but they underestimated the power of the bush telegraph. The speaker outside the door of Midas proved an ingenious marketing tool because it immediately captured the attention of curious locals, as well as those visiting Ballyhaunis from neighbouring towns and villages.

"People would hear the music playing and they'd stop and say 'What's that?'" recalls Paul. "It was like the spread of a bushfire; it just took off within a matter of weeks."

One day in early December, Paul called into the nearby Freyne's Garage to get some work done on his troublesome Fiat. As he waited outside, he saw a middle-aged farmer climb out of a decrepit Ford Cortina that looked almost as battered as his own Fiat. The man approached one of the mechanics.

"Have ye heard of that new radio station Midwest?" the farmer began. "How do I get it in my car?"

"It's 1332 medium wave," Paul shouted over helpfully.

"What's that?"

"Tune your radio into 1332 medium wave."

"Arra sure I don't know anything about that sorta craic. Can you show me?" the man asked, turning to the mechanic.

Paul later discovered this was no once-off episode: in the winter of 1985-'86, Freyne's Garage was inundated with people calling in to have their car radios tuned into this new local pirate station.

Gerry Reilly, who regularly visited Ballyhaunis in those early weeks to service the transmitter, recalls people calling into Midas with radios under their arms.

"People would buy a radio and then call in to get you to tune it to where Midwest was on the dial," he says. "There was an innocence at that time; it was an absolutely beautiful time."

The studio was a source of much fascination too, despite it being as rudimentary as one might find anywhere in Ireland.

"It was the only radio station where they'd bring the whole station home with them when they'd finish," Gerry Reilly says laughing.

It was true. On at least three or four nights each week, Chris unplugged and dismantled the equipment, loaded it into his van and set off for a disco. He then returned at 2 or 3am to set it up all over again for Paul's morning show.

The studio itself was tiny – it was where the bands got ready before shows – and its windowless walls created a feeling of claustrophobia, but at least the lack of windows meant it was naturally sound-proofed... well, apart from the occasional noise from the adjoining toilet.

"You had to pee at the start of a record so the flush would be finished by the end of it!" recalls Paul.

The rapid success of Midwest Radio – its listenership in Ballyhaunis and the surrounding hinterland grew exponentially in the early weeks of December 1985 – came as a pleasant surprise to Chris and Paul who hadn't really expected such a spontaneous reaction. Chris puts it down to the authenticity of the station; unlike a lot of the pirates of the era, they weren't trying to ape RTÉ or Radio Luxembourg or some of the so-called fashionable pop stations.

"People identified with us because we were who we were," he says. "We weren't trying to be Gerry Ryan or Gay Byrne, we weren't trying to have mid-Atlantic DJ accents.

"Anyone can press the buttons to play two songs; it's what you bring to the show that makes you different. The most important thing is not to try to be something you're not because people won't identify with you."

It also helped that Midwest's pirate status meant it could get away with things that today would land a fully licensed station into all sorts of trouble. For example, one Friday evening in the early days, Paul had just finished his show and Chris was preparing to dismantle the gear for another night in the Don Arms, when Joe Cunniffe, who was the sound engineer at Midas, wandered into the studio, accompanied by a couple of friends. They sat around chatting for a while and Paul – as was his wont – commenced telling a few jokes.

"They were the bluest of blue jokes," Chris recalls, laughing. "Of course, what we didn't realise was that Paul had left the mike on when he'd signed off."

While Paul regaled the lads with his vast collection of risqué jokes, a man was going door to door in Ballyhaunis, telling his neighbours: "Quick, turn on Midwest, turn on Midwest, Jaysus, it's mighty stuff!"

The following evening Chris called into the local Wimpey's.

"That was the best hour of radio I've ever heard," the owner Rita O'Sullivan told him. "Sure the whole town was listening."

Paul and Chris were prepared for criticism when mistakes occurred but instead people loved Midwest all the more for the unexpected and innocent gaffes.

"I learned a lot from my experience with the radio station the first time around in Castlerea when I was trying to be too polished and too professional," explains Paul. "Other stations who set up around the same time weren't successful because they were determined to be so good.

"On the other hand, we were very unorthodox. Anything we did, we did it wrong; but we did it wrong in the right way, if you understand!"

Paul had been keen to get Midwest up and running before Christmas 1985 because he wanted to use the station to promote the festive entertainment in Midas. But something unexpected happened in early December. Paul was in the station one afternoon when Paddy Ryan from the local SuperValu arrived at the door.

"I've a heap of tins of USA biscuits up there in the shop and they're not shifting," Ryan said. "Would you ever stick a few ads on the radio and maybe I'll be able to move a few of them."

The supermarket owner then thrust £100 into Paul's hand, a huge sum in those days. Midwest immediately went USA biscuit mad. After three days, Ryan called down to ask the lads to pull the ads.

"All those biscuits are gone," he said. "I only wish I'd ordered more!"

For Paul and Chris, it was the first glimpse of the potential of local radio but they still weren't sure they had a business proposition on their hands. For one thing, they had no idea how they were going to continue with this exhausting daily schedule; if they kept it up, they'd surely be burned out by the start of spring.

It didn't take long for Midwest to extend its reach beyond Ballyhaunis. In the little village of Granlahan, on the Roscommon-Mayo border, teenagers like Gerry Glennon experienced a mixture of wonder and excitement when word started to filter through in the dying days of November 1985 that a new pirate radio station was broadcasting from Ballyhaunis.

"We were all listening to it," Gerry recalls. "I wasn't even into radio let alone music but I was absolutely fascinated by this new station, Midwest Radio. We all were. We couldn't get over it. Everyone around the place was talking about it. Some people didn't even believe it existed in Ballyhaunis!

"Radio 1 seemed so alien and so far away. Obviously we'd grown up with the Gay Byrnes and the Mike Murphys but they seemed so distant. Then, all of a sudden, something like this had come to Ballyhaunis. It was unbelievable."

In the early days, one of the thrills for Gerry and his friends was to ring requests into Midwest.

"To get a request played on Radio 1 or Radio 2 for that matter was unheard of so the novelty of phoning in and getting a request played and hearing your name back on the radio literally two or three minutes later, well that was unbelievable altogether. It's something we take for granted now because of local radio but at that time it was a totally new phenomenon and people loved it, they absolutely loved it."

The studio phone – telephone number 0907-30169 – was, in fact, a callbox located in the box office at Midas so it was something of a challenge in the early days for Paul and Chris to field calls while simultaneously spinning the discs.

Broadcasting was certainly not on Gerry Glennon's career radar in the winter of 1985-86. In an Ireland where job opportunities were few and far between, Gerry had made up his mind to move to England later in 1986 to pursue a career in psychiatric nursing. But until then he was at a loose end.

Even before Midwest launched, Gerry knew Chris Carroll who occasionally went out to Granlahan with some friends to shoot pool in the local pub. One day, Chris invited the teenager to call into Ballyhaunis to see the Midwest Radio studio for himself.

"Call in for the craic when I'm doing the afternoon show," Chris suggested.

Gerry duly hitched a lift from Granlahan to Ballyhaunis, arriving at Midas just as Chris was about to go on the air. He sat in the studio and watched his friend spinning the discs but the Granlahan youngster felt no gravitational pull towards the microphone. In fact, it was the opposite: he was in mortal dread of having to sit in front of the 'live mike'.

One evening in late January, Gerry was seated in the far corner of the studio – at a suitably safe distance from the microphone – when Paul arrived to present his evening show.

"Howye lads," Claffey said in a rasping voice that was barely decipherable. "I don't know if I can do this show at all. I have the mother and father of a sore throat."

"Sure Gerry can do it," said Chris turning to his friend. "You know the way it works by now... that's turntable one, that's turntable two and that's the microphone...

"Yeah, Gerry," said Paul. "You cover for me because I'm fecked."

"No way," said Glennon. "I can't do a radio show."

And with that the youngster leapt up and made a dash for the door. He was back in Granlahan within the hour. When Gerry tuned into 1332MW to hear how Paul was managing, he was greeted by radio silence; Claffey had gone home to his sickbed.

The following day Gerry was back in the studio for Chris' afternoon show. Paul had managed to get through the morning show but the voice was gone again.

"We can't leave the slot blank two days in a row," he said to Gerry. "You'll have to do something."

"Okay," said Glennon. "I'll give it a go but I'm not talking into that microphone!"

Gerry was as good as his word until the end of the fourth record; by then, he had grown comfortable in the DJ's hot seat and was happy to say a few words. By the third hour of the show, he was totally at ease in his new role and was even – dare we say it – enjoying himself!

While Gerry was in the studio in Ballyhaunis, Paul and Chris were out at Spadagh where they were inspecting the transmitter for faults having received a report of poor reception. Gerry Reilly had erected the transmitter on a platform of beer barrels and plywood and it consisted of six huge valves covered by metal plates with glass in between because glass wouldn't conduct the heat.

On the day he installed it, the Cavan man explained that the valves were guaranteed to fail from time to time but there was only one safe way to check whether they were working.

"You spit on the metal plate," he said. "Like this."

Reilly duly spat on the nearest plate and his spittle ricocheted at speed towards the ceiling, settling neatly in a cobweb.

"Jaysus," said Claffey gazing in wonderment at the ceiling. "That's wild stuff altogether."

"Now if the valve is gone," said Reilly. "That spit will just sizzle and stay on the plate. It's that simple."

"And what happens if I touch the plate?" ventured Claffey

"That wouldn't be such a good idea," said Reilly in his drawl Cavan accent.

"Would it be dangerous?"

"Well, do you see them false teeth over there," Reilly said, pointing towards the dresser. "Touch one of those plates and you'll be meeting the owner of those teeth!"

"Feckin' hell," exclaimed Claffey. "I'll leave Chris to look after this yoke so!"

"Wait there and I'll show ye something," said Reilly before disappearing out to his van. He returned with a faze tester that immediately lit up as soon as he walked into the room.

"Now that's the sort of radiation that's in here," he said. "So don't touch those plates whatever ye do. This feckin' place is spooky enough without having one of ye're ghosts wandering around here too!"

The day Gerry Glennon took to the airwaves for the first time, Paul and Chris were carrying out the spittle test and having isolated the failed valve, set about changing it. They then turned on the radio to check everything was in order. An unrecognisable voice greeted them.

"Who's that?" Paul asked. "That's Radio 1 you've got on there."

"No, it's not," replied Chris. "That's Gerry Glennon."

"It is not, sure that fella talking there is a pure natural."

"It is Gerry, look, it's 1332…"

"Jaysus, he's mighty. Sure he's made for radio."

Midwest Radio had just found its third presenter.

Paddy Ryan continued to place advertisements in the early months of 1986. A few other local businesses, including Billy Rochford in Rochford Motors, also gave early support to the new station. But there was no concerted effort by Paul or Chris to seek out advertisers; they had enough on their plate presenting programmes seven days a week and holding down regular jobs.

Both men had a sense the station was gathering momentum – certainly the number of requests coming into the Midas callbox was increasing every week – but there was no scientific way of establishing whether Midwest was making an impact beyond Ballyhaunis. The station had been set up in a fairly haphazard fashion with no clear business plan or long-term growth strategy; the only aim really was to keep spinning the discs and never, ever answer the door to a Garda.

"We never foresaw what Midwest became," explains Chris. "We were two chancers who saw a gap in the market and went for it. The gardaí were raiding and closing radio stations everywhere but we still went on the air because it just seemed like an exciting thing to do at the time. But we never thought it could become a fully-fledged business that would employ staff."

Everything changed, however, one Friday morning in the spring of 1986 when an envelope bearing the distinctive logo of the ESB landed in the letterbox at Midas. Upon opening it Paul turned pale.

"Christ, will you look at this?" he said to Chris, shoving the piece of paper towards him.

It was a bill was for almost £300. Gerry Reilly had promised to build a high-powered transmitter and he had certainly lived up to his word. Midwest was consuming electricity as fast as the power station down in Bellacorick could generate it.

"How are we going to pay that?" asked Chris. "They'll cut us off if we don't find the money right away."

"Leave it for now," said Paul. "We'll sit down this evening and figure out what to do."

Paul thought of little else for the rest of the day. The bill was much bigger than he had anticipated and it presented Chris and himself with a very stark choice: either shut the station for good or start to make some money from it.

Paul, Chris and Gerry Glennon sat down later that evening and agreed to close the station for two days to allow them to go on the road selling advertisements. If they raised sufficient money to pay the ESB bill, they'd re-open the station; if not, they'd be as well to close it there and then because there was no future in it.

Of the three, Paul was the most determined to make it work because he had the most to lose.

"This was my fight for survival," he explains. "It was how I was going to put bread on the table for my family. I could see how Midwest had started to lift the crowds in the nightclub so I was desperate to keep it open."

On the following Tuesday morning, 1332MW went silent for the first time since November 25 as Paul set off in the direction of Kilkelly while Chris and Gerry made tracks for Gurteen in Co Sligo, making their first stop at O'Dowd's car dealers. They introduced themselves to the owner Brendan O'Dowd.

"Who'd ye say ye're with?" he asked.

"Midwest Radio."

"Ah yeah, the pirates in Ballyhaunis! Sure I listen to ye all the time. But ye're not on this morning?"

"No, we'll be back on again later in the week."

"Good stuff, I love the music ye fellas play. Lookit, sign me up for £100."

It was that easy. Chris and Gerry couldn't believe their luck. They walked out the door of O'Dowd's with a cheque for £100; they were already one-third of the way to paying the ESB bill. Meanwhile, over in Knock, Paul had also struck it lucky with his first sales pitch, picking up a cheque for £10 from King's Garage.

It was late in the evening when all three returned to Midas.

"You won't believe it lads," said a breathless Paul as he burst through the studio door, brandishing a fistful of cheques and cash. "I've got the guts of £300 here! How did ye do?"

"Ah we did alright, I suppose," said Chris, shooting a knowing glance over at Gerry.

"Well, did ye get a hundred even?" said Paul.

"I think we finished with about… let me see… I'd say it was £900 in the end!"

Almost 35 years later, Paul can recall that evening as if it was yesterday; finally, he could see a way out of the financial quicksand in which he had been floundering for the past few years.

"I thought all of our birthdays had come together," he says. "I was certain now that this was going to be a commercial success. That evening was the first time I became convinced we were on our way to making something big out of Midwest Radio."

CHAPTER EIGHT

A Garda raid with a difference

ALMOST a year to the day that Paul Claffey and Chuck Owens had their fateful conversation in the bar of Midas Nightclub, Gene Stuart and the Homesteaders were back in Ballyhaunis for a mid-summer gig. This time Midas was packed to the rafters and there was a buzz around the place that Owens hadn't seen in an Irish Country music venue in a long time. There were even minibuses lined up along Clare Street at closing time, a sure sign people had travelled long distances to be there.

"Didn't I tell you," Owens remarked to Claffey. "A radio station was the very thing you needed. It's going well, is it?"

"It's going mighty, Chuck; it's going mighty," replied Claffey.

And it was. Midwest was enjoying a great summer as more and more advertisers came on board. Listenership was also increasing steadily and Paul and Chris had a mounting sense that Midwest was gradually establishing its own unique identity. The number of telephone requests was increasing so fast they felt the need to employ a part-time receptionist, Mary Reilly, from the nearby village of Tooreen, while postal requests were coming from places they didn't even know the transmitter could reach.

With a few pound in their pockets, Paul and Chris were even able to upgrade the studio from the dressingroom to the ladies' cloakroom while also installing a telephone extension, which meant there was no longer a need for lung-bursting sprints to the callbox at the front of the building.

Crucially, the early success of Midwest was having a very positive effect on attendances at Midas, giving Paul the lifeline he needed to commence paying down the mountain of debt accrued in the first half of the decade. Sensing the pirate station might have a short lifespan, Paul threw himself into the promotion of Midas during the first half of 1986, figuring that if the pirate were closed he would at least have put the nightclub on a reasonably solid footing.

But there was a price to be paid, too, for the gruelling work regime. Between the radio station and the nightclub, Paul was spending more time in Ballyhaunis than in Castlerea, which meant he was away from his wife Maureen and their children, Geoffrey and Rachel, for long periods.

"Maureen was fantastic during those years because the job was non-stop for me between the radio station and Midas," he recalls. "It was very difficult to juggle all of the commitments. Later, when Midwest was made legal, Maureen took over the running of Midas and made a great success of it as a nightclub throughout the 1990s."

Operating a radio station was an all-consuming occupation, especially when there were so few presenters involved. By the summer of 1986, Midwest still only had three regular presenters – Paul, Chris and Gerry – and while some modest sums of money were coming in on advertising there certainly wasn't sufficient spare cash to pay a team of DJs. The problem with a radio programme was that, unlike most other types of work, it couldn't be cancelled or deferred. It was a bit like a crying baby: it demanded your attention there and then.

Paul's work-life balance was brought into sharp focus the day after Gene Stuart's latest gig in Midas. It was a warm Sunday in early August and Paul had hoped to bring Geoffrey and Rachel, then toddlers, to the swimming pool in Castlerea, but another baby was demanding his urgent attention too. A four-hour afternoon slot on Midwest needed to be filled and he was the only person available to do it, Gerry having already taken the morning slot with Chris due to come in later that evening.

Paul took to the airwaves shortly after 1pm and played a succession of Country records, among them Big Tom's *Four Country Roads,* which had reached No 5 in the Irish charts five years earlier.

Four country roads, winding to a town in County Galway
Four country roads, leading to the friends I left behind
Four dusty roads, winding to the town of Glenamaddy
Four dusty roads, forever in the caverns of my mind

As he sang the song's lyrics, Paul rooted through a box of records on the floor, selecting the ones he intended to play for the second hour of the show. At first he failed to hear the loud knock on the front door and when he did his initial inclination was to simply ignore it.

"Who the hell is calling here on a Sunday afternoon?" he thought.

KNOCK-KNOCK-KNOCK.

There it was again. Whoever was out sounded like someone used to having doors opened promptly when they knocked.

Four roads to Glenamaddy
Four roads that drift apart
Four roads to Glenamaddy
Are the four dusty byways to my heart…

Paul continued to sing as he strolled along the corridor towards the front door.

KNOCK-KNOCK-KNOCK.

"Alright, alright," shouted Claffey. "I'm coming, I'm coming."

Reaching the door, Paul prepared to pull the lever-handle when he instinctively glanced through the peephole, his eyes feasting on a sight that caused him to leap backwards so fast he almost landed below in the studio with Big Tom. Standing outside the door of the fastest-growing pirate radio station west of the Shannon was a stern-looking Guard in full uniform with an envelope in his right hand.

"JAYSUS," Claffey muttered under his breath. "Of all the feckin' things…"

Removing his glasses, Paul peered through the peephole again, hoping against hope this unwelcome vision might have miraculously disappeared… but the Guard was going nowhere.

KNOCK-KNOCK-KNOCK.

Claffey stepped away from the door and paced up and down the hallway. He needed time to think. If he opened that door, everything he and Chris had worked for over the past nine months would be gone so maybe it was best to just go back to the studio and ignore the Guard altogether.

Paul peered through the peephole again and then something odd struck him: the Guard was in full uniform right enough but he wasn't wearing his cap. An ancient memory stirred somewhere in the caverns of Paul Claffey's mind. He'd once heard that Gardaí always wore their caps when they were on official duty. Whether it was true or not was debatable but, at any rate, he better open the door because this fella showed no signs of shifting and he'd have to go out and face him at some point anyway. Putting his glasses back on, he pulled the lock across and drew the door ever so slightly ajar.

"Hello Guard, what can I do for you?" he said, peering warily through the slit in the door.

"Howya Paul," said the man in uniform. "John Duggan here from Glenamaddy, I've an oul tape for you and I was hoping you might give it a play on the radio. It's a tape Seamus and myself just recorded."

Claffey nearly sank to his knees in sheer relief. John and Seamus were a popular traditional group who had been playing the western pub and cabaret circuit for years. Duggan was a long-serving garda in Glenamaddy and was known as a bit of songwriter too.

But the pirate remained a little wary. He was well aware of the famous raid at Capitol Radio in Dublin a few years earlier when a Garda tried to gain entry to the studio on the pretext of giving a tape to the on-air disc jockey; minutes later a 16-man team of Gardaí and department inspectors were taking the place apart.

Leaning out the door, Paul glanced cautiously up and down Clare Street but could see no signs of a cavalry... on horseback or otherwise.

"Are you sure you're on your own?" he asked Duggan suspiciously.

"Yes, yes, of course I am," the Guard replied, thrusting the envelope into Paul's hand. "You will give this an oul play or two, won't you?"

"Sure come in, John, come in," said a mightily relieved Claffey. "Would you like to see the studio?"

"God, I'd love to," said Duggan. "I've been listening to ye for months. Ye're fierce popular over in Glenamaddy."

Paul closed the door and the two men continued down the corridor and into the studio where John took a seat in the corner while Paul resumed his show, pirate broadcaster and Garda chatting freely as the records played.

"You've written songs, haven't you?" Paul asked Duggan. "You've a great knowledge of music. You'd be perfect for this sort of craic."

"Ah, sure you wouldn't have much of my kind of music here," said John.

"Look at these," replied Paul, pulling out several boxes of records. "There's everything you need here for a good Irish music show."

"Begad, there is," said Duggan, warming a little to the idea. "But I wouldn't have a clue how to work those gadgets."

"Sure it's easy," said Paul. "Just sit in there and I'll show you. That's turntable one, that's turntable two..."

By now, Claffey had reached the conclusion that this Garda, far from being an enemy of Midwest, was, in fact, one of the station's biggest fans and had an excellent voice for radio. If he could persuade Guard Duggan to hold the fort for an hour, he'd have enough time to shoot over to Castlerea to take Geoffrey and Rachel to the swimming pool.

"Why don't you take over for a while?"

"Oh, I couldn't," said Duggan. "I'm a guard. It'd be illegal for me to present a show on this station. I could be fired."

"But sure who'd know apart from you and me? What's your middle name?"

"My middle name?" asked a bemused Duggan.

"Yeah, your middle name."

"Edward."

"Perfect," said Claffey, pressing the 'ON' button on the microphone as the last strains of Johnny Cash's *Folsom Prison Blues* faded into the background. "And now, listeners, we have a great treat in store for you on this beautiful Sunday afternoon. Our next programme will be presented by the one and only John Edwards who has some great Country favourites lined up."

And with that Paul Claffey bolted out of Midwest's little studio, leaving a garda in full uniform to look after a pirate radio station.

Like the four roads in Big Tom's iconic anthem, the dusty byways of John Edward Duggan's life seemed to have led him inexorably to the Midwest Radio studio on that auspicious Sunday afternoon in August 1986. Duggan was a born broadcaster, a natural communicator whose gentle, laid-back speaking style may have sounded effortless but was, in fact, impossible to imitate.

By the time he made his life-changing visit to the pirate radio station in Ballyhaunis, the Longford native was in his mid-fifties and had spent most of his adult life in An Garda Síochána. But he had also acquired a lifetime love of music that made him the perfect candidate to present a music show on local radio.

Growing up in the village of Killashee in the dreary Emergency era of the early 1940s, the young John Duggan's life was immeasurably enhanced by the many talented traditional Irish musicians who performed in local halls and house-dances across south Longford.

"My father was a music fanatic," John recalled in an interview shortly before his death. "He'd stand in his waist in snow listening to a good reel or a jig."

When he was about 10, John saw an advertisement in the *Longford Leader* for a fiddle for sale in nearby Lanesborough and immediately rushed out to his father who was digging potatoes in the backfield.

"Dad, dad, there's a fiddle for sale in Lanesborough, will you give me the money for it?"

"Get away outta that," came the father's blunt reply.

Times were tough and the Duggans, like many more in their village, hadn't the money to spend on musical instruments, regardless of how much they might enjoy music.

In 1950, John was a student at Longford Vocational School and had aspirations to become a carpenter or maybe even set sail for England to make his fortune as a big-time builder. One day, while on his way home from school, the foreman of Magan's, a large hardware and grocery store in Killashee, asked Duggan if he'd like a job.

"When do I start?" the youngster asked.

"Come in tomorrow morning at 10 o'clock."

John talked the offer over with his parents who were not averse to the idea of him quitting school for Magan's. There weren't too many opportunities in 1950s' Ireland and Magan's had a reputation as one of the best employers in the Midlands. Young Duggan duly commenced his career in Magan's the following morning and when he got his first pay packet, he put as much aside as he could because there was something he desperately wanted to purchase for the family home: a wireless.

There was only one other wireless in the village (in Conway's, who lived next door to John) and that had come all the way from America, its transatlantic voyage making it all the more exotic. When Kerry played Cavan in the famous Polo Grounds All-Ireland football final in 1947, nearly every able-bodied person in the entire village crowded into and around Conway's little cottage to listen to Micheál O'Hehir's breathless commentary.

After several months of diligent saving, John had sufficient funds to go to Flaherty's in Kilashee where he purchased a battery-operated wireless that he had his eyes on for months. His father fell for the device as soon as the son turned it on.

"He listened to it every night and no-one dared open their mouth while the wireless was on. He loved to listen to the news and to music shows on Radio Éireann; it became a big part of his life."

In 1954, John embarked on a correspondence course with Kilroy's College in Dublin to prepare for the tough entry examination for An Garda Síochána. Later that year, he and his brother Danny joined the force on the same day.

"We got on the train together in Longford, went to digs together in Dublin and arrived together at the training college in the Phoenix Park the next day," he recalled.

Garda training in those days was completed in a matter of months and John was posted to Donnybrook Garda Station, which was not to his liking.

"There were 12 ambassadors living in Donnybrook in those days and you had to be watching these fellas day and night. If they complained about a stray dog you'd better go and look for it!"

John was desperate to escape the 'Big Shmoke' so he lodged an application with the Commissioner's office for a transfer, following it up with an informal telephone call in which he expressed a desire to "get down the country". However, the message got lost in translation and John was instead dispatched to Crumlin. It was a case of out of the pan and into the fire.

While in Crumlin, John started writing humorous little musical ditties about the characters he met in his day job or even some of the events that occurred in the lives of colleagues.

"I got into trouble with some of the lads in the station because of the stuff I was writing!" he recalled. "There was nothing serious about the songs; they were just a bit of fun really."

John finally succeeded in 'getting down the country' when he was posted to Carlow in the early 1960s and then to Glenamaddy in 1966. The latter was supposed to be a staging post on the way to Castlerea – the town where he intended to spend the rest of his career – but for a music lover like John Duggan it was difficult not to fall in love with the Glenamaddy of the Swinging Sixties.

The North Galway town was a mecca for the booming showband scene and dancers flocked in their thousands every weekend to Joe O'Neill's Sound of Music ballroom, which was the beating heart of a vibrant and flourishing town. The Sound of Music was, of course, immortalised in Big Tom's *Four Country Roads*, penned by O'Neill's great friend, the London-based singer-songwriter Johnny McCauley, who even gave a nod in the song's lyrics to the famous ballroom.

"Once in a while," wrote McCauley, *"I hear the Sound of Music in the winter nights."*

Apart from the dancehall, Joe O'Neill also owned a music shop on the Kilkerrin Road, supplying instruments and equipment to the countless bands then emerging from the West of Ireland's ever-expanding showband scene. John Duggan regularly called into O'Neill's shop to chat with Joe and the staff and to play a bit of music.

"I'd go in and take down an accordion and go rasping away on it," he recalled. "I was only a short time in Glenamaddy when I bought an accordion and taught myself to play."

John was in O'Neill's "rasping away" one afternoon when he fell into conversation with Seamus Mannion, who was one half of a well-known local musical duo (Gerry O'Neill was the other half).

"I could badly do with you," Mannion said to Guard Duggan, "because Gerry has just left the outfit."

From that chance encounter came 'John and Seamus', a two-man band who, like the Joyce Country Céilí Band of Sawdoctors' fame, were soon performing at 'dos and functions, weddings and wakes'.

They played various venues several nights each week and once managed four gigs in a single Saturday – an early evening performance in Bernie McInerney's pub in Ballygar sandwiched between two weddings (in Longford and Ballygar) before finishing with a housewarming party in Kilkerrin that went on until 4am!

Dubbed the 'Nashville of the West', Glenamaddy in the 1960s and 1970s was a truly magical place for anyone possessed of an artistic or musical spirit and John Duggan's creativity blossomed in this fertile milieu. He wrote his first proper musical composition, *I'll Go Back To Glenamaddy*, shortly after his arrival in North Galway but the song remained unrecorded for almost two decades. The lyrics were inspired by the sight of a married man with a young family having to leave his native place to go to work in London during the winter months to keep food on the table back home. The man spent Christmas alone in London because he needed to save money to return to Glenamaddy in the spring.

John continued to pen lyrics to music throughout the 1970s without ever really doing anything with the songs. All that changed, however, in 1981 when Brendan Shine called to Duggan's home.

"I hear you're writing an odd oul song," Shine began. "Would you send me a few of them?"

To have someone of Shine's stature show an interest in his work was a huge boost for John who, up to then, wasn't even sure if his songs were any good at all. In the early 1980s, Brendan was presenting a Country music show on RTÉ Television called *Nice and Easy* and was still featuring fairly regularly in the Irish charts. In fact, a year earlier he'd had a top ten hit with *Catch Me If You Can.*

A few weeks later, Duggan was in Glenamaddy Garda Station when one of his colleagues shouted across the office.

"There's a fella on the 'phone here pretending to be Brendan Shine! He wants to speak to you."

Although the call was no prank it took some time for John to fully comprehend what Shine was telling him.

"I'm putting three of those songs of yours on my next album. Is that okay?"

Was it okay? One of the songs was *I'll Go Back To Glenamaddy*, which had been gathering dust in a cupboard in Duggan's kitchen for over 15 years and now the biggest hit maker in Irish Country music was putting it on an album along with two other more recent compositions *The Rose of Castlerea* and *The Races of Killadoon*... Was it okay? John Duggan couldn't believe his luck.

"I felt I was made," he recalled. "I couldn't believe it was happening to me."

It was only the start. Shine's version of *The Rose of Castlerea* entered the Irish charts in 1982 and stayed there for 17 weeks, reaching No 16 and winning Irish Country Record of the Year. That early and unexpected success proved the catalyst for several other Duggan compositions, including *The Roads of Kildare,* which was recorded by at least ten different artists in the mid-1980s, including the great Brian Coll.

John spent the early months of 1986 listening to Midwest Radio and was impressed with the new pirate station's wholehearted commitment to Irish Country music. He was hearing songs on Midwest that wouldn't get a look in on RTÉ.

"You know we should record a song and give it to those lads in Midwest," he told Seamus Mannion in the summer of 1986. "I've just finished writing an oul ditty so why don't we go over to Joe [O'Neill] and get him to record it."

They recorded the song on a Saturday and John took the tape with him to work the next day. Glenamaddy station was always a quiet place on a Sunday afternoon so John reckoned he'd have plenty of free time to skip across to Ballyhaunis and drop the tape into Midwest. It couldn't take more than an hour, could it?

Three hour later, Duggan's perplexed sergeant was asking a colleague:

"Where in hells fire has that bloody Duggan got to?"

If the sergeant had only turned on Midwest Radio he'd have got his answer. In the space of a single sun-drenched afternoon, long-serving Garda John Edward Duggan had entered a radio studio in Ballyhaunis and morphed into pirate disc jockey John Edwards, making a little bit of broadcasting history in the process.

This was certainly a Garda raid with a difference.

CHAPTER NINE

Listening to the listeners

THE first record John Duggan placed on the turntable in the old Midwest Radio studio on that August day in 1986 was Makem and Clancy's *Rambles of Spring*. While it was playing, he rooted through the boxes of records at his feet and selected several that took his fancy, mainly Irish artists who wouldn't get a lot of airplay on RTÉ.

In between the records, Duggan chatted easily about everything and anything, from the hot weather to the All-Ireland championships to the latest headlines in the Sunday newspapers – the *Independent* and the *Press* – which he found on the small cluttered studio desk. It seemed the most natural thing in the world to be playing music and chatting and it wasn't long before the garda-turned-pirate DJ was lost in a stimulating world of songs and stories.

Meanwhile, over in Castlerea, Paul was having an equally enjoyable afternoon with Geoffrey and Rachel at the swimming pool, the cool water a welcome refuge for the youngsters on this humid August day. Afternoon slipped into early evening and Claffey, now lost in a blissfully relaxing environment, forgot all about the rookie DJ whom he had left running the station back in Ballyhaunis. It was only when another parent asked him how Midwest was coming along that Paul was catapulted back to reality. He rushed over to where he'd left his clothes and pulled out his watch. It was 4.45pm.

"Jaysus, your man is still on the feckin' radio," he exclaimed, hastily toweling himself down as he pulled on his clothes. "Geoffrey, Rachel, come on, come one, it's time to go home."

When he got outside to the car – the dodgy Fiat had been replaced by a green Renault – Claffey immediately switched on Midwest, expecting dead air but instead Johnny Logan's Eurovision winner from a few years earlier, *What's Another Year,* crackled from the speaker. After leaving the children back to the house, Paul continued to listen to Duggan as he drove at breakneck speed towards Ballyhaunis, figuring that if he was to be stopped for speeding he'd have the most original excuse in the history of motoring offences: he was on his way to relieve a Garda from his duties as a pirate disc jockey!

Bursting into the studio, Claffey gave Duggan a slap on the back.

"Jaysus John, you're doin' mighty. I'm sorry I left you here on your own for so long."

"No problem at all, Paul, sure I loved every minute of it. How long have you been gone?"

"It's nearly three hours, John."

"Three hours? God, I've done checkpoints for three hours and they seemed to last forever but those last few hours just flew by."

"Well, why don't you come back again next Sunday? We'd love to have you."

"Oh I don't know, Paul, I could get into fierce bother altogether."

However, the broadcasting bug had bit Duggan and there was no turning back. Later that week, he met Paul and Chris and agreed to broadcast a Sunday show under the pseudonym John Edwards. The garda took to the airwaves again the following Sunday and continued to broadcast throughout September.

But secrets are not easily kept in rural communities and rumours started to reach the Garda Commissioner's office in Dublin that a serving officer was broadcasting on a pirate station called Midwest down in Mayo. *Magill* magazine even carried a special feature on Midwest in September 1986. Eventually, Garda headquarters made contact with Duggan's superintendent who said he'd investigate the matter. A week later, the Galway superintendent reported back to top brass in the Phoenix Park.

"I listened to that show last Sunday," he said. "It's a very good show. In fact, it's so good it couldn't possibly be a serving garda presenting it. This John Edwards fella is clearly a professional DJ."

Years later, Duggan would liken broadcasting to another of his favourite pastimes: golf.

"If you get into it at all, it's like a disease," he commented.

By the autumn of 1986, the Glenamaddy garda was so captivated by his part-time role as a pirate disc jockey he was willing to consider ending his career in An Garda Síochána altogether. Having served for over 30 years, he was eligible for early retirement and knew there was a full-time job waiting for him at Midwest if he decided to take the plunge.

"We wanted to expand our hours so we offered John a slot from 7pm to 10pm," recalls Chris. "But it would have been impossible for him to take on that role while still working as a Garda."

In early October, John travelled into Tuam for a meeting with his superintendent.

"I'm thinking of retiring," he began.

"What the hell are you doing a thing like that for? You can do another seven years if you want."

"I know," said Duggan, choosing his words carefully. "It's just that I might have another job coming up…"

The superintendent raised an eyebrow and a faint smile crept across his lips.

"And what might that job be?"

"I'd rather not say," Duggan replied awkwardly.

The superintendent nodded gravely.

"I understand," he said. "But I'll let you in on a secret. I heard ya and you're damn good!"

They shook hands and the superintendent wished his officer well on his retirement, which, of course, wasn't really a retirement at all. The following day, John called over to Ballyhaunis and shook hands with Paul and Chris, agreeing to a deal that would see him broadcast a three-hour show five nights a week.

"Will you miss the Guards," Chris asked John as the three men stood outside the door of Midas in the chill dusk of a late October evening.

"I won't," said John. "I've done my time – over 30 years at this stage – and now I'm looking forward to this change of career. You lads have given me a new lease of life."

"Do you know," said Paul. "I've been meaning to ask you something for ages. Is it true that a Guard always has to wear his cap when he is on duty."

"Begad," said Duggan. "I never heard tell of that."

"So when you called here last August without your cap... that didn't mean you were off duty then?"

"Jaysus no," replied the now retired officer. "The only reason I left the cap in the car that day was because of the blasted heat."

"Well feckin' hell," said Claffey, bursting into gales of laughter. "If I'd known that I'd have never let you into the place at all!"

In the summer of 1986, a reporter from the *Sunday Independent*, Kevin D. O'Connor, went on a tour of Ireland in search of 'witches, witchery, the casting of circles, spells and strange beliefs'. On his arrival in Galway, somebody directed him deep into the hills of Connemara, to Coilleach Mór in Leenane where he encountered Bina McLoughlin, then aged 57 and running a sheep farm on her own in some of the most inhospitable terrain in the country. Standing in a field above the Killary fjord, surrounded by her sheep, Ireland's only shepherdess laughed cheerfully at the suggestion she might be a witch.

"A witch?" she shrieked in delight. "Go on outta that! A witch? Ho, ho, ho!".

However, Bina conceded she might have 'inherited a special power from the saints', having been born on November 2 – between All Saints' Day and All Souls' Night. She professed to 'seeing and knowing what's in a person's face', offering several personal insights to O'Connor that he admitted were 'fascinating' but were also unrepeatable because Bina 'swore me to silence'.

O'Connor's article offered a captivating glimpse of a remarkable woman who was steeped in the heritage and lore of her native area, a remote and isolated part of Ireland more accessible by sea than land up to the 1800s. Bina belonged to a generation who grew up in an Ireland without television and, in many cases, without even a wireless. She and her ilk were raised on fireside tales of local myths and legends, magical cures, strange superstitions and supernatural curses. Theirs was a religion that pre-dated Christianity, or as Bina told O'Connor:

"Connemara never came under Rome. We differed and went our own way."

By the mid-1980s, mystical women such as Bina McLoughlin represented a fast disappearing Ireland as the country made up for lost time in its headlong rush towards modernity. Kevin D. O'Connor had described the Leenane native as being 'lost in the mists of Connemara antiquity' and it was absolutely true; she and her generation were relics of an Ireland before rural electrification when people had to make their own entertainment. National and local newspapers occasionally featured articles about these 'local characters', as they were wont to be described, but more often than not the headlines were penned after the person passed on. Indeed, it was rare for these people to be given a voice in life. Rare, that is, until the pirate Midwest Radio installed a phone extension in its cloakroom studio in Ballyhaunis.

The direct line meant members of the public could now be put on the air for the first time and Paul immediately saw the potential of giving his listeners a voice; a voice that was just waiting to be heard.

"There were so many people out there in those days that were natural entertainers," he explains. "They'd grown up in an era when storytelling was all the rage and they had a turn of phrase that was just incredible. They had all of the cures and old wives' tales that people had heard about in their childhood but maybe forgotten due to the passage of time. The people I started to bring on the radio captured the rural way of life in bygone years and everyone could relate to them. In fact, the listeners just loved them and they became a big part of my show."

One of the first of Paul's regular callers was the elderly Kathleen Loftus, from Logboy, who was the organist in her local church and also happened to have an electric organ in her house, which she was more than happy to play for the listeners. Kathleen had a terrific sense of humour and was an extremely intelligent, well-read woman with a great knowledge of local history. She also took immense pleasure in telling stories about some of the strange happenings in the South Mayo countryside in days of yore.

During one of her early telephone calls to Midwest in the summer of 1986, Kathleen revealed that her family – the Loftuses – could trace their roots all the way back to a mermaid who one day – *fadó, fadó* – emerged from a lake near the town of Ballyhaunis.

"She was a beautiful woman who had come up out of Lavallyroe Lake," Kathleen explained, "and as she sat by the side of the water, a Loftus man came along and abducted her."

"And did he marry her then?" asked an intrigued Claffey.

"Oh, wait till I tell you what happened next, Paul."

"Go on…"

"Well, he brought this beautiful woman home, hid her golden comb – in which her strange powers seemed to be located – and married her. They had a very big family and so it was that the Loftuses came into being…"

"Well, holy smoke," said Claffey.

But there was a twist in the tale… there had to be for a gifted seanchaí like Kathleen Loftus. The 'fairywoman' – as she called her ancestor – managed to find her magic comb, succeeded in escaping from Lavallyroe while her husband was at a fair and disappeared, never to return.

Thus ended the story but Kathleen wasn't quite finished yet. She then sat down at her organ and launched into a lively rendition of *South of the Border,* an old Frank Sinatra number that had its roots in a 1939 film of the same name.

By late 1986, Kathleen's almost daily calls to Midwest Radio were becoming an important feature of Paul's morning show and she was almost as well known as the presenter himself. She began each call with her 'newses' – as she described the latest happenings in her life – before sitting down at the organ to play *Danny Boy, South of the Border* or a self-penned song *If I had Paul in the Woods,* which soon took on a legendary status.

Gerry Glennon, who worked as a producer on Paul's show in those early years, says Midwest's informal style of broadcasting was one of the reasons the 'phone calls from the likes of Kathleen Loftus worked so well. There was nothing contrived about what was happening; this was the very definition of 'live' radio.

"As far as somebody like Kathleen was concerned, she was just talking to Paul one-to-one. I think that's why it was so natural. Radio was still a bit of a mystery at that time and people couldn't imagine themselves on the radio because the voices of ordinary people from rural Ireland were never heard on radio back then. So I think Midwest really benefitted from the fact that people like Kathleen came on the airwaves with no inhibitions and no pretensions; they were as natural as if you were sitting by the fireside having a cup of tea with them."

Kathleen was the first of Paul's many regular contributors – from Hilda Creaby in Kiltimagh, Hazel Leonard in Ballinrobe and May Hunt in Ballymote to Paddy Joe and Maggie down on Achill Island and the *enfant terrible* himself, JJ in Ahascragh who could start a row in an empty room. But the doyenne of them all was the inimitable Bina McLoughlin, the shepherdess from the hills of Leenane, who lived in glorious solitude in a little cottage high over the fjord at Killary where successive generations of farmers had existed at one with nature since pre-Christian times.

It would be another few years before Bina fully emerged from 'the mists of Connemara antiquity', but when she did, the Queen of Connemara became the undisputed star of Midwest, thereby staking her place in the folklore of the West of Ireland.

The summer of 1986 was bookended by two hugely significant events in the modern history of Co Mayo – the opening of Knock Airport on May 30 and the sudden death of its 75-year-old founder Monsignor James Horan in Lourdes on August 1. Midwest Radio was still a fledgling pirate station with a limited current affairs output but Paul, Chris and Gerry understood the need to reflect the huge wave of public emotion that accompanied both occasions. The sudden death of the monsignor evoked a particularly immense outpouring of grief and Midwest's single telephone line was inundated with listeners who wanted to pay their personal tribute to a man whose indefatigable campaign to build an airport had captured the collective imagination of so many people.

"One of my biggest regrets is that Midwest never got to experience Monsignor Horan in his prime," says Paul. "I was a great admirer of his and it is such a pity he didn't live another ten years because I'd have loved to have seen the relationship that Midwest would have developed with him. He was a man born for the radio."

In the spring of 1987, local singer Carmel Kilgallon, from Shraheens, Balla, released a tribute song entitled *A Man Apart* and it quickly became the most popular song from Midwest's pirate era.

"It was played off the airwaves," recalls Gerry Glennon. "People were still mourning Monsignor Horan and this song perfectly captured the mood at the time. The West had lost a leader; someone that was admired and liked by everyone – regardless of their political persuasion."

The success of *A Man Apart* – it was one of the bestselling singles in music shops west of the Shannon in 1987 – was an early barometer of the growing power of Midwest. Here was a song that would have barely got a look-in on RTÉ Radio but singers like Carmel Kilgallon now had a pirate station that was more than happy to give local artists their due recognition and put them on the same playlists as the more established names in music.

Midwest's willingness to give a voice to the so-called plain people of the West of Ireland was its greatest calling card in those early days. Whether it was Carmel Kilgallon or Kathleen Loftus, Midwest gave its listeners a sense of ownership of the airwaves that was unprecedented up to then, thereby forging a fierce loyalty that would serve the station well when challenges arose in later years.

In many ways, Midwest's listeners were the same people who, at the depths of an economic recession, rallied to the cause of Monsignor Horan after a skeptical government pulled the funding for his beloved airport.

Paul and Chris had started their radio station at the most inopportune time – the west of Ireland was beset by the twin evils of unemployment and emigration in the mid-1980s – but Midwest, in those early pirate days, captured something of the spirit of defiance that characterised the building of Knock Airport. After more than half a century of political independence, people in the West were tired of being dictated to by successive Dublin-centric governments and pandered to by a national media that paid scant attention to the real issues impacting the lives of ordinary folk beyond the Pale.

From the outset, Midwest Radio was unapologetically rural in its outlook. Its playlist was dominated by Country and Western and Irish traditional music while its airwaves were open to anyone who had a song to sing, a story to tell or a missing dog to find. The Ballyhaunis station differed greatly from other pirates in that listeners were made to feel part of a broad church – a family even – and that spirit of togetherness gave Midwest an identity all of its own.

"Whereas other stations were trying to set the agenda, we let the listeners set the agenda," explains Gerry Glennon. "Our attitude was to listen to the listeners and follow their agenda rather than trying to set it on our own."

Paul and Chris were also willing to take risks other station owners might have baulked at such as giving a three-hour nightly show to a retired garda in his mid-fifties with absolutely no broadcasting experience. Yet it was John Duggan's down-to-earth and often unconventional style that made him such an instant hit with listeners.

Fr Colm Kilcoyne, who was a curate at Knock Shrine in 1986 and an early supporter of Midwest Radio, often told a story of visiting an elderly woman one winter's night and finding her alone in the kitchen listening to John Duggan.

"What are you doing listening to that oul pirate station?" asked Fr Kilcoyne good-humouredly. "Sure that fella Duggan is breaking the law – and him a Guard!"

"Father," said the old lady, "John Duggan is all I listen to every night. Sure you'd think he was sitting here in the kitchen with me."

When he first came up with the idea of establishing a radio station, Paul viewed it as little more than a useful vehicle to promote his struggling dancehall, but by the end of the 1986, he and Chris were starting to realise they had created something much bigger than either anticipated when starting out just 18 months earlier. By listening to its listeners, Midwest Radio was fast becoming an authentic voice for a vast swathe of rural Ireland that for years had struggled to be heard at a national level.

On New Year's Eve 1986, RTÉ Radio 1's *Looking West* programme featured none other than Kathleen Loftus from Logboy who regaled the entire country with South Mayo tales of mermaids and harsh landlords and New Year's celebrations of bygone times before finishing with a blast of *Auld Lang Syne* on the electric organ.

The pirate station Midwest Radio and its band of loyal listeners were now setting a national agenda.

CHAPTER TEN

Zanier than zany

JOHN Duggan wasn't the only new addition to Midwest's expanding schedule in the summer of 1986: a second young man from Granlahan was also boarding the pirate ship. Michael Neary and Gerry Glennon were childhood friends and it didn't take much to convince Neary to try his hand at broadcasting.

"I had a great love of music anyway but it would have been mainly chart music at that time," Michael recalls. "But I got more into Country after I joined Midwest. In fairness, though, I never felt under pressure to play any particular type of music. There were no playlists then – and there are still none today. Instead Paul and Chris were willing to put their trust in whoever was presenting a show and I think that generally paid off for everyone involved."

Michael recalls being invited into Midwest to meet Chris to discuss the possibility of presenting a show. There was no interview or proper audition; Michael just had a microphone thrust under his nose and away he went.

"Before I knew it I was presenting a weekend show… I think it was the next day! There were no disclaimers signed; it was right in at the deep end."

There was an urgency in identifying new broadcasters in the autumn of 1986 because Gerry had decided to up sticks and move to London to try his hand at psychiatric nursing.

"My intention when I'd left school was to do psychiatric nursing so when an offer came through to train in England I decided to take it up," he explains.

Gerry joined the thousands of emigrants setting off for London as Ireland experienced a new wave of emigration that was almost as bad as the 1950s. But he found it hard to settle into his new career. The broadcasting bug had bitten deep and he couldn't find any cure for it in the pyschiatric hospital in London. He set off for home that Christmas and upon reaching Ballyhaunis, Gerry's first port of call was the radio studio in Midas. Chris and Paul welcomed him with open arms.

"Do you mind staying around to record some Christmas ads?" Chris asked. "I'll give you a lift out home afterwards."

"No problem," said Gerry, delighted to be asked to get involved again so soon. He quickly discovered that Midwest had undergone a rapid expansion in the short time he'd been away. The station was now employing a part-time advertising sales executive, Jimmy Deasy, and the old dressingroom was back in use again, this time as a recording studio for ads.

"Our earliest ads were recorded on cassette tapes – the same cassette tapes used by teenagers to record songs off the radio," explains Chris. "If you made a mistake recording a 30-second ad you'd have to go back to the beginning and start all over again. And, trust me, we made plenty of mistakes!

"We had a three-cassette deck in the studio so when one ad ended you'd have to stop it and then press play for the next one. While that was playing you'd be removing the first cassette tape and putting in a new one because each ad required its own cassette tape."

By the Christmas of 1986, Paul and Chris were using blank cassette tapes at a faster rate than the entire teenage population of Co Mayo. Advertising was rolling in that December as Jimmy Deasy, armed with a tidy-looking briefcase, toured the towns of Mayo, Roscommon, South Sligo and even North Galway.

"This was the pirate days so there were no restrictions on the length of advertising breaks," explains Chris. "We had ad breaks around Christmas that ran for ten minutes!"

An increasing number of ads meant an increasing number of cassette tapes, which inevitably caused an increasing amount of confusion for the on-air presenters. On one occasion, Chris let a tape run on for too long.

"Paul had made a mistake while recording the ad and roared 'Shit' at the end of it. He then went back and re-recorded the ad but the expletive stayed on the tape. I put the ad out on air and let the tape run on too long, which meant everyone listening heard Paul roaring 'Shit' at the top of his voice!"

Seconds later, the telephone rang and Mary Reilly called out to Paul:

"Can you take this call right now? It's Maureen and she wants to speak to you immediately."

Claffey picked up the phone.

"Paul, that's lovely language to be putting out on air."

"What do you mean?"

"Well, I'm listening here in Castlerea to you cursing on the radio, that's what I mean!"

"Sure, I'm not on air at all. It's Chris!"

"Well, you want to listen back to your ads so!"

On the second last Saturday in December, Paul and Gerry were recording the last pre-Christmas ads when there was a tentative knock on the door of the backstage dressingroom. Gerry opened it to find a tousle-haired young man standing outside with a bunch of records under his arm.

"I'm Johnny Oosten," the man began nervously. "Jimmy Deasy told me to call over. He said you're looking for new DJs."

"Come in, come in," Paul called out. "Yeah, Jimmy told me about you. Why don't you go into the studio and record something for us. Gerry will show you around."

Johnny had never been in a radio studio in his life and was, by his own admission, a "nervous wreck" but the aspiring presenter became a little more relaxed when he saw the rudimentary equipment in the old cloakroom. There were two record players, a three-cassette deck, two microphones, a mixing desk and a set of headphones. It didn't look that complicated and Gerry made it sound incredibly easy.

"Sure why don't you record something now and we'll have a listen to it," suggested Gerry.

"Okay," replied Johnny. "But will you be here listening to me?"

Having experienced his own tentative, anxious journey into broadcasting just a few months earlier, Gerry was happy to give the newcomer the space he needed.

Johnny sat down and familiarised himself with the equipment before recording a 15-minute 'show' on cassette, which he immediately wanted to erase. He was about to record a second tape when Paul and Gerry returned to the studio.

"Well," said Paul. "How'd you get on? Let's hear this tape."

Johnny excused himself while the tape was playing, disappearing into the sanctuary of the toilet, convinced he had just flushed away his best chance for a career in broadcasting. But he was in for a pleasant surprise after returning sheepishly to the studio.

"That's exactly what we're looking for," Paul said enthusiastically. "When do you want to start?"

"What?" the astonished Johnny exclaimed.

By January, the Westport native was presenting a Saturday show and was soon a key member of the expanding Midwest team.

"It was really haphazard in those days," recalls Gerry. "You just shoved people in live on air to see how they got on. There was no paddling pool; it was straight in at the deep end and if they swam they swam or if they sank they sank."

Johnny Oosten and Michael Neary were among those who swam but these young men were about to discover that broadcasting was just a small part of the varied life of a pirate disc jockey. In fact, the couple of hours spent in front of the microphone were often the most relaxing part of the day.

Johnny Oosten slipped easily into his new role as a radio presenter. Like so many who drifted into broadcasting in the 1980s, Johnny's career path was guided by his abiding love for music but there were also a unique set of circumstances that steered him in the direction of Ballyhaunis that December afternoon in 1986.

"When I was 16 I was involved in a serious motorbike accident that left me in a coma for four months," he explains. "The accident happened near Partry on May 18, 1979 and I didn't wake up from the coma until September 23 of that year. It took me a long time to recover from my injuries and music was my salvation."

Johnny had been dabbling in the music business before his accident, spinning discs at 'hops' organised by the local youth club in Westport Town Hall, but he really threw himself into his work as a disc jockey after his accident. There was a thriving DJ scene in Westport in the early 1980s and Johnny's contemporaries included future RTÉ Radio 2 DJ Dermott Langan, Dick Bourke of Dazzle Disco and Ronnie Ring. The explosion in the local disco scene meant there was work for all of them and Johnny was soon providing the musical entertainment at various events across West Mayo, including discos in Castlebar Town Hall where he met his future wife Ann.

In early December 1986, Frank McCann, of the Tile Centre at Tucker Street in Castlebar, approached Johnny with a suggestion: why not broadcast music on the streets of the county town to create a bit of a festive atmosphere? Johnny thought it was a great idea and erected a public address system on a few poles, then connected it to a record player located in a portakabin beside McCann's premises and, hey presto, he was up and running. This was outside broadcasting in its most primitive form.

After a couple of days, a few traders asked if they could broadcast some of their Christmas deals, even offering to pay for the ads. Seeing an opportunity to make a few bob, Johnny went around the town and sold advertisements to the other traders, which then made the whole venture financially viable for the month. Jimmy Deasy, who was touring Castlebar in search of ads for Midwest Radio, was none too impressed to learn that a kid in a portakabin on Tucker Street had already laid claim to the bulk of the town's advertising budget.

"Jimmy was the drummer with the Brose Walsh Band and I knew him well," recalls Johnny. "He was a gentleman so when he called into the portakabin and asked if I might do a bit of work with Midwest I was immediately interested. I'd heard about this Country music station that had started up in Ballyhaunis but I didn't know a whole lot about it really. I didn't even know that Jimmy was involved with it."

Deasy explained he was in Castlebar selling advertisements for the new radio station.

"You're selling ads for a pirate radio station?" asked Johnny in disbelief.

"Yeah, same as you're selling ads!"

"And are you sure they're looking for presenters?"

"Course they are. You should go over and meet the lads. I think you'd get on great with them."

That was all the encouragement Johnny needed. A few weeks later he was hosting a new Saturday afternoon show on Midwest, merging his love of '70s and '80s music with the station's staple diet of Country music. Michael Neary also embraced a similar formula on his weekend show, thus providing Midwest with a greater diversity in its playlist, something Paul and Chris were keen to encourage.

"Nothing was ever set in stone as far as Midwest's playlist was concerned," says Chris. "Country music was a very important part of it but we gradually brought in a bit more pop and tried to cater for as many musical tastes as we could, especially when we started to expand our schedule."

By the early summer of 1987, Midwest Radio was broadcasting from 10am to 10pm seven days per week but the expanded schedule required more presenters, placing additional pressure on Jimmy Deasy to bring in new advertising. One evening he arrived in the studio in Ballyhaunis and wearily flung his trusty briefcase on the desk.

"How'd you get on today?" asked Paul cautiously.

Deasy silently opened the briefcase and pointed inside. The case contained a single cheque and little else; no cash, no money orders, just one bloody cheque.

"Christ," said Paul. "That's not good."

"You reckon?" said Jimmy, a faint smile creeping across his lips. "I actually think it was a very good day's work."

"How do you figure that out?"

"Here," said Deasy, tossing the cheque across the desk. "Have a look at that boy!"

Paul stared at the cheque for what seemed like an eternity before leaping off the chair and grabbing Jimmy in a bear hug.

"Didn't I tell you it wasn't a bad day's work?" said Deasy.

The cheque, from Western Pride Bakery in Ballinrobe, was made out for £3,000. THREE THOUSAND POUNDS! That was more than Midwest might have hoped to earn in a whole month let alone a single day.

"Nellie Keady was the boss of Western Pride at the time and she doled out this cheque for £3,000," Paul recalls. "We couldn't believe it. It wasn't just about the money either. Obviously it was a great financial boost at the time, but it also meant so much that she was placing such faith in us as a pirate radio station. It was one of those magical days from the pirate era I will never forget."

The increasing number of ads meant there was more voiceover work for presenters like Johnny Oosten… and more opportunities to make mistakes too.

"The music for the ads was coming from records so you were essentially talking over a record. Nowadays, you do the voiceover first and it's a lot easier to correct mistakes but back then if you made a mistake you had to start all over again. You'd have to line up the record again, go right back to the beginning of the voiceover and hope you didn't make another mistake. You could have multiple takes of the one ad and it could get very frustrating."

When a presenter finished playing a batch of advertisements, the cassettes were left out to Mary Reilly on the reception desk.

"Mary had a tape recorder on her desk and one of her duties was to rewind all the cassettes and line the ads up to be played again," explains Johnny. "She'd have to cue them perfectly so they were ready to go as soon as we pressed play. Kids today wouldn't believe what we had to do back then but at the time we thought it was so high-tech!

"The names of the ads were written onto the cassettes and we'd use Tipp-Ex to remove them; then we'd record a new ad on the same tape. Midwest Radio was ahead of its time when it came to recycling!"

At least one cassette didn't require any Tipp-Ex in 1987. Three thousand pounds went a long, long way back in the 1980s and Western Pride's advertisement got as much airplay on Midwest Radio that year as Carmel Kilgallon's *A Man Apart*. The Ballinrobe bakery had certainly delivered the dough.

By the summer of 1987 Midwest Radio was a modest financial success, but it still wasn't generating a full-time income for its two founders. Chris continued to depend on his private DJ business while Paul was wholly reliant on the profits from Midas, which was enjoying something of a renaissance courtesy of the unexpected success of the radio station.

A firm believer in the old Irish adage that it is wise to make hay while the sun shines, Paul decided the time was ripe to launch a new late-night radio show, one that would break new ground for pirate broadcasting in Ireland. *Sunday Night Live at Midas* soon became synonymous with Midwest, attracting thousands of listeners and establishing the station as the most innovative pirate broadcaster in the country. This was the first time a local radio station had broadcast an entire concert live on air and it was an enormous undertaking, especially as there were so many different components to the show.

Underpinning the entire evening was music from some of the top Country artists of the day, whether it was Brendan Shine, Big Tom, TR Dallas or one of the new wave of Country singers emerging in the mid-1980s. But music was just a small part of the attraction of *Sunday Night Live*, which also included the *Search for a Star* entertainment competition, with John Duggan as compère, and a gameshow hosted by Paul.

"It was the era of the television gameshow," he explains. "There was one on ITV at the time called The *Price is Right* so I gave it a Ballyhaunis twist and called it *Come On Down, The Price is Right.*"

The concept was simple. Paul would invite members of the audience on stage to take part in a competition that involved guessing the price of a wide variety of items, everything from household goods to farmyard animals… even a few lions and tigers were thrown in for good measure. Michael Neary, who was part of the production team for this mammoth broadcast, quickly learned that his new boss had torn up the broadcasting rulebook a long time ago.

"What you got to remember is that Paul was always zanier than zany in his thinking! From a technical point of view, there was a lot of work involved because you were working with bands and with contestants in a singing competition so you had to have the sound right for those in the hall and then you had to have the sound right for people listening at home. Now they were two different sounds altogether so that was a challenge in itself.

"But even if we were technically ready at 9.55pm, we were still operating on a wing and a prayer because no-one had the foggiest idea what was going to happen once the show started.

"Paul didn't work off a plan. He wouldn't have a clue at ten to ten what he was going to do let alone a few hours earlier!"

When Paul first came up with the concept of an on-air gameshow, he went to Michael Gunning who owned an electrical appliances store on Main Street in Castlerea and convinced him to travel to Dublin to seek sponsorship from Zanussi.

"Zanussi gave us £2,000 in prize-money, which was a huge amount at that time, but they also gave Michael a selection of their products – washing machines, dishwashers, fridges, freezes, etc – for raffle," says Paul.

The various electrical appliances were placed on stage and contestants had to guess their value, but there was also a big screen on which other 'items' could be displayed.

"We'd put a Friesian heifer on the screen with full sound effects so the fella listening at home would wonder if we had a cow on the stage!" Paul recalls. "There were goats and sheep and rams and even lions and tigers on that screen. We'd have sound effects for them all. It used to really fire up people's imaginations and they got great enjoyment from it."

Watching from behind the mixing desk, Michael Neary wouldn't have been a bit surprised if a lion or a tiger had appeared on stage. The live broadcast itself was a complicated affair but there was a big team involved, including Chris Carroll who mixed the sound for the radio and the live band.

"*Sunday Night Live* wouldn't have been possible without the support of O'Neill's in Glenamaddy," he says. "Joe Cunniffe and Michael O'Hara were working in O'Neill's and they were crucial to the success of Midwest in the early days. Joe set up all the equipment while Michael repaired everything. We came to depend on them enormously and the truth is we wouldn't have been able to manage without them. Another important man was our electrician, Michael Morley from Bekan, who was constantly on call and went way beyond the call of duty to assist us at every opportunity. Those men played a big part in the early success of Midwest.

"*Sunday Night Live* was a bigger undertaking than some of the things RTÉ was doing at the time and it certainly wouldn't have happened without the support of a big backroom team. In the end, we surprised ourselves by what we were able to achieve with that show."

Believing he needed a particular look to present the gameshow, Paul 'borrowed' Joe Dolan's white jacket on the first night, put on a twinkling bow-tie and arrived on stage calling himself 'The Man With The Flashin' Dickie'. A name like that would be almost enough to get a man arrested in today's PC world but, thankfully, people still possessed a sense of humour back in the 1980s.

"As well as the gameshow itself, I'd give out spot prizes to members of the audience and have a bit of banter with them," he explains. "It was great craic and people who were there loved it and people listening at home loved it too."

In fact, *Sunday Night Live* became something of a phenomenon and was soon one of Midwest's most important calling cards.

"It helped build the brand, there's no doubt about it," says Chris. "Midwest's popularity shot up during that period because there wasn't a whole lot on radio or television on a Sunday night so people were suddenly drawn to us; these were people who might have been RTÉ listeners up to then."

The entertainment competition, *Search for a Star,* was another important component of the show, especially as it had a first prize of £2,000. Four contestants took part each night culminating in a grand final, which was filmed by Channel 4 in late 1987 on a night when Jacqui Burke from Clonbur was crowned the inaugural winner. Jacqui went on to front her own band, Speak Easy.

"*Search for a Star* was way before television talent contests like *The X-Factor, Pop Idol* and *You're A Star,*" explains Paul. "It was incredibly popular and was another big part of the show."

The popularity of *Sunday Night Live* meant it became easy for Paul to attract the biggest names in Irish music, including a new generation of Country stars who were benefiting greatly from the rise of local pirate stations like Midwest. Among them were John Hogan, Mick Flavin, Declan Nerney and a young singer from Kinclasslagh in Co Donegal named Daniel O'Donnell.

"Daniel was a huge favourite in Midas in those years," says Paul. "But we had all the music stars of the era and they all attracted massive crowds because people wanted to be part of the *Sunday Night Live* experience. It was something totally different and the public really embraced what we were trying to do."

It also helped that the admission price before 11pm was a very reasonable £2.50.

Midwest Radio had provided Paul with a crucial lifeline at a time when Midas was struggling to stay open but *Sunday Night Live* propelled the nightclub into the stratosphere, generating the sort of hype its owner dreamt of a mere two years earlier. There were now queues along Clare Street at nine o'clock on a Sunday evening as people flocked from all over the province to soak up the unique *Sunday Night Live* experience. Even Gerry and Charlie Reilly came down from Cavan to see what all the fuss was about.

"I have a lot of memories of going into Midas for *Sunday Night Live*," Gerry jokes, "but I have no memories whatsoever of coming out!"

Sunday Night Live put Midas on the map and Paul was soon running discos on Saturday nights starring some of the top disc jockeys from RTÉ Radio 2. The increasing popularity of the nightclub allowed its owner to accelerate payments on the debts accrued in the preceding years and he was soon in the black for the first time in almost a decade. Ireland was plumbing the depths of a brutal economic recession in 1987 but the owner of Midas was enjoying an economic resurgence that defied logic.

"I always say that I have no fear of a recession because I was a failure during the boom!" Paul remarks. "And it's absolutely true. When everyone else was making money in Ireland I was losing it hand over fist and then I cleared all my debts at a time when the country was banjaxed. Now, go figure that one out!"

Michael Neary was right: The Man With The Flashin' Dickie really was zanier than zany.

CHAPTER ELEVEN

The Midas Express

MIDWEST Radio was barely two years in existence when Paul and Chris faced a watershed decision. As sole directors of the company, they could pocket the modest profits now being generated from advertising revenue or invest in additional transmitters, thus giving Midwest a much wider geographical reach. It was a classic choice between short-term gain and long-term growth, and in recession-battered Ireland of the 1980s, the temptation was to select the former. But unlike a lot of other pirate operators, Paul and Chris had alternative sources of income and saw the value of expanding Midwest's broadcasting footprint.

"Mayo is obviously very large from a geographical perspective and we were never going to cover the whole county from a single transmitter in Ballyhaunis, no matter how powerful it was," explains Chris. "So, in 1987, we began to look at other locations for transmitters to allow us to get a signal into north and east Mayo. I was particularly keen to re-invest in the business because I had been doing that since becoming a DJ. As far as I was concerned, it was the best way of securing the future."

Kiltimagh was identified as the optimum location for a new medium wave mast and another empty cottage was rented for the purpose of housing the transmitter, which was again installed by the Reilly brothers. This time there were no false teeth on the dresser but Gerry reckoned the cottage had the same eerie presence as the one in Ballyhaunis and wasn't inclined to spend too much time there on his own. The Cavan man's nerves were already shot from an incident a few weeks earlier in Spadagh when he responded to an urgent call from Chris to repair the transmitter.

"I was working in Carlow one Saturday afternoon when Chris rang to say that Midwest's transmitter was down so I got in the van and arrived in Ballyhaunis around 9pm," he recalls. "There was nobody at the station and I couldn't see Paul or Chris anywhere around Midas so I reluctantly went out to the house on my own."

It was a late spring evening and darkness was closing in as Gerry stepped out of his van. He walked warily towards the deserted cottage, the sound of his boots echoing amid the stillness of the gathering dusk. Stepping inside the cottage he instinctively reached to grab a torch that was always kept on a window ledge inside the front door but the device wasn't in its usual place. Reilly fumbled around in the half-light, glancing over at the dresser to see if the torch might be there… and then he felt it, something cold was touching him.

The Cavan man froze, feet rooted to the spot as an icy hand slid across the back of his neck and when he looked over at the dresser those blasted false teeth seemed to be grinning back at him. Reilly let loose an almighty roar that must have resounded all the way back to Kilnaleck and made a mad dash for the door only to hear howls of laughter from the corner of the room… and the laughter sounded very familiar.

"Gerry Glennon and Mick Morley had waited for me to come out and they hid when they saw my van approaching. They knew how much I hated that feckin' house so Morley decided to hide in a corner and surprise me! Well, he didn't just surprise me, he nearly gave me a bloody heart attack!"

The transmitter in Kiltimagh made a huge difference because it introduced Midwest to another audience in the north of the county, stretching as far as Ballina and Crossmolina. The requests came flooding in as more and more people became aware of this new Country music station called Midwest Radio that could be found on 1233 medium wave, which was the wavelength for the Kiltimagh transmitter. There were new listeners in Ballyvary, Bohola, Foxford, Swinford and over to the foothills of Nephin in places like Pontoon and Lahardane. But after little more than a week the inevitable calls started coming through… *This is Paddy here in Knockmore and I can't get ye anymore… Have ye changed the wavelength…? It's Betty here in Swinford and I'm getting nothing but static. It's driving me crazy… It's PJ here in Ballina, have ye closed down already?*

Paul and Chris set off for Kiltimagh to repair the transmitter, expecting one of the valves to have blown, but when they arrived at the old cottage, a scene of utter devastation greeted them. A sheet of protective plastic used to cover a hole in the roof had collapsed inwards, dumping a torrent of rainwater onto the transmitter, which now stood forlornly in a small pond.

Everything was ruined; there was no question about it. Paul and Chris had invested the best part of £2,000 on this new equipment and now it was all destroyed; their ambitious plans for expansion were – quite literally – under water. Both men barely spoke to each other on the return journey to Ballyhaunis; they were utterly despondent.

The following day Gerry Reilly arrived to assess the damage and see if anything could be salvaged.

"Why don't we take her apart, bring her back to Ballyhaunis and dry her out?" he suggested to Paul.

"Dry her out?" asked an incredulous Claffey. "What do you plan to do… hang it on a clothes line? Sure how could you dry that thing out?"

"Well, what about those big ovens you've got there in the restaurant in Midas? I could take her apart and stick her into one of those."

"Hould your horses," said a now bewildered Claffey. "You want to put a radio transmitter in a feckin' oven?"

"Well, have you got a better idea?"

"I suppose I don't," said Claffey wearily.

Gerry Reilly spent the morning dismantling the sodden transmitter and loading it into his van before setting off for Ballyhaunis. He seemed surprisingly cheerful on arrival.

"Do you know, I think this could actually work," he told Paul.

"So what exactly do you plan to do?" asked Chris warily.

"Well, I'm going to put the transmitter into the oven and bake it at a low temperature for about three to four days. That should dry it out."

Michael Neary, who had helped unload the transmitter, leaned over to Claffey and chuckled: "And here was I thinking you were the one that's zanier than zany!"

In the absence of a better idea, Paul and Chris had little choice but to go along with Reilly's unorthodox recipe. The ovens in the Midas restaurant hummed away for the rest of the week and by the time Reilly returned on Saturday afternoon, the transmitter was as dry as a bone. Loading the parts into his van, the Cavan man could barely contain his delight.

"You know, I have a good feeling about this," he told Paul. "I'll call in on the way home and let you know how I got on."

But curiosity got the better of Claffey and he drove over to Kiltimagh after the *Mid-Morning Show* to see how Reilly was progressing. The technician had almost finished reassembling the transmitter.

"You couldn't have timed it better," he said to Paul. "I'm going to switch her on now in a minute."

"What'll happen then?"

"Well, she'll either work perfectly or she'll blow us up."

"BLOW US UP?"

"Sure feck's sake, how do I know what's going to happen? I never baked a transmitter before!"

"Christ. Well I'm standing well away so."

Reilly finished connecting the transmitter to the electric generator and flicked the switch as Claffey stood nervously in the doorway, wondering if they were both about to be martyred for the cause of pirate radio. But the transmitter slipped seamlessly into its standby mode. He should never have doubted Gerry Reilly; the man might be unconventional but he was a technical wizard.

"See," said Reilly triumphantly. "She's as right as rain!"

"Jaysus, Gerry," said Claffey, pointing up at the roof. "Don't mention the feckin' rain!"

"Oh yeah," said Reilly chuckling. "Will you get that bloody roof fixed cos I'm not baking another transmitter for you! Now, have you any oul free passes for *Sunday Night Live*...."

It would take quite the aerial to pick up Midwest Radio on Achill Island in the summer of 1987 but a young man named Michael Duggan had just the job.

Car radio antennae were all the rage in the 1980s. The manufacturers had yet to develop inbuilt boosters for radio reception so motorists took it upon themselves to purchase aerials that came in just about every conceivable size.

Attached to the roof of Duggan's car was a fibreglass car antenna of such towering height it was almost a danger to low-flying aircraft.

The young electrician was driving across the island one afternoon when he happened upon a radio station called Midwest that seemed to be broadcasting out of Ballyhaunis. Duggan pulled in at The Grove in Bunnacurry where his boss, Peadar McHugh, operated an electrical appliance business.

"Here, take a listen to this station," Michael said. "They're playing some mighty music."

Peadar sat into the passenger seat but as soon as he did the reception started to fade. However, he could make out faint traces of John Hogan's *Brown Eyes,* one of the big Irish Country hits of the year.

"I wonder would they come down here?" Duggan asked.

"Sure why don't you take down their 'phone number and I'll give them a call later tonight," said Peadar. "Maybe we can help them to get set up on Achill."

If any man could bring Midwest Radio to an audience on Mayo's Atlantic coastline it was the indefatigable Peadar McHugh who had been pioneering new technology in some of the most remote outposts along the western seaboard for over 30 years. Only a decade earlier, Peadar had been instrumental in bringing electricity to Inishbiggle Island, one of the last areas in Ireland to be connected to the national grid.

"I was always interested in electricity," he explains. "When I was 12 years old – that would be in the 1940s – I erected lights in my uncle's house here in Bunnacurry operated by a wind generator."

Peadar grew up in the village of Bullsmouth on the east of the island at a time when a battery-operated wireless was the height of modernity. It was only when he went to the Vocational School in

Westport that the young McHugh really gained an insight into the new-fangled technology that was electricity.

"I had a science teacher from Ballina, Mr Mongey, and he ran electrical courses for us," he recalls. "I was really interested in those courses and I got a job working evenings and weekends with an electrician in Westport. When I finished school in 1949 I got a full-time position with him."

By 1951, Peadar was working as a projectionist at the Ideal Cinema and Ballroom in Westport and was also serving as a local promoter for some of the well-known music stars who played the Irish ballroom circuit in those years. Among the international stars he persuaded to visit Achill Island were the renowned English trumpeter Eddie Calvert and the legendary big band leader Victor Silvester.

In 1952, Peadar left the Ideal to open his own mobile cinema, which he brought to small parish halls across Achill and Erris for the next decade.

The big movie of the era was, of course, *The Quiet Man,* and Peadar gave that famous film its debut in community halls from Currane to Blacksod and everywhere else in between. He estimates he must have watched the movie about 800 times in his life... and he'd still watch it again, no problem.

As television grew in popularity in the early 1960s and cinema began to wane, Peadar decided he, too, needed to move with the times.

"Television wiped out the concept of the mobile cinema," he explains. "I was going into halls where there was no central heating so it was very primitive stuff and it couldn't survive the arrival of television."

Peadar brought the first television to Achill in 1963 and was soon running a thriving electrical appliance business from the rear of his home at The Grove, which was conveniently located at a busy crossroads. His wife Phil, a woman of endless energy, ran an equally bustling grocery shop and newsagents from a caravan adjacent to the large two-storey house, as well as a bed and breakfast from the building itself. The Grove in Bunnacurry was, therefore, the very epicentre of life on Achill Island when Paul and Chris arrived there on a summer's day in 1987.

"I recall getting a call from Peadar who was very keen on bringing Midwest to Achill," explains Chris. "We had a chat with him and Michael that first day and immediately knew they would be of great assistance in getting us set up on the island."

Peadar and Phil agreed to house the transmitter in a room at the back of The Grove and to erect a 20-foot mast on the chimney. It was quite a big commitment given that pirate stations were still being raided across the country.

"Midwest would never have got launched on Achill in the pirate days without the support of the McHughs and Michael Duggan," says Paul. "They were so accommodating to us and did everything they could to help."

Chris has very fond memories of making the long cross-county journey from Ballyhaunis to Achill.

"Phil would insist on us having something to eat before the work was done. Their hospitality was amazing and they were the finest people to work with."

Gerry Glennon can still recall that summer's evening when Gerry Reilly turned on the transmitter for the first time.

"Dozens and dozens of cars started to appear and they all congregated at The Grove," he says. "Everyone wanted to get their radios tuned into Midwest. The word spread like bushfire – 'Midwest was in Achill'. It was something else to witness."

Peadar McHugh likens the arrival of Midwest on Achill to the advent of electricity some three decades earlier.

"When I was driving into Westport in the early 1950s to work in the Ideal Cinema, I'd see the teams of ESB workers as they erected the poles from Mulranny out to the island. It took five or six years – from about 1950 to 1956 – to connect up the whole of the island to the national grid and that was a hugely exciting time in Achill.

"Midwest Radio arriving in the early 1980s created a similar stir. There had never been a local radio station before so it was a real novelty and people really bought into it. Midwest took off straight away on Achill and it's never looked back since."

Before he departed the island on that historic first evening, Paul stuck his head in the door of McHugh's grocery shop where Phil, her daughter Catherine and a friend, Mary B Gallagher, were sorting through newspapers and magazines.

"Here girls," Claffey began. "You know we're running these live shows on the radio on Sunday nights from Midas? Why don't ye get a bus and come up next weekend? I've a few free passes for ye here."

More than 30 years later, Mary B recalls with humour the moment she took those tickets from Paul.

"That was the rock we perished on!" she says cheerfully.

The Midas Express was about to be born.

By the late summer of 1987, *Sunday Night Live* had reached such levels of popularity people were travelling from all over the province to savour the unique atmosphere of Sunday nights in Midas. Buses and cars were parked along both sides of Clare Street and far out the Claremorris Road while a lengthy queue, several people deep, snaked its way around the side of the nightclub. Many of the mini-buses came fairly long distances – from Ballina or Tubbercurry or Tuam – but there were none to beat the Midas Express, which left The Grove in Bunnacurry each Sunday evening at 7.30pm, reaching its destination shortly after 9pm. The driver Jackie Rumley, from Tiernaur, near Mulranny, recalls the heroes' welcome that awaited the islanders on arrival at Midas.

"It got to the stage we were like celebrities! Paul and Gerry would be waiting outside to open the doors of the bus to greet everyone. The fuss they made of us was something else.

"I don't know who christened it the Midas Express but the name stuck and even to this day I meet people who travelled on that bus all those years ago and it's the first thing we talk about."

Mary B Gallagher, Catherine McHugh and Michael Duggan were regulars but Jackie never had any trouble filling the 14-seater vehicle, collecting patrons in Achill Sound, Tiernaur, Currane and other villages where Midwest had quickly become the radio station of choice.

"I don't think we were prepared for how popular we became on Achill in the pirate days," says Paul. "Obviously, it was a very distant place from Ballyhaunis and when we put up the transmitter in The Grove we weren't even sure if it was going to be worth our while."

Phil McHugh recalls with amusement the initial reaction locally to the giant 20-foot mast that now towered over The Grove.

"Sure it was the talk of the place! There were old women down in the village saying it was a bad sign because we had Midwest blasting out of a speaker beside the shop. They were blessing themselves whenever they went by!"

Peadar wasn't entirely keen on the mast either but for different reasons: he worried it might attract the attention of the forces of law and order on Achill.

"We'll be lucky if we're not raided," he told Johnny Oosten who was up on the roof one day carrying out some repairs to the transmitter.

"Raided?" replied Johnny merrily. "Sure they'd never get up here. They'd need a ladder and they'd have to get through about three doors. I wouldn't worry about it. We haven't been raided in Ballyhaunis yet so they're not going to raid us down here."

The young man's confidence put Peadar at ease and The Grove continued to be Midwest's base for several more months. The mast was able to send a signal across the Atlantic as far as Bangor Erris but Chris and Paul, having seen the success of Achill, were keen to spread Midwest's wings deep into Erris.

Commonage on Minaun Heights in Achill was identified as the optimum location for a new, more powerful FM transmitter and it became operational in late 1987. Michael Neary will never forget his first visit to the site.

"Achill was scary, hairy and death-defying," he recalls. "Everything was so wild and barren. You had to park the car and walk for half a mile up to that first site with nothing but the Atlantic underneath you!"

Peadar McHugh had a television deflector – the only legal one in Ireland – located at the same site so there was a ready supply of electricity for the transmitter, which was located in a steel hut that Johnny Oosten reckons "looked like a bank vault".

"The hut was buried into the ground," recalls Michael Neary, "and there was no floor in it so if you were there on a bad night it was hard going because once you opened the door you'd have a foot of water underneath you within 20 minutes. You'd be working away in that with the wind howling around you. Sure it was all great craic at the time!"

Chris Carroll says the assistance of Peadar and Michael Duggan was crucial in the early days of Midwest because it meant the staff in Ballyhaunis didn't have to make the long journey to Achill whenever there was an outage. But there were occasions when Chris and others had to scale Minaun Heights to ensure Midwest's growing fan base on the Atlantic seaboard had their service restored as quickly as possible.

"I remember going down there with Paul one evening. He waited in the car while I went up to the transmitter. Now this was in the days before mobile 'phones so the idea was that he'd honk the horn when he could pick up Midwest in the car. Anyway, I spent half the evening wandering around with a torch up in the clouds trying to find this transmitter and hoping I wouldn't fall into a boghole!"

The reward was worth the risk though. The powerful FM transmitter on Minaun Heights introduced Midwest to the vast barony of Erris – a region with the same geographical size as Co Louth – and it also gave the pirate station a reception that extended as far south as Galway City. Indeed, such was the success of the Achill foray into FM broadcasting – then a fairly revolutionary wavelength for a pirate station – a decision was taken to locate a second FM transmitter on Crucspullagadaun Hill near Balla.

"We bought a transmitter for £5,000, put it in a dog kennel and six of us carried it up the hill in the dead of night because we were still illegal," explains Paul. "When we got back down to the cars we tuned them in and the reception was perfect. We'd got a great signal."

Midwest blasted out on 97.1FM the following day and several listeners called in to compliment the station on the improved signal. However, the next morning the FM signal was completely gone.

"There wasn't a meg," recalls Gerry Glennon. "We went across to Balla and found the kennel containing the transmitter at the bottom of the hill. There had been a bit of a storm the night before and it blew the kennel the whole way down the hill but, thankfully, the equipment was okay."

With four transmitters – two medium wave and two FM – Midwest now had a greater geographical reach than almost any other local radio station in the country. But it was still a pirate and could be closed overnight if the State was so minded. Political inertia had characterised the government response to the rapid growth of pirate stations such as Midwest throughout the late 1980s but something had to give sooner rather than later. However, in the meantime, the only thing Paul, Chris and the rest of the team at Midwest could do was to keep expanding their listenership in the hope that Midwest would be at the top of the queue when licences were finally handed out.

That day was coming faster than many believed.

Paul Claffey chats with a contestant in 'Come On Down The Price is Right' during *Sunday Night Live* at Midas Nightclub in Ballyhaunis in the late 1980s.

Chris Carroll takes the last record off the turntable and hands it to receptionist Denise Moran, Ballyhaunis, following the closure of the pirate Midwest Radio on December 30, 1988.

Picture: Michael Connaughton

Midas Nightclub was packed to the rafters on December 30, 1988, as the pirate Midwest Radio held a farewell concert. Picture: Michael Connaughton

Midwest Radio presenters and friends – including members of the famous Midas Express from Achill Island – join TR Dallas and a host of stars onstage at the end of the farewell concert on December 30, 1988.
Picture: Michael Connaughton

It was standing room only in Midas Nightclub on December 30, 1988, as the pirate Midwest Radio said farewell to its loyal listeners.

Picture: Michael Connaughton

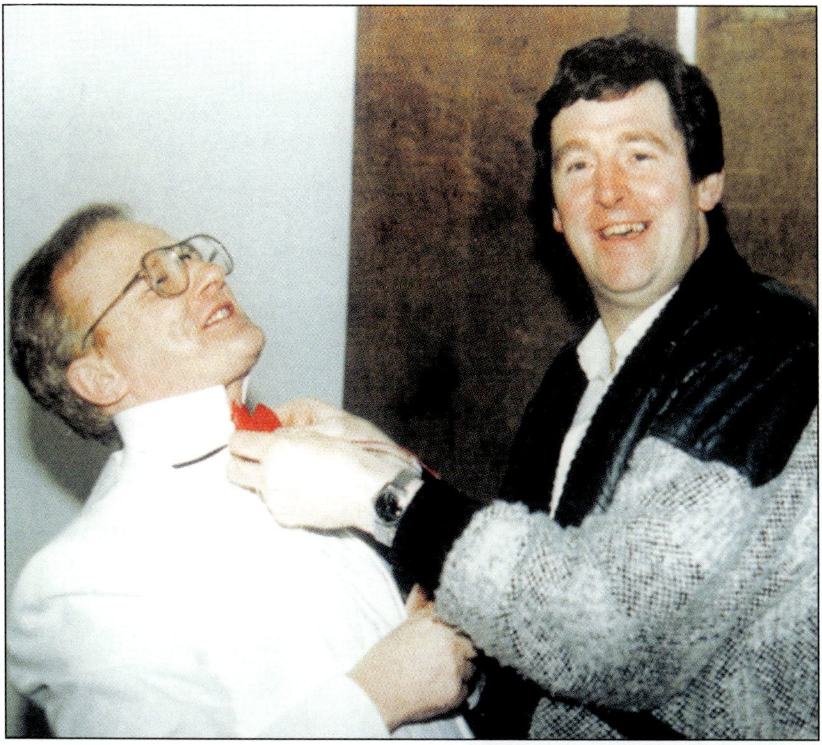

Mick Flavin puts the finishing touches to Paul Claffey's famous flashing dickie!

Retired garda John Duggan presented the final show on the pirate Midwest Radio before its closure on December 30, 1988. Picture: Frank Dolan

Directors and staff of County Mayo Radio Ltd pictured at the Ardilaun Hotel in March 1989 ahead of the oral hearing for the Mayo radio franchise.
Picture: Michael Connaughton

The directors of County Mayo Radio pictured at the Ardilaun House Hotel in Salthill, Co Galway, on March 3, 1989, ahead of their submission to the Independent Radio and Television Commission (IRTC) for the Mayo radio franchise. Front row, from left: Tom Courell, Paul Claffey, Michael Hughes (chairman), Terry Reilly, Louis McRedmond (advisor). Back row: Dr John Connolly, John Martyn (advisor), PJ Hennelly, Willie Sammon, John Reilly, James Jennings (advisor), John Dillon-Leetch (advisor) and Michael O'Malley (Mayo Co Council manager). Picture: Michael Connaughton

Presenter Adrian Eames holds up a copy of Kevin Prendergast's record *The Pride of the West,* which included the song *My Old Home In Mayo,* penned by Michael Commins. It was the first song played on Midwest Radio on July 24, 1989. Picture: Frank Dolan

Granlahan native Mary Raftery holding the first request, which arrived via telephone, on the morning of July 24, 1989 after Midwest returned to the airwaves. Mary continues to work at the station. Picture: Frank Dolan

THE VOICE OF THE WEST: At the launch of Midwest Radio in 1989 were Justice Seamus Henchy, IRTC chairman; Paul Claffey, Midwest Radio CEO; Minister for Communications Ray Burke and Michael Hughes, Chairman, Midwest Radio. Picture: Western People Archives

Enjoying the official launch of Midwest Radio in 1989 were, from left: Tom Courell, Fr Johnny Doherty, Bishop of Achonry Thomas Flynn, Rev Jack Heaslip and Fr Des Fahy.
Picture: Frank Dolan

The directors of Midwest Radio and dignitaries pictured in the grounds of Breaffy House Hotel, Castlebar, on July 24, 1989, for the official launch of the station. Back row, from left: Tom Courell, Paul Claffey, Cathal Duffy, Minister for the Environment Padraig Flynn, Jim Ryan, Michael Durcan, Terry Reilly, Michael Farrell, John Connolly, PJ Hennelly, John Reilly. Front row: Justice Seamus Henchy, Michael Farrell, Minister for Communications Ray Burke, Rita de Vere-Durcan, Archbishop Joseph Cassidy, Fr Colm Kilcoyne.

Picture: Frank Dolan

Renowned US attorney and Bohola native Paul O'Dwyer (left) chats with Mayo Co Council manager Michael O'Malley and council chairman Martin J O'Toole at a reception in Breaffy House Hotel, Castlebar on July 24, 1989, to mark the official launch of Midwest Radio, which was the first local radio station outside Dublin to take to the airwaves. Picture: Frank Dolan

Paul Claffey holds Midwest's first Christmas card, sent by Kathleen Staunton, Kilmeena, Westport, on the first week of October 1989. Picture: Frank Dolan

NWR 102.5 FM

NWRfm
Market Yard,
Sligo, Ireland.

Telephone (071) 61555/60108

THE COUNTDOWN BEGINS
NORTH WEST RADIO
Commence Broadcasting
ON FRIDAY NOV. 2, '90
at 10 a.m.

FREQUENCIES: 102.5 FM (SLIGO)
96.3 FM (DONGEAL)

TEST TRANSMISSIONS BEGIN THIS WEEKEND

TUNE IN TO THE VOICE OF THE NORTH WEST FRIDAY NOVEMBER 2

THE N.W.R.
CELEBRATION CONCERT

To celebrate the launch of our new station North West Radio invites you to join in a night of celebration and entertainment...

THIS MONDAY (5th) NOVEMBER
IN THE ABBEY HOTEL, DONEGAL TOWN

ON STAGE:

★ JOHN HOGAN AND HIS BAND
★ MICK FLAVIN AND HIS BAND
★ JOANNA AND TEQUILLA SUNRISE
★ DECLAN NERNEY ★ THE CONQUERORS
★ AND THE LIMITS

HOSTING THE EVENING'S CELEBRATIONS WILL BE N.W.R. PRESENTERS –
HENRY McGLADE, PAUL CLAFFEY
AND TOMMY MARREN

Doors open 9.00. Concert starts 9.30.
Full Bar Extension. Tickets £5 at the door.

M W R
is on
96.1 FM

Consult your Electrical Dealer in case of difficulty.

MID-WEST RADIO
On the air MONDAY, JULY 24th, from 10 a.m.

Playing all your favourites . . . plus news, as the stories break . . . sport . . . farming feature items . . . quizzes and fun.

MID-WEST RADIO on 96.1 FM ● *See Special Souvenir Supplement next Tuesday to celebrate gala opening.*

Mid-West Radio proudly presents

GALA CELEBRATION CONCERT
in TRAVELLERS FRIEND HOTEL, CASTLEBAR

on Monday, 24th July, at 9.30 p.m., to mark the opening of MWR FM, featuring . . .

BRENDAN SHINE & HIS BAND

MICK FLAVIN & HIS BAND

JOHN HOGAN & HIS BAND

JOANNA & TEQUILLA SUNRISE

TONY ALLEN & HIS BAND

JOE DOLAN & THE DRIFTERS

Plus a host of other stars

Doors open 8.45 p.m. ... £5.00. Show starts at 9.30 p.m. sharp.

COMING SOON

FRIDAY 2ND NOVEMBER

AT 10.00 A.M.

TUNE YOUR RADIO TO FM 96.3 or 102.5

NORTH WEST RADIO

GOES ON AIR FOR THE FIRST TIME

NWR 102.5 96.3FM

TO CELEBRATE WE'RE GIVING AWAY £100'S IN CASH

Gala Dance

WITH IRELAND'S TOP ARTISTES

MICK FLAVIN & HIS BAND · JOHN HOGAN & HIS BAND · JOANNE & TEQUILA SUNRISE · DECLAN NERNEY & HIS BAND · THE CONQUERORS · THE LIMITS

Comperes: HENRY McGLADE, TOMMY MARREN & PAUL CLAFFEY

THE ABBEY HOTEL, DONEGAL TOWN

MONDAY 5th NOVEMBER

DOORS OPEN 8.30 · SHOW STARTS 9.30 · ADM. £5

COME EARLY TO AVOID DISAPPOINTMENT

FULL BAR EXTENSION · TICKETS AT THE DOOR

Tune in

NWR gives you what you want.

Comprehensive Local & National News.

The perfect music mix! Golden Oldies Classic Hits, quality Irish & Country recordings, middle of the road and a Sprinkling of Chart Favourites.

Plus - win lots and lots of Cash.

NORTH WEST RADIO

MARKET YARD · SLIGO

TEL / FAX 071-60108

REQUEST HOTLINE 071•61555

TO ADVERTIS[E] CALL: 071• 60108

M W R

In association with

Michael Gunning Electrical

PROUDLY PRESENTS

"Sunday Night Live"

Ireland's biggest live variety show

STARTING SUNDAY, AUGUST 6th at 10 p.m.

Starring:

Brendan Shine & his band

Plus special guest Sean Cuddy

Ireland's newest country star

And the £8,000 game show

'COME ON DOWN'

ALL BROADCAST LIVE ON MWR-FM

... 9.15 p.m. Show starts 10 p.m.

Balla Oil ...

Tel.: 094-65237

Wednesday, 26th July, 1989 Price: 30p

Mid-West blasts into radio history books

The Minister for Communications Mr. Ray Burke, seated at the controls following the opening of Mid West Radio. On his right is Mr. Justice Seamus Henchy, chairman of the IRTC, with the chairman of the Mid West Board, Michael Hughes, on his left. Standing at the rear is Paul Claffey Mid West Radio CEO

TWO ... teamed up to tunefully launch ... Radio ... Monday, ... from Logboy ... Home In ... d on a...

festivities and he was joined by Minister for the Environment, Padraig Flynn and Minister of State, Sean Calleary.

The Minister said: "For too long there has been a feeling in ... provinces that the national broadcasting ... cater adequately for the needs of rural ...

... MWR fm gives the people of Mayo a ... influence ... they listen to ...

... Radio and Tele...on

M W R

TUNE TO MID-WEST RADIO

96.1 FM

ON AIR FROM JULY 24th

- Now testing signals, music and tone. Has your set FM? Your electrical dealer will advise.
- Testing shortly, 97 FM, to cover West and North Mayo region.

GALA CELEBRATION CONCERT

JULY 24th -:- TOP ACTS

Full details next week.

Best wishes and a very welcome back to MWR – FM from

Mary B. Gallagher
Catherine McHugh
Ann Gallagher
Kathleen Gallagher
Alice O'Donnell
Michael Durcan
Michael McGinty

And all on the

Midas Express

BUNNACURRY

Paul Claffey pops the champagne outside Midwest Radio's old offices at Abbey Street in Ballyhaunis in the 1990s to celebrate record-breaking listenership figures for the radio station.

Chris Carroll with colleagues Paula Donnellan and Gerry Glennon back in the days when record players were a feature of radio studios.

The staff of Midwest Radio in the early days of the station in the 1990s. Left to right: Gerry Glennon, Maria Mullarkey, Padraic Walsh, Paul Claffey (CEO), Tommy Marren, Paula Donnellan, Chris Carroll.

There have been days when Midwest Radio had to battle against the elements to keep on air. In January 1993, winter storms caused serious damage to the station's transmission equipment.

John Duggan in conversation with fellow Midwest broadcaster Séamus Duffy.

Liam Horan and the late Ivan Neill filing copy for the Western People from a hotel room in Dublin in the late 1980s. Ballinrobe native Liam undertook the first live commentary for Midwest Radio when he stepped behind the mike for the Connacht Senior Football Final Replay in 1989. Ivan was also a sports contributor to Midwest in its early days.

Picture: Western People Archives

The Beat on the Peat in New York has gone down in history as one of the great events organised for the Irish Diaspora. Pictured at the second annual Beat on the Peat reunion dinner dance for committee and friends, held in the TF Royal Theatre, Castlebar were, front row, l-r: Ann Roper, Assistant Treasurer; Angela McLoughlin, Treasurer; May Hunt, Paul Claffey, Midwest CEO; Sarah Keane, Assistant Secretary; Elsie McTigue, Secretary. Back row: Kevin Ruane, Marjorie Nolan, Michael Keane, Chairman; P.J. Sammin, Assistant Chairman; Mary Whittington, Padraic Moran and Paddy Moran, PRO.

Bangor Erris native Maria Mullarkey began her career at Midwest and later worked for the *Nationwide* television programme on RTÉ.

Martin McHugh from Castlerea holds the record as Midwest's longest serving Sales Executive, having served from 1989 to his retirement in 2011.

Former drama producer Geraldine Lavin was a key figure in Midwest's Radio Drama series over many years.

Former staff members Mary Whittington and Tina Mitchell.

Padraic 'Stan' Moran is the man behind Midwest's Radio Bingo and clocks up the miles each month distributing bingo books across the region.

The former secretary of Knock Airport Jim Ryan with his great friend Monsignor James Horan celebrate the opening of the airport in 1986. Jim was one of the first directors of Midwest Radio.

Picture: Western People Archives

Joe Byrne displays some of his extensive collection of archival material on Irish traditional music and culture. Picture: Western People Archives

International singing star Daniel O'Donnell chats to Midwest Radio's Gerry Glennon during an outside broadcast in Belmullet. Daniel was one of a new generation of Country music singers who became household names in the 1980s through the airplay they received on pirate stations like Midwest.

Paul Claffey is pictured with the legendary Joe Dolan (right) and Paddy Cole at an event in the Galway Bay Hotel in 1999. Joe was a great friend of Midwest and performed at the station's opening concert in the TF Royal Theatre in 1989.

One of the best-known guests on the *Mid-Morning Show* was May Hunt, from Ballymote, who is pictured with another great Midwest Radio supporter Mary B Gallagher from Achill Island.
Picture: Courtesy of Mary B Gallagher

Midwest Radio's news team achieved major success in 2011 when it won gold at the annual PPI National Radio Awards. The popular *Lunchtime News* programme beat off stiff competition from national and local radio stations, including RTÉ, to land the coveted title of 'News Programme of the Year'. News editor Teresa O'Malley is pictured holding the award with Paula Donnellan (left) and Angelina Nugent.

Ballinrobe native Mike Finnerty prepares to broadcast Sky television's first GAA match on June 7, 2014, in the company of Tipperary hurling legend Nicky English. Mike began his career at Midwest Radio in the early 1990s and was the station's GAA commentator for over a decade.

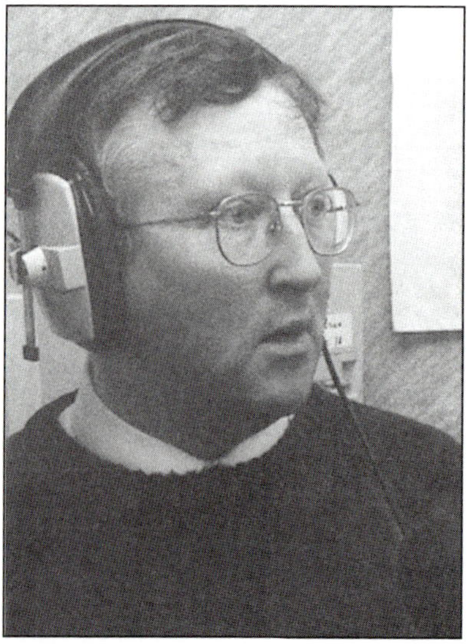

Willie Ryan, from Ballyhaunis, was the voice of GAA for Midwest Radio throughout the 1990s.

Former Mayo football star Billy Fitzpatrick was GAA analyst for Midwest for many years.

The one and only Willie 'The Shoe' McNeely pictured with a copy of the *Mayo News* sports supplement outside Midwest's office in Castlebar in 2001.

East Mayo native Noel Grogan has been the man behind the wheel of Midwest Radio's famous satellite cruiser for many years.

Ballina man Tommy Murphy was involved in pirate radio in his hometown throughout the 1980s before taking up a role as a presenter with Midwest Radio when it became legal in 1989.

Sir Alex Ferguson during the 2002 interview with Anthony Hennigan in which he confirmed the record-breaking transfer of Rio Ferdinand from Leeds United to Manchester United.

Entertainers Sean Keane, Mike Denver and Robert Mizzell prepare to saddle up for Craic at the Track music event at Ballinrobe Racecourse in 2005.

David Cawley has been Midwest Radio's earliest riser and presents the most popular breakfast show on local radio in Ireland.

Former Taoiseach Enda Kenny with Midwest presenters David Cawley and Angelina Nugent at the Pink Ribbon Cycle in Castlebar, which takes place each May Bank Holiday Weekend to raise funds for cancer charities.

Western Alzheimers is one of many local charities that Midwest Radio has supported over the years. Our picture shows CEO Paul Claffey preparing for their annual Tea Day in the company of John Grant and other representatives of the charity.

Marjorie Morrow-Nolan launching one of her cookbooks in the company of Midwest CEO Paul Claffey and presenter Gerry Glennon.

At the launch of Midwest Irish Radio in 2005 were, from left: Noel Grogan, Gerry Glennon and Una Flanagan.

Tommy Marren shares a lighthearted moment with Belmullet's Ian McAndrew during an outside broadcast from the Erris capital.

Michael Neary was one of the presenters on the original pirate Midwest Radio in the mid-1980s. He is pictured with Foxford's Frankie Devaney during an outside broadcast at the local craft fair some years ago.

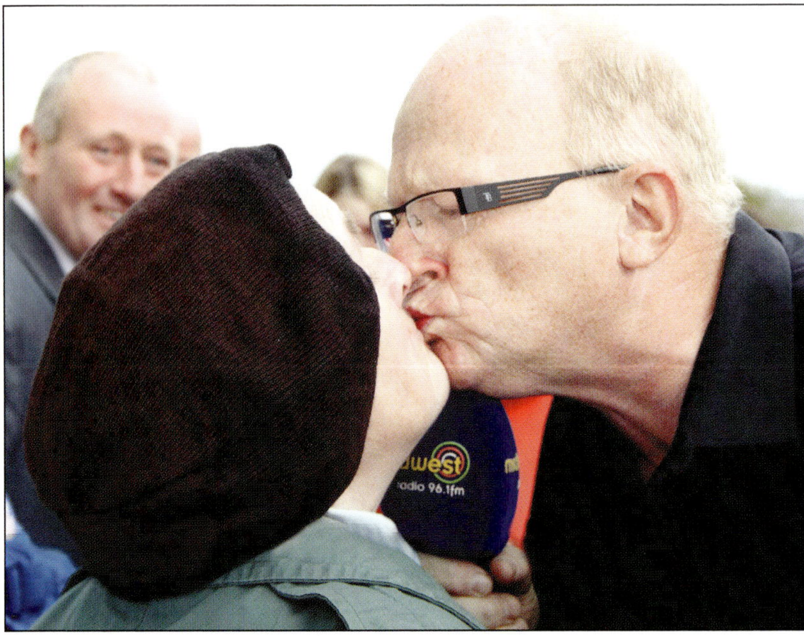

Zanier than zany: Paul Claffey administers his famous Bohola kiss to Ellen Mary Boland, Rathlee, Easkey.

Padraic Walsh trying to find a victim for his Alphabet Quiz.

CHAPTER TWELVE

The pirate who lived in a castle

BY the start of 1988, Midwest was facing competition from another pirate station, Independent Radio Mayo (IRM), which launched in Castlebar earlier that year. Broadcasting on 738 medium wave, IRM was using a powerful transmitter sourced from the defunct Dublin-based pirate Radio Leinster, giving it a transmission range that rivalled Midwest. Among those involved in the new station was Hollymount man Gerry Delaney, who had founded Mayo's first proper pirate station, Atlantic Radio, almost a decade earlier.

Atlantic Radio began as a student project in the summer of 1978 and had its roots in a community radio initiative that took place in Claremorris the previous year when RTÉ facilitated the establishment of a local station for the duration of the town's Ham Festival. This project was identical to the one Michael Commins participated in during his time in Abbeyleix and proved so successful that some of those involved decided to set up their own pirate station in South Mayo. Commins, who returned to the West in 1978 to take up a position as a reporter with the *Western Journal*, was part of the Atlantic Radio team for a brief period.

"Atlantic Radio was the brainchild of Gerry Delaney," he says. "Gerry was always a radio head and technically very good and had a bit of a rebel spirit too!"

The launch of Atlantic Radio made headlines in regional newspapers across Connacht with the *Western Journal* describing it as "the first pirate of any size in Mayo". The new station was certainly not underselling itself: the promoters claimed to have a library of 40,000 records and were part of the rather grandly named 'Atlantic Broadcasting Corporation' or ABC!

Using the pseudonym 'Alan Dean', Gerry went on a media blitz ahead of the launch of Atlantic Radio, telling the *Western People:*

"People may say that we are doing this for the fun of it but this is totally untrue. We are broadcasting illegally because the national radio service, RTÉ, is not providing the service people want.

"We in Mayo have little chance of ever getting what we deserve from RTÉ so it's up to ourselves to provide the service that is required for our people."

Delaney's view was wholeheartedly endorsed by the likes of Michael Commins who did his best to promote the new station through his weekly music column in the *Western Journal.*

"I always had a soft spot for the pirates," he explains. "They were fulfilling a need and I never saw anything wrong with what they were doing. Nobody considers putting out music and giving people happiness breaking the law. How could they? Sure it's the most natural thing in the world to give people what they want. As long as radio is not used to overthrow governments – and none of us were pushing it that far!"

Not everyone in print journalism shared Commins' benign view of the pirates. The Irish branch of the National Union of Journalists (NUJ) and the Provincial Newspapers' Association of Ireland, which represented owners of regional newspapers, issued statements in the late 1970s condemning the pirates and claiming they were a threat to print journalism, which was then employing thousands around the country. Indeed, Michael Commins was one of only a handful of print journalists who became involved in pirate radio, firstly with Atlantic Radio and later Midwest.

"Provincial newspapers saw the emergence of local radio as a threat to their advertising revenues, in particular, and that was understandable," he explains. "I used to give Midwest the odd mention in my column in the *Connaught Telegraph* [Commins moved to the *Telegraph* when the *Journal* closed in 1982] but it would be frowned on a bit. The feeling was that we shouldn't be giving the pirates publicity."

There had been a spate of raids on Dublin-based pirates in 1983 but by the time Midwest was launched in 1985, the Department of Posts and Telegraphs had resigned itself to the fact there was little it could do to curb the rapid growth of the pirate radio movement. In fact, the situation became so absurd that the Department ended up providing telephone facilities for the very stations it was meant to be shutting down.

Such was the explosion in the number of new stations taking to the airwaves in the mid to late 1980s that Gerry Reilly was servicing transmitters from Malin Head to Mallow and from Achill Island to Carlingford.

"In 1987, I changed two new vans because I was doing 100,000 miles every six months," he recalls. "The reason I remember it so well is that 1987 was the year the new car registrations came in and I had CN 288 and CN 988 within six months of each other."

Michael Commins made his first broadcast as a pirate disc jockey from Caltra sandpit, near Claremorris, in 1979, which was the same year Atlantic Radio closed down after just 18 months on the airwaves. Like so many pirates of the late 1970s, Atlantic's playlist of pop and rock music was targeted at a teenage audience and the local station simply couldn't compete with RTÉ Radio 2 when it launched in May 1979. But Gerry Delaney wasn't giving up on local radio, telling the *Western People* he looked forward to the day when licences would be made available to operators of stations like Atlantic Radio.

"With a licence we will provide a well-run local radio station for the West, plus a dozen jobs at no cost to the taxpayer. It gets me why the Government is so against this type of development. We are doing nobody any harm and providing a service that's badly needed."

Almost a decade later, Gerry was back on the pirate radio scene with IRM, which had Castlebar man John Morrin as one of its principal backers. IRM was mainly targeted at a younger audience and its playlist was not dissimilar to RTÉ Radio 2 but it also had a strong local feel to it and was a credible rival to Midwest.

IRM made national headlines in the spring of 1988 when it was announced that Sharon Flynn, the 23-year-old daughter of Minister for the Environment Padraig Flynn, was to broadcast a weekly Irish language programme on the new station. The revelation that a minister's daughter was broadcasting on an illegal radio station was grist to the mill for critics of the pirates, although Flynn wasn't losing too much sleep over it, telling the *Sunday Independent* he was more than happy for his daughter to chart her own course in life.

"When people are over age they don't ask their parents," he wryly opined, adding that he had no comment to make "one way or another" about pirate radio.

But Flynn's cabinet colleague, Minister for Communications Ray Burke, had plenty of strident remarks to make about pirate broadcasters and was preparing to bring legislation before the Dáil that would put them out of business for good. There would be no ifs, buts or maybes any more; this time the pirates really were going to walk the plank.

Midwest and IRM weren't the only pirate stations vying for radio listeners in Co Mayo in the late 1980s. Ballina-based Twin County Radio (TCR) was broadcasting across a fairly large swathe of North Mayo and West Sligo – hence the station's 'Twin County' name – and had built up a loyal listenership by 1988. Its manager was Tommy Murphy, a man who later became synonymous with listeners of Midwest Radio, both as a broadcaster and the driver of Midwest's outside broadcasting unit up to his death in 2012.

"Tommy Murphy was Mister Radio in Ballina," says Dermot Rice, one of countless local disc jockeys to get their first break from the genial Tommy.

There were a plethora of different stations in Ballina throughout the 1980s, including Castle Radio, located at Belleek Castle, Alternative Radio West, Westward Radio and finally Twin County Radio. Tommy's interest in broadcasting came from his lifetime love of music, which was fostered as a youngster in his native Enniscrone in the 1940s and 1950s when he'd fall asleep to the glorious sounds of the big bands drifting across the Atlantic waves from the Marine Ballroom.

One summer's evening, Tommy made his way to the famous dancehall and watched the musicians as they performed, fascinated by the seemingly effortless way they could play their different instruments. Sensing the youngster's curiosity, the drummer invited him to sit behind the kit and put a pair of drumsticks in his hands. That was it:

Tommy Murphy was hooked. Music was to be his guiding star for the rest of his days.

Like so many of his generation, Tommy left school in his early teens and immediately got a job as a drummer with the Jimmy Honeyman Band, which had a residency at the Olympic Ballroom in Dublin. Born in London on the eve of World War II, Tommy decided to return to the country of his birth in the mid-1950s and got a job working in an office. He was still only 16 but there was companionship to be found among the many other Irish emigrants – some as young as himself – who came in their tens of thousands to cities like London, Manchester, Birmingham and Leeds throughout the 1950s. Tommy missed home, however, and particularly pined for the Irish music scene, so he decided to return after a year and promptly got a job as a drummer with the Ballina-based Jack Ruane Band.

It is a measure of the teenage Murphy's musicianship that he was considered good enough to be part of one of the most popular and longest-established dance bands of that era. The Jack Ruane Band had been performing since the 1930s and was the first Irish band to undertake an overseas Lenten tour, playing a number of venues in post-war England in 1947. The Lenten tours of the UK – so-called because the Catholic Church did not permit dancing in Ireland during Lent – gradually became a vital source of revenue for full-time bands, especially after Irish emigrants started to flood into Britain in the 1950s.

Tommy joined the Jack Ruane Band at a time when it was transitioning from an orchestra to a showband. The 'big band' sound of the early 1950s, epitomised by sit-down orchestras such as Mick Delahunty's, was giving way to the likes of the Clipper Carlton Showband, which was influenced by the rock 'n' roll tsunami sweeping across the Atlantic. The Jack Ruane Band was one of the very few acts to survive the shift in musical tastes and it did it so by employing young musicians such as Tommy Murphy and Ruane's sons, Judd and Jack Jnr.

In 1962, the Jack Ruane Band broke into the Irish charts with the single *The Grand Old River Moy* and they also embarked on a six-week tour of America, opening at the famous City Center Ballroom in New York and playing to full houses in several other cities too.

By now, Tommy had married the love of his life, Reenie Corcoran, and settled down to raise their family at Lord Edward Street in Ballina. The Jack Ruane Band continued to perform up to 1977 when it, too, fell victim to the rapid demise of the dancehall scene. Tommy continued to perform as a backing musician for various well-known artists from Slim Whitman and Sandy Shaw to Dana, but he also became an enthusiastic pirate radio broadcaster and was like a father figure to many wannabe DJs in Ballina.

"I have such great memories of Tommy," says Dermot Rice. "He was a gentleman to work for and was really proud of the various radio stations he was involved with. Of course, it was all very ad hoc at that time. In fact, before setting up the transmitter, Tommy would often call over to the Garda barracks and the fire station to find out what frequencies they were using so he wouldn't interrupt their work!"

Tommy Murphy must be the only broadcaster in the history of Irish pirate radio who checked in with the local Gardaí before going on the air and it is measure of the man's popularity in Ballina that nobody in the barracks ever considered raiding one of his stations. He was just a genuine, passionate music man who was – in the words of Michael Commins – bringing a little bit of happiness into the lives of his listeners.

"I've always enjoyed presenting programmes," Tommy remarked in an interview in 1997. "I find there is great satisfaction in entertaining people."

His signature sign-off – both in the pirate days and later with Midwest Radio – summed the man up:

"Be kind to each other," he'd tell listeners, adding in the 1997 interview, "I find it costs us nothing to be kind."

Tommy was so devoted to broadcasting he even converted a room in his house into a small studio and made a little bit of pirate radio history in the spring of 1988 when he broadcast an hour-long programme from 33 Lord Edward Street, Ballina to the small US town of St Patrick in Missouri via local station WGFM, located in Illinois. The partnership came about through a remarkable chain of events that began when Tommy spotted a small article in *Ireland's Own* magazine.

"The article was by a Mrs Druger who lived in St Patrick and she was offering a service where she'd send special St Patrick's cards to addresses anywhere in the world on St Patrick's Day," he recalled. "The cards were unique because the town of St Patrick was the only place in the world where the envelopes were stamped with green ink. I happened to have a couple of dollars in my pocket from an earlier trip to America so I decided to give her my own name and another person's for the hell of it."

Tommy ended up getting a lot more than a card with a green postmark. Upon hearing of the Ballina man's involvement in local radio, Mrs Druger contacted her own local station, WGFM, and asked its manager Leo Henning to telephone Tommy. The two men discussed the idea of a one-hour broadcast from Ballina and it was agreed that Tommy and Leo would record a special show on St Patrick's Day 1988 for WGFM, which was based in the city of Quincy, Illinois and had a vast audience in both Illinois and Missouri. Indeed, it was a case of the twin-county radioman meeting his twin-state counterpart.

The show was broadcast and at the end of it, Henning issued an invitation to his new Irish friend:

"Come on over next year, Tommy, we'd love to host you in St Patrick."

"Give me a ticket and I'll go!" Tommy jokingly replied.

"We'll pass around the hat," countered Henning.

Tommy thought no more of it and went back to the day job at Twin County Radio, but Leo Henning and the folks in St Patrick had other ideas. The Ballina pirate would soon be setting sail across the Atlantic.

One of the daily presenters at Twin County Radio was a Sligo man whose career in radio had almost ended before it even began. In October 1979, Tommy Marren entered a competition on the newly launched RTÉ Radio 2 to become a DJ for a day.

"I had just completed my Leaving Cert in Banada Abbey and sent RTÉ a very basic tape pretending I was presenting a radio programme," he explains. "I got called to the final in Limerick and was instructed to go to the Glentworth Hotel where the competition was to take place.

"Obviously, I was absolutely thrilled. This was a huge deal at the time. Ronan Collins and a DJ from Radio Luxembourg were the judges so I felt this was a great opportunity."

A career in radio had been Tommy's cherished ambition for as long as he could remember. A show-jumping commentator, of all people, got the Tourlestrane youngster hooked on the enchanting world of broadcasting.

"Brian MacSharry was RTÉ's show-jumping commentator and as a child I wanted his job more than anything else in the world! I'd be out in the field at home leaping over makeshift fences and commentating at the same time. I was the horse, the rider and the commentator all in one."

Sports broadcasting continued to capture Tommy's imagination into his teenage years. In 1975, Sligo's senior footballers won their first Connacht title in 47 years after a dramatic replay against Mayo and went on to meet Mick O'Dwyer's young Kerry team in the All-Ireland semi-final. Tommy followed their progress through the colourful commentaries of the inimitable Micheál O'Hehir.

"I was just intrigued by his commentaries," he recalls. "He was the voice of GAA at that time and was an inspirational figure for anyone who was even remotely interested in broadcasting."

It was one thing being interested in radio but trying to pursue a career in broadcasting in the late 1970s wasn't easy. There were no third-level courses and Sligo hadn't a tradition of pirate broadcasting, which was surprising for a county with such a large urban centre. Indeed, in September 1978, the *Sligo Champion* bemoaned the fact that Sligo was "the only area of the country without a local station", so when the young Tommy Marren was selected a year later as a contestant in RTÉ Radio 2's 'DJ for a Day' competition he was convinced this would be his one and only opportunity to forge a career in broadcasting. It was going to be his date with destiny.

Tommy, his brother and two friends set off down the N17 on an October afternoon, arriving at the Glentworth Hotel with plenty of time to spare. A competition involving Ireland's newest national broadcaster might be expected to attract some degree of fanfare but the Glentworth seemed eerily quiet that afternoon. Tommy approached the reception desk and asked where the event was being held but was met with blank stares. In an era before smartphones and instant communication, there was little to do except wait around until the competition finally commenced because it was fairly obvious there had been a change in the starting time. Tommy and his supporters lounged around reception as one hour crawled into a second and then a third... if John Duggan thought a three-hour checkpoint was tedious he'd want to try this.

Eventually, after nearly four hours, a man in a suit burst through the front door and made a beeline for Tommy's group.

"Which one of you is Tommy?" he asked.

The teenager stood and introduced himself.

"I'm really sorry about this," began the man. "But there has been an unfortunate mix-up. You were sent to the wrong hotel and the competition is over but we do want you to come up to spin a few discs anyway."

Tommy recalls the story now with the humour that comes from an adult perspective but back then it was a crushing disappointment for a teenager with such an enthusiasm for broadcasting. As he made the long trip back up the N17, the youngster genuinely believed fate had cruelly conspired to quench his dream of a career in radio.

By the following week, Tommy was back in Banada Abbey Secondary School where he participated in a one-year post-Leaving Cert Commercial Course. He was the only male in a class of 17 girls, which wasn't the worst fate to befall an 18-year-old lad; maybe the gods weren't against him after all.

Upon graduation the following summer, he started working in the purchasing department of local firm Basta before moving to Ballina around 1981 to take up a position in the Credit Finance Bank.

An avid reader of local newspapers, Tommy was flicking through the pages of the *Western Journal* one day when he noticed an advertisement for presenters on Ballina's first pirate station Alternative Radio West (ARW). Deciding it was time to resurrect his radio dream, the Tourlestrane man recorded a demo tape and dropped it into ARW's offices for fear it might get lost in the post. This time those fickle gods weren't going to deny him.

"A few days later I was called in for a meeting with Tommy Murphy and he offered me a job as a full-time presenter there and then," he recalls. "Tommy was constantly on the lookout for new talent and was always willing to give people a chance even if they lacked experience."

As pirate radio stations came and went in Ballina, Tommy Marren moved between them, always managing to secure full-time employment whenever one pirate replaced another. ARW gave way to Castle Radio, located in the impressive surroundings of Belleek Castle whose manager was particularly keen to use pirate radio to promote his new nightclub Candles. Tommy reached a plum arrangement where he was offered accommodation in an apartment at the rear of the stately residence, giving him the dubious distinction of being the first Mayo pirate to live in a castle since Grainne Uaile.

Castle Radio lasted about a year before it was subsumed by Tommy Murphy's latest foray into broadcasting, Twin County Radio, which had the support of several prominent local businessmen, including Joseph Murphy of Murphy's Mills who provided accommodation at his premises on Lord Edward Street. Tommy was one of six full-time staff and the station broadcast seven days per week, serving up a non-stop diet of music, music and more music.

"There was no talk in those days and there wouldn't have been much by way of news bulletins either," he recalls. "We played music from the '80s in the main. Country wouldn't have really got a look in. We viewed Country as music people didn't want to hear but if we'd only asked them it was exactly what they wanted to hear. TCR had its own audience though and it was doing as well as any of the other pirates."

When he wasn't in the radio studio, Tommy was the resident disc jockey at the newly opened Tingles Nightclub, located in the old Central Hotel (now the Broken Jug) and owned by John Barrett. In the 1980s, Tingles was the place to be seen in Ballina; it was – as its slogan cheekily proclaimed – *where sensations begin.* And quite a few sensations began in Tingles.

"It was the first nightclub in Ballina with strobe lighting and helicopter lighting," recalls Tommy. "John was really progressive and was forever doing the place up, putting in more strobe lighting or upgrading the upholstery or whatever."

For someone whose childhood ambition had been to make a full-time living from broadcasting, the dual roles with TCR and Tingles were providing Tommy with everything he hoped for when setting out for the Glentworth Hotel in Limerick almost a decade earlier. But as winter turned to spring in 1988, the Tourlestrane man was acutely aware that the days of the pirate broadcasters were numbered and felt the need to "get a proper job". He applied for a position at AIB's branch in Sligo and when an offer came through, Tommy and his wife-to-be Mary Ryan, a native of Ballina, decided there would never be a more opportune time to make a move because pirate radio looked like it was about to "fizzle out".

It was a prescient decision. The new Television and Broadcasting Act was published that summer, setting a non-negotiable deadline of New Year's Eve 1988 for the shutdown of all pirate radio stations in the Republic of Ireland. Pirates who broadcast beyond that date faced financial penalties of up to £20,000 (from a token £50) and would also be automatically disqualified from receiving a licence from the newly established Independent Radio and Television Commission (IRTC).

It had taken the State the best part of a quarter of a century to get to grips with the pirate broadcasters but, finally, the authorities had them exactly where they wanted them: on the plank. And as any self-respecting pirate knew, once you were on the plank there was no turning back.

CHAPTER THIRTEEN

The sound of silence

1988 was the year of two halves for the team at Midwest Radio. The first six months were spent waiting for Minister Ray Burke to make his long-expected announcement on the future of pirate radio, and the wait was almost worse then the news itself.

The minister possessed a dim view of the pirate broadcasters and had previously stated they were law-breakers who should not be entitled to apply for radio licences if, and when, a new regime was put in place. But temperate voices at the Cabinet table sought a more conciliatory approach and ultimately won the day. There was a certain amount of self-preservation at stake for the Fianna Fáil minority administration. The government, under the stewardship of a certain Charles J Haughey, was electorally savvy enough to recognise that the pirates now commanded a lot of public affection, especially in rural areas where stations such as Midwest were offering a service previously unavailable. Nowadays it is difficult to imagine the broadcasting environment of the pre-pirate era where something as simple as having a request played was virtually impossible. John Duggan understood the appeal of local radio better than most.

"Many people get a kick out of hearing their names mentioned and their favourite piece of music played," he remarked in an interview in 1997. "I remember many years ago my late father was in hospital and I wrote several letters to try and have a request played on Radio Éireann. Eventually his name was mentioned but the music requested was not and he was offended somewhat at the choice of music that was requested, thinking I had requested it!"

Not only were Paul, Chris and the team at Midwest playing every request that was sent their way but they were also bringing listeners live on air, making household names of wonderful local characters who, up to then, lived in total anonymity. When Kathleen Loftus passed away in May 1988, her death made headlines in the local newspapers and the church in Logboy was packed to capacity for her funeral Mass as Midwest's listeners came from near and far to bid their final farewells to a unique woman who had become such a part of their lives through her regular on-air chats with Paul.

In many ways, Kathleen was the standard-bearer for the kind of listener Paul and Chris had in mind should Midwest be offered a licence for Co Mayo. She was one of a family of nine born and raised in a little farmhouse in Logboy in the pre-war years, a cottage that teemed with life in Kathleen's childhood. But by the time Midwest took to the airwaves in 1985, the Loftus family had been spread to the four winds, ravaged by the scourge of emigration that emptied so many houses in rural Ireland in the 1950s and 1960s. Five of the siblings were residing in England, another was in New York while two brothers remained in Ireland – one a monk in an enclosed religious order in Dublin and Jim, who lived at home with Kathleen until ill-health forced him to move to the Sacred Heart Hospital in Castlebar. Indeed, one of Kathleen's rituals during her frequent conversations with Paul was to play a request for "her brother James in the Sacred Heart Home in Castlebar and for all the staff, doctors and nurses, male and female, and to all who know me".

Midwest Radio was much more than just an entertainment vehicle for people like Kathleen Loftus; it was a companion, a friend and a welcome distraction from the trials and tribulations of everyday life. It cannot have been easy for Kathleen to see silence descend on that once lively cottage at Logboy as siblings left, parents died and then her sole companion, Jim, moved to Castlebar, a place very distant for someone without a car.

There were thousands of elderly people like Kathleen Loftus living alone in towns and villages across Mayo and its neighbouring counties and Midwest had become a really positive force in their lives by 1988. The pirate station's relationship with its listeners was unique in that Paul and Chris fostered a community-minded ethos that permeated everything the station did. Johnny Oosten got an early insight into Midwest Radio's very special bond with its audience when Paul pulled him aside not long after he started working in Ballyhaunis.

"Will you be going back to Castlebar this afternoon?"

"I will," replied Johnny.

"Would you ever call over to Logboy and pick up Kathleen Loftus? She wants to go in and see her brother in the Sacred Heart Home but there is no bus going in today."

Johnny usually spent his weekends blasting out Free's *Alright Now* to air guitar-playing rockers in Westport and Castlebar and he certainly hadn't expected his new career as a pirate radio DJ to involve ferrying little old women around Mayo. But Midwest was a radio station like no other and Oosten quickly bought into its unique culture to such an extent he once ended up doing some wallpapering for Bridgie Cuffe, a regular contributor to Chris' show who lived at Brabazon Heights in Swinford.

"I don't think there is another radio station in Ireland that has such an intimate relationship with its listeners," he says. "And that all stems from the pirate days when the staff got to know so many of the listeners personally."

One of the best decisions Midwest made in the pirate era was to bring a scaled-down version of *Sunday Night Live* on a tour of venues across Co Mayo during the summers of 1987 and 1988.

"We went to Julian's in Midfield, the Beaten Path in Brize, the Palm Court in Belmullet, Ted Lavelle's in Achill, McGoldrick's in Elly Bay – we went all over the place," Paul recalls. "It got us right out into the community and we got a great first sense of what people liked and, more importantly, what they didn't like. It was a brilliant training ground for us."

The loyalty of Midwest's growing band of listeners was put to the acid test in January 1988 when a winter storm brought down the entire transmission infrastructure, causing the station to go off the air for over two days, which was the longest break in broadcasting since it started.

"Within five minutes of us going back on air the 'phone started ringing," recalls Gerry Glennon. "We couldn't believe it. People had left the dial where it was, or even if they hadn't, friends or family rang them to say that Midwest was back on air. The immediate response was remarkable really."

But the loyalty of listeners would not be enough to keep Midwest on the airwaves once the new broadcasting bill came into law on January 1, 1989. Paul and Chris had already decided to bid for a radio licence so it was in their best interests to bring their pirate ship to dry dock before the end of 1988.

The last leg of the voyage would be emotional and unforgettable.

Midwest launched a second series of *Sunday Night Live* in October 1988 and took the show on the road in the final weeks of December as a novel way of saying goodbye to its radio audience. There was no way of knowing whether they would get a licence or not so the farewell tour was quite possibly the last chance the Midwest team would have to interact with their listeners, many having become friends of Paul, Chris, Gerry and the rest of the staff.

"We did four massive shows in the Beaten Path, the Royal Theatre, the Palm Court and, finally, in Midas on the night we closed down," recalls Gerry. "There were huge crowds at each and I especially remember the one in the Beaten Path because that was the night of the Lockerbie Disaster – December 16, 1988."

Paul and Chris were in agreement that Midwest should cease broadcasting on December 30, thus avoiding any possibility the station might breach the New Year's Eve cut-off date. When they made the formal announcement on Paul's show a few weeks before Christmas, the telephone line (there was only one!) went into meltdown. Jim Higgins, then a backbench TD on the opposition benches, was at the forefront of a public campaign to have the controversial ministerial order rescinded.

"I have a huge file of heart-rending and pleading letters from distraught listeners who are absolutely devastated at the prospect of the loss of the service," Higgins told the *Western People.* "A substantial number of them are from elderly people living alone in isolated areas. To the vast majority of them, their whole day revolved around the unique community service provided by stations such as Midwest Radio. These stations have done a tremendous amount of good and as

I told Minister Burke in the Dáil, to continually brand them as 'illegal' or 'pirates' is a most unfortunate misnomer."

One of the most vocal critics of Burke's decision was Hilda Creaby, herself a staunch Fianna Fáil supporter. The Kiltimagh resident had become a regular caller to Paul's show over the course of the previous year, regaling listeners with stories of growing up in Manchester during the war years. One of her favourite tales related to the night in 1945 when she and some friends queued for two hours at the Palace Royal in Manchester to get front-row seats for the legendary Frank Sinatra. Such was Hilda's devotion to Ole Blue Eyes she even christened one of her sons 'Albert', which was Sinatra's middle name.

People like Hilda simply could not comprehend why a station such as Midwest, which was providing a valuable public service, was being forced off the air. The pirate had become a big part of the local landscape over the past three years, so much so it had got to the stage where Gardaí were now ringing Midwest – a station deemed illegal by the State – with news of car accidents and road closures. Dunnes Stores, then the largest supermarket chain in the country, frequently ran advertisements, as did many other prominent firms. Therefore, it seemed wholly illogical that a station so firmly rooted in the community should be outlawed by government edict.

But the protestations of politicians and public were in vain. Midwest Radio ceased broadcasting as agreed on Friday, December 30, 1988, a day that will live forever in the memory of Gerry Glennon.

"When we opened the doors of Midas at 10am that morning there was literally a stream of people queuing outside and they continued to arrive throughout the day. It was like queuing for a funeral and, in many ways, it was an old-style wake really. People just wanted to come in to have one last look at the studio before we went off the air.

"Midwest had become a vital part of people's lives and there was a huge relationship built up with the listeners. People had become accustomed to it over the previous three and a half years and all of a sudden there was this realisation that come Saturday morning it wasn't going to be there anymore so they wanted to say goodbye and, for many, that meant travelling to Ballyhaunis."

Paul, Chris and the rest of the Midwest crew were completely overwhelmed by the spontaneous public reaction and took it for what it was: the ultimate endorsement of a job well done.

"In the end, the Guards rang to tell us to stop people coming to Ballyhaunis!" Paul recalls, shaking his head in wonder even after all these years. "There were that many cars coming into Ballyhaunis that they had to put a couple of officers on point duty to divert the traffic. It was incredible really."

John Duggan was the man behind the mike on that emotional evening; the garda really was shutting the pirate station down this time!

"I recorded the final half hour of the show in advance," he recalled. "I don't think I'd have managed it otherwise. After that show I received several letters from total strangers. There was a particular one from Cloghans Hill area that encompassed so many of the ideals I had tried to portray and attain in my show. It was a lovely tribute."

Down on Achill Island, Peadar McHugh and Michael Duggan made the long, lonesome walk across Minaun Heights – or 'Old Smokey' as they called it – to disconnect the transmitter. Back at The Grove, Mary B Gallagher and the McHughs were in tears as they listened to John Duggan say farewell on behalf of the Midwest team.

"It was really, really sad because this radio station had become such a huge part of our lives and we had got to know all of the Midwest crew really well by then," recalls Mary B. "I'm sure we weren't the only ones who shed tears that evening."

Later that evening, the Midas Express cranked into gear once again as the Achill contingent set off for the farewell concert in Ballyhaunis. They even made their own banner emblazoned with the message: *Thanks Midwest From Your Achill Friends.*

"We were proper groupies!" jokes Mary B.

But the friendships forged in those pirate days have endured to this day. Men like Michael Neary and Johnny Oosten came to love their trips to Achill – even if it sometimes meant scaling a mountain in gale-force winds with nothing underneath except a stormy sea.

"Going to Achill was an excuse to meet Phil and Mary B in the shop," recalls Johnny Oosten. "We were always given the warmest welcome and would be served sandwiches and tea and a full dinner if we wanted it."

The generosity was reciprocated whenever the islanders visited Ballyhaunis. In the early days of the Midas Express, Jackie Rumley used to sleep in the minibus while *Sunday Night Live* was in progress.

"I'd bring a quilt and try to grab a few hours' sleep because I had a school run in the morning and often wouldn't get back to Achill until 6am," he recalls. "The Midwest lads heard about this and insisted on giving me a camper bed in a room at the back of Midas. Obviously it was noisy enough but at least I got to have a little bit of a rest in comfort – whatever about falling sleep!"

It would have been easier to take a nap on an electric fence than catch forty winks at Midas amid the glorious madness that was *Sunday Night Live* in the late 1980s. Paul and the crew were already keeping half the province awake so there was absolutely no hope for the backstage sleeper, even one as weary as the indefatigable pilot of the fabled Midas Express.

Midwest's farewell concert was one of those magical nights that will live forever in the collective memory of the one thousand-plus loyal Midwest fans that packed into Midas on that Friday night. There was a stellar line-up of music stars but it was the emotion of the evening that caught everybody by surprise.

"We knew Midwest meant a lot to people but it was only on that farewell tour around Mayo, and especially on the final day, that we truly appreciated the incredible impact the station had had in a fairly short period of time," says Chris. "We got loads of things wrong in the pirate days and made lots of mistakes but people liked us as much for the mistakes as anything else. They related to what we were trying to do and came to regard Midwest as an authentic voice of rural Ireland."

The magic of that December night is wonderfully encapsulated in an anecdote from Chris who ended up on stage performing in Midwest's version of the Fab Four.

"We were short an act so Paul, Gerry and myself decided to act as a backing band for John Duggan. Now I had an idea how to play the guitar but Paul and Gerry hadn't a clue how to play any instrument so we decided to use John's backing tracks.

"Out we go with John Duggan singing and none of the instruments even plugged in! We brought the house down after the first song *The Farmer* and the crowd roared for more. We did a second and the crowd screamed for another.

"Unfortunately, there were only two backing tracks but the crowd still wanted more so we had no choice but to 'perform' *The Farmer* again. We could do no wrong!"

Michael Duggan has a memory of being on stage with TR Dallas and the rest of the Achill crew as the curtain came down. In the midst of the islanders was Michael Commins who had started broadcasting a Sunday night show with Midwest a year earlier. Commins epitomised the down-to-earth, unpretentious style of broadcasting that came to characterise the Ballyhaunis pirate; in many ways, Midwest's secret was that it was different because it made a virtue of being authentic.

"I grew up in a generation where we didn't do celebrities," Michael notes. "My heroes growing up were the local people in the local villages that surrounded me – places like Cloonmore, Cuiltybo and Mace. They came from farming stock and made us the people we are today. We were taught to help people if we could and be proud to speak with our own local accents; in other words, to be rooted and not have any notions about ourselves."

Whether it was by accident or design – or maybe a combination of both – Midwest Radio instinctively tapped into old-fashioned community ethos, *that spirit of meitheal,* which had been the bedrock of life in rural Ireland for centuries.

Paul, Chris and the rest of the team knew the goodwill generated from the pirate days would hold them in good stead should they be successful in their application for a licence, but nothing was guaranteed. They hoped the farewell concert would be just a temporary parting of the Midwest 'family' but what if it was for good? What if Midwest didn't get back on the airwaves?

As a new year dawned the Midwest team didn't know whether to celebrate the arrival of 1989 or mourn the passing of 1988. The only one who remained steadfastly optimistic about the prospects of Midwest returning to the airwaves was John Duggan, the man who had walked away from a full-time career in the Gardaí to throw in his lot with a gang of pirates.

"We'll be back on the air, you mark my words," he told Claffey at the end of the farewell concert.

"How can you be so sure?" asked Paul.

"Cos if anyone can find a way to get back on the air it's you!" replied Duggan cheerfully.

For Paul, December 30, 1988, was a day of very mixed emotions because he genuinely feared that history was repeating itself. A decade earlier he had owned one of the most successful dancehall businesses in the country only to see it fatally undermined by the shifting sands of time. Having stared into the financial abyss, Claffey managed to restore his fortunes through the unlikely success story that was Midwest Radio but now this latest enterprise had fallen prey to the fickle finger of fate just as it was beginning to realise its true potential.

"It was a very uneasy and worrying time," he recalls. "I went back into Midas the next day and it was really eerie to walk in there and hear nothing but silence. I think that's when it really hit me; that's when I realised this thing is gone now and it mightn't be coming back."

That very same silence was resonating across the West on New Year's Eve 1988 as homes from Belderrig to Bunnacurry and Blacksod to Ballyhaunis adjusted to a world without Midwest Radio. This pirate station had struck a chord with so many people in such a short space of time but now it was gone and its waveband had been taken over by an eerie sound that seemed to echo all the way from the little studio in Ballyhaunis into kitchens and living rooms the length and breadth of the province. It was the sound of silence.

PART III

CHAPTER FOURTEEN

A station for the people

ON the afternoon of January 2, 1989, a middle-aged woman alighted from a taxi outside Abbeville, the stately home of the then Taoiseach Charles J Haughey in Kinsealy in Dublin. Having paid her fare and bid adieu to the very helpful driver, she proceeded to march up the sweeping driveway, handbag swinging to the beat of her purposeful stride. As the woman neared the front door of the imposing 18th-century mansion she encountered Haughey's daughter, Eimear, who was bringing one of the family's horses out for a ride.

"I want to see your father," the woman declared. "It's about a very urgent matter."

"I'm not sure if he is able to take visitors today," Ms Haughey ventured. "He's on holidays at the moment."

"Never mind that," countered the woman. "Tell him it's Hilda Creaby from Kiltimagh in Co Mayo and I want to talk to him about Midwest Radio… and I won't be leaving either until he sees me!"

Eimear Haughey dutifully climbed off her horse, tied the animal to a gatepost and wandered off into the sprawling country house in search of her father. After a short while, the great man himself appeared at the front door and graciously invited his unexpected visitor into the drawing room.

"Have you come all the way from Kiltimagh just to see me?" asked the Taoiseach.

"I have," said Hilda. "I got the bus up this morning."

"It must be something very urgent, Hilda?"

"It is very urgent, indeed, Mr Haughey. It's about Midwest Radio, our station in Mayo, it's been taken off the air since last Friday."

"Oh yes, the pirate station."

"It's not a pirate station, it's my local station and I want you to put it back on the air immediately. We all miss it terribly."

"But I am afraid I cannot do that," Haughey patiently explained. "Midwest Radio will have to apply for a local licence and, hopefully, they will be successful."

"Well they better be, Mr Haughey," said Hilda. "Because if they're not I'll be back up here to see you again and the next time I'll bring a full bus with me!"

Ever the courteous host, Haughey arranged for his driver to leave Hilda back to Busáras from where she caught the next bus to Kiltimagh, arriving home late in the evening. The first thing she did on entering the house in Goulboy was to ring Paul Claffey.

"You did what?" exclaimed Claffey in disbelief. "Jaysus Hilda, you're some woman for one woman!"

"I told him that if Midwest doesn't get that licence there'll be hell to pay!"

"And what did he say?" asked Claffey, chuckling.

"He told me I must be an awful big fan of Midwest to come the whole way from Kiltimagh just to see him!"

Hilda Creaby's novel cameo was unlikely to sway the Independent Radio and Television Commission (IRTC) but it reflected the depth of feeling among Midwest's army of listeners in the early days of 1989.

Raw emotion, however, would not be enough to get the station back on the airwaves; the only way Midwest would return was if Paul and Chris could put together a sufficiently strong application for one of the 25 local broadcasting licences now available under the new regulatory regime. The problem was that IRM was also in the hunt for the sole licence in Co Mayo and they were already assembling a fairly formidable consortium, spearheaded by the Westport-based *Mayo News* and Castlebar Community Development Association (CCDA) under the chairmanship of well-known local businessman Paddy McGuinness of Albany.

Chris Carroll was under no illusions about the monumental task facing Midwest.

"We had to get a consortium of our own together because the IRTC would never give a licence to private individuals. The new station would need financial backing to get through its early years because it would have to invest in news coverage and other public service-type programming that wouldn't have been a feature of the pirate era when the vast, vast majority of our daily output was music and more music.

"We knew that if we were to have any chance against the opposition we'd need to put together a good community-based application."

The previous summer, Paul and Chris had held tentative talks with Tom Courell, the editor of the Castlebar-based *Connaught Telegraph*, who looked favourably on the idea of marshalling a strong consortium to bid for the radio franchise in Mayo.

"Tom Courell and PJ Hennelly [then the manager of the *Telegraph*] had a real appreciation of the entertainment industry because they'd both been involved in the Castlebar Song Contest," notes Michael Commins. "In fact, the *Connaught* used to organise its own concerts in the Royal Theatre back then and the two lads would have known all the big Country bands so they'd have had a real interest in Midwest. I was also doing my bit to persuade them to get involved because I could see the potential of Midwest too."

Courell turned to his cousin, George Waters, the former director general of RTÉ and a native of Ballina, for advice and asked him to come to Mayo to meet with Paul and Chris. That got the ball rolling.

Courell was adamant the consortium must be representative of the disparate strands of community and business life in Mayo and spread the net wide in the search for shareholders. Knock Airport, North Connacht Farmers (NCF) and the Federation of Western Churches were all asked to come on board and they readily agreed. So, too, did the *Western People*, where editor Terry Reilly was enthused about the project from the moment Courell contacted him.

"There was a fair bit of concern in local newspapers at the time about the impact these new radio stations might have on circulation and advertising revenue and I was criticised by staff in the *Western* for getting involved in the Midwest bid," he recalls. "But the way I saw it was that this was a new media company and we were a media company so it made sense to join forces. The owners of the *Western* at that time, my uncle Vincie [de Vere] and Rita [de Vere-Durcan], understood where I was coming from and fully backed the decision to take a 15 per cent stake in Midwest. As it turned out, it was the best investment I ever made!"

Terry says the Midwest licence bid would never have materialised without the tireless efforts of the affable and hardworking Tom Courell, a man who was hugely respected in journalism in Mayo. It's a view shared by Paul Claffey.

"Tom Courell was the cement that brought everyone together," he says. "He was the one who did the most work on the application but the likes of Terry [Reilly], PJ Hennelly, Michael Hughes (NCF) and Michael O'Malley [then the manager of Mayo Co Council and deputy chairman of Knock Airport] were also key figures. Chris and I were very reliant on them for advice and we spent many long afternoons drinking pots of tea and eating salad sandwiches in the International Hotel. I think a lot of the early meetings were in dark corners of the hotel because they couldn't possibly be seen with pirates!"

By early January 1989, the consortium had made good progress on preparing its application but there was one major bone of contention: the location of the new station. Paul and Chris wanted to keep it in Ballyhaunis but several members of the consortium believed it would be wiser to relocate to the county town of Castlebar, especially as the sole rival for the licence, IRM, was already headquartered there.

"We came under intense pressure to move to Castlebar," recalls Paul. "In the end, we reached a compromise where we'd remain in Ballyhaunis but put satellite studios in Castlebar and Ballina."

Chris says Midwest ended up getting the best of both worlds – a chain of studios across Mayo and the retention of its provincial base.

"We were concerned that we would lose the listenership we had attracted from our neighbouring counties of Roscommon, Sligo and Galway if we relocated to Castlebar or Ballina, and for the franchise to work we needed the revenues from these counties. The satellite studios were needed anyway because they brought us closer to our listeners so we were happy with the outcome in the end."

Midwest submitted its application on the day of the deadline – January 19, 1989 – and, as expected, there was only one other contender for the Mayo licence, IRM, which had assembled its own heavy-hitting consortium with the *Mayo News* and CCDA joined by Ballina

Chamber of Commerce, Castlebar Credit Union and Balla Co-op Mart.

Tommy Marren, now working for AIB in Sligo, was asked to do some voiceovers for the IRM submission.

"IRM put in a serious bid. John Morrin was very professional and left no stone unturned in putting in the best possible application. I think the view of most people at the time was that the competition for the Mayo licence was simply too tight to call."

The two consortiums were invited to attend an oral hearing at the Ardilaun House Hotel in Salthill, Co Galway in early March at which they would get the chance to make their pitch before a panel of IRTC members, chaired by Justice Seamus Henchy. A couple of weeks before the hearing, Paul and Chris – as sole directors of the old Midwest Radio company – received a hefty bill from the Revenue Commissioners for outstanding tax liabilities.

"It was for £13,000," recalls Paul. "A huge, huge sum in 1989."

One of the peculiarities of the pirate radio industry was that although the stations were adjudged by the state to be illegal, everyone employed in them still had to pay PAYE and PRSI while the companies themselves were liable for VAT and corporation tax. There was a temptation to simply ignore the Revenue letter because, at the end of the day, Midwest Radio no longer existed and a new firm, County Mayo Radio Ltd, had been formed for the purpose of applying for the IRTC franchise. But Paul and Chris were damned if their one shot at acquiring a commercial radio licence might come unstuck as a result of an unpaid tax bill.

"What if we get asked at the oral hearing whether we are tax compliant?" Paul said to Chris. "Sure we'll be goosed there and then if we haven't paid this bloody bill."

Later that afternoon, the two men put their names to a cheque for £13,000 – the largest single payment they'd ever issued – and sent it off by registered post to the Revenue Commissioners. The irony of the task wasn't lost on them: even pirates must pay their taxes.

"It was tough signing a cheque for such a large amount, especially when we didn't even know if we'd ever be in business again as a radio station," says Chris. "But we also knew the future of Midwest was at stake. Of course, it was a win-win for the Revenue Commissioners because ultimately they got a lot more afterwards!"

The Midwest consortium prepared diligently for the oral hearing. A week before the group's date with destiny, Tom Courell organised a mock hearing under the chairmanship of district court judge John Garavan, a man of sharp intellect who was more than capable of putting the various speakers through their paces.

"He gave us a good grilling," recalls Terry Reilly, "and that certainly prepared us for what was to come in the Ardilaun."

Gerry Glennon, who had been retained along with Michael Neary to assist in the preparation of the licence application, says no stone was left unturned in putting forward the strongest possible case for Midwest. On the morning of the hearing – Friday, March 3, 1989 – Paul recalls waking up and saying a prayer to his late father Gerry and to Kathleen Loftus, the woman who had come to epitomise the spirit of Midwest.

"I was very nervous about the licence application because I knew IRM would mount a serious challenge and everything was going to Castlebar at that time," he recalls. "If we didn't get the licence I was out of a job again and that was a really sickening feeling."

The applications for the Galway franchise were due to be heard in the morning – there were three applicants for the sole licence – while it was Mayo's turn in the afternoon. When the commission reconvened after lunch, IRM were the first to make their case and it was a strong one as expected. The consortium intended to invest £250,000 in establishing the new station and had another £105,000 in share capital to call on if required. Midwest, on the other hand, only had shareholder funds of £135,000 and intended to rent studio space in Ballyhaunis compared to IRM, which was going to be headquartered in a CCDA-owned premises at MacHale Road in Castlebar.

The two applicants found common ground in other areas, most notably their revenue projections with IRM predicting it would generate £315,000 per annum and break even within three years while Midwest's figure was £328,000 on an identical breakeven time-frame. Both stations intended to broadcast for 17 hours per day and to offer a diverse schedule of programming from music and current affairs to sport and community events.

One of the key contributors to Midwest's oral submission was Michael Hughes, then the marketing manager of NCF and an articulate advocate of the consortium's low-cost business model, which might have been seen as a weakness in some quarters.

"The low-cost approach is vital to ensure commercial viability and to survive the start-up period, thus allowing us to develop the service," he explained. "Such an approach will not be achieved at the expense of programme quality but rather will involve greater creativity in programme design and audience appeal."

Tom Courell and Terry Reilly were important, too, in outlining the station's editorial strategy with both men emphasising the consortium's commitment to allowing the new broadcaster to "act independently of the newspapers involved".

"There was to be an arrangement where journalists from both newspapers would provide editorial content for the station," recalls Terry. "But Midwest was very much the master of its own destiny and there certainly wasn't going to be editorial influence brought to bear from either the *Connaught* or the *Western*."

One of the key changes under the proposed new regime was the migration of all local stations to the FM wavelength, a plan that was strongly resisted by IRM, which claimed it would lose about a quarter of its potential audience unless it was allowed to continue to broadcast on medium wave as well as FM.

Midwest, however, did not share its rival's concerns. The station had already established a strong following on FM through its masts in Balla and Achill Island and believed it could retain its listenership despite the shift in wavelength.

There was one other significant point of departure between the two applicants. Justice Henchy wanted to know if both former pirate stations had met all of their liabilities including any outstanding debts to the Revenue Commissioners. Paul glanced over at Chris and the two men exchanged relieved smiles: that cheque for £13,000 might yet prove the smartest investment they ever made.

IRM, on the other hand, still had an unpaid tax bill for £8,000, a revelation that caused Justice Henchy "most concern", according to newspaper reports at the time. On a day when there was little to choose between two excellent applicants, the issues surrounding FM transmission and unpaid taxes may well have swung the decision in Midwest's favour. But Paul Claffey was taking nothing for granted. In his submission, which closed out the Midwest application, he made a plea straight from the heart.

Noting that one-fifth of Mayo's population of 100,000 was over the age of 65, and many of these elderly people lived alone and in isolated areas, Claffey said he wanted to provide a radio station that would "be a friendly voice" for the whole community. It would be, he declared, "a station for the people" but, most especially, for older people.

"We are acutely aware of the loneliness and hopelessness among so many people in this area," Claffey told the commission. "We want these people to relate to us and we welcome them into the family of Midwest Radio."

It was powerful stuff and totally unscripted. Many of the applicants for local licences were making slick presentations in which their target audience was set at the key 15-25 demographic but Paul was not going to compromise on the formula that had made Midwest Radio such a success as a pirate. He told the commission the new station's audience would be mainly in the over 25 age category, and while the younger age group would be catered for through nightly pop music programmes, the principal focus in terms of musical output would be Country and Western, Irish traditional, ballad, folk and middle of the road.

It was a brave move and one that might easily have backfired were the commission minded to award the licence to a more youth-orientated station, which was clearly the pitch coming from the IRM benches. But Claffey was convinced the only way a newly licensed radio station would survive in a rural county such as Mayo was if it stayed true to the tastes and values of an older audience. Terry Reilly and the rest of the consortium fully backed the somewhat unorthodox strategy.

"Paul and Chris knew the market very well because Midwest had been broadcasting for three and a half years up to that point and it had built up a very loyal listenership," says Terry. "Mayo was a largely rural county. It wasn't like Galway where you had this big monolith city with a very young population. Although there were several big towns in Mayo, there was no real disparity between urban and rural as far as radio listeners were concerned and the two guys understood that."

Having sat through IRM's presentation, Chris was growing in confidence as the oral hearing progressed.

"I was relieved we were not asked too many questions about our studios and transmission system. Obviously, the commission was happy with what they had seen in our submission. Overall, I felt we produced a great presentation on the day and although we were aware the battle for the licence was going to be tight, I was quietly confident we had the edge on the opposition."

Terry Reilly was equally optimistic, especially when he heard Claffey's closing remarks, which really struck a chord with everyone present.

"I think Paul's passionate speech at the end of the oral hearing left the commission in no doubt that were Midwest awarded the licence, Paul and the rest of the team would leave no stone unturned to provide the best possible radio service to the people of Mayo."

Claffey wasn't so sure about the impact his heartfelt plea might have had on the members of the commission, which included communications consultant Terry Prone and future labour relations supremo Kieran Mulvey, but at least there was one thing he was pleased about as he and Chris walked out of the Ardilaun that spring evening.

"Thank God we paid that feckin' tax bill," he said. "I'd have never forgiven myself if I'd lost that licence for the sake of a tax clearance cert."

While many in the national media might have wondered about the wisdom of placing so much emphasis on older listeners and Country music, at least one prominent journalist on the press bench in the Ardilaun understood the philosophy espoused by Paul Claffey. John Waters had come a long way since the days of the original Midwest Radio in Castlerea when he was compiling weather reports by sticking his head out of the window of Claffey's garden shed. Now a columnist with the *Sunday Independent*, Waters was widely regarded as the natural heir to the legacy of the great John Healy, the Charlestown-born journalist who had been the authentic voice of rural Ireland for over a quarter of a century.

At the start of 1989, Waters penned an article in which he bemoaned the demise of the pirates, especially the rural pirates who "tell us most about what is happening to this country". Having briefly operated a radio station with Claffey that played nothing but rock and pop music, Waters was intrigued by Midwest's very different playlist in its second incarnation.

"[The music] is mostly of a kind which, a dozen or so years ago, perched high on our platform shoes and thinking we could see for miles, we pronounced as good as dead, and good riddance. It was the music of a darker past, of the kind of sentimentality, which went hand-in-hand with resignation and despair.

"Today, local halls which rocked ten years ago to Horslips, Thin Lizzy and the other heroes of the emerging pop culture, now jive once more to local stars like Kevin Prendergast, Mick Flavin and Michael O'Brien, all of whose names have been made through exposure on stations like Midwest. Daniel O'Donnell owes his entire career to people like Paul Claffey."

It was an interesting and prescient observation. Looking back now, from the elevated position of 30 or more years, the emergence of stations such as Midwest Radio can be viewed as the catalyst for a renaissance in Irish Country and Western music. Michael Commins says there is a greater acceptance of Country music among all age groups in Ireland today but it wasn't always like that.

"I came through an era when there was a very snobbish attitude to Irish Country music," he explains. "To me it was a musical equivalent of apartheid. People looked down their nose at you for liking Country music; in fact, it got to the point where there was almost an attitude of 'how could you even have any intelligence if you're into that kind of music'.

"The prejudice was very widespread and you were made feel it at times too if you let it get to you. But I always held onto what I believed in."

Despite enjoying several number one hits, Brendan Shine was often on the receiving end of disparaging remarks from a Dublin-centric music industry that refused to recognise Irish Country music as a credible genre.

"If it wasn't for honest people like Larry Gogan and Paschal Mooney who believed there was a world outside the Pale people like myself would never have got a break," he says.

Ironically, Shine received a warmer reception from younger audiences in London than Dublin.

"I remember a young Shane McGowan coming to one of my gigs in the Galtymore in Cricklewood in the early 1980s. He was in a punk band but was also looking for his Trad roots and, ultimately, he managed to combine the two in The Pogues, which had a brilliant mix of Irish music and punk attitude."

Shine is in no doubt that RTÉ left the door ajar for the likes of Midwest Radio by allowing Radio 2's young DJs to play nothing but pop and rock music.

"The Radio 2 DJs were promoting that kind of music cos they were down the country playing at discos so why would they play Brendan Shine or Big Tom or Larry Cunningham if they were going to be playing something totally different on Saturday night? I could completely understand that and I had no problem with it. But RTÉ let all that happen. There was nobody monitoring it and, as a result, they created a gap in the market for local radio."

But the big question in the spring of 1989 was whether the IRTC would grant a licence to an unconventional station such as Midwest whose outlook was so unapologetically rural it planned to headquarter itself in a market town like Ballyhaunis instead of moving to the expanding metropolis that was the county town of Castlebar. The answer came just a fortnight after the oral hearing: the Midwest Radio consortium had been awarded the franchise for local radio in Co Mayo.

"It was the best day of my life professionally, no question about it," says Paul. "It had been a frightening time really because I had no Plan B at all. If we failed to get the licence, I'd have been back struggling with Midas again and God knows how that would have ended up."

Chris was equally relieved. He didn't want to spend the rest of his adult life travelling the highways and byways of Ireland as a DJ and was already putting a backup plan in place should the application for the radio franchise fail.

"Martina and I got married in August 1988 so we needed security," he explains. "I decided to investigate the possibility of opening my own nightclub and discussed the idea with Martina who has always been a rock of support to me throughout my career. She suggested speaking with Andrew Durkin, a local hotelier in Ballaghaderreen."

Chris met with the Durkin family and a few months later, Studio 57 – a nightclub catering for over 21s – opened.

"Andrew and his family could not have been more accommodating and I was lucky to have found such genuine partners. Studio 57 was great because it meant that if the licence application was successful I could resume the radio career and promote the nightclub."

Chris can still recall that fateful Friday when the news came through from Dublin.

"I was just elated because I could now make a full-time career out of something that started as a hobby. All of a sudden I could start planning for the future."

The joy was not confined to Ballyhaunis either. Far away in a stately manor in Kinsealy in north Co Dublin, a certain Mr Charles J Haughey was breathing a heavy sigh of relief: the redoubtable Hilda Creaby from Kiltimagh would now be leaving him in peace to enjoy the small comforts of fine wine and Charvet shirts.

CHAPTER FIFTEEN

'Always remember the old lady by the fire…'

A FEW weeks after receiving the Mayo radio franchise, Paul Claffey found himself walking into the luxurious offices of a design and marketing firm in Dublin 4. It was the last place he wanted to be. There were a million and one things to be done back in Ballyhaunis, from furnishing the new rented headquarters to ordering the necessary studio equipment from England, but there was no way he could avoid this early-morning engagement in 'The Big Shmoke'.

The design and marketing firm had been tasked with arguably the most important assignment in the complicated rollout of Mayo's new local radio station: it was to rebrand Midwest Radio by way of a fresh logo and, crucially, a new name.

Claffey had an uneasy feeling about the whole exercise and his heart was sinking as deep as his shoes as he walked across the deep-piled carpet of the plush reception hall and into a private meeting room. He readily acknowledged the name 'Midwest Radio' made absolutely no sense from a geographical perspective – Ireland's mid-west was at least 50 miles south of Ballyhaunis – but nobody ever complained about it in the past. And, anyway, why should he jettison a name that was already well established as a brand from the pirate days and replace it with something entirely unknown?

There was also the small matter of sentiment and superstition. The name 'Midwest' might make no geographical sense but it had been good to Chris and himself and it would be a crying shame to get rid of it now; it would be like renaming a ship that had brought its crew through many a storm... no good could come from that.

But as he sat down at the table with Tom Courell and Fr Colm Kilcoyne – the latter now representing the Federation of Western Churches on the Midwest board – Claffey decided he needed to be a little bit more open-minded about the job in hand. Maybe the board was right: Midwest was a geographical misnomer that needed replacing.

The agency came strongly recommended and the sharp-suited marketeer, who positioned himself at the head of the table, certainly looked like he knew what he was about. A blackboard with a cloth covering it was strategically positioned nearby, adding to the sense of drama and occasion: this really was going to be a grand unveiling.

Yet as he gulped down a glass of water, the only thing Claffey could think was: "This fecker is going to charge me a bloody fortune!"

The marketeer proceeded to launch into a lengthy discourse about the process involved in selecting the new name and logo before finally – some 30 minutes later – reaching the nub of the matter.

"You are an enterprise in the West of Ireland involved in radio," the man concluded. "So we have tried to encompass all of these components into this new name and logo, and we are pleased to announce that we have settled on the following..."

And with a dramatic flourish the marketeer ripped away the cloth to reveal the new identity of Midwest Radio... from this day forth it would be known as 'West of Ireland Radio Enterprise' or 'WIRE FM' for short. Paul Claffey didn't know whether to laugh or cry.

"What a crock of shite!" was all he could mutter to himself. "WIRE FM! He must be pulling my wire! Sure we'll be the laughing stock of Europe."

But if the main course was tough to digest, the dessert, namely the bill, was unpalatable altogether.

"It was for £1,200," Claffey recalls. "I nearly had a calf!"

There was much animated discussion in the car on the long journey west about what to do next. All three men were in agreement that a radio station named WIRE FM would nearly be as bad as a boy named Sue but alternative names were not exactly tripping off the tongue either. Paul left his colleagues in Ballyhaunis and continued on to Achill Island where Chris and Michael Neary had spent the day working on the new FM mast to be located at the top of Minaun Heights. Later that evening, they all gathered in the cozy front room of The Grove where Phil McHugh served them a hearty evening meal.

"What do you think would be a good name for the station?" Paul asked Peadar McHugh.

"But sure don't you have a great name already?" replied Peadar.

"I suppose," said Paul. "But some people would say the name doesn't make sense geographically."

"I'll tell you what doesn't make sense," said Peadar in that sincere, soft-spoken manner of his. "It doesn't make sense to change the name of a very successful radio station. You'll have to educate the people all over again and why would you want to do a thing like that when there is no need for it?"

The homeliness of The Grove in Bunnacurry was about as far as one could get from a marketeer's swish offices in Dublin 4 but Paul instinctively knew what 'expert' advice he'd be bringing to the next board meeting.

"Do you know, I just wasted a whole day in Dublin," he said to Peadar as he was getting up to leave, "when all I had to do was come down here and listen to the likes of you."

The board of County Mayo Radio Ltd convened the following week and unanimously agreed that Midwest Radio (abbreviated to MWR FM) would keep its original name. The Ballyhaunis pirates might have surrendered to the State but there would be no renaming of the sturdy vessel that had served them so well up to now.

The good ship Midwest Radio was almost ready to set sail again.

The race to become the first independent commercial radio station in Ireland commenced as soon as the IRTC revealed the identity of the successful applicants for the country's 25 local franchises. Paul and Chris knew they might struggle to keep pace with the Dublin stations, who were better positioned for a quick return, but both men were determined that Midwest would be the first station outside the capital to take to the airwaves. They were setting themselves an onerous task, especially as Mayo was one of the most difficult counties in which to set up a transmission system, but they had one big advantage, although it actually looked like a disadvantage.

"We were very frugal because we had started off from having nothing," explains Chris. "Paul had already gone through financial problems and wasn't prepared to go through that again. I'd always been frugal. I came from a family of seven and saw my father going over to England to work so he could send money home. There was no way either of us was going to be spending loads of money launching the station – even if cash was available to us."

Paul says Midwest spent a mere £40,000 before it took to the airwaves in the summer of 1989, a fraction of the hundreds of thousands being spent by other local stations who were investing in palatial new offices and purchasing state-of-the-art studio equipment. Midwest, on the other hand, rented a two-storey house at Abbey Street, converting one bedroom into a studio and another into a newsroom. It was as low budget as one might find but it was entirely in keeping with the prudent philosophy of the station's founders who were strongly backed by a board that did not want to waste money on frivolous expenses.

"Michael Hughes, who was elected chairman at our first board meeting, used the same word again and again and again," recalls Terry Reilly, "and that word was 'generic'. We were going to grow the business slowly, grow it by what we brought in and nothing was ever going to be done that we couldn't afford.

"It was a strategy Tom [Courell] and myself strongly supported because we had asked the owners of our newspapers to pony up money and we didn't want to be going back looking for more money."

Most of the equipment was acquired second-hand from the BBC in England, the only exceptions being two Technics turntables purchased for the grand sum of £4,800 and a new FM transmitter for Kiltimagh.

"We'd done a good bit of research about the kind of equipment we'd need ahead of the oral hearing," recalls Chris. "Joe Cunniffe and Michael O'Hara from O'Neill's accompanied me to the massive Frankfurt Trade Fair and we also went to Manchester, Leeds and London to source second-hand equipment."

The trio visited the BBC radio studio in Manchester and fell into conversation with an electronics supplier who was about to take the studio apart and replace it with entirely new equipment.

"The supplier came to Ballyhaunis to ensure the equipment was correct and suitable," says Chris. "It all came from BBC regional stations and it was hardly used. We made a big saving by buying second-hand. Other stations were spending fortunes kitting out their studios but we were determined to stay within a strict budget."

There was no extravagant spending on the station's music library either.

"We had a library of six CDs and one of them was the Elvery Brothers!" recalls Gerry Glennon. "CDs were growing in popularity at that stage but we were still on vinyl."

Chris Carroll, who was now the production manager, was charged with the unenviable task of adapting a modest, old-style townhouse into the headquarters of a modern radio station, while also ensuring the new studios fulfilled the fairly stringent requirements laid down by the IRTC.

"The regulations insisted that the studios had to be soundproofed. We were on a busy street so if a lorry came up the street it would rumble all the way through to the studio so we had to insulate against the noise from outside while at the same time creating a soft surface to dampen the sound inside.

"Now this was all totally new to us because we never had to worry about these sort of things in the pirate days. In the end, we built a second partition away from the wall and covered it with a soft surface, which was carpet!"

Chris admits he would have been lost without the invaluable assistance of Joe Cunniffe, Michael O'Hara and the crew at O'Neill's but there were aspects of the project that even went beyond their expertise. Michael Neary recalls standing on a hill in Kiltimagh on a beautiful summer's day with Joe Cunniffe and ex-RTÉ employee John Martyn, who had sourced the new FM transmitter in Italy. Having removed the device from its box and connected it to the power supply, Martyn turned to Neary and Cunniffe and asked the million-dollar question:

"Does either of ye lads know how to tune in this yoke?"

He was greeted by bemused shrugs and chuckles.

"We were hoping you knew that!" replied Neary.

In the end, the three men sat on a rock, amid the wild heather and glorious sunshine, leafing through a 40-page manual, desperately trying to figure out how to tune the device to 96.1FM, the waveband the IRTC had assigned to Midwest. Thankfully, the manual wasn't in Italian and the transmitter was up and running by the evening.

The switch from medium wave to FM was a cause for genuine concern ahead of Midwest's launch date. While listeners on Achill Island and some in north and east Mayo had grown accustomed to FM, the vast majority of Midwest's audience was still accessing the station via the old medium wave band.

"Every house in the country had a medium wave radio or transistor," recalls Michael Neary. "We worried that it would be hard to educate people to go to FM because most people had been using medium wave all their lives. For example, people would have grown up accessing the likes of Radio Caroline or Radio Luxembourg on medium wave transistors so FM was alien to them."

The quality and consistency of FM was much superior to medium wave but the latter gave Midwest a near global reach, albeit on rare occasions.

"Medium wave was totally dependent on atmospheric pressure," explains Chris, "so if you were over in England you could get Midwest at night-time if the conditions were right. It was a bit like us getting Radio Luxembourg in the old days. I remember Kevin Prendergast telling me he was on a tour of England and could pick up Midwest in Liverpool one night."

Johnny Oosten says staff occasionally received letters and cassettes from radio enthusiasts in far-flung places all over Europe and further afield.

"They'd have picked Midwest up at night on medium wave and would record it to prove they were able to hear us! Then they'd send the cassette in the post and ask us to respond in writing, confirming that this was, indeed, Midwest Radio. I remember those letters coming in from the UK, Holland, Germany and even the US."

Chris says the transition from medium wave to FM was essential to ensure the smooth running of Ireland's new commercial radio industry.

"The only way the Department of Communications could control the radius of a radio signal from travelling too far was to confine it to the FM band. In that way, there wouldn't be too much overspill into neighbouring counties. They achieved this by limiting the height of your mast and the power radiating from a transmitter."

By mid-summer, Midwest's new studios were equipped and the transmitters at Kiltimagh and Achill Island were fully operational. A launch date of Monday, July 24, was set but there was still so much more to be done, not least the appointment of a raft of new presenters and support staff. The new licence stipulated that Midwest had to deliver 17 hours of continuous broadcasting per day, including comprehensive coverage of all local news, current affairs and sporting events, so fresh voices were going to be required.

Paul and Chris spread the net wide in the search for new broadcasters and weren't disappointed: there was a veritable wealth of radio talent in Connacht just waiting to be given its chance to flourish.

Midwest Radio was about to become a launch pad for a whole generation of talented young broadcasters.

Adrian Eames was aged just 25 when he uttered the first words broadcast by the newly licensed Midwest Radio. The Sligo-born disc jockey was young in years but had already built up a lifetime of broadcasting experience, having worked in a plethora of pirate stations in the northwest since his late teens after catching the radio bug at a very young age in his native Ballinode. He also boasted considerable experience in theatre – both in stage management and acting – and had experienced pressure-filled opening nights at renowned venues such as the Hawk's Well in Sligo and the Olympia in Dublin. But nothing from his past could adequately prepare Eames for the drama of that opening morning in the bedroom-cum-studio in Ballyhaunis.

"When I was initially told I'd be the first voice to be heard on Midwest I was really honoured but as the countdown to opening day drew closer it all became somewhat nerve-racking," he recalls. "Being the first legal station to go on the air outside Dublin meant it attracted a lot of media hullabaloo so I was adamant I wouldn't let the side down and that it would all go without any hitches."

It was difficult to remain suitably detached, however, amidst the hoopla unfolding around him. Every time Adrian looked out of the studio window he saw another photographer or cameraman or member of the Midwest board. RTÉ had sent a television crew to record the momentous occasion for the *Six-One News* while the local and national newspapers were also on hand as well as most members of the board and a large number of staff. No pressure then…

"I must have rehearsed that opening script hundreds of times so it fitted the 30-second music-bed we chose to go with it," Adrian recalls. "In hindsight, it would have been a lot less stressful to pre-record the introduction but we went with the live format and once I was up and running it all went to plan."

The moment the studio clock struck exactly 10am, Adrian pressed the on-air button, leaned into the microphone and uttered the historic words: "Good morning! It's Monday, July 24, 1989, and this is Midwest Radio…"

After completing the 30-second introduction, Adrian leaned across to one of the two new turntables and pressed play on Kevin Prendergast's vinyl version of *My Old Home In Mayo.*

It's many years ago now since I left my Mayo home
Searching for those green hills somewhere across the foam
I was young and foolish and I longed for city life
Away from my Clare Island and its lovely scenic sights.

Adrian recalls there was much debate in the days preceding the launch about the choice of first song, which was nearly more important than the opening words to be broadcast.

"I remember the discussions around what the first song on the station should be and, in truth, I don't think there could have been a better choice as the lyrics depicted what the ethos of Midwest Radio was both then and now – a station that is home."

The song was, indeed, an inspired choice since it was sung by a man from just down the road in Logboy and written by a man who was standing outside the studio on the very day Adrian Eames launched the new, fully-licensed Midwest Radio.

"I wrote *My Old Home In Mayo* after a visit to Clare Island around 1982-83," recalls Michael Commins. "I was still working for the *Western Journal* and I went there with Frank Dolan, that great photographer from Westport. I'd never been to Clare Island before and I was really struck by the beauty of the place."

The launch of Midwest Radio on that summer's morning was a momentous occasion for men like Commins who had been championing the cause of local radio for more than a decade. In a souvenir supplement in that week's *Connaught Telegraph,* the Claremorris journalist described the arrival of pirate radio as a "direct answer" to RTÉ.

"The advent of local radio heralds a brand new and exciting era in all our lives. Gone forever are the days when the national radio service 'imposed' what they thought we should be listening to rather than what we ourselves demanded to hear. Midwest Radio hopes to reflect the people of the West as they are and copper-fasten the things that make us uniquely West of Ireland people."

Adrian Eames was barely a wet week in Midwest but was rapidly becoming immersed in the ethos of the station, especially its heavy bias towards Country music. His favourite bands were 1980s' cult pop outfits like The Cure and New Order but he knew that sort of music was not going to sit easily with a Midwest audience. Three decades later, Adrian recounts the "immortal words of advice" he received from Paul on his first day in the job: *Always remember the old lady sitting by the fire and you won't go too far wrong.*

The old lady sitting by the fire was unlikely to be a 'Curehead' so Adrian was quite happy to embrace music that might not necessarily be his cup of tea but was, more importantly, the listeners' choice. *My Old Home In Mayo* was followed by several more Irish Country classics as Midwest picked up where it left off seven months earlier. With the all-important introductory remarks out of the way, Adrian settled into his new role and before he knew it, the Sligo man was handing over to his boss for a special *Mid-Morning Show*... in the afternoon.

"I clearly remember the spontaneous round of applause that greeted me when I walked into the outer studio with my first day's work under my belt," he says. "The feelings of stress were replaced by total relief and a dash of Lucozade!"

Paul, Chris and Gerry needed quite a few dashes of Lucozade to keep them going that day. The station was due to be officially launched at a gala reception in Breaffy House Hotel later that evening with Minister Burke and Justice Henchy among a long list of dignitaries that included the Archbishop of Tuam Dr Joseph Cassidy and renowned New York human rights lawyer Paul O'Dwyer. The launch was being broadcast live, which meant Midwest was about to make two pieces of history in one day by becoming the first legalised local station to launch outside Dublin and the first to host an outside broadcast.

If that wasn't enough, a celebratory concert was scheduled for the TF Royal Theatre later that night with a star-studded music line-up that included Mick Flavin, John Hogan, Joanna and Tequila Sunrise, Tony Allen and the biggest attraction of them all, the legendary Joe Dolan.

"My abiding memory of that day is of the 'phones starting to ring as soon as Adrian uttered his opening words," recalls Gerry Glennon. "People had read in the local papers that we were going to be on air at 10am on Monday, July 24, and they had their dials set and were as ready to go as we were! The 'phones were literally hopping for that entire day as hundreds and hundreds of people rang in, not to play requests at all but just to wish us well."

Among the messages of congratulations was one from Taoiseach Charles Haughey, although Hilda Creaby managed to get her 'spake' in before him, having gone on air with Paul earlier that afternoon. Meanwhile, down on Achill Island, Peadar McHugh and Michael Duggan were fine-tuning the new transmitter on the top of Minaun, some 1,500ft above the Atlantic.

"It was a blazing hot day and there were no vents in the container that housed the transmitter so we had to keep the door open to allow the equipment to cool off," recalls Michael. "The heat in there was unreal – it was like 10 convectors going at once – so we left the door open for the night and headed off to the TF for the big party!"

Midwest and the Midas Express were back on the road again. It was like they'd never been away.

CHAPTER SIXTEEN

The summer of innocence

MAYO was in the grip of football fever in July 1989. The day before Midwest Radio went live, the county's senior footballers played out a drawn provincial final against Roscommon in MacHale Park in Castlebar and the replay was fixed for Dr Hyde Park in Roscommon town the following Sunday.

Nowadays, in the back-door era, provincial football doesn't pack the same punch but in the summer of '89 the thrill of a winner-takes-all clash against the neighbours proved intoxicating. There was a sense that Mayo football was on an upward trajectory after a couple of summers in the doldrums following the unforgettable campaign of '85 when a relatively inexperienced Mayo team took Dublin to a replay in the All-Ireland semi-final. Liam Horan, then a novice reporter with the *Western People*, was convinced '89 could be a breakthrough year for Mayo's senior footballers who had gone 38 years without reaching an All-Ireland final.

"Mayo won the Connacht championship in '88 and pushed a really good Meath team close in the All-Ireland semi-final. That was the Meath team of Colm O'Rourke, Brian Stafford, Gerry McEntee, Martin O'Connell and Mick Lyons, to name but a few, and they went on to retain their All-Ireland title later that year so I felt Mayo were in a right good place going into '89."

Horan had a busy few days prior to the drawn Connacht Final after Terry Reilly put him in charge of the *Western's* souvenir supplement to mark the launch of Midwest Radio. The young Ballinrobe man spent the last few days of the week in the new studios in Ballyhaunis, interviewing the likes of Paul, Chris, Adrian Eames and other prominent presenters before dashing over to the railway station in Claremorris to send his typewritten copy to Ballina.

On Sunday, the 21-year-old set off for MacHale Park to watch a decidedly under-par Mayo share the spoils with Roscommon in a dour game that hinged on a dramatic, late save from Mayo's rookie 'keeper Gabriel Irwin. By the time the young reporter had sent the last of his copy through to Ballina on Monday afternoon he was flat out exhausted and looking forward to a few days' well-deserved rest.

Meanwhile, in Ballyhaunis, the sudden realisation that the county for which he now possessed the local radio franchise had gone football bananas was presenting a major problem for Paul Claffey. He already had plans for the last Sunday in July – Midwest intended to mark the annual Reek pilgrimage by broadcasting morning Mass from the top of Croagh Patrick – and now he was being told his station needed to do a second outdoor broadcast later that afternoon from 'The Hyde'.

"How can I go about getting the rights to broadcast the replay," Paul asked Terry Reilly on Tuesday morning.

"Leave it with me," said Terry. "I'll talk to Donal Keenan."

Dr Donal Keenan was the patron of Connacht GAA and a former national president of the association. He was a most obliging man and was happy to section off a small area in the main stand at Dr Hyde Park as a commentary box to be shared by Midwest and RTÉ. Joe Cunniffe had a brother working in Telecom Éireann and the two men went over to Roscommon and checked that a telephone line could be installed in the hastily erected box. Michael Neary was pleased to report to Paul that everything was in order on the communications front.

"How exactly will it work?" Paul asked.

"Well, we're going to have to send a line over to Shannonside studios in Longford and that'll send a signal back to Kiltimagh, which will bounce a signal onto the studio here in Ballyhaunis and that'll go back out to Kiltimagh…"

"Stop right there, Mick," said Claffey. "Will it work?"

"I think it will. The lads in Telecom think so too."

"Right, let's do it," said Claffey before picking up the telephone and ringing Terry Reilly.

"I got that sorted for Sunday. We have a line set up from The Hyde."

"Oh great, and have you a commentator?"

"A commentator?"

"Yeah, who's going to do the broadcast for you?"

"Christ I never thought of that!"

"Let me think about it," said Terry, laughing, "and I'll talk to Tom [Courell]. He might have a few ideas."

The two editors exchanged several telephone calls over the next couple of days but no obvious candidate sprang to mind. There hadn't been a tradition on pirate radio of providing sports commentaries or even post-match reports so Midwest was breaking new ground in attempting a live commentary of something as high profile as a provincial football final. By the end of the week, a commentator had yet to be identified and Terry Reilly was becoming decidedly uneasy about the entire project, especially when Paul announced at a board meeting in Ballyhaunis on Friday he was thinking of taking on the role himself.

"Paul, what in the name of God do you know about Gaelic football?" asked Tom Courell.

"Sure it can't be that difficult," Claffey replied. "All I have to do is describe what is happening out on the field."

"Right so," said Tom, giving Terry a playful nudge. "Tell me what colour flags are raised for a goal and a point?"

"Flags?" asked Claffey incredulously. "Sure what have the supporters' flags got to do with anything?"

That exchange put paid to the brief sports commentary career of 'The Man With The Flashin' Dickie' but the problem remained: who was going to step forward and make a little bit of broadcasting history on Sunday, July 30, 1989?

Terry Reilly was in the office in Ballina on Saturday afternoon when he got a telephone call from Paul.

"I've got the man to do the job, the commentary," said Claffey.

"Who?" Terry asked with a certain amount of trepidation.

"A guy called Billy Horan from Ballinrobe, one of your reporters..."

"Surely you mean Liam Horan, surely you *don't* mean Liam Horan," Terry volunteered.

"The very man. We'll have everything hooked up tomorrow at The Hyde."

There was a deathly silence at the other end of the telephone before Terry eventually spoke.

"Paul, are you really going ahead with this?"

"Well I can't pull out now. I've just announced it on the radio!"

Meanwhile, over in Ballinrobe, young Liam Horan was furiously leafing through old match programmes in an effort to compile some titbits of information to fill the dead air during the inevitable breaks in play. He'd never sat in a radio studio before or provided any post-match reports to the likes of RTÉ or even worked as a disc jockey. In fact, his broadcasting experience amounted to little more than a several workshops while a student at Rathmines School of Journalism and "a few bits for videos around town". Now he was about to embark on the most audacious experiment of all: a full live commentary where the margin for error was nil.

Novices had been thrown into the fray in Connacht finals before but none were as wet behind the ears as the man from Ballinrobe. The summer of innocence was truly about to begin.

Liam Horan worked late into the night in Ballinrobe, jotting down copious notes, but he wasn't the only youngster preparing to make broadcasting history the following day. Further west, on the shores of Clew Bay, Gerry Glennon and Michael Neary were slowly ascending the Reek, each guiding a donkey heavily laden down with the equipment needed for the broadcast of morning Mass. Both had yet to turn 23 and were about to embark on a most elaborate mission, one RTÉ hadn't even attempted in its 60-year history, namely an outside broadcast (OB) from the top of a mountain.

Michael wasn't a bit surprised when Paul came up with the novel idea because he was only too familiar from the pirate days with the boss's offbeat style.

"Do you think it can be done?" Claffey asked.

It was a question Neary would hear again and again in the years ahead and it was always best to answer in the affirmative because Paul would find a way to make it work no matter what.

"Well, height wise you couldn't have a better spot for an OB," Michael replied. "If we can't get a signal from the top of the Reek we might as well give up on this broadcasting craic altogether!"

But Midwest had never attempted anything remotely like this before. The *Sunday Night Live* broadcasts were complicated affairs but at least they were taking place only yards from the studio or in big music venues with secure electricity and telephone connections. Mass from the Reek, however, was a different ballgame. Gerry and Michael weren't just jumping in at the deep end; this was more like leaping from Minaun Heights into the broad Atlantic.

"The most technical OB we'd done up to that point was from Paddy Ryan's SuperValu shop back to the station, which was a distance of about 300 yards," recalls Michael. "Now that was pretty straightforward compared to firing a UHF signal from the top of Croagh Patrick to the mast in Kiltimagh and on to Ballyhaunis!"

As they trudged wearily up the stony slopes of the Reek in the muggy evening sunshine, the old school-friends debated who were the bigger donkeys: the four-legged creatures carrying the gear or the two-legged plebs who had volunteered for this mad expedition.

"We were bringing a lot of gear with us," Michael recalls. "We had a desk, mikes, an aerial and a transmitter so there was no way we'd have carried all of that ourselves."

Before leaving Ballyhaunis, Paul presented them with something called a mobile telephone, a huge, ugly block of a thing that nearly required its own donkey to carry it.

"She's state-of-the-art, lads," he proudly declared. "There are only a few of them in the country so don't lose it."

"Lose it?" said Glennon. "It'd be hard to lose that yoke!"

It was agreed that on scaling the mountain, they'd set up the equipment and make a quick telephone call back to base to check that everything was in order. Then they'd settle down in the old chapel for a night's rest and, hopefully, the equipment would still be behaving itself come the morning.

"John McIntyre from Swinford was presenting a show that Saturday evening and he was going to be on again on Sunday morning so we got set up and then put the call through to him," recalls Michael. "Everything was perfect. The signal was excellent and John was hearing us loud and clear in Ballyhaunis."

It all seemed too easy… and it was. Having gone out to feed the two donkeys, tethered beside the chapel, our pilgrims settled in for the longest night of penitence the Reek had known since the days of St Patrick. Initially everything seemed fine but things took a turn for the worse around 2am when Neary awoke to the sound of voices approaching the chapel. Who in the name of God could be on top of the mountain at this very unholy hour? He was about to find out.

Determined to uphold the ancient tradition of the midnight pilgrimage, a large group of late-night revellers had scaled the summit in the dark and were understandably curious to discover two sleeping donkeys at the side of the chapel. To make matters worse, the intrepid pilgrims sounded like they had been drinking a lot more than water on the long, arduous climb and were now most decidedly the worse for wear.

"They knew there was something inside the chapel but they didn't know what," recalls Michael, laughing. "They thought maybe it was all-night Confessions or Mass or something! So they were banging on the door trying to get in and we were both leaning against it trying to keep them out!"

Meanwhile, the two weary donkeys, who only hours earlier had carried an entire radio studio to the top of a 2,500ft mountain, were not especially pleased to be rudely awakened from their well-deserved slumbers and were quick to voice their irritation. To make matters worse, a row erupted among the group of impatient pilgrims whose brains were struggling to cope with the lack of oxygen at these dizzy heights… or maybe it was just the alcohol. At any rate, a scene was soon unfolding at the top of the sacred Reek that was biblical in its fury; there were roars and curses from the men, wails and screeches from the women, an incessant banging on the chapel door and the braying of two very angry donkeys. If poor St Patrick didn't turn in his grave that night he never would.

Finally, after what seemed like an eternity, dawn broke over the holy mountain and the large group of drunken pilgrims decided they had offered up enough penance for one year and began to chaotically retreat down the cone-shaped upper slope. Glennon and Neary, who by then had completed sufficient penance to last several lifetimes, slumped to the chapel floor in exhaustion, having spent the previous couple of hours silently singing Kris Kristofferson's classic *Help Me Make It Through The Night.* However, it was too late now for catching up on lost sleep; there was an outside broadcast to be done.

Picking up the bulky mobile phone, which had been placed carefully in a corner of the chapel out of harm's way, Gerry began to dial through to Ballyhaunis only to stop in midstream... there wasn't a murmur from this piece of so-called state-of-the-art equipment. Unfortunately, the 'phone's battery – unlike the hardy Midwest Radio team – had failed to make it through the night.

"Without the telephone we had no way in the world of God of knowing what was happening in Ballyhaunis," recalls Gerry. "How would we know if they could hear us back at base when we couldn't contact them? It was a disaster."

By 9am the duo was no nearer to solving the dilemma and Mass was due to commence in little more than an hour. Gerry had brought a small transistor with him so they were able to listen clearly to John McIntyre who was due to hand over to them at 10am.

"The only thing we could do was to keep talking down the line and hope that John would give us a signal on air that he could hear us," recalls Gerry.

While Michael checked and rechecked the various connections, Gerry spoke again and again into the microphone: "John, if you're listening can you say something... John, please let me know you can hear me..."

The minutes ticked by and 9.15am became 9.30am with still no indication from McIntyre that he was picking up the signal from the Reek. Gerry was becoming increasingly desperate as he repeated again and again the same phrase or slight variations of it: "John, can you *please* let us know you're hearing us... John, can you say something... John, are you hearing us at all?"

At 9.45am, McIntyre stuck another record on the turntable and then took an advertising break, which only added to the sense of frustration above on the Reek where Gerry and Michael were now in total despair, believing their Herculean efforts during the previous 12 hours had been little more than a spectacular failure. Fr Colm Kilcoyne, who was due to celebrate the historic Mass, had now joined them and was pacing from one end of the little chapel to the other, beseeching God and St Patrick to intervene on their behalf.

Upon returning from the break, McIntyre went straight into yet more music, prompting groans from Croagh Patrick that could nearly be heard all the way to Ballyhaunis, but suddenly the record faded and Michael and Gerry heard their colleague's voice crackle through the transistor.

"And now, listeners, we are delighted to report that we have established contact with our technical team on Croagh Patrick and Mass will be coming to you live at 10am."

For the second time that morning, Neary and Glennon sank to the chapel floor in weary relief. St Patrick's epic pilgrimage of 40 days and 40 nights had been a piece of cake compared to this broadcasting lark.

As soon as Fr Colm Kilcoyne completed the Mass, Gerry and Michael were packing up the equipment and loading it onto the donkeys because they needed to make haste to Roscommon town for the Connacht Final replay, which was due to commence at 3.30pm.

"We only had one UHF transmitter so it was a case of a hop, skip and jump from Croagh Patrick to The Hyde," recalls Michael Neary. "I left Gerry in Ballyhaunis, collected Joe Cunniffe and we got to Roscommon about an hour before the throw-in."

Another man making haste to The Hyde was Terry Reilly, an avid Mayo football supporter, who found himself in the curious position of being more worried about what would happen off the field than on it.

"I never thought I'd have seen the day when priorities could have been so deflected, even warped," he recalls.

On arrival in the press box he encountered a nervous-looking Tom Courell who had just discovered there was a poor two-way link to the studio, the mobile telephone still having failed to revive itself.

"Call if off," urged Courell, mopping his brow with a handkerchief.

But Michael Neary, who was still floating on air after his epic night and morning on Croagh Patrick, wasn't a bit fazed by the inability to establish a two-way link to Ballyhaunis. Once again, he had a battered transistor – this time owned by Michael Commins – to serve as a connection of sorts and was confident he could pull off another 'Miracle of the Reek'.

"Michael, Joe and the Telecom man worked away feverishly as we counted down to throw-in," recalls Terry, "throwing out a few mikes that looked puny by comparison to RTÉ's million-punt cameras and radio facilities in the adjoining box. One Midwest mike dangled down from a rafter… to catch the atmosphere.

"The coolest dude around was young Liam Horan, who was about to become the first man to do a full commentary on a provincial final on local radio."

As broadcasting baptisms of fire go, the Connacht final replay of 1989 was as scorching as it gets. The game began at a helter-skelter pace and continued in that vein throughout the next 70 minutes as the sides served up an exhibition of attacking, free-flowing football that was totally at odds with the dull, cagey first encounter.

But if the players had started at a blistering speed, so too had the Midwest Radio commentator, who set off at a gallop that would have left the great Shergar trailing hopelessly in his wake.

"I started at 100 miles per hour and tried to lift it from there," Horan wryly recalls.

Terry Reilly, who was on co-commentating duties with Tom Courell, was fairly confident the Mayo players would stick the pace but wasn't so sure about Midwest's young commentator. Horan's task was made all the more difficult when a gust of wind swept his sheaf of carefully-prepared notes into the crowd but the Ballinrobe man battled on heroically, even resisting the urge to leap out of the box after them.

As the game reached an unforgettable climax, an increasingly animated Liam Horan abandoned all pretence of impartiality and treated Midwest listeners to a breathless commentary the likes of which they had never heard before. Mayo led by two points with only a minute of normal time on the clock only for the great Tony McManus to win – and then score – a penalty. Almost immediately the men in green and red hurtled back down the field and Michael Collins booted the ball to the net but the score was disallowed by referee Mickey Kearns who instead awarded a free to Mayo, which Michael Fitzmaurice calmly converted to send the game into extra-time.

A now hoarse Horan brought the extra-time drama to thousands of listeners across the province… and what drama it was! Roscommon established a three-point lead but Mayo kept plugging away until the game swung back in the champions' favour at the death when burly full-forward Jimmy Burke scrambled the ball across the line for a goal that Horan memorably described as "the most slobbery of all time". Slobbery or not, it was the winning score and Mayo had claimed back-to-back provincial titles for the first time since 1951, while Midwest Radio and its effusive greenhorn commentator had set an electrifying tone for the next two months.

The summer of '89 would be like no other in Mayo.

Terry Reilly recalls meeting hoards of Tyrone fans as he made his way down from the commentary box after the final whistle. The Red Hand men had already won the Ulster title and their supporters were bullish about their prospects in the upcoming semi-final against Mayo. But Reilly and Liam Horan both believed the men in green and red would never get a better chance to reach their first All-Ireland Final in 38 years.

"Connacht and Ulster were the weak provinces in the 1970s and 1980s," explains Liam. "The only time teams from one or the other made it through to the All-Ireland final was when they played each other, which was once every three years. That pattern started in 1974 and continued right through until '89 and I strongly fancied Mayo to do it that year."

Terry and Liam returned to the Midwest studio in Ballyhaunis for a post-match analysis programme where the guests included Minister of State Seán Calleary, former GAA referee PJ McGrath, Ivan Neill of the *Western People* and Tom Courell. Terry presented the show in which listeners were able to call in and offer their views on a game that was being hailed as one of the greatest Connacht finals of them all.

Liam was still on a high from his commentary but in an age long before social media he wasn't entirely sure how the public had received it. He got his answer when one elderly listener rang into the evening show. The old man explained how he had travelled to countless Mayo matches over the years but was no longer able to attend the games due to failing eyesight.

"You were my eyes today," the old man said, barely able to contain his euphoria. "You were my eyes."

The comment made Horan stop and think about the power and potential of local radio. Writing in the *Western People* the following Tuesday, the young journalist described the man's remark as "five words which touched my heart, five words which perfectly sorted out the mish-mash of thoughts [that] had raced through my crowded mind..."

Paul Claffey was, by no means, a sports fanatic but he knew when something appealed to listeners and the match commentary really struck a chord across the province. He planned a similar extravaganza for the All-Ireland semi-final.

"We have to get a report from Croke Park after the game, win or lose," Claffey told a perplexed Terry Reilly.

"How do you plan to do that? Do we have mobile 'phones or a studio? Or even a pigeon?"

Midwest had already sought permission to broadcast a full commentary of the semi-final but was informed that RTÉ had exclusive rights. Instead it was decided to do a post-match show, similar to the one broadcast from Ballyhaunis after the Connacht final replay. But where would they set up the makeshift studio?

"Paddy Moran of Bonniconlon, who was an officer of the Mayo Association in Dublin, and director of C.P. Security, happened to have an office outside Croke Park," recalls Terry. "It was from there that we broadcast a live post-match show immediately after Mayo had beaten Tyrone. I remember Paddy was wheeling in the likes of Seán Boylan, former Mayo great John Gibbons, as well as team members like Jimmy Browne, Dermot Flanagan and county board secretary John Prenty.

There was great excitement because this was the first time Mayo had reached an All-Ireland senior final since '51. We were all saying 'The Famine is over, the Famine is over'!"

Among those present was Foxford-born Noel Howley, chairman of the Mayo Association in Dublin, who had hosted a function in the Garda Club on the evening before to raise funds for the team. Writing in the Mayo GAA Yearbook later that year, Howley remarked:

"I have been to Croke Park many times and have witnessed many momentous occasions there, but I have never experienced anything like this before. Men and women were just overcome with emotion as tears of joy streamed down their faces. Our dreams and aspirations were fulfilled – we were in the final at last!"

The newly established Midwest Radio surfed the waves of euphoria and excitement that swept through Mayo in the ensuing weeks. Paul, Chris and the rest of the team couldn't have timed their arrival on the local media landscape any better; it truly was the summer to beat all summers.

"All of a sudden Mayo was aflame," recalls Terry Reilly. "Qualifying for a final after a lapse of nearly 40 years released a sea of emotions and we were all lifted like boats on the tide. Green and red material was snapped up, flags flew from every vantage point, towns and villages put out bunting and the quest for tickets helped to accentuate the atmosphere."

Mayo football supporters later became accustomed to the hype that inevitably comes with an appearance in an All-Ireland final but it was all so intoxicatingly fresh in that enchanting summer of '89 and Midwest contributed enormously to the fever-pitch atmosphere that gripped the county in those early weeks of September. Songs by the likes of Frank McCaffrey, Dan The Street Singer, Tommy Battle and Doc Carroll were soon filling the airwaves as the novelty of having your county's anthem played regularly on the radio inspired one green and red ditty after another. Supporters were soon belting out verses from their personal favourites such as *Up Mayo* by Doc Carroll:

With Eugene Lavin injured sure we stumbled on a gem,
Known as the angel Gabriel, his second name's Irwin
If anything passes Maher, which should be rare enough
Kilgallon, Finn and Collins will be there to sweep it up.

Part of Midwest's brief under the terms of its IRTC franchise was to connect with the Mayo Diaspora so it was decided the station would broadcast a big match special in an attempt to unite people at home and abroad. The spectacular sell-out event was held at Midas on the Thursday before the final against Cork with all funds raised going to the team's training fund. It was a mammoth undertaking involving a host of special guests as well as on-air calls to Mayo natives in London, Manchester, New York, California, Sydney and the Lebanon.

The Ballina Brass and Reed Band and the Balla Pipe Band were even on hand to rally the Mayo troops ahead of their county's date with destiny.

The final, of course, ended in a narrow defeat but somehow that loss has always seemed much less painful than the many more that came after it. Writing in the Mayo GAA yearbook, Terry Reilly brilliantly captured the spirit of a magical, memorable summer when Mayo football and Midwest Radio came of age together and became forever inextricably linked in the hearts and minds of GAA fans all over the world.

"1989 was, above all else, a summer of innocence. We stumbled along, we got up and running, and we nearly cleared the greatest hurdle of them all in a romantic adventure.

"I doubt if we can create that atmosphere, that innocence again, for if we make Croke Park on the big day in 1990 or 1991, we will be streetwise, seasoned, call it what you will. The team will be more hardened in its attitude, the radio more professional in its approach. Both, unfortunately, will have shed that innocence, which bestows such an aura of well-being on all who walk in its shadow."

After flying into Knock Airport, the Mayo team embarked on a tour of the county that continued for the best part of a fortnight. Johnny Oosten was dispatched in a Midwest Radio-branded Daihatsu Charade to report live on the extended homecoming.

"How will I report back to the studio?" he asked Paul.

"Here," said Claffey. "Take this. It's called a mobile telephone, state-of-the-art technology, you can make a call from anywhere."

"You're joking me," said Oosten.

At the other end of the office, Gerry Glennon and Michael Neary simultaneously threw their eyes to heaven. State-of-the-art, how are ya!

"Just keep that yoke turned off until you need to make a call," advised Neary. "The old battery isn't great."

Oosten, however, was in his element. The only place he had seen a mobile telephone before was in the Hollywood movie *Wall Street*, which had been a big hit in cinemas a year earlier.

"I was chuffed to be going around with this brick-like 'phone and to be making calls standing from the top of hills or standing on walls!" he recalls. "I'd have the 'phone attached to my belt because I was so proud to carry it around; now you'd be ashamed to be seen with a thing like that!"

Johnny spent more than a week with the Mayo footballers, visiting places as far-flung as Healy's in Glenamoy in North Mayo, the home village of goalkeeper Gabriel Irwin. He'd usually ring into John Duggan's evening show to give an update on the progress of the team bus as it rambled around the county from town to village, stopping at just about every crossroads in between. He was in Mitchell's in Moygownagh on the famous night when Anthony 'Larry' Finnerty, the acknowledged joker in the Mayo team, gave an unforgettable address to the packed pub. The corner-forward, with the distinctive mop of curly blonde hair and penchant for Irish dancing, had scored Mayo's only goal in the final but missed arguably an easier chance for a second. Standing on a barstool, Finnerty solemnly told his audience it was with great regret he had been unable to bring Sam Maguire back to his home village and admitted he had to shoulder at least some of the blame for the defeat.

"But," he added, perking up considerably. "I can't be too downhearted because if I'd scored that second goal ye'd have been talking about me for the whole winter, whereas now that I missed it ye'll be talking about me for the rest of my life!"

It really had been the summer of innocence.

CHAPTER SEVENTEEN

'Wired to the moon'

PAUL Claffey's *Mid-Morning Show* set the tone for much of what Midwest became famous for, especially in its early years. It was whacky; it was old school; it was risqué, but never in an offensive way; it was middle-of-the-road; it was far out there; it was a bit of everything really. Claffey's on-air persona was, by necessity, carefree, good-humoured and mad for a bit of craic but away from the mike he had to be deadly serious because Midwest was a business that needed to be run in a sober, responsible manner.

Unlike RTÉ, the new local broadcasters could not rely on licence fees or any state funding whatsoever; they had to sink or swim on their own merits and several found themselves in deep, deep water within a year or two of launching. Claffey was determined Midwest would not be listed among the failures. He'd endured his share of financial woes during the previous decade and wasn't prepared to go back there.

"When I'm on air I'm wired to the moon [but] the minute I come off, I become wired to the pound note," Paul told John Waters in an interview for the *Sunday Independent* on the eve of Midwest returning to the airwaves. It was a catchy line that neatly encapsulated the chief executive's attitude to commercial broadcasting: it was all fine and dandy having fun on the airwaves but the party had to stop once the microphone was turned off. In that sense, the couple of hours spent each weekday on the *Mid-Morning Show* was Paul's downtime; the rest was hard work.

The only source of revenue for Midwest was advertising and the new station wasn't going to get anything easy in a county where there were three paid-for newspapers (*Western People, Connaught Telegraph* and

Mayo News) and a freesheet (*Mayo Post*). The initial annual revenue projection was £380,000, which meant the station needed to average over £30,000 per month, a pretty ambitious figure in a period of continuing economic recession and in a part of the country blighted by unemployment and emigration.

But at least Midwest had a financial base dating from its spell as a pirate when it attracted a lot of advertising from a wide geographical area. Key to that revenue stream was the station's Ballyhaunis location, which placed it at the very heart of the province.

"When we went legal everybody was telling us to move to Castlebar or Ballina," says Chris Carroll. "But Paul and I knew we had built up a loyal listenership in North Galway, Roscommon and South Sligo – in good business towns like Castlerea, Tubbercurry, Ballaghaderreen and Tuam. We felt that if we moved out of Ballyhaunis people might no longer identify with us as their local station and we knew we'd never be able to depend on the revenue from Mayo alone."

Harry McGowan, a former schoolteacher from Castlerea, had sold advertising in the pirate days and returned once the licence was granted to head up a new advertising department that also included John Murphy, Tina Mitchell and Mary Whittington.

The feelgood factor surrounding the success of the Mayo football team meant Midwest hit the ground running and the station was soon selling wall-to-wall adverts extending good wishes to John O'Mahony and the boys. Terry Reilly recalls the delight at board level when it was revealed in early September that Midwest had generated £35,000 in its first full month in business.

"The figures were very encouraging from the start but there was still a lot of nervousness among the members of the board. People like Tom [Courell] and myself came from a newspaper background where circulation revenue was the backbone of our business model but Midwest was totally dependent on advertising, which can be very cyclical so there was no complacency despite the positive signs early on."

There were also strict regulations governing the number of minutes per hour the new commercial stations could devote to advertising.

"Back in the pirate days, we could run a 10-minute advertising break and nobody paid a blind bit of notice but now the IRTC were supervising everything," explains Chris. "That created its own pressures too because we had to make sure everything we broadcast was kept for 90 days in case the IRTC wanted to check anything."

Chris's appointment as production manager was very deliberate because it was a key role in the new organisation. The production manager was responsible for the recording of all adverts, live music sessions, debates, quizzes and drama.

"The biggest part of my day in those early years was recording ads," recalls Chris. "I still kept my hand in on the broadcast side by presenting a weekend show but the recording of ads was very time-consuming back then and sometimes that's all I'd do in a day."

There were three studios in the new headquarters and one was largely devoted to the recording of ads. The days of speaking over vinyl and recording to cassette tapes had long gone but the work was still very laborious and intensive. However, Chris was always happy when an abundance of adverts needed to be recorded because it meant the money was rolling in; the alternative would have been a disaster.

"The transition from pirate to commercial was nerve-wracking," he says. "All of a sudden this was professional and we had to be as professional as possible. There was also a lot more at stake and the cost of failure was so much higher.

"Everyone worked incredibly hard in those years. It was a small, tight team and there was a real sense of camaraderie, a feeling we were doing something that had never been done before and we were absolutely determined to make a success of it."

Fear of failure was Paul's biggest motivational tool in those early days when memories of frequent court appearances for unpaid debts were still fresh in his mind.

"You know, it got so bad the judge was calling me 'Paul'!" Claffey joked to John Waters in that *Sunday Independent* interview before quickly becoming serious again.

"When I go on air I always think of how I felt in the dog days, when I would want to get away from it all, just for an hour or two. I think of the people out there who feel like that – who are lonely, or unemployed, or not feeling the best. Give the punters what they want, give them a lift and you can't go wrong."

The pirate's garb might have been shed but the captain was staying true to the ship's original course.

One of the key stipulations from the IRTC was that 20 per cent of Midwest's weekly output must consist of news and current affairs. For a station that had, in its pirate incarnation, been heavy on light entertainment and light on hard news this was a big ask, but it had to be done or the licence would be swiftly revoked.

Chris Clesham, a native of Cong in South Mayo, who had previously worked as a current affairs presenter on IRM was appointed newsreader, while an arrangement was agreed that journalists in the *Western People* and *Connaught Telegraph* would supply a regular stream of local news and sports stories.

Initially, there had been plans to locate the newsroom in a studio in Castlebar while the sports department would operate from another satellite facility in Ballina but it became apparent after a short while that such an arrangement would be impracticable. However, the two smaller studios were opened as per the terms of the IRTC contract. They were very modest affairs in keeping with the board's thrifty approach, and Terry Reilly actually recalls that the original Midwest studio in Ballina was destined to be a Portakabin in the car park of the *Western People.* However, Paul sourced a small unit on Teeling Street at the very last minute and it was soon home to Ballina-based staff members like Mary Whittington, who had previously worked at Twin County Radio.

"Mary played a big role in establishing Midwest in Ballina and North Mayo in the early 1990s," says Tommy Marren. "She had great organisational skills and was hugely regarded around the town so she was a great ambassador for the station. She was the perfect person really to take charge of the Ballina office."

Twin County's founder Tommy Murphy was also drafted onto the Midwest team as a presenter of a Saturday afternoon show while Tommy Marren was asked to head up the station's three-hour sports programmes on Saturday and Sunday.

"When Midwest got the licence they were looking for full and part-time presenters for a whole series of programmes," he recalls. "I applied and was offered a part-time role as a sports presenter, which suited me down to the ground as it meant I could continue with the day job in AIB."

Chris Clesham and the two Tommys weren't the only former employees of rival Mayo pirate stations to join the Midwest team. Several ex-DJs from IRM were charged with providing younger listeners with a nightly pop music programme from 10 to 11pm, which again was part of the agreement with the IRTC.

While Midwest's playlist was largely its own business, there was an expectation that the station would provide relevant programming for all age groups. Former IRM DJs such as Kevin McNeela ('Webster') and Frankie McDonald were assigned to the nightly show along with Brendan Redmond, John McIntyre and Joe Finnegan.

Another prominent presenter in the early days was Henry McGlade, from Castlebar, who had been involved in the entertainment business since the mid-1970s and presented some popular shows on Midwest in the pirate days, including *Sunday Choice,* which featured the very popular *'Hospital Requests'* segment.

A former director of Castlebar International Song Contest, Henry's lifelong love of music was fostered through long nights listening to Radio Luxembourg in the early 1970s. A talented guitarist, the Sligo native played in several bands in his younger years, including one with Gerry Gallagher of the famous Kim Newport Band. Henry opened a record shop in Castlebar in the late 1970s and also booked gigs for bands, as well as writing a weekly pop music column in the *Connaught Telegraph,* acting as compere at various events and working as a DJ. His involvement with radio was a natural progression and he was an enthusiastic supporter of the pirate stations in the late 1980s.

Henry pulled off a real coup in the first week of the newly licensed Midwest when he secured a studio interview with American Country singing star Nanci Griffith, whose song *From A Distance* had been a worldwide smash-hit two years earlier.

Weekdays on Midwest began at 8am with Adrian Eames followed by Paul's *Mid-Morning Show* from 11am to 1pm. Sponsored programmes were broadcast from 1 to 1.30pm while Chris Clesham's afternoon news show took to the airwaves from 1.30 to 1.45pm. Michael Neary and Johnny Oosten shared duties on the afternoon show from 1.45 to 3pm followed by *Helpline*, a phone-in show presented by Henry McGlade that offered listeners an opportunity to raise issues of concern to them. In many respects, this programme was a precursor to the modern-day *Tommy Marren Show* and it played a major role in fulfilling the IRTC requirements for topical content other than music.

Gerry Glennon presented *Homeward Bound* from 4 to 6pm before John Duggan picked up the baton after the evening news with his hugely popular *John Duggan At Home* show, which ran from 6.30 to 9.30pm.

A series of topical and current affairs shows, including religious affairs and farming, were broadcast nightly from 9.30 to 10pm before the airwaves were handed over to a teenage audience for one hour of pop music. The concept of different DJs for each night was abandoned after a few months and a new slot from 9 to 10pm was created for younger listeners to be filled by *Dial A Disc*, presented by Westport's Brendan Redmond. An A-Z list of songs, mainly consisting of chart music, was published in the *Western People* each Tuesday and listeners rang in with their song choices and requests.

"We tried different things in those early days and it was hit-and-miss at times," explains Chris. "Pop music would not have been our strongest suit at that time and RTÉ Radio 2 was hugely popular back then. DJs like Gerry Ryan, Dave Fanning and Ian Dempsey had enormous followings so, unlike some other local stations, we had no intention of going head-to-head with them and trying to lay claim to that teenage audience. But *Dial A Disc* proved a big success for us and became one of our really popular shows in the 1990s after it moved to the new slot from 9 to 10pm and became *The Hot Hits Hour.*"

The late-night slot alternated in the early days between Gerry, Paul, Michael Commins, Henry McGlade and Tommy Marren. Michael, who broadcast his first Wednesday night show in February 1988, was thrilled to return to the airwaves.

"It's only 30 years ago – and it seems like yesterday to me – but the world really was so different then," he says. "I remember I used to run a thing in the pirate days called the postal quiz, which was specifically aimed at people who didn't have telephones and couldn't take part in the phone-ins, which were becoming so popular in radio at that time."

In fact, a big portion of the requests would have come in by post in those early years because home telephones were still fairly uncommon, especially among older and isolated listeners, and mobile 'phones were only for yuppies like Johnny Oosten. It wasn't uncommon for people to wander down to their local telephone box to ring in a request or even go live on the radio, oblivious to the traffic rumbling along the street or the queue forming outside.

Those who recall the telephone boxes of a bygone era – with missing doors and broken panes of glass – will know they were not the most discreet facilities in which to hold a conversation and people using them needed to exercise a certain degree of caution. On one occasion, not long after Midwest returned to the airwaves, Paul – in one of his more 'wired to the moon' moments – invited listeners to ring in with animal impersonations and he'd give a prize to the best one. A man from a certain town in Mayo called in and proceeded to treat listeners to a vast selection of animal noises that were downright uncanny. The man could impersonate every four-legged creature in the farmyard and a few in the jungle too.

The only problem was that the self-same individual was ringing from a telephone box on a busy street and by-passers were more than a little alarmed to witness a middle-aged man in a telephone box howling like a wolf, roaring like a lion, braying like a donkey and squealing like a pig. The bemused onlookers did the only thing a group of responsible citizens could do in the circumstances: they called the local gardaí.

A couple of officers were promptly dispatched to investigate these extraordinary reports that a madman, who seemed to only communicate in animal-like noises, had commandeered the local telephone box. When the gardaí jumped into the nearest patrol car they switched on their radio station of choice… Midwest Radio. Well, they didn't need to go any further; it was a case of 'Elementary, My Dear Watson', case closed.

Chris Carroll readily admits his long-time business partner has always been a fountain of creative ideas. Paul was often at his most resourceful when Midwest needed to find new ways to generate revenue. Some ideas flew, some flopped but nobody could ever accuse Midwest of failing to demonstrate an innovative or enterprising spirit.

"A lot of businesspeople are afraid to fail but I never had that problem because I had failed long before I set up Midwest," says Paul. "I had no fear of failure whatsoever and, in a way, that was a great strength for me because it meant I was willing to do things other people would have probably ran a mile from."

The newly-legalised Midwest was barely a few days' old when Paul tossed a radical idea out at a board meeting that left the members utterly perplexed.

"I'm thinking of broadcasting death notices," he said.

"Death notices?" asked Tom Courell.

"Yeah, every morning we'll announce the people in the area who have died."

There was a sharp intake of breath.

"Well I've heard of dead air," said Fr Colm Kilcoyne. "But this is a new one on me."

"Trust me, it'll work," said Claffey. "People will want to use this service."

In fairness, Paul had an advantage over the rest of the board in that Midwest tentatively trialed the concept of death notices in the pirate era.

"Radio Limerick used to read out death notices from the papers in a very informal way and we did a bit of that too, reading deaths haphazardly from the *Indo*," explains Gerry Glennon. "But it was all very loose, there was no real structure to it and we stopped after a while."

When Paul revived the death notices in 1989 he quickly discovered there were unexpected hazards in offering an easily accessible service to the public. Matters came to a head when Gerry Glennon answered the telephone one day and got the shock of his life.

"Hello," said a male caller. "I'm inquiring about that death notice you just had on there for Paddy Murphy from down in Bangor Erris."

"Hold on a minute and I'll check the details," replied Gerry. "You'll want to know the funeral arrangements, is it?"

"Well there is no funeral."

"No funeral? How do you know that?"

"Because I'm Paddy Murphy and I'm not dead yet!"

Gerry chuckles at the memory but the seriousness of the call was not lost on him either.

"The man [who wasn't named Paddy Murphy from Bangor Erris] took it in good spirits but it set alarm bells ringing and we knew that if we didn't put some sort of structure in place we were up the creek."

It was decided it would be safest to introduce personal pin numbers for each of the undertakers supplying the death notices. A charge was also imposed because there was now a lot of administrative work involved.

"We got some negative feedback from undertakers about the new system but we stuck to our guns," recalls Paul, "and the death notices were soon an integral part of our daily schedule.

"You see, at that time people might come into town once or twice a week and by the time they heard about somebody's death he or she could be buried. We're talking here about pre-Internet, pre-Facebook days; there was no other way to find out the news on a daily basis because the local papers just came out once a week."

Today, death notices are a common feature on local radio stations all over Ireland, but in 1989 the phenomenon was so unprecedented the BBC actually sent a camera crew to Ballyhaunis to investigate the Irish radio station making money from dead air. Terry Reilly says the concept attracted a lot of derision in the national media in the early days.

"Midwest got a fierce ribbing over it and there was a lot of mirth about this radio station down in the west that was reading out death notices."

But Paul ultimately had the last laugh. When the JNLR listenership figures were published in September 1990, Midwest had a bigger share of its respective market than any other station, and the death notices were the most listened to section of the day. Indeed, the death notices became a really useful device for nabbing listeners at 9am when they might have otherwise drifted away to Gay Byrne on

RTÉ Radio 1 or Gerry Ryan on RTÉ Radio 2. Ryan was so frustrated about this new phenomenon, he dedicated an entire show to death and death notices! It was the ultimate in backhanded compliments.

Gerry Reilly's involvement in local radio petered out with the advent of the legalised stations. December 31, 1988, truly was the end of an era for the likeable Cavan man and he knew it.

"I knew the fun was gone when the pirates were put off the air," he says. "At that stage, I was doing a good bit of television work and I was also doing bits of radio for BBC in Northern Ireland and later RTÉ."

However, Reilly and his brother Charlie continued to visit Mayo to provide much-needed assistance for the many outside broadcasts Midwest undertook in the early days. The Midas tours of 1987 and 1988 had been a great learning curve for Paul, Chris, Gerry and the rest of the team, giving them an appreciation of the impact an OB could have on a local community.

"There were thousands of people coming out for OBs in those days," says Gerry. "Local radio was totally new and people were fascinated by the idea that Midwest could be broadcasting live from their town or village."

Some OBs stand out more than others. Gerry Reilly recalls meeting an old man at the opening of the SuperValu shopping centre in Castlebar in 1990.

"He told me he'd cycled 10 miles just to meet Paul Claffey," recalls Gerry, laughing. "It was the same when I'd be working on OBs up in Donegal, people would be queuing down the street just to get the chance to play a request on the radio."

Outside broadcasts were fraught with all sorts of unexpected problems and there was a lot of preparatory work involved. In the case of Midwest, a transmission mast, aerial and three-way poles needed be erected to bounce a signal to the FM mast in Kiltimagh. Gerry Reilly recalls one particular OB from Cormac Hanley's Equestrian Centre in Claremorris when things didn't exactly go according to plan.

"Gerry Glennon and myself set up the site," he recalls. "There were a few cars there from the previous Thursday night's auction

[Hanley also operated a weekly car sales' auction from the premises] so I asked Cormac if anybody intended to move the cars before I set up. He said they'd be staying put, which was great because it meant I could fix up a three-way pole and tie it to the tow-bar on one of the cars."

It was a Bank Holiday Sunday and the broadcast was to take place the following day. Once everything was set up and the test connection made to Ballyhaunis, Gerry retired for the evening but was back in Claremorris in plenty of time the following morning for Paul's *Mid-Morning Show.* Test connections were made again and everything was as he had left it the night before. Conditions were calm so there was no danger of the mast being blown down either.

"I went into the van to listen to the show as it as being broadcast, just to make sure it was all okay," Gerry recalls. "It sounded great, the FM signal was really strong."

Gerry stretched back in his seat, understandably pleased at a job well done. He closed his eyes and was half-dozing when suddenly there was the unmistakable sound of severe static. Reilly sat bolt upright and watched in astonishment as the transmission tower drifted slowly past the window of his van, like some sort of mid-morning ghost.

"A fella had decided to move his car and was pulling the whole thing out the gate with him! I had to leap out of the van and go chasing after him!"

Michael Neary, now the station's chief technician, was only too familiar with the trials and tribulations of outdoor broadcasts. When Mayo played Tyrone in the National League in October 1989, Neary found himself on the roof of MacHale Park's old stand, waving an aerial over his head in a desperate attempt to get a signal to the mast in Kiltmagh.

"I pointed the aerial in the direction of what I thought was Kiltimagh but I later discovered it was pointing towards Nephin," he recalls. "Incredibly, the signal bounced off Nephin and hit the mast in Kiltimagh so the commentary went out loud and clear."

The Mayo senior football county final between Knockmore and Hollymount in Fr O'Hara Park in Charlestown was another first for Midwest in the autumn of '89.

"There was still a real feelgood factor around the place after the All-Ireland so Midwest decided to do a full commentary on the county final and I was drafted in again," recalls Liam Horan. "I think I may have paced myself a little better the second time around!"

Midwest was making one piece of broadcasting history after another. In November, it became the first local radio station to broadcast Mass live after St Cormac's Church in the North Mayo village of Moygownagh was chosen for Sunday Mass. Michael Neary recalls travelling down on Thursday evening to set up a transmission system that involved a telephone cable running 200 yards from a local house, through a field and into the church. He wasn't convinced it would work but was pleasantly surprised to discover the connection was perfect and returned to Granlahan a happy man. He was less pleased, however, on Sunday morning when he arrived in Moygownagh to discover his telephone link had been mysteriously severed.

"I checked everything and came to the conclusion there must be a break in the telephone cable so I started tracing it back the full 200 yards from the church to the house."

There were many scenarios Neary envisaged but the actual cause wouldn't have even crossed his mind.

"A few cattle had wandered into the field and they'd ate the cable in not one, but two, places! So Mass is at 10am and here I am at 9.35am still walking the field wondering how much more grazing the cows have done on the cable! I'm literally flicking the switch at 9.55am to go live, that's how much we lived by the seat of our pants back then."

Chris says there was a can-do spirit in Midwest in those early years that contributed enormously to the station's success.

"We inherited this unique spirit from our pirate days so we were never fazed by the prospect of trying something new. Whenever we wanted to broadcast an event there was never an attitude that it could not be done. We were unorthodox at times in the way we achieved things but, ultimately, we got it done, and a lot of the time thanks to the genius and determination of Michael Neary."

Terry Reilly says the frequent outside broadcasts were crucial in the rapid growth of Midwest, allowing the station to develop a relationship with its listeners that was absolutely unique.

"Fellas like Paul, Gerry, Chris and Michael were on the road continuously back then," he says. "They were at every dog fight going and I think a lot of those guys in Midwest never slept at all in those years! Make no mistake about it: they worked very, very hard to build that brand. Nothing came easy to them."

Midwest's historic year of outside broadcasts ended in Foxford on Christmas Eve when Sunday Mass was relayed live from St Michael's Church. It had been an eventful and exhausting 12 months but the work was only just beginning. A new decade beckoned, the last of the 20th century, and the team in Ballyhaunis was determined to take the 1990s by storm. Much had been achieved in a short time but the golden era of Midwest Radio was only just beginning.

CHAPTER EIGHTEEN

'Bringing radio to the people'

LOCAL radio was flourishing in Co Mayo by the spring of 1990 but it was a very different story in Co Sligo where attempts to establish a new station were floundering badly. Ironically, there had been fiercer competition in Sligo for the radio franchise than in many other counties and no less than four consortia made submissions to the IRTC when the oral hearing was held in July 1989. The four were North West Communications Ltd, Sligo Community Radio, Glencoe Radio and the eventual winners Rosses Radio, which had the *Sligo Champion* as its principal backer.

The Sligo franchise was unusual in that it was not confined to a single county and instead included South Donegal and North Leitrim, which together offered a potential audience of about 100,000. Initially, the vibes from the Rosses Radio consortium was very positive with chairman Niall Townsend telling the *Donegal Democrat* in September 1989 that he hoped the station would be on the air by December.

But Christmas came and went without any sign of Sligo's new station making its first broadcast. Unlike Midwest, Rosses Radio had no links to the pirate era and was instead trying to get up and running from a standing start, not an easy task at the best of times but one made all the more difficult because its potential market was already becoming very crowded. The splintered territory meant stations were encroaching from all sides with Midwest already popular in south Sligo, Shannonside being heard throughout all of Leitrim and Highland Radio about to launch in Donegal.

By the early spring of 1990, the board of Rosses Radio was having grave reservations about the whole enterprise, believing its potential advertising base would be too small to support a commercial radio station.

Matters came to a head on February 20, 1990, when an extraordinary general meeting was called and shareholders voted by a substantial majority to hand the licence back to the IRTC. In making their decision, the shareholders said they believed Rosses Radio would incur "major losses for most of its first seven years", which was the duration of the licence.

Niall Townsend, in an interview on RTÉ, claimed the franchise area was too small to be viable and shareholder funds would be "decimated" in a short period if they went ahead with the project.

"The national advertising cake we feel will not come in the quantity that it should to make up the figures we need," he explained. "The news and current affairs requirement, as laid down by the Act, are expensive and the levies and royalties are too high at present."

The decision to hand back the franchise took everyone by surprise, not least the IRTC whose spokesperson Michael O'Keeffe told the *Donegal Democrat* that Rosses Radio was the first applicant to say an area was not viable. He also promised the licence would be re-advertised and expressed confidence there would be interest in it. He was right. Paul Claffey and the board of Midwest were watching events in Sligo with a very keen eye.

"We believed Sligo would be an obvious extension for us," Paul recalls. "We were already broadcasting into south Sligo and had been doing so since the pirate days so we had a pretty good understanding of the market."

In the same way it had obtained the franchise in Mayo, Midwest set about assembling a representative consortium to pitch for the now unwanted licence in Sligo. North Connacht Farmers (NCF) agreed to come on board again while the North-Western Health Board and Federation of Churches in the Northwest also signed up along with the *Donegal Democrat* newspaper, Magees men's clothes shop and several prominent businessmen including Donegal football manager and hotelier Brian McEniff.

The business model was identical to the one that had worked so well for Midwest during the past year. Capital investment would be restricted to £100,000, with an additional £50,000 on call if required, and the new station, which was to be called Northwest Radio, would share some programming with its sister station.

But Midwest wasn't the only radio station with eye on the vacated Sligo franchise. Shannonside, which broadcast in the Midlands, and Highland Radio in Donegal joined forces to establish a consortium backed by Cable Management Ireland Ltd, a cable television firm chaired by well-known RTÉ personality Mike Murphy. They planned to call their station Innisfree Radio and believed it could generate revenues of £240,000 per annum and reach a breakeven point within two to three years.

Both consortia made their cases to the IRTC at an oral hearing in Sligo in May 1990. There was a general acknowledgement that the potential audience was limited – it was estimated at about 98,000, broken down into 56,000 in Sligo, 30,000 in Donegal and 12,000 in Leitrim. The only really large urban centre was Sligo, which meant the potential advertising base was restricted, and there was also a worry that a younger population in a student-dominated town like Sligo might be more inclined to stay faithful to RTÉ Radio 2.

The Inishfree consortium predicted it would lose £56,000 in its first year on a turnover of £240,000 but hoped to break even in year two on an increased turnover of £360,000.

The Northwest consortium was equally pragmatic in its financial projections. It also set its target for annual turnover in year one at £240,000 and predicted a breakeven scenario after two years with "moderate" surpluses recorded thereafter. The Midwest Radio chairman, Michael Hughes, was among those to address the oral hearing and succinctly explained the realities of the Northwest enterprise when responding to a question about the investors' expectations of a return on their investment.

"We have told our investors quite clearly that if they are investing to get a quick return they would be better off putting their money in the post office."

Two weeks later, the IRTC announced that the Northwest Radio consortium had been granted the franchise for Sligo, South Donegal and North Leitrim. Ever the optimist, Paul Claffey told the *Sligo Champion* the new station would be on air in time for the All-Ireland Fleadh Cheoil in Sligo, which was a mere 12 weeks away. It was wishful thinking. Northwest Radio was without staff, a headquarters and even studio equipment but at least Paul had somebody in mind for the crucial role of station manager.

Step forward one Tommy Marren.

After the excitement of Mayo's march to an All-Ireland Final, things were a little quieter in the Midwest Radio sports department for the winter months but with summer looming large again, anticipation and expectations were mounting as Mayo prepared to defend their Connacht crown against Galway.

"As a Sligo man, it took me about five years to understand this phenomena of Mayo football," Tommy Marren explains. "The passion was quite incredible and I really got an education in it through the summer of '89."

Tommy presented the three-hour sports programmes on Saturday and Sunday afternoon with match reports coming from journalists employed by the *Western People* and *Connaught Telegraph*, as well as freelance contributors. The key man in pulling the show together was Willie Ryan, son of local supermarket owner Paddy, who produced the weekend sports shows in those early days.

"Willie was very detailed and he'd have everything ready when I'd arrive," recalls Tommy. "He'd have all the scripts waiting for me on Saturday afternoon and then he'd head off to do a shift in the shop while the show was on! He used to stick around for the show on Sunday because the supermarket would be closed."

Having made his debut as a GAA commentator the previous winter, Willie was in the commentary box for Mayo's short-lived championship campaign in 1990, which ended on the day it began with defeat to Galway in the provincial semi-final. Tommy Marren, meanwhile, was headed back to his native Sligo.

"Once I was offered the position of station manager with Northwest I decided to leave AIB and return to broadcasting full-time," he says. "It wasn't a hard decision to make. Northwest was a really exciting project and I was more than happy to give it a go."

The autumn of 1990 was one of the most hectic periods in Tommy's life. As expected, the late-August deadline was not met but

Northwest was determined to take to the airwaves in plenty of time for the crucial Christmas advertising period.

While it had been agreed in advance with the IRTC that Northwest would share a significant amount of programming with Midwest, the new station had to provide its own news, current affairs and sports service, as well as other programming reflective of the geographical area it served. An office was acquired at Market Yard in Sligo town while a team of permanent staff gradually took shape, eventually numbering 13 by the time the station opened on Friday, November 2.

The launch of Northwest on 102.5FM also offered new opportunities for Midwest, which was able to expand its schedule of programmes. For example, Tommy Marren launched a morning show from 9 to 11am, which was broadcast on both stations and became as popular in Ballinrobe as in Bundoran. Similarly, some of Midwest's more established shows, such as Paul Claffey's *Mid-Morning Show* and *John Duggan At Home*, found a new audience among Northwest's listeners.

But Northwest had its share of fresh and exclusive programming too, beginning with Daire Nelson's *Rise 'n' Shine Breakfast Show* from 6.30 to 9am and including the likes of Alan Russell, Ita McMorrow and John Ryan. About two-thirds of the programmes were shared between the stations in the early days but Tommy was keen to ensure Northwest had its own identity.

"I think Northwest built its own listenership base very quickly but there was a logic to sharing a lot of content. Obviously it made sense from an economic perspective but it also worked for the listeners too because essentially the audiences of the two stations were very similar and some listeners – for example, people in west and south Sligo – were already listening to Midwest anyway."

The issue of shared programmes and the unique identity of Northwest became the subject of much debate in later years when the IRTC made the decision to withdraw the franchise but Paul Claffey says it would have been virtually impossible to get the Sligo station off the ground without the Midwest alliance.

"The shareholders in Rosses Radio had investigated the market and concluded there was no way a standalone station would work on its own," he explains. "We recognised that too and knew the dual approach was the only way to go. We had package deals for advertising on both stations and were able to do outside broadcasts across the two stations. So I could be broadcasting from North Galway one day and the next I'd be up in Donegal town. It worked for everyone; it was a marriage made in heaven."

Chris says he and Paul had a very clear vision from the outset of what they wanted to achieve with the two stations.

"Midwest had always enjoyed a strong listenership in the Sligo area from the pirate days so it wasn't as if we were entering new territory. The secret was to make the collaboration as seamless as possible while maintaining the individual identity of each station. Essentially we were taking the model that had made Midwest such a great success and sharing it with Northwest."

Terry Reilly edited a newspaper straddling the Mayo-Sligo border so he knew only too well the obvious benefits of the partnership between Midwest and Northwest.

"I'd have given advice to the Northwest board in the early days because I knew the market in south and west Sligo where the *Western People* was traditionally very strong. I think Northwest was an incredible success story. It hit the ground running in November 1990 and Tommy Marren did a fantastic job running it. He was absolutely superb because, not only was he a broadcaster, but he also had his eye on the ball from a business perspective."

The rapid success of Sligo's new station astonished even its shareholders. When the JNLR figures were published in early September 1991, Northwest Radio emerged as the country's leading local radio station with a reach of 63 per cent in its franchise area compared to RTÉ Radio 1's 51 per cent and RTÉ Radio 2's 39 per cent. Asked by the *Donegal Democrat* to reveal the secret to Northwest's success, Tommy Marren remarked:

"Programming has a large part to play in it. We've devised what we feel is a very good programme schedule – a good mix of news, sport and music.

"That's why it has been successful, plus the fact that we have put enormous emphasis on going out and meeting people, with outside broadcasts and roadshows. We're bringing radio to the people. It's what they want."

The listenership statistics certainly didn't lie. In the space of just two years, Mid and Northwest Radio (or M&NWR as they became known) had effectively wiped out RTÉ's long-held monopoly across a vast swathe of Connacht and south Donegal.

The message from the JNLR figures couldn't be clearer: local radio was here to stay.

Northwest Radio may have failed to make it onto the airwaves in time for the Sligo Fleadh but its sister station was certainly doing its bit to keep the music of our forefathers alive. Indeed, even in the pirate days, Midwest Radio was a bastion for lovers of traditional music and one man, above all others, became synonymous with the 'Fleadh sound' that emanated from the little studio in the cloakroom of Midas nightclub.

Séamus Duffy had travelled his share of highways and byways since the days when he was living on the border with Northern Ireland, writing paeans to fallen Republican volunteers. The Aghamore native met his wife-to-be Bríd at the Fleadh Cheoil in Ennis in 1956 and married the following year.

"I'd have done it a lot sooner but for the fact that we had no house!" he explains. "I was being paid £22 per month as a teacher and couldn't afford to buy a house. But, in 1957, a job became available as *príomhoide* in Ballymacward National School and, crucially, it came with a teacher's residence. I immediately applied and got the job."

Séamus spent nine years in Ballymacward, a village in south Galway about 15 miles from Ballinasloe, and loved every minute of it.

"I was involved in everything," he says, "Macra, drama society, Pioneers... I had a wonderful time there."

But home was never too far from his mind and when the position of *príomhoide* of Aghamore National School became vacant in 1966, Séamus didn't need a second invitation to apply. His return to Mayo coincided with a renewed popularity in traditional music and Séamus, through his membership of Comhaltas Ceoltóirí Éireann, was at the vanguard of the renaissance. He believes Comhaltas was as important to Irish culture in the twentieth century as the GAA was to Irish sport, and the cultural organisation's establishment in 1951 was the start of a process that marked the gradual reversal of two decades of decline for traditional music.

"In the late 1920s, small dance halls started to mushroom all over the country, sometimes only five miles apart," he explains. "Conradh na Gaeilge encouraged céilí dancing and the GAA had a rule in its constitution that permitted céilithe only as fundraisers by its various units.

"Initially, small bands or groups supplied the music in these halls but the music was Irish traditional. About this time also, Paul Whitman heralded the jazz-rage in America and the disease spread to Ireland soon after till it reached rave proportions, luring the dancing age group away from the scene they knew and marking a further decline in the sprees [country house dances], which had already waned as a result of the popularity of dancehalls.

"The 1930s was the end of an era and though the country house dances did not become totally extinct until about 1950, the traditional musician had lost a major platform on which to parade his talent."

Comhaltas gave the traditional musician a platform again and Séamus Duffy certainly used it well. Describing himself as a "run-of-the-mill" fiddle player, Séamus focused instead on the ancient art of sean-nós singing and excelled at it.

"It has always been maintained that the greatest musical instrument of all is the human voice so that singing always formed a large part of Ireland's musical tradition," he explains.

In a glorious 20-year spell, Séamus won 23 All-Ireland senior competitions and also won the Oireachtas five times as a sean-nós singer. Of the 23 All-Ireland titles, 16 were for singing and four for newly-composed songs. Indeed, when Fleadh Cheoil na hÉireann came to Swinford in 1961, Séamus' *Lament for Mick Flanagan* claimed top prize, the song having been composed only months earlier in tribute to the former Mayo GAA football star and member of the 1950-51 All-Ireland winning team who passed away in January 1961 after a long battle with cancer.

On his return to Aghamore in 1966, Séamus immersed himself in the Mayo branch of Comhaltas where he met a kindred spirit in Joe

Smyth, the *príomhoide* of nearby Kilmovee National School and a native of Straide.

"Joe and myself were bosom pals," he says. "We travelled far and wide together and we even retired from teaching at the same time – in 1993."

By the time Midwest came on the airwaves in 1985, Seamus had been secretary of Comhaltas in Mayo for six years and was looking for ways to gain greater exposure for the county's many talented traditional musicians.

"It was deemed advisable for the cause we were working for if we could get a radio show," he says. "There was no problem getting a show on Midwest. Paul and Chris were very happy to facilitate us."

Séamus was aged 56 when he broadcast his first show on February 18, 1987, but the Aghamore *priomhoide* possessed the enthusiasm and energy of the children he taught. From the outset, Séamus vowed that no half measures would be permitted in delivering a show true to the time-honoured traditions of the Irish music he loved since childhood. He also had very strong views on the kind of music he would – and, more importantly, wouldn't – be playing.

"With traditional music and song, there's no such thing as accompaniment. It should be kept to fiddle, accordions, concert flutes, tin whistles, concertinas, pipes and the harp, and what's more, singers should have no accompaniment at all. That's my take on it and that's the end of it."

And what about a rhythm section that might, perhaps, add a little beat to those other melodious instruments?

"The man is yet to be born who can get music out of a drum or a bodhran," Séamus declares emphatically. "There is no music in them, only noise!"

Duffy's weekly show became an integral part of the Midwest schedule in the pirate days, playing a crucial role in providing a platform for local musicians who would never have gained airplay on RTÉ Radio. Indeed, when Midwest applied for the franchise in the spring of 1989, programmes like Duffy's and John Duggan's were held up as examples of the cultural significance of local radio, a significance that went way beyond mere short-term entertainment.

Once the newly-licenced Midwest launched in 1989, Séamus Duffy was installed as the station's voice of traditional music but the *príomhoide* had an able accompanist in Joe Byrne, another schoolteacher and musical troubadour who happened to live just across the road from Séamus. Joe also began broadcasting his weekly show, *Ceol agus Ealaíon*, in 1989 and it perfectly complemented his neighbour's already established programme.

"Séamus, be it as a songwriter, singer, adjudicator or official, has a role akin to the elders of the Jews, the High Priests, the ones with the beards and the hats, who would be the guardians of the tradition," Joe humorously remarked in an interview in 2008.

But Joe – as we will discover later – wasn't a bad keeper of the flame either and, together, the Aghamore double act quickly established Midwest as one of the foremost promoters of Irish traditional music, ensuring a regional musical genre that might otherwise have been lost forever was captured for posterity.

Midwest wasn't just bringing radio to the people; it was bequeathing the rich cultural heritage of our forefathers to a new generation.

CHAPTER NINETEEN

Hilda and The Hay-Carrier

THE launch of Northwest Radio offered opportunities for all sorts of partnerships between the two stations. One of the earliest, and most successful, initiatives was the Radio Drama Awards, sponsored by First National Building Society and launched only weeks after Northwest took to the airwaves.

There had always been a great tradition of amateur drama in the West of Ireland and festivals in towns like Tubbercurry and Claremorris were well established by the late 1980s. Radio offered a new outlet for the members of these drama groups to parade their talents to a much bigger audience across a vast region – and they certainly embraced the chance. Entries soon flooded into the headquarters of both stations and a shortlist of 22 was selected for the competition's opening season, which culminated in a mini-Oscars' style gala awards ceremony in spring 1991.

The driving force behind the Radio Drama Awards was Foxford woman Teresa O'Malley, then a schoolteacher at St Attracta's National School in Ballaghaderreen and the host of Midwest's weekly current affairs programme, *Wednesday Report.* Like so many of the station's early presenters, Teresa was thrown in at the deep end after tentatively inquiring about doing some broadcasting work.

"I was planning to go to America for the summer of '89 but had heard through the school secretary in St Attracta's that Midwest was looking for broadcasters," she explains. "I'd never done radio before but I was always interested in broadcasting. I decided to call them up to see if they were looking for any part-time presenters. Next thing I knew I had a weekly current affairs programme."

Wednesday Report dealt with a range of topical issues, including the rod licence controversy and the TV deflector system, both hot topics in 1989. Boston-born Teresa also focused on the plight of the illegal Irish in America, interviewing a number of emigrants desperate for visas so they could continue to work in the States.

The show became very popular and Teresa quickly realised she had a flair for broadcasting; however, she continued to stick with the day job while taking on various one-off projects for Midwest, including the Radio Drama Awards.

"The Drama Awards were a big undertaking but very enjoyable," she recalls. "Everything was done in studio so the members would sit around a table and act out the various parts. We'd have to do the sound effects as they happened because we couldn't insert them like nowadays so it really was live in every sense of the word.

"But the groups were absolutely amazing. A few of them had done radio drama with RTÉ but the majority had no experience whatsoever of a recording studio. They were amateur groups but were totally professional in everything they did."

The members of the local drama companies weren't the only ones experiencing a baptism of fire. A young radio technician from Castlerea, Padraic Walsh, who was studying for a diploma in radio and studio operations at Ballyfermot Senior College in Dublin, was also drafted in to assist with the project. It was a dream come true for Padraic who had harboured ambitions of working in radio since his early teens.

"The first thing I remember asking for as a young fella was a transistor radio and when I got it I would tape songs off RTÉ Radio 2 and make up my own compilation cassettes. That was how it all started for me and then when I was in Castlerea Community School a group of us set up an in-house radio station for charity and that's when the bug really started to bite."

The Radio Drama Awards became the Castlerea student's university of broadcasting and he revelled in the responsibility placed on his young shoulders. He was also blessed to have an excellent mentor in Chris Carroll who was central to the success of the Drama Awards in its first season.

"This was the reel-to-reel era when editing was done by splicing where you had to physically cut unwanted words or sounds from the tape," explains Chris. "It was very intricate and painstaking work that required lots of patience and time!"

Teresa O'Malley says the likes of Chris and Padraic played vital roles in ensuring the success of the Radio Drama Awards over several winters. The first recipient of the First National Building Society Trophy (and a cheque for £500) was Louisburgh Drama Group with its production of Tom Murphy's play *On The Outside.* There were also prizes for Mary Mannion, Phoenix Players, Tubbercurry (Best Actress); Michael O'Malley, Louisburgh (Best Actor), Martin Boland, Kilkee Drama Group (playwright); Donegal Drama Circle (production); and Paddy Henry, Charlestown (producer). The awards were presented at a gala ceremony in the Sligo Southern Hotel attended by Mr Justice Seamus Henchy, the chairman of the IRTC, who described the Mid and Northwest Radio Drama Awards as "a model for all other radio stations in the country".

It was rich praise, indeed, especially coming from the body charged with supervising Ireland's new commercial radio industry. The awards ceremony also marked the end of a memorable period for Teresa who had spent the autumn of 1990 covering Ireland's historic presidential election in which Ballina's Mary Robinson became the country's first woman president.

"The presidential campaign of 1990 was a really big deal for Midwest because of the Mayo connection," she says. "We had Brian Lenihan, Mary Robinson and Austin Currie on *Wednesday Report* at various times throughout the campaign and I was fortunate to be in Dublin Castle for Mary Robinson's inauguration on December 3, 1990. It's a day I'll never forget and it is certainly one of the highlights of my career in broadcasting."

A few months later, Midwest was in Teresa's hometown of Foxford for the visit of President Robinson who launched the new visitor centre project at the local Woollen Mills.

"The early 1990s was a really positive time in Mayo and across the West in general," says Chris. "There was so much happening in every town and village whether it was community development groups such as the IRD in Kiltimagh and Foxford or local festivals, etc, and

Midwest was able to get involved at a grassroots level with all of these organisations. I think it was a time when the West really came alive after the recession of the 1980s."

Midwest Radio's willingness to make itself a promotional vehicle for the many new initiatives that sprang up in the early 1990s was crucial to its long-term success. Chris, Paul, Gerry and the rest of the team were determined that Midwest would be, above all, accessible to each and every local volunteer, whether they were organising a week-long international festival in Ballina or a knitting club in Ballycroy. Midwest was there to serve the people, and while it might be a commercial radio station in name, its ethos was that of a public service broadcaster with a real determination to make a difference for the community it served.

One of the early supporters of pirate radio in Mayo was Fr Brendan Hoban, a priest of the Diocese of Killala and a highly regarded columnist with the *Western People* since 1980.

In March 1989, Fr Brendan wrote about the immense potential of a legal, local radio service in Mayo.

"A whole new agenda in radio coverage is about to emerge," he wrote. "A sense of being part of the Mayo community will be reinforced. Information appropriate to our needs will be available. Debate on issues of local interest will be an accepted pattern of our own radio service… in fact, nothing will ever be quite the same again."

Religious affairs coverage was always going to be an important part of the new station's programming and Fr Brendan was an obvious choice as a broadcaster alongside Fr Colm Kilcoyne and Monica Morley of Knock Shrine. The three met in a room in Knock in the late spring of 1989 and hammered out what they hoped would be a winning formula for their new 30-minute programme.

"Topicality was a priority," recalls Fr Brendan. "No matter how worthy a subject was unless there was a topical hook to hang it on, people weren't interested. So our first programme was on the hot issue of the day: the proposal to mine for gold on Croagh Patrick."

They decided to call their show *Faith Alive.* It was a title that certainly reflected the mood of the time. Faith was very much alive in

Ireland in 1989. Only ten years earlier, an estimated 2.5 million had turned out for the visit of Pope John Paul II, including 450,000 at Knock Shrine. Mass attendance levels were still in the 90 per cent plus bracket and vocations to the priesthood, while falling, were at reasonably respectable levels.

But the 1990s was to usher in a turbulent era for the Irish Catholic Church, a period of turmoil and recrimination that continues to this day. If there was a turning point, it came on a May morning in 1992 when The *Irish Times* published the sensational revelation that the Bishop of Galway Eamonn Casey had fathered a child with an American woman Annie Murphy.

Topicality had been the touchstone in Knock three years earlier but suddenly the word took on a whole new meaning for the *Faith Alive* team.

Writing in his column in the *Western People* on May 20, 1992, Fr Brendan described the 'Bishop Casey Affair' – as it became known in Ireland – as a 'GUBU moment for the Church' (GUBU being the famous Charles J Haughey acronym from a decade earlier – Grotesque, Unbelievable, Bizarre and Unprecedented).

But there were many more GUBU moments to come for the Irish Catholic Church, and Midwest Radio's *Faith Alive* team had to negotiate them with honesty, compassion, fairness and wisdom.

"Gradually we established a formula and our reputation," says Fr Brendan. "Whatever the issue of the day was we wouldn't avoid it. We'd try to have a mix in each programme so variety became another priority. Interviews, reflective pieces, letters and comments and local interest pieces became the staple diet of our schedule. The focus was on respect for position and person but also on truth."

One of the interesting dynamics for Midwest Radio in relation to its coverage of religious affairs was its shareholder structure. The Federation of Western Churches owned a stake in the station and a similar arrangement existed in Northwest. Terry Reilly says there might have been a perception that the dual shareholding allowed the Church to influence Mid and Northwest's editorial policies but nothing could be further from the truth.

"In all of my years on the board I never recall the Church making any complaint about coverage. Fr Colm, Fr Brendan and Monica would have addressed a lot of topical and divisive issues on *Faith Alive* but the Church never tried to exert control over it.

"I think there was an unspoken understanding from the very beginning that none of the shareholders would try to unduly influence the direction the station was taking in editorial matters, and certainly not in instances where there would have been a conflict of interest. Michael Hughes, our chairman, would definitely not have tolerated interference in the editorial independence of the station."

The board's focus in the early 1990s was directed principally at governance issues and the need for financial prudence. As the station expanded, space in the rented house on Abbey Street became more and more limited but Paul, Chris and the other directors resisted the temptation to borrow heavily for a shining new headquarters.

"I know staff might have been wondering when they were going to get out of the house and into new studios but the cautious strategy we adopted was the right one," says Terry Reilly. "We didn't race ahead of ourselves and we were the better for it."

If the board of Midwest needed a salutary lesson in the dangers of running too fast too quickly, they need only look to Century FM in Dublin, launched amid much fanfare just a few weeks after the Mayo station. Century had Terry Wogan and Chris de Burgh among its investors and embarked on a £400,000 publicity campaign with the express aim of deposing RTÉ Radio, even making a £1m offer to Gay Byrne. However, the new station was plagued by signal problems – people outside Dublin could not even find it on their radios – and it collapsed into bankruptcy in November 1991 having racked up staggering losses of £7m in just over two years.

While Century FM was frittering millions of pounds, Paul Claffey was busy trying to find new angles to generate a couple of bob here and a couple of bob there.

Like the death notices, Radio Bingo was one of those unexpected success stories for which Midwest became famous. Claffey had dabbled with the idea of broadcasting bingo during the pirate era but ran up against all sorts of problems.

"I recall Paul coming to me looking to advertise some kind of radio bingo around 1988 but I couldn't agree to it because there were all kinds of regulations around advertising bingo at that time," says

Terry Reilly. "In addition, we weren't allowed to promote pirate radio stations so this would really have been a case of double jeopardy!"

Claffey put the bingo balls away but was determined to revisit the concept. In 1991, he contacted bingo and lotteries firm Playprint and asked if they could investigate the possibility of designing a book suitable for radio bingo.

"The only mistake I made was that I should have got it patented for Midwest because every station was soon at it," he recalls. "People who loved going to bingo but couldn't go for one reason or another started playing it. Before you knew it we were selling several thousand books per week."

One of the key men in popularising Midwest's Radio Bingo was the late Joe Fahey, from Brickens, Claremorris, who passed away in 2019.

"Joe was fantastic in those early days of Radio Bingo," recalls Paul. "He toured the province delivering bingo books to countless outlets and worked tremendously hard building up the brand."

The original Midwest Radio Bingo was organised as a fundraiser for the parochial hall in Ballyhaunis but other charities soon benefitted. Among them was Western Alzheimer's Association, which was established by Claremorris man John Grant in 1990 after his father-in-law was struck down with the debilitating illness. Western Alzheimer's is headquartered in Ballindine and offers respite and outreach services to people with dementia in counties Mayo, Roscommon and Galway.

John, who retired as chief executive in 2016, says the revenues generated from Radio Bingo were crucial to the charity during his period in charge.

"I couldn't emphasise strongly enough how important Midwest Radio Bingo has been to Western Alzheimers. It gave us a steady income and allowed us to provide more carers to help both the sufferer and families affected by dementia.

"Everyone at Western Alzheimers was always extremely grateful to Midwest for choosing us as the charity to benefit from Radio Bingo and I can assure you the money we got over the years made a huge difference to hundreds of families out there."

The man who makes Radio Bingo happen today is Padraic 'Stan' Moran who takes to the roads every couple of weeks to deliver bingo books to dozens of shops across the province.

"I've clocked up a fair few miles and I've got to visit places I hardly knew even existed," he says. "Delivering bingo books might sound like a mundane job but far from it. I get to travel a huge geographical area and I've met some really great people who I regard as friends as well as customers.

Radio Bingo has been running for more than a quarter of a century but it remains as popular as ever. With a daily minimum payout of €300 and a minimum jackpot payout of €3,000, it's not surprising Radio Bingo still has so many fans.

"Radio Bingo is definitely here to stay," says Stan. "As the jingle says 'The magic's in the numbers'! It's part of the social fabric of the station now and we're going to continue to promote it for another 30 years!"

Radio Bingo was one of those left-field ideas from Paul that many might have dismissed as farfetched or, at best, a short-term craze. However, it has stood the test of time and its success has even surprised the man who invented the concept.

"Radio Bingo took off like nobody's business," he says. "The charities did well out of it, we made a few bob and the listeners had – and continue to have – great fun playing it."

It's been clickety-click all round for everyone involved in Midwest's Radio Bingo.

Local radio had already put down deep roots by the start of 1992 but it was given a huge boost in January of that year when 1,600 staff at RTÉ decided to go on strike. The industrial action was sparked after two-person camera crews were introduced without agreement from SIPTU. Other prominent unions, including the NUJ, soon became involved and strike action was declared on January 21.

The dispute continued until February 17, resulting in the effective shutdown of the national broadcaster. Leading radio personalities like Gerry Ryan spent their mornings out on the Stillorgan dual carriageway holding banners instead of being in the studio entertaining their regular listeners.

The strike, of course, presented an enormous opportunity for local stations like Midwest who were able to attract a whole new tranche of listeners that, up to then, might have stayed loyal to RTÉ Radio. Suddenly, the commercial stations were able to monopolise the airwaves. The public reset the dial and many never switched back. And why would they when stations like Midwest were bringing a cast of unforgettable local characters into their homes.

Paul Claffey's *Mid-Morning Show* had many memorable contributors down through the years but few were as popular as the inimitable Mary (May) Hunt from Ballymote in Co Sligo. May was already in her late sixties when she made her debut on the airwaves and was an instant hit, striking a chord with listeners from Donegal town to Dunmore.

"Everybody could relate to May," recalls Paul. "She was like a grandmother to the listeners and people loved to hear her on the radio. She'd have cures for different ailments and would always offer good, old-fashioned commonsense advice when listeners called in with various problems."

May had been something of a local legend in Ballymote long before she became a regular contributor to Midwest's *Mid-Morning Show.* A native of Templehouse, she operated a lodging and dining house at Wolfe Tone Street and was renowned for her fine helpings of dinner for the farmers attending fairs and marts in Ballymote.

Among her former lodgers was future Taoiseach, Albert Reynolds, who came to Ballymote in the 1950s to work for CIE. Indeed, May was a staunch Fianna Fáil supporter, serving as president and secretary of the local cumann.

May was a great community woman and was always prepared to do a good turn to neighbour and stranger alike. A good-humoured lady, a consummate host and a renowned cook, May's boarding house was the sort of place where people came for a week and ended up staying for a month (or maybe even a year!).

"It was nearly like a halfway house," recalls Paul. "It was in May's nature to look after people so nobody was ever turned away from her door.

"I think one of the main reasons she was so popular with listeners was she had a bit of devilment about her and she was always up for the craic."

Another woman who had 'a bit of devilment about her' was Hilda Creaby who continued to contribute to Paul's show on a regular basis. When Seamus Moore released his *JCB Song* in 1990, Hilda persuaded Paul to play it off the airwaves and it became one of the most popular songs in the station's history. The Kiltimagh woman possessed a larger-than-life personality and a straight-talking style that made her a wonderful guest on a live radio show. When it came to Hilda, you never really knew what was going to come next.

Gerry Glennon recalls a morning in the 1990s when Hilda was particularly exercised about some members of the Irish Army, stationed at Renmore Barracks in Galway, who had been struck down with a bout of food poisoning after eating contaminated mousse. Hilda had a slight hearing difficulty and the news report about the soldiers and the mousse became slightly lost in translation.

"I've no sympathy for those soldiers," she told Paul.

"No sympathy, Hilda? Sure the poor fellas are dying with food poisoning?"

"But isn't it their own fault?"

"How is it their own fault?"

"Well doesn't it serve them right for eating mice? Sure what did they expect would happen to them if they ate a mouse?"

It was one of those rare occasions when even Paul was rendered speechless.

In 1993, RTÉ television hosted a special *Late Late Show* to coincide with the Mayo 5000 celebrations and Paul was asked to bring along some of the most popular contributors to Midwest Radio. Hilda was always going to be high on the list and the Kiltimagh housewife was thrilled at the prospect of making her debut on national television.

But the show was a bit too tedious for her liking and Paul could tell she was getting a little restless in her front-row seat. The tipping point came when Gay Byrne introduced one of Ireland's most eminent poets, Paul Durcan, who had just penned a new poem entitled *The Hay-Carrier,* inspired by his great love of Mayo where he had deep family roots.

'Have you ever saved hay in Mayo in the rain?' Durcan intoned. *'Have you ever saved hay in Mayo in the sun?'*

Now Hilda Creaby hadn't come the whole way to Dublin to listen to some fella droning on about saving hay in Mayo. She let out an impatient sigh, which was only amplified by the echo in the television studio. Durcan glanced curiously in her direction but continued undeterred, eventually reaching those defining middle lines of his poem.

My father was a hay-carrier.
My mother was a hay-carrier.
My brothers were hay-carriers
My sisters were hay-carriers.

Hilda shifted again in her seat and Paul could hear her muttering to herself.

By now, Durcan was in full hay-carrier flow…

My wife is a hay-carrier.
My son is a hay-carrier.
His sons are hay-carriers.
His daughters are hay-carriers.

Hilda could take no more. Leaning across to Claffey and fiercely grabbing his arm, the woman from Raiftéirí Country delivered a withering assessment of one of the greatest Irish poets of the twentieth-century.

"Merciful hour," she whispered loudly in Paul's ear. "Did ya ever in all your life hear such a load of oul potwallop?"

It took every ounce of Paul's willpower to hold in the laughter as Uncle Gaybo shot a disproving glance in their direction. *The Hay-Carrier* certainly wouldn't be replacing Seamus Moore's *JCB Song* as Hilda Creaby's favourite party piece.

CHAPTER TWENTY

Going to the bog in a limo

IMPROVISATION was key to a lot of the things that made Midwest Radio such a phenomenal success in the 1990s. Paul and Chris openly admit there was no elaborate masterplan or strategic vision; things sort of fell into place in a seamless way that had as much to do with chance as anything else.

The *Mid-Morning Show*, with its cast of captivating, colourful characters, embodied the freewheelin' spirit of Midwest in those early years, and some of the more riotous shenanigans on Paul's show gave rise to the nickname 'Madwest' Radio.

"We never lost our streak of madness from the pirate days," Paul remarks. "Other stations changed when they became legal but we always tried to stay true to our roots."

Gerry Glennon, who produced the *Mid-Morning Show*, knew his best-laid plans could be set aside before the final strains of Brose Walsh's *Zambesi* had even faded. All it took was one caller to send the show in a completely different direction, something that was, in fact, one of the great strengths of Paul's spontaneous style of broadcasting. The host also had the propensity to agree to things on air that would have his producer holding his head in his hands off air.

One of the great examples of Paul's off-the-cuff approach was Betty's Birthday Bash, an event that began as a simple birthday party for one of his regular callers, Betty Roache from Moneen in Castlebar, and turned into a full-blown extravaganza.

Betty, who was affectionately known as the 'Moneen Blackbird', was a returned emigrant who had left her native Castlebar as a 16-year-old in the early 1940s to serve in the Auxiliary Territorial Service, the women's branch of the British Army in World War II. Like Hilda Creaby, May Hunt and Kathleen Loftus, Betty lived life to the full and was a familiar figure around Castlebar, cycling from place to place and occasionally stopping to tend to animals in need.

One morning, while chatting to Paul, Betty let it slip that she was celebrating her birthday the following week.

"And what are the plans for the big birthday?" asked Paul.

"Well, I don't have any plans," said Betty.

"No plans? Sure you'll be having a bit of an oul party, won't you?"

"Well, I don't really have anyone to celebrate my birthday with," Betty confessed.

"Ah sure we can't have that," said Paul. "We'll organise a birthday party for you, Betty."

As soon as the *Mid-Morning Show* ended, the planning for Betty's Birthday Bash started in earnest. A venue had to be found, musicians booked, food sourced for an unknown number of guests, etc, etc.

"Half the time we didn't know what we were doing," says Paul. "We'd agree to something and then panic!"

Betty's Birthday Bash captured the imagination of listeners who were soon calling in with promises of home-baked goodies, decorations and everything else needed for a proper birthday bash. A hotel was booked in Enniscrone to facilitate listeners from both Mid and Northwest Radio and companies soon started contacting the studio in Ballyhaunis to offer all sorts of support for the novel event. In the end, more than 200 people turned out on a Wednesday morning for a live broadcast to coincide with Betty's Birthday Bash, and the celebrations continued long into the evening. What began as a spur-of-the-moment offer to organise a birthday party evolved into a massively successful event that was talked about for months afterwards.

But the level of preparation for Betty's Birthday Bash paled into insignificance compared to another *Mid-Morning Show* 'special'. This event came to define Midwest's willingness to embrace projects so mad in their conception they were either destined to be a spectacular success or a phenomenal flop. As a businessman, Paul had learned to curb his propensity for risk-taking, especially when it came to the financial affairs of Mid and Northwest Radio, but as a broadcaster he loved nothing more than living on the edge.

Death notices on the radio were one thing but when Midwest announced in the summer of 1993 that it planned to organise something called a 'Beat on the Peat', an incredulous national media reached for the smelling salts. RTÉ Radio 2 had been organising the 'Beat on the Street', which was a nationwide tour involving some of its top DJs, for several summers but the 'Beat on the Peat'... now what could that possibly be?

Well, as was often the case with Midwest, the Beat on the Peat began with a simple telephone call to the *Mid-Morning Show* on a day when Gerry Glennon was sharing duties with Paul.

"The caller said it was a terrible shame that the old ways of cutting turf with the sleán were dying out and that a day on the bog was not the same since machines came in," Gerry recalls. "Before we knew it, more and more people were calling in with their memories of the bog in the old days."

In an era when landline telephone calls were the only way of instantly contacting a radio studio, Paul and Gerry were simply astonished at the response their discussion about old days on the bog had elicited from listeners. Before the show ended, Paul casually remarked: "You know, Gerry, maybe we should organise a day where we cut turf the old-fashioned way for one last time."

That was it. The Beat on the Peat was born. But where would they find a bog easily accessible to the public? A few days later, while taking a flight from Knock Airport, Paul absentmindedly glanced to his right as the plane was taxiing along the runway. Suddenly, Jim Mitchell's old barb about the 'foggy, boggy' airport sprang to mind.

"As I looked over I could see a big freight apron and beside it was a bog," he recalls. "When I returned home a week later I went down to the area in question and sure enough there was a bank of turf. It was ideal for what we had in mind."

Knock Airport was a shareholder in Midwest Radio and Paul had an excellent relationship with Jim Ryan, the then secretary of the airport and a director on Midwest's board. He tentatively suggested to Ryan that he might organise "a bit of an event" at the airport some Sunday afternoon and broadcast it.

"What's the event," Ryan asked.

"Well, we're calling it 'A Day in the Bog'," replied Paul. "We'll have a few hundred people here and we'll cut a bit of turf in the old-style way and play a bit of music."

"That'll be no problem," said Ryan. "The freight apron will be perfect to hold the people and we can put up a gate to seal off the runway so there'll be no disruption at all."

A delighted Paul returned to Ballyhaunis to share the news with Gerry Glennon.

"Why don't you call it the Beat on the Peat," remarked Teresa O'Malley who happened to overhear the conversation between her colleagues.

"The Beat on the Peat?" echoed Paul. "Jaysus, that's mighty Teresa. I wish I had thought of that myself!"

The following morning Paul announced on his show that the Beat on the Peat would take place at Kilgarriff Bog, adjacent to Knock Airport, on the August Bank Holiday Monday. Listeners were soon calling in with suggestions of what exactly the event should entail.

"It started out with turf-cutting but then people began to recall all the things that used to happen in the bog," explains Gerry. "Things like boiling an egg in a brown paper bag, churning butter, making the tea on an open fire… People's imaginations were absolutely fired up in a way we hadn't seen before."

The only thing that wasn't fired up was the weather. The summer of 1993 was largely a washout and heavy rain had been forecast for the Bank Holiday Monday, prompting the Midwest team to make an eleventh-hour decision to postpone the event to the following Sunday. It was a fateful decision.

"All we succeeded in doing was creating greater anticipation," recalls Gerry, laughing. "There were grandfathers and grandmothers who wanted to show their grandchildren how they used to cut the turf in olden times and there were whole families talking about travelling down from Donegal for the day. It became absolutely crazy."

Apart from the nostalgic appeal of spending a day on the bog, there was a fantastic music line-up that included Brendan Shine, Kevin Prendergast, Dave Lawlor, Mick Flavin, John Hogan, Dickie Rock, Frank McCaffrey and Brose Walsh.

By Thursday afternoon, Paul and Gerry were beginning to realise they had an event like no other on their hands and they'd want to start preparing for a few thousand rather than a few hundred turf-cutters.

Noel Howley was sitting in the office of his transport company in Dublin when he received a telephone call from a rather frantic Gerry Glennon.

"Noel, we need you to pick up some crowd control barriers for us in the Phoenix Park."

"When do you need them?"

"Now!"

Lorries were not permitted to enter the Phoenix Park but Howley reckoned if there was ever a time to break protocol it was when a Mayo woman was resident in the Áras. He hopped into one of his trucks, set off for 'The Park' and had the barriers loaded into the vehicle before you could say 'Mary Robinson'. By nightfall, he was depositing his cargo at Knock Airport much to the delight of Claffey who declared that if he ever again needed a job done Noel Howley would be the first man he'd call. That was it then: Howley's fate was sealed.

The crowd control barriers were badly needed. An estimated 20,000 people turned up at Knock Airport on that Sunday afternoon, creating traffic jams that stretched to Charlestown and upsetting the travel plans of an entire plane of London-bound Ryanair passengers. It was, quite simply, sheer madness and it was the talk of the region for months afterwards.

"We never in our wildest dreams expected the sort of crowd that came out," recalls Paul. "I was in the observation lounge with Brendan Shine, Gerry [Glennon] and May Hunt. The idea was we would travel by ass and cart down to the bank of turf to do our day's work. We couldn't see out and Shine was wondering if anybody would turn up at all but when we got out there it took a full three-quarters of an hour just to get to the freight apron!"

Shine, who had been playing the accordion on the journey down, nimbly leapt from the cart onto the bank of turf, grabbed the sleán and announced they were going to work. Paul's job was to catch the turf as Brendan deftly cut it in the old-fashioned way. All was going to plan until a few wet sods went astray, soiling Claffey's pristine pink grandfather shirt. Now who would wear a pink shirt to a bog? Well, only a man who would convince 20,000 people to travel from all over the country for something as mad as a Beat on the Peat!

"It was definitely one of the more crazy days in the history of Midwest Radio," Paul recalls, chuckling. "We hadn't planned for anything close to the numbers who turned out and it did create a big disruption for Ryanair. There was absolute war. People with suitcases were hopping on their heels and Michael O'Leary ate the socks off Jim Ryan afterwards!"

But it was all for a good cause. The Western Care Association received the proceeds of the Beat on the Peat while the event itself created a feelgood factor among listeners to Mid and Northwest that resonated for months.

It was generally agreed it would be impossible to replicate the event, and Jim Ryan certainly wouldn't be in a position to re-offer Knock Airport as a venue. So it seemed the Beat on the Peat had been a once-in-a-lifetime experience until one day a caller to the *Mid-Morning Show* made a suggestion that Michael Neary might describe as zanier than zany.

"Wouldn't it be something else," said the caller, "if you could bring the Beat on the Peat to New York?"

A day on the bog in New York... on the Richter scale of zaniness that really was at a whole other level, but the caller had come to the right place. By the following afternoon, Paul was wandering around the studio in Abbey Street humming a tune that sounded remarkably like an old classic from Hilda Creaby's favourite crooner.

Start spreading the news,
I'm leaving today.
I want to be a part of it...

It was as good as a done deal: the Beat on the Peat was bound for the city that never sleeps.

Noel Howley was sitting at his desk in Dublin on a spring afternoon in 1994 when the telephone rang. It was Paul.

"I've a bit of an oul idea, Noel."

"Go on," Howley said warily.

Paul gave a rough outline of what he had in mind. When he'd finished, Noel glanced over at his desk calendar. No, it wasn't April Fools' Day so either Claffey was deadly serious, stark raving mad or a combination of the two.

"Just so I'm clear, Paul, let's go back over this again," he started. "You want me to transport a bog to New York."

"Well not a whole bog, a bit of a bog."

"A bit of a bog?"

"Well enough so people can come and cut turf."

"How many people do you have mind?"

"Sure I don't know, as many as will turn up."

Paul admits the idea was so outlandish he didn't even put it to the board of Midwest and instead decided to fund it himself along with Pat Jennings of the TF Royal Theatre in Castlebar and US-based promoter Gertie Byrne, who was a native of Cong.

Teresa O'Malley was among those roped into the project in its infancy. Twenty-five years later, she is still not entirely sure why Paul decided to get her involved; perhaps it was her American links or maybe it was because she coined the phrase 'Beat on the Peat' or it could even be because she was about to begin a career break from her teaching job. Whatever the reason, she found herself travelling to Co Kildare in mid-June to view a section of bog which Bord na Móna believed was suitable for a transatlantic voyage.

"I have to admit I thought the whole idea was pretty far out there," says Teresa with heroic understatement. "But, probably because of my teaching background, I've always encouraged creativity, never quelling dreams. I am of the opinion if someone has an idea then let's see if it's possible. If no-one ever did it there's a reason to try it but there's also a reason why no-one ever did it!"

Teresa met Noel Howley in Co Kildare and together they inspected the bank of bog earmarked for 'emigration' to America. Yonkers Racetrack had been identified as the location for the event and the engineer from Bord na Móna handling the project, a man by the name of Tom McDonnell, seemed surprisingly optimistic about its prospects for success. Howley later drove back to Dublin wondering what in the name of God he was getting himself involved in.

"I thought it was crazy but the more I got involved the more I got consumed by it," he recalls. "Suddenly, I was no longer just providing the transport, I was part of the whole damn thing!"

Once it became apparent an Irish bog could, indeed, be transported to New York, the project took on a life of its own. A mere bog would be of limited appeal so Paul went in search of suitable artifacts to create the ultimate authentic Irish experience of a bygone era.

"The Sligo Agricultural Museum in Riverstown had recently opened so we emptied it out," he recalls. "We got ploughs, creels, wheelbarrows, churns and spinning wheels. Whatever we could lay our hands on we took it."

Someone suggested it might be a good idea to get an old Irish cottage. Paul went and found one. Somebody else thought a thresher and vintage tractor would be essential so Sligo farmer Davy Carroll, who often brought his thresher to heritage days across the province, was persuaded to travel. Having initially agreed to ship a single container to New York containing a bank of bog measuring 60ft x 6ft x 6ft, Noel Howley suddenly found himself transporting an entire Irish village across the Atlantic. By the time Claffey was finished, there were eight 40ft containers ready for shipping, although not immediately because the bog needed to be sterilised and placed into quarantine for several weeks.

"Customs officers had to be convinced the shipment was germ and pesticide free and that the turf was dead matter," recalls Paul. "Now that took some convincing! Bord na Móna extracted it in sections and each section was covered in polythene and packed carefully into a sealed container which held the moisture of the bog."

Every single article in the eight containers had to be itemised in order to meet the strict Customs' regulations. Paul wanted to have a poteen-making demonstration but knew there was no way he'd get approval to bring illicit alcohol into the US.

"We put the poteen in bottles marked 'Knock Holy Water'," he recalls with a laugh. "And, trust me, there was a lot of Knock Holy Water!"

Apart from eight 40ft containers packed to the brim with artifacts, turf and poteen, Claffey also intended to send a veritable army of Irish musicians, singers and set dancers, including Seamus Moore, The

Conquerors, Philomena Begley, Declan Nerney and Brendan Shine. Flights, accommodation, meals and a myriad other expenses needed to be paid for this elaborate festival, which was scheduled to run over two days, September 17 and 18, with no guarantee of success because there were no advance ticket sales.

"It went out of control on me," Claffey confesses. "I knew by the end of August I could lose a fortune on it but I'd gone so far in I couldn't get out. I just had to plough on and hope for the best."

Noel Howley also felt he was sinking into a bottomless bog hole and was determined that once the eight containers reached Yonkers Racetrack he'd wash his hands of the whole crazy caper. It had been agreed the containers would be loaded onto a convoy of Howley's lorries and driven through several towns in Mayo to create a bit of hype ahead of the event. After that, it was on to Dublin Port for an epic voyage to the US.

"There's no direct shipping from Dublin to the US so I had to put these eight containers onto a feeder vessel into Europe," Noel explains. "They were fed into Le Harve in France and then they had to be transshipped from Le Harve out to the ocean-going vessel that took them to New Jersey. The whole journey was two weeks or more and I needed to be in New York to meet them off the boat."

Howley enlisted the assistance of two trusty, able-bodied lieutenants – Paddy Moran and Kevin Ruane – to travel to the US with him to oversee the successful delivery of the precious cargo. Teresa O'Malley, who was handling the paperwork for the eight containers, travelled with the three amigos. After a largely uneventful flight, all four landed in New York to be confronted with the first of many crises.

"Customs officials wouldn't clear the eight containers," explains Teresa. "It was only four or five days before the event and I was very concerned they would start taking the artifacts apart because if they did the whole thing was gone."

Noel, who had considerable experience in handling shipments and had worked on the Northern Ireland border in the past, could completely understand the US Customs officials' position.

"You can imagine how amazed these officials in New Jersey are to discover they have a shipment on their hands that contains a cottage, a tractor, a thresher, ploughs and a bank of bloody turf! Would you blame them for being suspicious?"

Early on Wednesday morning, Noel called out to the docks to plead his case. A swarthy Italian-American Customs official greeted him with a look of bemusement, bordering on outright disbelief.

"What are you guys doing?" the man asked. "Are you transferring Ireland over here?"

It was a difficult one to explain but Noel, who had long years of negotiating the strange Byzantine world of Mayo GAA politics, was able to make a strong case for the immediate release of the eight containers.

"Let me think about it overnight," said the Italian-American. "But I'm kinda worried about where we're going with this. What else is going turn up here tomorrow?"

"There'll be nothing more," assured Howley. "Everything is here now."

"I see you've got 20 bottles of holy water on this list here. That's an awful lot of holy water. You guys havin' some kinda Mass there?"

"Oh there'll be a lot of prayers said alright," replied an earnest-looking Howley.

By Wednesday evening the eight containers were still under lock and key and Paddy Moran was starting to feel for his old friend.

"Noel was up the walls and understandably so," he recalls. "It was a huge responsibility for him because if these containers didn't get clearance then everything was cancelled."

By now, a team of 72 volunteers, who had each fundraised £2,000 for Western Care Association, were preparing to leave Ireland while the musicians, singers and dancers were also embarking on the transatlantic trip.

Pat Jennings, who had just arrived in New York, was making countless calls to Paul in Ballyhaunis and both men were seriously wondering if they should call off the entire event. Howley, meanwhile, returned to New Jersey early on Thursday morning to plead his case again. If the containers weren't released by that evening they were in big trouble because it would take at least one full day to set everything up.

Having received a half-hearted commitment from the head Customs official that the paperwork would be completed later that day, Howley, Moran and Ruane set off for Yonkers to prepare for the containers' arrival. But evening came without any sign of the all-important cargo. Disconsolate, the three men climbed into their hired car and set off back to New York City, resigned to the reality they were now in a hopeless race against time.

As the men's car cruised along the freeway into the setting sun of a typically autumnal American evening, Howley suddenly slammed on the brakes and veered towards the nearest exit.

"That's them, that's them," he shouted excitedly.

"That's what?" asked a startled Moran.

"The containers, the feckin' containers, I just saw them going up the freeway!"

He was right. As soon as the car got onto the opposite section of the freeway they could see far off in the distance the unmistakable green-and-red liveried containers of Howley Transport from the proud village of Curradrish in Foxford in Co Mayo.

Noel Howley breathed a deep sigh of relief. His job was almost done… or so he thought. But there was something Paul Claffey had omitted to tell him…

By Thursday night, the eight containers were delivered to Yonkers Racetrack and Noel Howley was preparing to embark on a well-deserved night on the town with his two able-bodied lieutenants.

"Who's in charge of the site," he asked Pat Jennings.

"Well, Paul says you are," replied Jennings.

"*I'm* in charge?" Howley exclaimed. "Jaysus, I'll put that feckin' Claffey into the thresher when he gets here!"

There was nothing to be done about it. The next day, Noel, Paddy and Kevin returned to the racetrack and started to supervise the unloading of the eight containers. They immediately hit a snag.

"The guys doing the unloading were the most unionised group of workers I ever met in my life," recalls Noel. "They wouldn't let us touch the forklifts and they were working at a snail's pace."

Finally, Noel lost patience and had a chat with the on-site union boss.

"Time is against us here," he explained. "We have to get everything done by tomorrow morning."

"You don't understand," said the union man. "We gotta take our breaks. We gotta go for *coffee*."

After the workers clocked off at 5pm, Noel jumped into a forklift and started unloading the containers at a furious pace. Tom McDonnell was on hand to reassemble the bog and by nightfall, the site was almost ready. The finishing touches were being completed on Saturday morning when Noel decided to put on a little performance for the intransigent union man.

"Listen lads," he said to Moran and Ruane. "When he walks over here I am going to give ye an almighty bollicking and let's see what happens."

As soon as the union man was within earshot Howley launched into a tirade.

"Ye fellas are good for nothing," he started, waving his fist in the air. "Ye're getting well looked after and ye're not earning ye're keep. I don't know why I brought ye over here at all."

He then stormed off. A few seconds later, the union man shot over to Moran and Ruane.

"That's awful abuse," he said. "I wouldn't take that kinda abuse from any man. You guys shouldn't have to put up with that."

"Well, he is the boss," Moran replied, shuffling sheepishly from one foot to another before lifting a bag of turf onto his broad shoulders.

"That don't matter!" exclaimed the union man. "Do you guys have trade unions in Ireland?"

"Here, Paddy," shouted Ruane, who was now standing on the bed of the turf trailer. "Can you carry a second bag? I'll put it across the back of your neck!"

"Oh, I will indeed," said Moran. "That's a good idea, Kevin!"

The union man turned on his heel and walked away in disgust.

Paul Claffey arrived at the racetrack for the first time that morning ('When all the work was done," jokes Howley) but his mood was dampened by a heavy rain-shower on the way from the city.

"I was sitting at the front of the bus carrying the 70 volunteers and all I could see was the rain beating down and the window wipers going over and back. I thought I was fecked. This was going to be an almighty disaster and I'd be the laughing stock of the country for trying it."

When he got to the racetrack, Paul took a quick look around and then disappeared into a container with Brendan Shine and a few of the other musicians.

"I'm a bag of nerves," he told Shine.

"Here," said Brendan. "Have an oul drop of holy water!"

The poteen nearly killed Paul.

"I'd never drank it in my life," he says. "I didn't realise how potent it was."

By the time he stuck his head out the door, Paul was convinced the poteen was playing tricks with his brain because the crowds were literally streaming into the racetrack, stretching as far as the eye could see.

"It was phenomenal," recalls Noel. "They came from all over America. I met people there from the Mid-West, from Kansas. The crowds were just unbelievable and everybody was so thrilled to be there."

Paddy Moran thought the event would be just 'a bit of craic' but he quickly realised it had a much deeper and poignant significance for the emigrants who flooded Yonkers Racetrack on that unforgettable weekend in September 1994.

"To be in the company of men and women who left Ireland back in the 1920s and 1930s and to see what this meant to them was really something else. The thresher was a big attraction because the hum of it reminded them of childhood.

"I always remember an old man in a white hat getting up on the bank of turf. He picked up the sleán and cut four or five sods and the tears were streaming down his face."

Davy Carroll's tractor was a source of much fascination.

"You know that tractor left here about 50 years ago," a man told Noel after inspecting it for what seemed like eternity.

"What do you mean?" asked Noel.

"That tractor was made here in America and must have been shipped to Ireland back in the 1940s," said the man. "And now it's back here in New York working a thresher. Well, holy cow!"

Howley, who was trying to wind down after a pressure-cooker week, was totally unprepared for the outpouring of raw emotion on that first day. It made those chaotic weeks of preparation seem very worthwhile after all.

One moment, in particular, stands out for him. When Brendan Shine started to cut the turf to mark the beginning of the two-day festival, a man at the front of the crowd burst into tears. Noel later spoke to him.

"I left Ireland 47 years ago and I never got to go back, not even for my parents' funerals," the man explained as the tears flowed freely. "The last thing I did for my mother and father before I left was I cut the turf for them. I never thought I'd see the old bog again."

Amid the tears there was humour too. A local television company had heard about the event and sent a camera crew to Yonkers.

"Are you one of the organisers?" the presenter Colleen asked Noel.

"Apparently I am!" replied Howley.

"Can you explain to me about this crop you call the peat?"

"Colleen, just a second," said Noel. "I have the very man for you."

Step forward able-bodied lieutenant Paddy Moran.

"Now Paddy Moran," said Colleen, standing on the bank of turf as the cameras rolled. "Do you ever foresee the day when the peat bogs of Ireland will become extinct?"

"Ah Jaysus not at all," replied Moran cheerfully. "Sure don't they grow 17 inches every year!"

Paddy thought no more of the interview until later that night when the volunteers were gathered in Rory Dolan's pub in Yonkers. NBC's *Evening News* was blaring from a television in the corner and nobody was taking a bit of notice until the newsreader unexpectedly announced: *And now we're going over to Yonkers Racetrack for a special report from the Irish festival that's been taking place there today.*

Suddenly, there was the bould Paddy Moran, filling the television screen and telling the American nation that the bogs of Ireland grow by 17 inches every year.

"Christ, he'll ruin Bord na Móna," was all a stunned Tom McDonnell could muster.

The weekend spawned a thousand and one hilarious anecdotes. There was the story of Davy Carroll driving down the freeway in his tractor looking for some diesel or the volunteer who was so suspicious of the newfangled keycards in the hotel he left his boot in the jamb of the door all weekend for fear he'd be locked out of his room. But Paddy Moran's tale of his 'journey to the bog' on the first day of the festival takes some beating.

"Noel, Kevin and myself were staying in the Pennsylvania Hotel and we got a limo out to Yonkers on that Saturday morning," he recalls. "Now I went to the bog in Bonniconlon on a bike, on the ass and cart and I even walked there, but I never thought I'd see the day when I'd be going to the bog in a limo!"

It was that sort of weekend.

CHAPTER TWENTY-ONE

Red-eye radio

WHEN applying for the radio franchise, Midwest told the IRTC it would strive to connect Mayo's vast and scattered Diaspora to their native county. It was a pledge that could easily have become a hostage to fortune because global communications technology was still fairly primitive at the end of the 1980s. This was the pre-Internet, pre-digital days when the broadcasting of a programme from one country to another required days, if not weeks, of planning and, even then, there was no guarantee of success.

But Paul and Chris were determined to reach out to Mayo emigrants across the globe, those who had departed in previous decades as well as the current generation who were also leaving in their droves. In January 1989, the *Western People* revealed that 8,250 people had emigrated from Connacht during the previous year, including 2,225 from Mayo.

A survey by the priests of the Diocese of Killala, which covered North Mayo and West Sligo, painted a similarly grim picture. Some 600 people emigrated from the diocese in 1988 alone, and it was no longer just young, single men and women who were leaving either. The Killala survey revealed that 117 young couples, 60 with children, had left the diocese while another 138 fathers of families also emigrated in search of employment.

History was repeating itself all over again. The 1980s were darkly reminiscent of the 1950s; the only differences being the emigrants were better educated now and were taking airplanes instead of ships. Knock Airport, built as a beacon for western development, soon became the departure point for a whole generation of talented young men and women from western counties who flocked to London and Manchester and Birmingham in search of job opportunities that couldn't be found at home.

Notwithstanding the limitations of the technology, the newly launched Midwest Radio was determined to give Mayo's emigrants a stake in their native county's latest media company by involving them in as many broadcasts as possible.

The pre-All-Ireland final broadcast from Midas was a case in point when connections were made with Mayo emigrants in various parts of the world. In fact, Paul loved nothing better than to spontaneously link up with Mayo people living in far-off places, much to the consternation of Michael Neary who would have to make the connections, often during outside broadcasts.

"Paul might be doing an OB in Belmullet when suddenly he'd meet Mary from Doohoma in the crowd. He'd know straight away there was a bit of craic in Mary so he'd zone in on her. Now Mary might mention that she had a sister Ann in New York who hadn't been home since 1944 so Paul would get it into his head that it would be great radio to put the two sisters on the 'phone talking to each other.

"So the next thing I'd have to patch in the lady from New York who'd probably be slightly deaf and get her to talk to the lady from Doohoma who'd probably be stone deaf and the whole feckin' thing would be live on the radio.

"Yet for some bizarre reason it nearly always worked!"

In the early days, Tommy Murphy was charged with producing a series of shows from Irish centres across Britain, as well as linking up with broadcasters in Australia and New Zealand. Midwest had a relationship from its pirate days with veteran Australian broadcaster Sid O'Malley, while the New Zealand connection was developed through Oliver Lee, a native of Kilkerrin in Co Galway, who was broadcasting a programme called *Ireland Calling* on a local station in Auckland.

There was no better man than Tommy Murphy to develop Midwest's ties with Mayo's Diaspora. The Ballina man's experimental link-up with WGFM in Quincy, Illinois, on St Patrick's Day in 1988 evolved into an unexpected transatlantic broadcasting partnership.

Tommy had joked with Leo Henning about visiting the town of St Patrick in Missouri for St Patrick's Day but got the shock of his life some months later when Henning contacted him to say that the trip was very much on for 1989. Henning explained that WGFM would pay for Tommy's flights and put him up in one of the media company's hotels in Quincy. The former pirate would also get to broadcast a special St Patrick's Day show on WGFM. Meanwhile, Henning planned to fly to Ireland to take in the St Patrick's Day parade in Ballina and to broadcast a special show from the town.

Tommy couldn't believe his luck. What had began as a quirky quest for a postcard from the town of St Patrick was now turning into an all-expenses paid trip to the American Midwest. But it got even better. When Tommy arrived in St Patrick he discovered the townspeople had decided to elect him honorary mayor! In Quincy, he was also asked to give lectures at the local Rotary Club and Notre Dame College, with the topics ranging from the state of Irish radio to the Single European Act of 1992. Such was the Ballina man's celebrity status he was even given a two-hour trip through the city in a police cruiser!

Tommy Murphy's series of broadcasts from Britain was just one aspect of Midwest's strategy to connect with its Diaspora. The Mayo Association in Dublin was also keen to work with the new station. The All-Ireland semi-final and final of 1989 was the first example of that partnership but there were others too.

"I recall Henry McGlade broadcasting a programme from the Shelbourne Hotel in the early days of Midwest that was attended by about 200 Mayo people living in Dublin," says Noel Howley. "We had a really healthy debate about the future of Mayo and we also linked in with London and New York."

At the start of the 1990s, Midwest began broadcasting one-hour specials from the annual Mayo People of the Year dinner in Dublin, organised by the Mayo Association, while representatives of the station also attended Mayo gatherings in the UK and US. Indeed, it was in New York in 1990 that Paul first encountered the renowned Irish-American broadcaster, Adrian Flannelly, whose show on WNWK Radio was one of the most widely listened to among Irish emigrants in the city.

"We should do something together," Claffey suggested. "Some kind of joint broadcast for the Irish in America."

The two men agreed to discuss a few ideas the next time Flannelly was in Ireland but the partnership between WNWK and Midwest Radio was forged a lot earlier than expected. The plight of the undocumented Irish in America was the common cause that brought together two radio stations on opposite sides of the Atlantic.

Adrian Flannelly was aged just 17 when he left his native Attymass in 1959 to start a new life in New York. He had strong ties to the city. His uncles Paul and William O'Dwyer, from Bohola, were among the best-known Irish-Americans in New York with William having served as mayor in the 1940s.

Flannelly, whose parents Padraic and Linda were both schoolteachers, had a keen interest in music and played the piano and piano-accordion with various Irish-American bands. In 1970, Adrian commenced hosting a radio talk show on WNWK FM with the intention of highlighting issues of concern to the Irish-American community as well as providing a platform for Irish culture and heritage. The show, entitled *Top of the Morning*, proved a phenomenal success and the Attymass man was soon regarded as one of the leading Irish-American voices in New York.

Flannelly was possessed of the same campaigning zeal as his uncle, the renowned human rights lawyer Paul O'Dwyer, and he became an ardent supporter of the undocumented Irish in America, who numbered some 100,000 by the end of the 1980s. Having been fortunate enough to emigrate to the States at a time when visas and opportunities for citizenship were readily available, Flannelly had great sympathy for this new generation of exiles who were being forced to live under the constant threat of arrest and deportation.

In 1987, Boston-born Congressman Brian Donnelly introduced a visa programme aimed at emigrants from countries like Ireland, which had been disproportionately impacted by changes to US immigration laws in 1965. Some 1.5 million people from 36 countries applied for the so-called Donnelly Visas in 1987, but with just 10,000 available, there were inevitably a lot of disappointed applicants.

Donnelly made no effort to disguise his Irish-American bias by insisting that over 40 per cent of the visas be awarded to emigrants from the land of his forefathers. In fact, over the next three years, some 20,000 Donnelly Visas went to Irish applicants, but as many as one in four were unused in 1990, the recipients still undecided on whether or not to emigrate to the US.

A second visa programme, initiated by another US Congressman, Bruce Morrison, was announced in 1991 and the response from Ireland was extraordinary. An estimated 250,000 people applied for the 16,000 visas that were available in the first year of the scheme, and a huge number of the applicants came from the catchment area of Mid and Northwest Radio.

Earlier in 1991, Paul and Adrian Flannelly had started a simultaneous broadcast each Friday morning via a satellite link and the subject of Morrison Visas was inevitably one of the main talking points. Just as people in Ireland were preparing to submit their applications, an industrial dispute erupted at An Post, prompting fears the applications would not make it to the States on time. Mid and Northwest Radio, in association with Adrian Flannelly, took it upon themselves to collect some 10,000 applications from the West of Ireland and fly them over to the United States.

"I remember travelling with Michael Neary to Shannon Airport with four sacks of applications," recalls Gerry Glennon. "They were put on the plane for New York and Adrian Flannelly picked them up on the other side."

In fact, Flannelly was collecting Morrison Visa applications from all over Ireland and transporting them directly to the US visa lottery office in Merrifield, Virginia. Paul and Henry McGlade travelled to America to assist the Attymass man with the sorting process and were later joined by the then Minister of State Máire Geoghegan Quinn and her husband John. In total, some 240,000 visa applications from Irish people – some living illegally in America but most still in Ireland – were submitted via Adrian Flannelly's office in New York, a mammoth administrative exercise that took a huge effort on Flannelly's part. The Attymass man subsequently received Mayo Person of the Year in 1992 in recognition of his work on the Morrison Visa programme, as well as his long years of promoting Mayo and Ireland on his weekly radio show.

One of the highlights of the transatlantic partnership between the two radio stations came on St Patrick's Day in 1992 when Paul, Henry McGlade, Michael Commins and Knock man John Kelly travelled to the US for a special two-hour show, which was broadcast simultaneously on Mid and Northwest Radio and WNWK FM. En route from Shannon Airport, they met actor Kevin Kennedy, who was then playing the character of Curly Watts in the hugely popular ITV soap opera *Coronation Street.* Kevin and his father Fred were also travelling over to New York for the St Patrick's Day festivities and the actor was among a veritable who's who of prominent guests for Adrian Flannery's 10-hour marathon show on March 17. Others included writer Maeve Binchy, Congressman Bruce Morrison, Mayor of New York David Dinkins, former mayor Ed Koch, Paul Hill of the Guildford Four and Hill's then partner Courtney Kennedy, daughter of the late US Senator Bobby Kennedy.

Midwest were to broadcast a two-hour live segment from 11am to 1pm Irish time, which meant Paul and the crew would need to be up at 6am on St Patrick's Day. Now this was not an easy task amid the temptations of New York's legendary nightlife scene. Paul went out for dinner and drinks the night before and was preparing to return to his hotel at a respectable hour when one of the New Yorkers in the group suggested he should reconsider his plans.

"I can't," said Paul. "I'm on the radio at 6am in the morning!"

"Why don't you do a red eye?"

"A red eye? What in God's name is that?"

"Just stay out all night and go straight to the studio in the morning."

By now, Paul was in a New York frame of mind and foolishly agreed to the idea. He turned up the next morning at the WNWK FM's plush studio on Madison Avenue, overlooking Fifth Avenue, feeling utterly exhausted and more than a little nervous about what awaited him. He had reason to be. The impending arrival of the mayor meant the building was crawling with security men who were noisily walking in and out of the studio while the live broadcast was taking place.

The mayor was scheduled to arrive for the last half hour of the show but there was still no sign of him at 7.30am, prompting Paul and Adrian to extend their interview with Kevin Kennedy. Meanwhile, the bould John Kelly who had been part of Claffey's 'red eye' brigade – was desperate to play a request for his wife Nuala and the family back home in Knock. Conscious that time was running out, John was signalling furiously to catch Paul's attention just as excitement mounted down the corridor as even more security men and officials hurried in and out of the building. At 7.50am, the door burst open and Mayor Dinkins swept in with an entourage so big it would have filled the nearby Bloomingdales let alone a small radio studio. It took some time for the Mayor to be seated comfortably, which meant the clock was now ticking towards 7.55am and John Kelly was becoming very concerned. He'd waited all morning to play his request and was damned if he was going to be denied now, especially after staying up all night. Meanwhile, a weary Paul Claffey was trying to muster one last bit of vigour to get him over the line in this never-to-be-repeated experiment in the art of 'red-eye' broadcasting.

"And now," said Claffey, "We're delighted and honoured to be joined by the Mayor of New York, Mr David Dinkins. Mayor Dinkins, what does St Patrick's Day mean to you?"

"Well," said the Mayor, settling in for what he clearly thought would be a lengthy interview, "I've been going to St Patrick's Day parades since I was a boy and..."

Suddenly, the Mayor felt two hands on his shoulders and when he turned around he came face-to-face with a man who had more important things on his mind than the speechifying of New York's first citizen.

"Excuse me, mayor, excuse me," said John Kelly as he leaned in towards the microphone. "Hello Nuala, it's John! I'm here in New York with Claffey and Curly Watts from *Coronation Street.* Nuala, I'm going to sing a bit of an oul song now for the mayor...

There's three pubs in Bohola, as everybody knows
McDonagh's, Clarkes and Roches, where the craic like honey flows"

Meanwhile, back in Ballyhaunis, the clock had struck 1pm, prompting a very wide-eyed Gerry Glennon to fade out this anarchic broadcast from New York just as Mayor Dinkins gesticulated frantically to Claffey that he still had lots of important things to say to the people of the West of Ireland if only that crazy man would stop singing about these three goddamn pubs in some place called Bohola.

This was red-eye radio at its very best.

In the days before the Internet, a shortwave radio was required to connect with foreign radio stations and, even then, the reception could be undependable. But for radio enthusiasts like Michael Commins, there was a thrill to be had from stumbling across stations in far-flung places like Cuba and Ecuador. It always amazed Commins that so many so-called Third World countries boasted shortwave stations but Ireland, despite its huge history of emigration, had none. Éamon de Valera had made efforts in the mid-1940s to put Radio Athlone on the shortwave frequency but the project was quickly abandoned when the First Interparty Government came to power in 1948.

"The absence of Ireland from the shortwave bands over the years was a complete mystery to me," Commins explained in an interview in the *Western People* in 1998. "Almost every other country had an external service. Yet here was Ireland, with one of the biggest Diasporas of all, and no government, with the exception of the de Valera government in the 1940s, had the vision or foresight to proceed with such a vital service.

"The Irish view was silenced by nobody but ourselves. It was a great shame and showed how little the Irish governments down through the years cared about the many thousands and thousands of Irish people in all parts of the world who would have loved to hear some music, history, news and culture from the homeland."

After receiving an old shortwave radio from Padraig Gilmore in Claremorris around 1994, Michael started chronicling in his 'Radio Focus' column in the *Connaught Telegraph* the various international stations he was picking up each night. There was Voice of America (VOA), Radio Moscow, HCJN in Ecuador, Radio Havana in Cuba, Radio Prague, Radio Korea, Radio Deutsche Welle in Germany and countless others. Michael quickly realised there were many other shortwave radio enthusiasts across the West of Ireland and decided to organise a seminar in Castlebar in the summer of 1995.

The principal purpose of the seminar was to canvass politicians of all persuasions to support the establishment of a State-funded shortwave radio station in the West of Ireland but Michael pulled off a real coup when he persuaded Simon Spanswick of the BBC World Service to deliver the keynote lecture.

The well-attended seminar set in train a series of events that culminated in Mid and Northwest Radio broadcasting on shortwave to a worldwide audience on St Patrick's Day 1996. It was the first time an Irish radio station had attempted anything like this and it was a complicated affair with Midwest having to 'hire' six hours of broadcasting time from the BBC World Service at a cost of £2,400.

"Paul and Chris were very supportive of the project and Midwest deserves a lot of credit for doing it at the time," Michael Commins remarks. "There was a lot involved because we had to be vetted in advance in case we might broadcast Republican propaganda."

Michael was the producer of the marathon broadcast, which involved programmes in seven languages – English, Irish, German, French, Spanish, Italian and Swahili, the last provided by Denis Mulkeen from Knock, a medical student at University College Galway who had spent time in Kenya the previous summer.

"It was the first time that an Irish station broadcast in seven languages," explains Michael. "The venture was an overwhelming success with reception reports pouring in from many parts of the world. We received messages from the US and Canada, Lima in Peru, Sweden, Switzerland, France, Spain, Portugal, United Arab Emirates, Australia, New Zealand, Malaysia, Nigeria, Italy, Canary Islands, many parts of Ireland and Britain, Austria and a huge response from Germany. In fact, one of our final calls came from the small island of St Helena in the South Atlantic Ocean!"

The programme included messages to missionaries and aid workers in Africa as well as St Patrick's Day greetings from Archbishop of Tuam Michael Neary and Church of Ireland Bishop John Neill, as well many other pre-recorded messages from well-known Mayo people.

One of the key men behind the broadcast was Michael's old friend from Atlantic Radio, Gerry Delaney, who was also a shortwave radio enthusiast. Later in 1996, the two men established West Coast Radio, a shortwave radio service that broadcast for 15 months before eventually going off the air on January 31, 1998.

"We got a huge response and built up a great circle of friends around the world," says Michael. "But it was a costly business as we had to hire time from Radio Deutsche Welle in Germany and we kept it on the air with support from South Mayo LEADER and by running concerts and dances."

Ultimately, State support was not forthcoming for a shortwave radio station and the rapid growth of the Internet at the turn of the millennium changed the course of broadcasting history forever. But the broadcasts of the 1990s – be they through shortwave radio or via link ups with stations in New York and London – were really important in creating an awareness among the Irish Diaspora of Mid and Northwest Radio and connecting emigrants to home in an era when the world was not the global village it is today.

John Duggan, who shared broadcasting duties with Paul and Adrian Flannelly each Friday morning, often recalled the tale of the Mayo man who listened to the Angelus on Midwest Radio while stuck in a line of traffic crossing Brooklyn Bridge on his way to work at 7am. Or the elderly emigrant, terminally ill in a hospital in New York, who persuaded his niece to tape the Midwest/WNWK show each Friday so he could listen to it again and again for the rest of the week.

"It's the nearest I'll ever get to being back on the old sod," he poignantly remarked in a letter to Adrian Flannelly.

The man passed away a few weeks later.

CHAPTER TWENTY-TWO

'No good-looking woman ever touched sugar'

IN the early summer of 1995, the young Fianna Fáil TD for Galway West Éamon Ó Cuív contacted Midwest Radio to seek the station's assistance in promoting an upcoming fundraising dance in Peacocke's in Maam Cross.

"It's to raise money for a lady out in the Maam Valley who had a bad house fire a few months ago and lost nearly everything," Ó Cuív explained to Paul. "Would you mind having her on your show to talk about the fire? It would create a bit of publicity for the dance."

"Is she a good talker?" asked Claffey.

"A talker?" exclaimed the TD. "Oh, she can talk alright! Her name is Bina McLoughlin. She's a sheep farmer and a great old character."

The following day, Paul put a call through to Bina who was living in temporary accommodation a short distance from her old home at Coilleach Mór, near Leenane. The county council and Western Health Board had concluded that the fire-ravaged house was beyond repair and suggested she should be housed elsewhere but Bina was having none of it. A shepherdess doesn't desert her flock, she said. And so, the people of Leenane, Maam Cross and the wider North Connemara area rallied to Bina's cause, thereby instigating a chain of events that would turn their neighbour into one of the best-known personalities in the West of Ireland. From the moment Paul heard Bina's distinctive, mellifluous Connemara accent – with its lyrical blend of Irish and English diction – he knew Midwest had unwittingly discovered a broadcasting gem.

"Once she uttered her first few sentences I knew I was talking to an absolutely wonderful character oozing with stories and songs and humour and wisdom from an era that was quickly passing us by," he recalls. "Bina had many abilities but it was her ability to be so natural over the airwaves that impressed me most. She just had a seamless ability to be herself whenever she was on the radio – and that is a real skill."

In the true style of the quintessential seanchaí, Bina recalled the fateful afternoon several months earlier when an unexpected fall of snow prompted her to put extra turf onto the open hearth in her living room. Retiring to the back room of her little cottage, she emerged a short time later to find the living room ablaze and immediately rushed to her neighbour's to seek help.

"Did you not think of 'phoning for help?" asked Paul.

"The phone was in the other room and if I went into it I was gone myself," said Bina. "But I knew what to do because I'd got a warning a week before that."

"A warning?" asked Paul.

"Yes, a warning."

"What kind of a warning."

"I heard a step coming in the door."

"A step coming in the door?" repeated the intrigued Calffey.

"Yes, I was preparing for dinner, peeling turnips and carrots for a bit of stew," explained Bina. "I always keep the outside hall door open and the inside one locked so when I heard the step coming in the door I shouted out to the person that I'd be out to them in a minute. As I was going to open the inside door, the step turned out and I heard the outside door bang. I ran out and there was not a human being to be seen. There was just the dogs and myself."

Bina said she took the "step turning out the door" to be an omen.

"I said to myself 'Now that's a sign for me. Whatever is coming I'll have to turn out myself.' As soon as I came down and saw the fire I knew that step was for me and I turned out and went down to my neighbour's. I wouldn't be on this 'phone talking to you today were it not for that step turning out the door."

It was an eerie tale that captivated listeners to Midwest and Northwest, but Bina had more, much more. She said the fire destroyed everything in her house except the religious paraphernalia that were so important to her.

"Not one of the Blessed pictures were burned," she proclaimed. "I have a beautiful Celtic Cross and the fire burned all around it but the cross is fine. It never touched the holy water or my prayer books or beads either."

Listeners may or may not have believed everything Bina was saying but she possessed an earthy authenticity that made her stories as compelling as the ones heard at firesides across rural Ireland in an age long before television and even radio. In many ways, Bina was bringing the old seanchaí tradition to a modern audience, using everything she had learned in her near seven decades living in a remote corner of North Connemara to enthrall and entertain listeners to Midwest and Northwest Radio.

The interview went on much longer than planned and when it finally concluded, Claffey went straight to an overdue ad break and stuck his head out the studio door to chat to his producer Gerry Glennon.

"Boy, that was some interview," said Gerry. "The 'phones are hopping here and it's the same over in Northwest."

"Keep that woman's number Gerry," replied Paul. "We're going to have to get her on again."

Aged 65, Bina McLoughlin had just got her big break in broadcasting. This masterful seanchaí would soon have a large regional radio audience gathered around her fireside… and the Queen of Connemara was not a woman to waste an opportunity to entertain.

"God might have done [the fire] for some good purpose… I hope so," she remarked before saying goodbye to Paul that first morning.

Bina, who placed so much faith in premonitions and portents, soon came to regard the fire as one of the greatest blessings in her life because without it she'd never have come into contact with Midwest Radio. For her, God had indeed moved in mysterious ways.

Long before she took to the airwaves, Bina McLoughlin was a renowned character in her native North Connemara and was a familiar – and colourful sight – at local festivals, patterns and pilgrimages for almost half a century.

"Thank God I am a real Connemara woman and proud of it," she once said, and it was true. Bina, with her colourful scarves and homemade shawls, was the classic Connemara woman of olden times, but there was also an exotic quality to her appearance that added to the intrigue. Her abundance of long black hair was usually ringleted and she tended to wear multiple necklaces and a collection of sparkling rings on her fingers.

"A lot say there is a bit of the tinker in me," she told the *Connacht Tribune* in an interview in 1991, although her roots were very much in the Maam Valley where her father and mother were both born and raised.

Sabina McLoughlin was born in her father's old home at Glenagimla on November 2, 1928, the third child in a family of six borne to Anne Seoighe and Peter McLoughlin. She would subsequently claim to have inherited mystical powers from her mother – a 'seer' who had the gift of prophecy – and, certainly, in later life, the shepherdess came to be regarded as a fortune-teller of some renown. The Joyces, according to Bina, were also the good-looking side of the gene pool – the *Seoighe Deasa* – and she was always quick to inform interviewers that her mother's family was not to be confused with the Seoighe Móra, hated landlords in the area.

Bina was raised in an Irish-speaking community that surrendered little to the march of modernity. Long into the twentieth century, the hill farmers of the Maam Valley continued to live contentedly in their little thatched cottages, eschewing many of the modern conveniences that had by then become commonplace in the towns and larger villages.

A child of sharp intellect, Bina immersed herself in a world where pre-Christian beliefs carried as much currency as the strong Catholic faith that was the cornerstone of her adult life. Whenever she took a visitor on a tour of her farm at Coilleach Mór, she could point to pagan marriage rocks and fairy trees just as easily as she could wax lyrical about her beloved Máméan where St Patrick was said to have rested on his journey through Ireland.

"Everything I have, it has been passed down from my people," Bina once remarked, and she certainly stayed true to the principles and traditions that defined her childhood. She was adept at spinning and carding and even made her own distinctive green dye from various sources, including the moss of the countless stone walls – many of them relics of Famine times – that created a mosaic pattern in the hilly landscape of Coilleach Mór.

"Green was always a tradition in our family," she once explained. "We go for the dye from thorn trees and ferns and moss.

"When the Fenians were hiding in Dáchruach, they used the green dye from the moss for their clothes and were able to stay out at night; and if they had to hide during the day they were able to hide against the stone walls and not be seen. When the English found out about this, they took all the cards [carding machines] off them. But one night one of my people had a dream and angels told her she could card with her hands. I can do that myself."

Like so many of her generation, Bina left school in her early teens and while several of her siblings took the emigrant boat to England, she was destined to remain in Coilleach Mór, where the McLoughlins had taken up residence in the early 1930s. Peter McLoughlin was a road contractor for Galway Co Council so someone was needed to help out at home. Traditionally, a son inherited the family farm but Bina had proven herself incredibly adept at handling animals.

"I have the gift for the animals," she once said. "They noticed it at home. They could not make a sheep eat or come beside them but when I called it the sheep came to me."

It was true. Anyone who ever visited Bina's farm would marvel at her peerless skills at taming the most recalcitrant animal. It was as if four-legged creatures became spellbound in the beguiling presence of this enigmatic woman who spoke to them in her native Gaeilge, the only language to cross her lips long into childhood.

As far back as the 1960s, Bina was a popular and exotic figure at the many traditional fairs and markets that took place in North Connemara, often selling homemade scarves, shawls and other items of clothing. She invariably caught the eye in her idiosyncratic garb and tourists were drawn to this cheerful, charismatic lady who regularly sang and danced at local festivals. Her many party pieces included

Sweet Leenane By The Sea, *Sweet Ashleigh Falls* and, of course, *The Queen of Connemara*, the song for which she became renowned. At the opening of the Rock Bar in Leenane in 1969, the popular Louisburgh entertainer Basil Morahan (better known as 'Dan the Street Singer') crowned Bina 'The Queen of Connemara', a title she retained with immense pride for the rest of her days.

When Richard Harris, John Hurt and Brenda Fricker sprinkled a little Hollywood sparkle on Leenane during the filming of John B Keane's classic play *The Field* in the autumn of 1989, Bina was among a large number of locals selected as extras. In her case, no period costume was required: Bina McLoughlin could easily have walked straight out of a John B Keane drama.

She continued to entertain at festivals and dances throughout North Connemara and was always one of the star attractions at the famous Bogman's Ball in Peacocke's in Maam Cross.

But the 1980s were a tough decade, too, for the unmarried Bina. The death of her brother Tom, who had been her sole companion since the passing of their parents, struck her particularly hard and that 1991 interview in the *Connacht Tribune* painted a poignant portrait of an aging woman who forlornly acknowledged she would be the last in a long line of McLoughlins and Joyces to farm those timeless Maamturk Mountains. She was still walking a quarter of a mile a day to draw water from the well and her only concessions to modern living were a bright red radio of 1960s' vintage and a cooking ring hooked up to a Calor Kosangas cylinder. On winter's nights she often entertained herself by playing the melodeon and singing for the mélange of dogs, cats, hens, ducks and sheep who had the run of her little cottage.

In many ways, Bina McLoughlin epitomised the sort of person Paul Claffey had in mind a few years earlier when he told the radio licensing hearing in the Ardilaun that he wanted Midwest to be a companion for the thousands of elderly people living on their own along the western seaboard. Bina was a gregarious person, blessed with wonderful neighbours who regularly visited her, but she was also a living embodiment of a rapidly disappearing Ireland, and was part of a generation who felt they had been left behind in a changing country.

In many ways, it was Bina's determination to stay absolutely true to the old traditions that made her such a hit with Midwest's listeners.

Here was this fascinating shepherdess, living high in the hills of North Connemara, possessed of a lifetime's knowledge of history, heritage, piseogs, myths and legends, the sort of hand-me-down pagan folklore and superstition that were once the accepted wisdom of rural Ireland. Bina and Midwest were a marriage made in heaven, something Paul recognised not long into that first interview in 1995.

A new radio star was about to be born.

Bina McLoughlin's regular conversations with Paul on the *Mid-Morning Show* from 1995 onwards quickly became the stuff of legend. Blessed with a singular turn of phrase that made her a truly one-off character, Bina was tailor-made for the off-the-cuff broadcasting style for which Midwest became synonymous; and she never disappointed, always delivering memorable, quotable pearls of wisdom that live on to this day. On one occasion, Bina revealed to Paul she didn't drink, smoke or take sugar.

"Why don't you take sugar?" asked Paul.

"Sugar? No good-looking woman ever touched sugar," Bina fired back.

One of her earliest campaigns on Midwest was to obtain a government grant or headage payment for donkeys. She'd just rescued four donkeys from the roadside and was convinced they were being neglected because there were no grants attached to them.

"But why would you get a grant for an ass?" asked Paul.

"Well, why would you get a grant for a goat or a sheep or a horse?" Bina countered.

"I suppose."

"Everyone else is getting a grant except the poor oul ass. He shouldn't be left out. Wasn't he the Lord's earliest friend?"

"Well he was," agreed Paul. "So how are you going to get this grant for the ass?"

"Well, if ye did a bit of battling down there."

Paul and the staff in Midwest started "a bit of battling", launching a petition that attracted plenty of signatures before dispatching it to the then Minister for Agriculture Ivan Yates who promptly ignored it. Bina, a dyed-in-the-wool Fianna Fáil supporter, wasn't a bit surprised and took immense pleasure in regaling Midwest's listeners with the unfortunate tale of Dillon's Hens, so-called because they were the brainchild of then Fine Gael Minister for Agriculture James Dillon in the early 1950s.

Dillon and his government were convinced they could revive Ireland's moribund rural economy by creating a poultry industry that would 'smother' post-war Britain with a never-ending supply of eggs, the British agriculture industry having fallen into decline during World War II. Department officials kick-started their ambitious project by offering grants for henhouses and distributing thousands of foul – at five shillings a clutch, according to Bina – to farm families in North Connemara. But there was a fatal flaw in the scheme, a gleeful Bina recalled.

"The cock wouldn't crow and the hen wouldn't hatch," she explained amidst much laughter. "And a Dillon's Hen would ate ya. She'd pick the eyes out of you!"

"Are there any Dillon's Hens left in Connemara today?" asked Paul.

"Not a one," came the emphatic response. "They're gone off to their eternal rewards!"

Listeners regularly called the station to seek Bina's opinion on a diverse range of topics from cures for arthritis to what should be done with a hen that crowed, and she always had her own inimitable solutions. Her remedy for arthritis was simple – 'If you sit down to it, it'll kill you' – while the crowing hen was also given short shrift.

"It's a sign of the law," she said.

"A sign of the law? What do you mean by that?" asked Paul.

"Having a hen that crows means you'll be caught up in the law, in the courts."

"So what would you do with a hen that crows?"

"Oh I'd get rid of her," she said emphatically. And, no doubt, if it were a Dillon's Hen she'd be getting rid of her doubly quick.

All of the talk of hens reminded Bina she needed a peacock for her lonely peahen.

"Sure I'll get you a peacock," said Paul. "Is there any listener out there who has a peacock for Bina?"

Within minutes, a farmer from Frenchpark had rung in to say he could supply a peacock if someone from Midwest called over to collect it. Never one to miss an opportunity for some good radio, Paul announced that the peacock would be delivered to Bina the next day live on Midwest with listeners receiving regular updates of the peacock's epic voyage from Frenchpark to North Connemara.

Early the following morning, before the peacock had even crowed, Michael Neary was bound for Frenchpark in Midwest's satellite cruiser. He met the farmer and the peacock, the latter looking decidedly nonplussed about its impending celebrity status. Soon the peacock was safely corralled into a box and placed in the back of the cruiser with an ample supply of grain and water to keep him nourished (and amused) on the long journey to Leenane.

Neary made a pit stop in Ballyhaunis to collect Gerry Glennon who was to undertake an outside broadcast from Bina's house to mark the historic arrival of a peacock that was fast-becoming the most famous bird in Ireland.

"When we arrived at Bina's we were greeted by hundreds of people who had turned out to see this peacock," recalls Gerry. "Pearse Doherty from the Sawdoctors was there and people had come from all over the place. It was mad."

The Queen of Connemara was, of course, in her element and afforded Gerry and Michael the sort of welcome that befits royalty, inviting them into her little cottage where she had prepared a special concoction to mark the momentous occasion.

"To this day I don't know what she served us," recalls Gerry laughing. "It was something out of a green bottle but we have no clue what we drank to celebrate the arrival of the peacock but all I know is I never drank anything like it before or since!"

It was Gerry's first visit to Bina's home and he was amazed at what he saw.

"There was a sheep thrown over an armchair and I'd be lying if I said he had his legs crossed but he was the most relaxed-looking sheep I'd ever seen in my life! He was just lying back, taking it all in and not a bother on him."

The peacock was of a different disposition, however. He had commenced his day in the glorious anonymity of a quiet farmyard amid the lush, peaceful plains of Co Roscommon but now, after several hours of a bumpy journey in a cramped box, the poor bird was discovering that its surroundings had greatly changed indeed. He had unexpectedly landed in the wilds of the rugged, windswept Maamturk Valley with its patchwork quilt of stonewalls, untamed terrain and bracing Atlantic air.

To make matters worse, upon emerging from captivity, the peacock was greeted by a theatrically-attired new owner, melodeon in hand, who was belting out a few verses of *The Queen of Connemara,* accompanied by Pearse Doherty on guitar while a few hundred Midwest Radio fans provided backing vocals, some standing on walls and cars as they craned their necks to catch a glimpse of the latest addition to Bina's famous farmyard. After briefly surveying this madcap scene, the peacock did the only thing a sane, self-respecting peacock could do in such circumstances: he headed for the hills.

"The minute he got out of the box the tail went up and he took off like the clappers," recalls Gerry Glennon amid fits of laughter. "He must have been stir crazy within in that box. Anyway, he took off for the mountains never to be seen again!"

Bina had lost her longed-for peacock but the whole saga made for some mighty, unforgettable radio. There was no doubt about it: the Queen of Connemara had become the undisputed Queen of the Airwaves.

CHAPTER TWENTY-THREE

The '90s Generation

THE Mayo broadcasting franchise came up for renewal in the spring of 1996. Paul, Chris and the other members of the Midwest board were fairly confident the licence would be retained but weren't taking anything for granted. There was always the possibility, however remote, that some powerful, deep-pocketed player might elbow into the competition process and pluck the franchise from under the nose of the incumbent.

Indeed, the fear was that Midwest could become a victim of its own success. Whereas several other local stations sustained heavy losses throughout the 1990s, Midwest demonstrated at any early stage that Mayo, for all its economic disadvantages, could sustain a financially viable broadcasting service, something many people in 'Radio Land' believed was impossible back in 1989. The shareholders did not have to invest a single pound in additional capital once the station was up and running and by the mid-1990s, modest profits were being posted as the rising national economic tide lifted the Midwest boat.

Midwest had stuck to the terms of its contract with the IRTC throughout the seven years and there had been a good relationship with the governing body, which was particularly evident each spring when representatives of the IRTC came west for the annual Mid and Northwest Drama Awards. There were occasional tensions, as there were between the IRTC and every other radio station in Ireland, but Midwest had unquestionably delivered on the commitments outlined at the oral hearing in the Ardilaun seven years earlier. Chris Carroll was charged with a lot of the supervisory work required under the terms of the IRTC's original contract.

"One of the conditions of the local radio licence was that everything we broadcast must be kept for 90 days in case the IRTC wanted to check anything. Today, with digital technology being what it is, that sounds like a relatively straightforward task but, in 1989, it presented all sorts of headaches because cassette tapes only lasted for 90 minutes at most.

"We actually used three-hour video tapes that we'd run at a slow speed, which gave us nine hours of recording from one tape. There had to be a live radio recording too so the IRTC knew if we went off air for any reason and how long we were off air, which meant we were using three video tapes per 24-hour period. We also had to make sure one tape started before the other stopped so there was a lot of administrative work that wouldn't have existed in the pirate days. But we did it because that was what was required under the terms of the licence and we were determined to have a good relationship with the IRTC. It was part of the contract we signed up to."

Midwest's weekly schedule had evolved in the seven years it had been on the air. The day now began with Paula Walsh's *Breakfast Show* from 7 to 8.30am. Castlerea native Paula first worked at Midwest in the pirate era when she was studying at Dublin City University. In those days, the teenage Paula was charged with compiling the news in the 'rip and read' tradition so beloved of low-budget pirate stations.

"Basically, rip and read involved taking stories from newspapers or essentially copying it from RTÉ Radio," explains Tommy Marren. "Every pirate station did it because there weren't the resources to have reporters on the ground. But all that changed when the stations were legalised and targets were set whereby 20 per cent of a station's content had to be current affairs."

When Paula became host of the *Breakfast Show* in 1992 she the first female presenter of a core weekday programme on Midwest, the main shows from Monday to Friday having all been presented by men up to then. Indeed, the pirate stations of the 1980s were largely male-dominated environments as were many regional newspaper newsrooms. However, by the mid-1990s, women's voices were being heard more frequently on local radio while young females were also playing a much more influential role behind the scenes. For example, a young woman from Bangor Erris, Maria Mullarkey, was producer of one of the most popular programmes in local radio, Tommy

Marren's *Connacht Gold Show*, from 9am to 11am, after joining Midwest's newsroom in the mid-1990s. The gradual evolution of the *Connacht Gold Show* was an early example of Midwest's willingness to regularly reinvent itself and go where the listeners wanted to go.

"The programme in its present form is a far cry from its inception," explains Tommy. "In those early days, the emphasis was on music and light entertainment but as time went on the programme took on more serious issues and gradually became the main chat/current affairs programme on the schedule."

The appointment of a full-time producer was key to the shift in emphasis. In those early years, people like Grainne O'Brien, Deirdre Lyttle, Margaret Carr-Flynn, Michael Herity, Fionnuala Clarence and Maria Mullarkey worked behind the scenes to develop the content, giving the *Tommy Marren Show* the broad appeal for which it is now synonymous.

"The programme has tried to cover every aspect of interest to the region, whether it is the lady from Kilkenny who says she saw the Virgin Mary or the only man in Ireland who can play the button accordion behind his back," explained Tommy in an interview in 1997. "We have always tried to provide variety. The success of the programme is attributed to the listeners and to the hard-working team who are the key to making it happen."

One of the interviews that really established the *Tommy Marren Show* came in 1995 when the renowned US-born healing priest Fr Peter Mary Rookey visited Ireland.

"We interviewed Fr Rookey and he recited his healing prayer, which left a really lasting impression on people," recalls Tommy. "For a full three weeks afterwards, An Post had to send our post in by the sack-load as listeners across the West and Northwest were desperate for a copy of the prayer. Today, we'd just post it online but in those days it was a case of sending the prayers out via stamped, addressed envelopes."

While programmes like the *Breakfast Show* and the *Tommy Marren Show* were reinvented over the course of the seven years, much of the core programming on Midwest remained true to the station's pirate roots. Indeed, the four original presenters – Paul Claffey, Chris Carroll, Gerry Glennon and John Duggan – presented programmes from

Monday to Friday that together made up the bulk of Midwest's daily schedule. Claffey's *Mid-Morning Show* continued to run from 11am to 1pm while *The Gerry Glennon Show* took to the airwaves from 2 to 4pm, followed by Chris Carroll's Goldmine between 4pm and 5pm and *John Duggan At Home* from 6.30 to 9pm.

"Paul and myself were adamant that any changes to the schedule would be introduced incrementally," explains Chris. "There was no point in change for the sake of change but we weren't going to stand still either so we always tried to strike a balance between keeping the things that worked and having the courage to make a change when it was necessary."

Whereas other stations relied on playlists, Midwest's presenters were granted autonomy to select their own music.

"My attitude has always been that if somebody like Michael Commins doesn't know his audience than he shouldn't be on the radio," explains Paul. "We have had presenters down the years that just didn't gel with the listeners so when that happened we just changed things around and tried something different until we found a formula that worked."

In fact, the key to Midwest's success was the sheer lack of a formula. Paul and Chris started their journey without any preconceived notions about where they wanted to go and ten years later the two founders were still as keen as ever to listen to the listeners and put their trust in the presenters.

"I have always believed that if a presenter is to enjoy presenting a programme you have to allow them some ownership on its content," says Chris. "Giving presenters the choice of music they play, whilst staying within the parameters of the genre the programme requires, is key. If the presenter enjoys the style of programme they are presenting then more often than not the listeners will too."

Midwest – with its daily diet of Country music and death notices – might have been portrayed in the national press as the epitome of staid, conservative, rural Ireland but the station was actually a lot more open-minded and creative than many of its counterparts, and nowhere was its enterprising spirit more in evidence than in the promotion of young broadcasters.

In the first decade of the legalised Midwest Radio, the cramped terraced house on Abbey Street became a 'university of life' for a whole generation of young broadcasters and sound engineers who were thrilled to be given a much-needed career break at their local radio station.

They were Midwest's '90s generation.

There is no better agent for change than the enthusiasm and fearlessness of youth and there were lots of young people – several fresh out of college – who were making notable impacts on Midwest's programming in the 1990s, providing valuable assistance behind the scenes while also delivering content that appealed directly to a younger audience. In fact, Midwest even had its own staff member in charge of Youth Affairs, Sinéad Freyne, and the station launched an Inter-Schools Debating competition in 1996 as part of its focus on providing content for a younger audience.

Sinéad was able to call on the expert assistance of Hilary Lally, a prominent member of Ballina Soroptimists, and Michael Neary, who continued to serve as Midwest's chief technician. In its first year, the competition, which had a prize-fund of £460, attracted teams from 16 second-level schools across the Mayo/Galway region with St Mary's Secondary School from Ballina defeating Presentation College, Tuam in the final. Northwest Radio was included in the initiative in 1997 and the number of participating schools increased accordingly to 26.

Mid and Northwest's Radio Drama Awards were also going from strength to strength and the workload had become so intense that Midwest had its own Head of Drama, Geraldine Lavin, who, in 1996, was handling the highest number of entries in the competition's six-year history. Indeed, such was the volume of applicants, the airtime had to be extended by two weeks and, even then, not every amateur drama group could be accommodated.

The annual awards ceremony continued to be held at the Great Southern Hotel in Sligo, and now included a special category for 'Dramaí as Gaeilge' while prizes were also handed out to the winners of Mid and Northwest's poetry and short story competitions, underlining the stations' wholehearted commitment to promoting arts and literature throughout the West.

Another of Midwest's '90s generation, Padraic Walsh, remained a key member of the drama awards team, but was also bringing his mastery of production and engineering to bear on the recording of advertisements, winning national awards for the quality of his work. Apart from utilising his technical skills, the young Castlerea man was also scripting and voicing advertisements, thereby relieving Chris Carroll, who was now the station manager, of a large body of time-consuming work.

"The recording of ads changed a lot throughout the 1990s," explains Chris. "We went from the pirate days where we were recording ads on cassettes to a system of carts [technically known as 'NAB cartridges'] where one ad kick-started the next, which meant we didn't have to switch tapes between ads.

"I later came across a digital programme called FastEddy that allowed us to mix multiple tracks with the voiceover.

"Once digital arrived, the recording of ads became so much easier and less time consuming and there was an awful lot more we could do for our advertising clients too. Digital was a game-changer from an advertising perspective, no question about it."

Patrina McDonnell and Ronan Courell were members of Midwest's '90s generation too. The move into broadcasting was certainly not part of Patrina's career plan and she only joined Midwest for a couple of weeks in the summer of 1995, having just completed a degree in Economics and Mathematics.

"I got chatting to Chris Carroll in Julian's of Midfield one night after a disco and he told me Midwest were looking for telephonists and asked if I'd be interested. I had just finished college in Galway and said I'd try it out. Little did I think it would end up as a career, but it did and I have no regrets."

Ronan Courell, on the other hand, had caught the broadcasting bug during his schooldays in Castlebar when IRM was operating from its little studio at the end of St Martin's Terrace in Moneen.

"A friend of mine, Frankie McDonald, was involved as a DJ and I'd call in to see how the ads were made," Ronan recalled in an interview in 2009. "That's when I got interested. From there, it was the love of music that got me involved. I'd do a bit of research and inserts for Frankie on what was happening on the band scene locally. Things went from there and I decided that was what I wanted to do when I finished school."

Ronan undertook a sound engineering course in Ballyfermot Senior College in Dublin and was soon working each summer at Midwest, the station his father Tom had done so much to establish. Indeed, Tom Courell's untimely death in 1995 after a brave battle with illness was a cause of immense sadness in Midwest where he was held in the highest esteem.

"The best compliment I can pay to Tom Courell is that I don't think we'd have got the licence in 1989 without his input," says Paul. "He was the kind of man who just had an amazing ability to bring everyone together and to somehow find a solution to every situation, irrespective of what the problem was. He was always calm and composed and saw things from all sides of the divide."

Chris hadn't known Tom prior to the licence application but he quickly came to regard the genial Ballina native as a real mentor.

"Tom was a very kind gentleman to work with. He had time for everyone and brought a wealth of knowledge and experience that proved invaluable to Midwest throughout the application for the licence and then as a director of the board and a contributor to various programmes in those early years."

A year later, the *Connaught Telegraph* and Midwest Radio lost another stalwart when the inimitable PJ Hennelly passed away.

"Those who knew PJ will immediately recall his buoyant personality, wit and foresight in all aspects of his life," remarks Paul. "Rather than seeing local radio as a threat to his beloved *Telegraph* he saw it as a media outlet that could work in harmony with the print media. How right he was.

"PJ's philosophy was always based on the glass half full and his business ethics and personal demeanour made him a highly popular man in all aspects of his life."

The loss of valuable supporters like Tom and PJ was a stark reminder to Paul, Chris and the rest of the board that time moves on inexorably. The only way for Midwest to remain relevant was to keep reinventing itself, which involved delivering a schedule of programmes that resonated across the generations.

Paul had made no secret in 1989 of Midwest's desire to focus the bulk of its programming on older listeners but by the time the second seven-year franchise came up for grabs, the station was repeatedly delivering JNLR figures that demonstrated its appeal across all age categories.

Midwest had various programmes targeted at teenagers, including the weekly *TeenTalk* hosted by Siobhán Carroll-Webb, but the cornerstone of its youth offering was undoubtedly Brendan Redmond's *Hot Hits Hour*, hosted each weekday from 9 to 10pm. Indeed, the show became iconic for the '90s generation and was a rare example of local radio taking on RTÉ 2FM at its own game – and beating it.

"The *Hot Hits Hour* still holds great memories for me," says Brendan, who relocated to Thailand in the mid-2000s. "It really was extremely busy and the requests came flying in every night. I know that for thousands of youngsters it was the release valve from study and homework. When the clock struck nine, the switchboard would light up and we'd be inundated with requests."

Brendan was one of the busiest nightclub DJs in Mayo in the 1990s so he knew exactly the kind of music his audience wanted to hear and never failed to deliver, focusing primarily on the chart hits of the day whether it was *Lemon Tree* from Fool's Garden, Peter André's *Mysterious Girl*, Del Rio's *Macarena* or the latest smash hit from Boyzone or the Spice Girls.

"It really was all about the music," he explains. "I always made sure it was fast-moving and we got through as many requests as possible but at the end of the day it was about playing the chart hits the young listeners wanted to hear. It was their dedicated hour on Midwest and they really responded to it and made it their own. It is always great to hear people who are now in their mid-30s or older say they remember that hour better than anything they learned it the classroom back in the '90s!"

Another key to Midwest's youth appeal was its weekend sports coverage, which set a standard that was the envy of other local stations. From the outset, Midwest had operated an open-door policy as regards novice broadcasters, providing invaluable experience while also entrusting youngsters with a level of responsibility that was character-forming as well as career-defining. Nowhere was this more evident than in the burgeoning sports department where Liam Horan was managing a team of young freelance reporters, the majority of whom had yet to complete their Junior Certificates but were already well on their way to possessing degrees in broadcasting.

Mike Finnerty was just 16 when Liam Horan convinced him to take charge of Midwest's coverage of the Connacht Colleges Senior 'A' Football Final. The teenager had been assisting his fellow Ballinrobe man in the station's sports department during the preceding two years but picking up a microphone and doing a live commentary was a daunting task for grown men let along a callow youth.

"I was racked with nerves as I held the microphone that first day," Mike recalls. "There was no trial run, no practice matches recorded; it was live and raw.

"The details are a blur now but I remember coming across the cassette tape of that first commentary a few years back and cringing at the sound of it. My mouth was dry, my voice had barely broken, and I was as nervous as a bag of cats. But I got through it!"

Horan and the *Tuam Herald's* Jim Carney had taken over the running of the weekend sports shows when Tommy Marren was appointed station manager at Northwest. The *Western People* journalist presented the Saturday show while Carney, who had worked for RTÉ, took charge of the Sunday programme.

"It was very much a case of learning on the job," recalls Liam. "I was learning as much as the young team I had around me. There was a real sense of mission among the team; a sense that local radio was becoming established and we were part of something that hadn't been done before."

Still in his mid-twenties, Horan believed in giving youth its fling and quickly assembled a team of teenagers that may have been short on experience but were fired with an infectious enthusiasm and a desire to establish Midwest as the leading local sports broadcaster in the country.

"I was 14 when I first started working in the sports department at the weekends," says Mike Finnerty. "It was mostly making and taking calls to and from club PROs seeking results. Looking back, they were some of the best days of my life."

One of the initiatives introduced by Liam and Jim was the Sunday evening sports results' programme from 6 to 7pm, which proved a massive hit with listeners. Horan's army of school-going reporters compiled most of the material for that groundbreaking show, teenagers like Finnerty, Jonathan Mullin, Majella Loftus, James O'Connell, Danny Carey, Kevin Murphy and Peter O'Malley.

"The young guys ran that show," says Liam. "They built up contacts in every club and sports organisation in the county, which gave us a really complete set of reports and results at the end of each weekend. The guys were also their own engineers because this was in the reel-to-reel era when you had to be technically proficient to produce the kind of show we wanted to deliver.

"Des Cahill's Sunday sports show on RTÉ was the barometer we'd measure ourselves against. We'd listen to what they did and learn from it. Jim Carney was very good in that regard because he had the experience from RTÉ and was a great colleague and mentor, as well as being fantastic fun. In fact, it's the fun as much as the work I remember. The younger guys wouldn't have been at all reverential towards me and would have been fairly adept at winding me up!"

Horan had no qualms at all about entrusting the live commentary of an underage schools' match to someone who was actually younger than the players themselves.

"Mike was precocious, he was the most natural broadcaster I ever encountered. He was doing the results' sequence at 14 in one take. I remember in the winter of 1993, Castlebar Mitchels were playing Clann na nGael from Roscommon in the final of the Connacht senior club championship and we had nobody to cover it so I went over to MacHale Park. Mike presented a 15-minute programme ahead of the game. He was 15 but he sounded older and carried it off effortlessly."

Even at 14, Finnerty wasn't the youngest in Liam Horan's broadcasting academy.

"I think Danny Carey was about 12 when he started with us," says Liam, chuckling. "There's not an employment law in the country that would sustain that one! But his family was very supportive and, most importantly, he was eager to learn and able to do the work. The fact there were no mobile 'phones or Internet meant there was always plenty to be done too so the help was needed. In fact, I remember doing sports bulletins from my house in Ballinrobe and Johnny Mullin and Majella Loftus would have helped out."

It's a measure of the calibre of the youngsters involved that they have all gone on to forge successful careers in broadcasting, print journalism, digital media and communications.

"You sometimes get periods in your working life that are really satisfying and those years in Midwest from 1992 to 1995 were a great time for me," remarks Horan. "All of the teenagers who worked with me in those years have gone on to become adult friends and it is great to see the success they have enjoyed."

The Horan School of Broadcasting closed its doors in the spring of 1995 when Liam was appointed Gaelic Games correspondent at the *Irish Independent,* a prestigious role in Irish sports journalism that necessitated the Ballinrobe man's relocation to Dublin. However, the foundations had been well laid and Midwest's sports department was in safe hands. Mike Finnerty had just turned 18, Jonathan Mullin was 17 while Danny Carey was all of 14; these grizzled veterans of broadcasting were ready to help steer the station's sports coverage through the second half of the 1990s.

The only question was whether Mayo GAA would offer them much to get excited about, the hype and optimism of 1989 having dissipated amidst a disastrous series of on and off-field events. It began with a managerial heave in 1992 and reached a nadir with a 20-point defeat to Cork in an All-Ireland semi-final in 1993 followed by a Connacht Final loss to Leitrim in 1994. When the old enemy Galway trounced the men in green and red in the 1995 Connacht Final it seemed as if the halcyon days of Midwest's summer of innocence would never again be replicated or, at least, not for a very long time.

And then came the swashbuckling summer of 1996 when Midwest Radio, fresh from the renewal of its seven-year franchise, got swept along on another wave of Mayo GAA euphoria as the whole county went football mad all over again.

PART IV

CHAPTER TWENTY-FOUR

'The Shoe' fits just fine

STEPHEN O'Grady's first full year at the helm of Midwest's sports department could hardly have been more eventful. The Ballyvary native joined the station in 1995, straight from University College Galway where he had majored in philosophy, a subject that would prove useful when coming to terms with the cruel fate visited upon Mayo football fans in the long and unforgettable summer of 1996.

Stephen was the station's first full-time sports editor and his appointment was a tacit acknowledgement by the board of the vital role of sport in developing a cross-generational audience for Midwest. Liam Horan and Jim Carney had operated on an ad-hoc basis for much of the early 1990s, incrementally building the weekend shows on a pretty modest budget. But Midwest would invest substantial resources in expanding its sports coverage during the second half of the decade and the watershed year was undoubtedly 1996 when the station provided live commentary from 24 different venues, including some as distant as Ruislip in London, Casement Park in Co Antrim and, of course, Croke Park.

The year was barely a few weeks old when Ballina – inspired by that magical duo of Liam McHale and Deora Marsh – won the Irish Basketball Cup at the National Arena in Tallaght. A few weeks later, St Gerald's College from Castlebar claimed the Connacht Colleges 'A' Championship for the first time since 1929. It was also the first time since 1981 a Mayo school had won the top prize in colleges football in the west.

St Gerald's failed to make it through to the Hogan Cup Final but Mayo GAA fans got a springtime trip to Croke Park anyway when the county's senior footballers, who were playing inspired football under new manager John Maughan, reached the semi-finals of the National Football League. Defeat to Derry would be their lot but the progress in the league – albeit in Division 3 – was a harbinger for better days ahead.

A young Mayo team went on to win the Connacht Senior Championship in emphatic style before setting off for Croke Park to meet hotly fancied Kerry in the All-Ireland semi-final. In truth, the Mayo supporters travelled more in hope than expectation on that mid-August afternoon and the players themselves were probably the only ones who truly believed they could topple the mighty Kingdom. After all, Mayo hadn't recorded a championship victory over Kerry since that famous All-Ireland winning year of 1951.

Willie Ryan had been commentating on Mayo GAA matches for seven years and the trip to Croke Park was a dream come true for the genial Ballyhaunis man.

"Even as a youngster I was interested in sports commentary, and the advent of local radio gave me the chance I needed," he recalled in an interview in 1997. "On November 15, 1989, Paul Claffey asked if I'd like to do a commentary on the following Sunday's National Football League game between Mayo and Roscommon at Ballina. I never looked back."

Willie was blazing a trail for local radio at a time when the facilities for broadcasters were primitive, to say the least. He once commentated on a National Football League game while standing on a stone and was particularly surprised at the lack of facilities for local radio in Croke Park.

"I had to commentate amongst the crowd, which is never easy."

Willie was also operating in an era when the concept of the co-commentator had yet to be fully developed so it really was a case of non-stop chat for a full 35 minutes, plus stoppage time.

"Unlike television, which is largely self-explanatory, a radio commentator must keep talking," he explains. "A good commentator must be armed with plenty of information on players and teams while remaining totally objective. A few seconds' silence and listeners think you are off the air."

There was no fear of any awkward silences when Mayo took to the sacred sod of Croke Park for their eagerly anticipated clash against Kerry on August 10, 1996. The men in green and red delivered a performance for the ages to book their place in the All-Ireland Final for the first time since 1989. The Midwest hype machine was about to be cranked up again.

As part of the build up to Mayo's showdown against Meath, Paul agreed a lucrative deal with Bank of Ireland, then the sole sponsors of the All-Ireland football championship, to broadcast a special show from New York, which would serve as an important fundraiser for the Mayo team. Noel Howley had strong links to the various Mayo associations in the United States and was persuaded to co-host the event with Claffey, having done something similar in Dublin on the night before the All-Ireland semi-final.

"I was organising the fundraiser prior to the Kerry game but I had nothing to do with the broadcasting side of things – or at least that's what I thought," Noel recalls. "I kept asking Claffey who was doing the broadcast for him and he kept telling me that the man who was doing it was somewhere in the room."

Howley scanned the function room, searching from face to face for this mysterious broadcaster who was worryingly anonymous for someone about to go live on air within a matter of a few minutes. Was it Micheál Ó Muircheartaigh or maybe Michael Lyster or perhaps even Gay Byrne himself? Finally, he gave up.

"Paul, who the hell is doing this broadcast?"

"You!" exclaimed Claffey. "You're doing it!"

"But sure I can't do it, I don't anything about radio."

"Look, you know everyone in this room so just get the mike and start asking questions. I'll butt in if you get into trouble."

The pre-final fundraiser in New York was in association with Adrian Flannelly who had booked the upstairs function room of Rosie O'Grady's pub for a gathering of the great and the good of Irish-American society, including many with Mayo connections. The plan was to record the show and send it back to Ballyhaunis via an expensive, new-fangled device called a telephone extender, which had cost

Midwest the rather considerable sum of £1,000. Michael Neary was on standby in Ballyhaunis to receive the show some time after 2am, edit it and then put it on the air at 9am.

Claffey spent most of the flight from Dublin telling Howley about this wonderful new piece of technology that would make it so easy to broadcast the show back to Ballyhaunis. He was so protective of it he even insisted on bringing it onto the 'plane in his carry-on luggage. On arrival in New York, the two men set off for Rosie O'Grady's in Times Square where they met the owner Mike Carthy who showed them to the upstairs function room.

"Now, lads, you know the electrical current is different here?" Carthy remarked as he watched Paul unpack his space-age machinery.

"No problem, Mike," said Claffey. "I've got it all under control."

Carthy went downstairs and Paul began setting up the equipment. Howley was at the other end of the room when he heard a loud bang followed by an ominous sizzling noise. Moments later, Carthy came running up the stairs

"Did you guys do anything to the telephone lines? All of our credit card machines are gone down."

"Jaysus, I did nothing," replied Claffey, positioning his body strategically in front of the telephone extender, which was now emitting a worrying amount of smoke.

Carthy went back downstairs to figure out how he was going to run a busy pub in the heart of New York City without credit card facilities. Meanwhile, a volcanic Paul Claffey was also emitting smoke as he surveyed the wreckage of his once magnificent telephone extender.

"What are we going to do? What are we going to do?" he pleaded with Howley. "Bank of Ireland are paying serious bobs for this broadcast."

"Is there any other way we can record it?" asked Noel.

Claffey paced back and over the room.

"I know," he finally said. "Let's get a Marantz."

The Marantz was a popular recording device among radio professionals and was frequently used when recording interviews away from the studio. Locating a Marantz at nine o'clock on a Saturday night was quite a mission but Howley and Claffey were hopeful they might strike it lucky in the city that never sleeps. They tore down the stairs and elbowed their way through the crowded bar where Mike Carthy was attempting to placate an angry army of credit-card waving customers. The search for the all-important Marantz ended successfully some 20 minutes later when they located a late-night electrical store in a side street. After bartering with the Vietnamese owner, who wanted to charge them double the price, the intrepid duo hightailed it back to Rosie O'Grady's just in time for the start of the show, which went surprisingly well considering the seat-of-the-pants preparation of its co-hosts.

When it was all over, a mightily relieved Claffey retired to his hotel room and put a call through to Michael Neary to report that everything was back on track and he'd be sending through the two-hour recording shortly.

"How do I get this through to you?" Paul asked his chief technician.

"Just connect a lead from the Marantz to the phone in your room," instructed Neary.

"A lead?"

"Yeah, a lead… you have a lead for the Marantz, don't you?"

There was a stony silence that echoed all the way across the broad Atlantic. Back in Ballyhaunis, the hush was eventually broken by the hollering of a party of late-night revellers making their way home from Midas. Neary glanced at the clock. It was already nearly 3am.

"Have you a set of headphones?" he asked Paul.

"Yeah."

"Right, connect those to the Marantz and hold the headphone up to the receiver."

Claffey did what he was told and Neary listened closely.

"There's too much background noise," he said. "I can hear all that noise from the street outside your hotel."

"Feck it," said Claffey, sinking back in the bed and gazing up at the ceiling in search of inspiration.

"Do you know what you could do," said Neary, pulling on his MacGyver hat. "You could put the headphone and the receiver into some kind of an enclosed space."

"An enclosed space? Like what?"

"A shoe, maybe?"

"A shoe? Are you serious?"

"Sure it's worth a try!"

Claffey despairingly removed one of his snazzy Clarkes' shoes and placed the headphone and the receiver inside. Neary listened again. There was still some background noise but it was much better than before.

"Right," he said to Paul who had momentarily retrieved the receiver from the shoe. "You need to find something solid to hold against the headphone for the next two hours to block out any remaining noise."

"What do you suggest, Mick?" said Claffey wearily. "Do you want me to go and find a concrete block somewhere?"

"Lift up the leg of the bed and stick it down on the headphone," said Neary. "That should do it."

The unconventional solution worked a treat. The following morning at 9am, tens of thousands of Midwest's listeners tuned in for the eagerly awaited two-hour Mayo GAA extravaganza from Rosie O'Grady's pub in the heart of New York City. What nobody realised was that the entire show had been broadcast back to Ireland via a shoe and the leg of a bed. So much for modern technology!

Unlike 1989, Midwest now owned an outside broadcasting vehicle – the satellite cruiser – and Paul was determined to make good use of it on All-Ireland Final Sunday. It was decided to undertake a live broadcast from outside Barry's Hotel on Great Denmark Street, a favourite haunt of GAA fans en route to Croke Park. The event was due to commence around midday and Paul expected no more than a few hundred people as it was still several hours before the match. But he was in for a big surprise.

"I remember walking up Parnell Square, turning right and the next thing I could see thousands of people gathered around the cruiser. It was absolute mayhem. There were so many there we had to broadcast from the top of the truck!

"It's one of those incredible memories I have from my time in Midwest. There was literally thousands of Mayo fans, all wearing their green and red, and singing full-throated versions of *The Boys from the County Mayo* and *Moonlight in Mayo.* The cops were gone absolutely daft and were telling us to abandon it but we wouldn't. I'd be arrested now if I tried something like that!"

It had been agreed that once the match commenced, Gerry Glennon and Michael Neary would take the cruiser back to Mayo ahead of the homecoming in Castlebar the next evening. However, with Mayo seemingly cruising to victory in the second-half, Paul had a sudden change of heart about what to do with Midwest's cruiser.

"Where are ye?" he shouted down the mobile 'phone from the back of the old Hogan Stand.

"We're just outside Longford," said Glennon.

"I think ye should come back. We have to be here in Dublin for this. They're going to win this time."

"Are you sure?"

"Look, I'll call ye at the end of the game and we'll decide then."

Mayo opened up a six-point lead just as the Midwest satellite cruiser passed St Mel's Cathedral in Longford. Sitting in the Hogan Stand, Terry Reilly afforded himself a rare moment of relaxation.

"I remember thinking to myself that I never believed it could be so easy to win an All-Ireland title. We had yearned for this day since 1951 and here it was unfolding before our eyes."

Meanwhile, Michael and Gerry had agreed to continue as far as Tarmonbarry to await further instructions. At the very moment Colm Coyle was unleashing his infamous long-range kick that sent Mayo's dreams of All-Ireland victory down the swanny, the satellite cruiser was crossing the River Shannon. Seconds later, the All-Ireland Final of 1996 had ended in an anti-climatic draw.

"What do we now?" a stunned Neary asked.

"Well, he told us to go west if they lost and go east if they won," mused Glennon, "so I suppose now that it's a draw we're as well to stay here!"

Two weeks later, the satellite cruiser was in Castlebar as 10,000 Mayo fans flooded The Mall for a bittersweet homecoming. Mayo had lost a fractious replay by a single point and the game would be best remembered for the unjust dismissal of the talismanic Liam McHale, who had been Mayo's Man of the Match in the drawn game. It was gut-wrenching stuff and totally different to 1989. This was the sort of coulda-woulda-shoulda defeat that would spawn much more than a single winter of regrets. Twenty-three years later, Liam Horan can still vividly recall the "funereal march" along Jones' Road on that bleak Sunday evening in late September as the Mayo fans began the long, dejected journey back to the west. The joyful optimism of two weeks' earlier when thousands had gathered around Midwest's satellite cruiser and lustily sang *The Boys from the County Mayo* seemed a long, long time ago.

Even the young sports editor of Midwest Radio was struggling to remain philosophical, although he had identified one shard of sunlight amidst the gloomy winter horizon. The performance of a young half-forward named James Horan, who kicked five majestic points in the replayed final, prompted Stephen O'Grady to look to the future with optimism. The Ballintubber man was a 'master of art', O'Grady declared in his weekly column in the *Mayo News*, and would surely paint many more green and red masterpieces in the years to come.

It wasn't a bad prediction, all things considered.

Mayo's broadcasting landscape was a little more crowded in the summer of 1996. A year earlier, the IRTC approved a licence for a community radio station in Castlebar, the first of its kind in the country. Castlebar Community Radio, or CRCfm as it became known, took to the airwaves on June 30, 1995, manned mainly by a team of volunteers drawn from the local community. The station manager was Henry McGlade and there were also several other former Midwest presenters involved, including Johnny Oosten, while a number of ex-IRM broadcasters returned to the airwaves too.

But the majority of the volunteer staff had little or no experience of radio. Foremost among them was the host of the weekend sports shows, a genial, gregarious sports fanatic named Willie McNeely who was better known around his native Castlebar as 'The Shoe'.

Willie turned 40 the same year CRCfm took to the airwaves and if ever a man was to prove the old adage that life begins at 40 it was The Shoe. The man from MacHale Road had enjoyed a varied career up to then, having started his working life in Tony Baynes' Moderne Shoes in the 1970s before moving to Dublin where he managed Boylan's Shoes on Henry Street for a period.

The Queen of Connemara Bina McLoughlin pictured outside her cottage in Leenane where she lived with her legion of dogs, cats, ducks, geese and sheep. A renowned singer, storyteller and dramatist, Bina first appeared on Paul Claffey's Mid-Morning Show in the summer of 1995 and quickly became one of the truly great characters of Midwest Radio.
Picture: Western People Archives

Enda Kenny is interviewed by Tommy Marren during a live broadcast from Kildare Street in Dublin on March 9, 2011, the day Mr Kenny was appointed Ireland's thirteenth Taoiseach.

Paul Claffey with then Minister of State Michael Ring and Senator Terry Leydon at an event in Leinster House in 2014 to mark the 25th anniversary of legalised local radio in Ireland.

Ireland's oldest broadcaster, 89-year-old Aghamore man Seamus Duffy, pictured in 2014 cutting turf with Ollie Robinson at Scárdán bog.

Mildred Beirne joins Seamus every week for an update on the céilí scene.

The Magnificent 7 from Midwest Radio pictured in 2007 with a cheque for €178,666.94, which they presented to various Mayo charities following a hugely successful week-long fundraiser. Front row, from left: Teresa O'Malley, Tommy Marren and Angelina Nugent. Back row: Viv Brennan, Chris Carroll, David Cawley, Paul Claffey and Padraic Walsh.

Staff from Midwest Radio present a cheque for €234,102 to Westport native Gena Heraty for her work in Haiti at the official opening of their new studio in Castlebar. Pictured at back from left: Tommy Marren (Station Manager), Martin McHugh (Advertising Sales Executive), Cllr Michael Kilcoyne, Mayor of Castlebar, Gerry Glennon (Presenter), Gena Heraty, Padraig Rabbitt (Advertising Executive Midwest Radio) and Michael Neary (Technician). Front Row from left: Enda Carberry (Financial Controller), Patrina McDonnell (Programming Department), Bernie Greally (Administration Department) and Mary Raftery (Traffic Department).

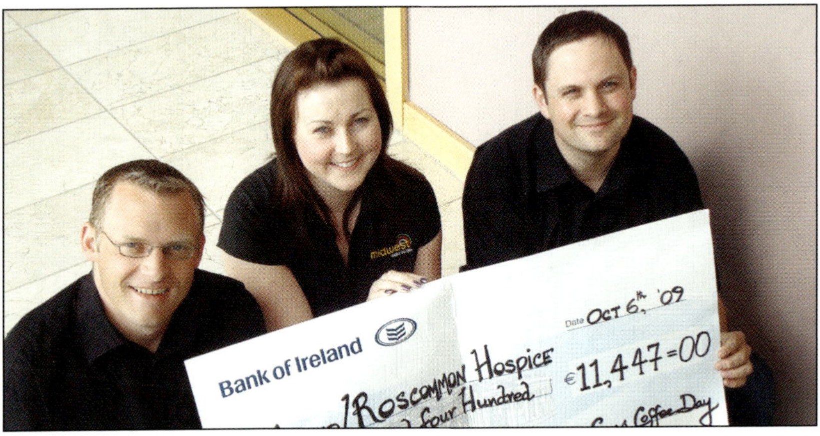

Padraic Walsh, Angelina Nugent and David Cawley pictured with the proceeds from their Hospice Coffee Morning in 2009.

Tommy Marren presents Erris woman Marie Carolan with a cheque for €37,907 towards her medical costs.

Getting ready to saddle up for Mayo Pink Ribbon Day were Midwest's Tommy Marren, Patrina Cunniffe and David Cawley.

Midwest Radio has been packing out the TF Royal Theatre in Castlebar for years and this photograph of Mike Denver was taken during the 25th anniversary concert in 2014.

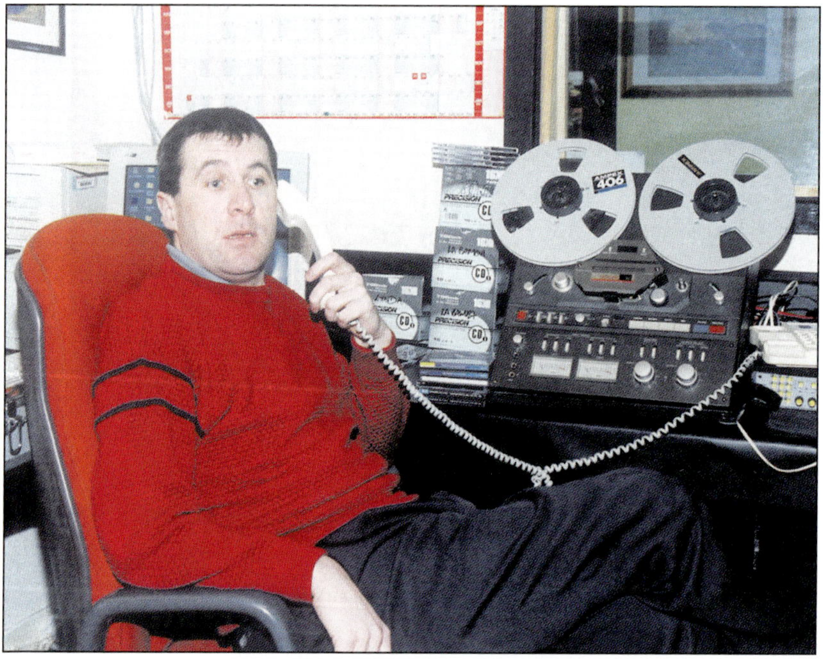

Gerry Glennon back in the days of reel-to-reel broadcasting.

Hard at work in our Castlebar studio in 2003 was Ronan Courell, whose father Tom played a vital role in establishing the station.

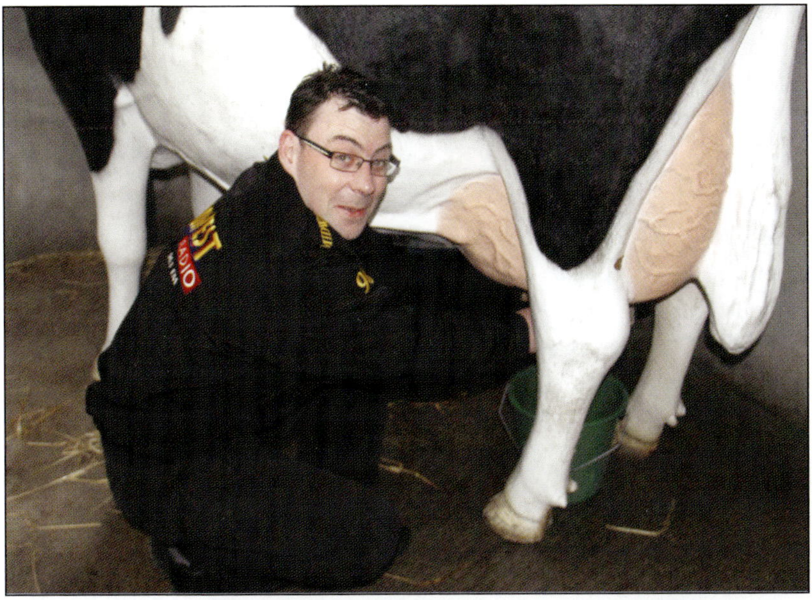

Brendan Nugent is never a man to milk it!

No, we weren't clamped, we were on the ferry to Clare Island!

Paul Claffey broadcasting the Mid-Morning Show live from the Castle Arms Hotel in Enniscrone, Co Sligo, on September 9, 2004, shortly before North-west Radio was forced to close much to the annoyance of its many thousands of fans.
Picture: James Connolly

Paul Claffey shares a joke with 91-year-old Johnny Moran from Ballina during Mid and Northwest Radio's live broadcast from the Castle Arms Hotel in Enniscrone, Co Sligo, on September 9, 2004. Picture: James Connolly

Thousands took to the streets on June 29, 2003, in a bid to save Northwest Radio after the Broadcasting Commission of Ireland failed to renew its licence. Picture: James Connolly

Sligo man Martin Forde spent eight days on the streets of Sligo in 2003 collecting over 9,000 signatures for a petition to halt the closure of Northwest Radio. Martin is pictured presenting the petition to Mid and Northwest chief executive Paul Claffey.

Picture: James Connolly

A group from counties Sligo, Leitrim and Donegal protest in the summer of 2003 in a bid to prevent the closure of Northwest Radio.

Picture: James Connolly

The closure of Northwest Radio was the biggest disappointment of Paul Claffey's long career in broadcasting. He is pictured with staff and supporters of the station during its final moments as it went off the airwaves on October 1, 2004.
Picture: James Connolly

All generations came out in force on June 29, 2003, to protest against the withdrawal of the Northwest Radio franchise. Picture: James Connolly

Mary Davis, the KIltimagh-born chief executive of the World Special Olympics 2003, unveils the plaque at the official opening of Midwest Radio's new broadcasting centre in Ballyhaunis on September 19, 2003. Also pictured is Martin Niland, the then vice-chairman of the station's board of directors. Picture: Henry Wills/Western People Archives

Canon Joe Cooney and Dean Ailstar Grimason perform the official blessing at the opening ceremony for Midwest's new broadcasting centre at Clare Street, Ballyhaunis on September 19, 2003.
Picture: Henry Wills/Western People Archives

Pictured at the official opening of the Midwest Radio broadcast centre in Ballyhaunis were, from left: Terry Reilly, Fr. John O'Boyle, Noel Filan, Joe Kennedy, Mary Davis, Paul Claffey, Martin Niland, Michael O'Keeffe and Chris Carroll.
Picture: Henry Wills/Western People Archives

Ready for action are some of the Midwest Radio staff on the opening day of the new broadcast centre in Ballyhaunis on Friday, September 19, 2003.
Picture: Henry Wills/Western People Archives

Mary Davis had the assistance of a large group of Special Olympians when she cut the tape to mark the official opening of Midwest Radio's new broadcasting centre at Clare Street, Ballyhaunis, on September 19, 2003.
Picture: Henry Wills/Western People Archives

Youngsters peer into the studio at the opening of Midwest's new broadcasting centre in 2003 while presenters Gerry Glennon and Teresa O'Malley chat to chairman of Knock Airport Joe Kennedy, Deputy Beverley Flynn and Deputy Jerry Cowley.

Picture: Henry Wills/Western People Archives

Two of Midwest's long-serving staff, Mary Raftery (right) and Bernie Greally made a presentation to Mary Davis after she opened the new broadcasting centre in September 2003.

Picture: Henry Wills/Western People Archives

Midwest staff members pictured in 2014, from left: Bernie Greally, Catriona McGuire, Sharon Behan-Woods and Mary Raftery. Sharon and Mary have worked with the station since it went legal in 1989 while Bernie previously worked at Midas Nightclub in the 1980s before later returning to Ballyhaunis from the UK to work in the accounts department.

Chief technician Brendan Nugent and sports editor Angelina McHugh fell in love while working at Midwest Radio and married in 2007.

Fr Brendan Hoban and Monica Morley recording another edition of the popular religious affairs programme *Faith Alive.*

A function in honour of John Duggan was held at the Western Hotel in Claremorris in November 2016 to mark his retirement from Midwest Radio after a career spanning 30 years. John is pictured with fellow Midwest presenters, from left: Gerry Glennon, Tommy Marren and Michael Commins. John passed away in July 2019.

Gerry Glennon takes a tractor for a test drive during an outside broadcast.

Michael Commins is one of Midwest's original 'pirates' and his renowned Sunday night show attracts listeners all over the world.

Midwest's outdoor broadcasts from Ballina Street Festival have been a popular feature of the summer schedule since 1991. Paul is pictured here with comedian Conal Gallen mingling with the crowds on Pearse Street.

Gerry Glennon chatting to some youngsters during an outside broadcast. Midwest has undertaken thousands of these broadcasts over the last 30 years.

Midwest Radio's spacious reception area at its broadcasting centre at Clare Street in Ballyhaunis is a far cry from the poky cloakroom in Midas Nightclub where it all began in the mid-1980s

Two of Midwest's presenters – Eunice Moran and Michael Commins – are pictured with songwriter Gerry Carney at the launch of the Kilkelly/Kilmovee Parish magazine in 2017.
Picture: James Hunt Photography

Paul Claffey and Gerry Glennon broadcasting their very popular television show for Ireland West Music TV. Midwest even built its own studio at Clare Street for the novel venture, which launched in 2011.

The Ireland West Music TV team pictured in 2014, back row, from left: Brendan Nugent, Patrina Cunniffe, Grainne Kivlehan and John Paul Heaney with Paul Claffey and Gerry Glennon seated.

Michael D McAndrew was appointed Midwest's sports editor in 2019 after Angelina Nugent took up a new role with Mayo Roscommon Hospice.

News editor Teresa O'Malley is pictured 'on the beat' some years ago. Foxford native Teresa first started producing current affairs programmes for the station in 1989 before being appointed news editor in 1997.

The legendary Noel Howley (nearest camera) is pictured with Deputy John O'Mahony, Deputy Pat Rabbitte and presenter Tommy Marren at Midwest's outdoor broadcast from Kildare Street in Dublin on March 9, 2011, to mark the election of Enda Kenny as Taoiseach. In 1994, Noel was the man responsible for transporting a section of bog to New York for the famous Beat on the Peat. Picture: Henry Wills

Deputy Dara Calleary shares a joke with a burger-eating Paul Claffey during a live broadcast from the Bonniconlon Show some years ago.

Renewing Midwest Radio's broadcast licence at the offices of the Broadcasting Authority of Ireland (BAI) in Dublin in 2013 were, left to right: Enda Carberry, CFO, Midwest Radio; Bob Collins, Chairman, BAI; Michael O'Keeffe, CEO, BAI; Paul Claffey, CEO, Midwest Radio and Chris Carroll, Director, Midwest Radio.

Paul Claffey was inducted into the PPI Hall of Fame in 2014 alongside the late 2FM disc jockey Tony Fenton, RTÉ Radio 1 current affairs broadcaster Áine Lawlor and Walter Love of BBC Radio Ulster.

Singing sensation Nathan Carter leads a host of stars at the 25th Anniversary celebrations of Midwest Radio at the Royal Theatre, Castlebar, in 2014.

Legendary local broadcaster Tommy Murphy, from Ballina, is pictured with Dana Rosemary Scallon. Tommy performed as a backing musican for Dana on occasions.

Winners at the annual Midwest/Northwest Radio drama awards held at the Great Southern Hotel in Sligo. The drama awards were a major event hosted by Midwest/Northwest Radio throughout the 1990s, attracting entries from drama groups across the West of Ireland.

Midwest Radio co-founders Paul Claffey and Chris Carroll pictured at the station's 25th anniversary concert in 2014.

In 1985, Willie returned to his native town to open The Shoe Market but also continued operating a footwear wholesaling business from Kilmainham in Dublin, importing shoes from Spain and Italy. It was around this time that Willie received the nickname that would become his calling card during his brief, but very impactful, broadcasting career.

"Fergal Murphy had a bookies shop in Castle Street in Castlebar back in the mid-1980s and I had the shoe shop at the Market Square," Willie explained in an interview with the *Mayo News* in 1998. "One day I called in to Fergal to back a horse, which I didn't know was being ridden by the US jockey, Willie Shoemaker."

The horse won and when Willie arrived to collect his winnings, George O'Malley, the well-known vet in Castlebar, let out a roar: "There he goes, Willie The Shoe!"

The unusual moniker stuck and Willie, being a larger than life character, was more than happy to give the name washkie, as he might say himself. When he took to the airwaves in the summer of 1995, Willie proudly announced that The Shoe was going to kick sports broadcasting in Mayo into the 21st century.

But it was easier said than done. The volunteers at CRCfm were discovering that a licence for a community radio station was a lot more restrictive than they had originally anticipated. For one thing, the station was only allowed broadcast six hours per day and it was also subject to strict regulations about the type of broadcasts that could take place. Willie wanted to provide listeners with live commentaries of major sporting events in Mayo but the IRTC was constantly telling him that such broadcasts were beyond the remit of the CRCfm licence. It was deeply frustrating for a man who was travelling from Dublin each weekend to volunteer at his local community radio station, especially as he was building up a big listenership in Castlebar.

"He built up a kind of cult following within no time," recalls his great friend and well-known Castlebar publican Mick Byrne. "He was the talk of the town. His way with words and his knowledge of all kinds of sports had become a topic itself. People tuned in every Saturday when he returned from Dublin after a week's work. They were tuning in just to hear him."

There was no doubt The Shoe had a unique turn of phrase that made him a natural-born broadcaster. He may have been a late vocation but he made up for it in enthusiasm and sheer force of personality. Only The Shoe could describe Mayo's agonising defeat to Meath in that replayed All-Ireland Final as "so bad it would bring tears to an onion". CRCfm had unearthed a broadcasting gem; Willie 'The Shoe' McNeely was soon the new station's bona fide star.

By now Willie was working as a sales and marketing manager for an energy-saving company based in Dublin but his family were living in Castlebar and he was heavily involved with the Mitchels and Castlebar Celtic. The one-hour radio shows on Saturday and Sunday were his favourite part of the week but he felt completely suffocated by the regulatory stranglehold the IRTC was imposing on CRCfm. He wanted to be in MacHale Park commentating on Mayo's latest National Football League encounter but instead the IRTC was telling him to stay in a studio on Linenhall Street. It just didn't make any sense and Willie, who had come to broadcasting late in life, hadn't time to waste on what he perceived as bureaucratic nonsense. On Sunday, February 16, 1997, The Shoe went on air and gave vent to his mounting frustrations, aiming an almighty kick at the IRTC, which he accused of "gagging" him.

"I have been putting a lot of my time into developing this show, sometimes up to 20 hours a week," he told listeners. "It is a voluntary input which I thoroughly enjoy. But I have become increasingly frustrated at the constraints placed on us as a station.

"I am not in a position to bring many major sporting events live on air, and this is hard for me to accept. I am a salesman and I feel I cannot sell my sports show properly with just two hours of programming every week."

The Shoe concluded that he would no longer be presenting the weekend sports shows and advised the local Dáil deputies to "get off their backsides" and come to the assistance of CRCfm.

As broadcasting resignations go, this was about as spectacular as it gets. It was incendiary stuff. However, Willie was keen to emphasise that his comments were entirely personal and did not reflect the views of station management.

Inevitably, the story made front-page news in the *Connaught Telegraph* and even appeared in several national newspapers. By then, The Shoe was back in Dublin and coming to terms with the painful reality that his nascent broadcasting career was already over. But he was in for a surprise. The following Friday afternoon he picked up the telephone and found Paul Claffey on the other end of the line.

"I'd heard Willie on CRCfm and was impressed by him," recalls Paul. "He was a born broadcaster, somebody who had a brilliant turn of phrase and a great way of relating to the listener. I'd heard he'd left CRCfm and thought he'd be an excellent addition to the Midwest sports team."

The *Connaught Telegraph's* John Melvin brilliantly lampooned the supposed 'conversation' between The Shoe and The Claff in his Melvine column in March 1997.

"Willie, I hear you're not just good but you're the best," says The Claff.

"Tell me something I don't already know," replies The Shoe.

"Listen, what about coming on board with us?"

"Talk to me about spondulicks," says The Shoe.

"Spon what?"

"Bread, man, you know, lucre, lire, yens, drachmas, rubles, deutschmarks, pesetas, you dig… are you getting my drift?"

"Oh you mean that dirty word 'money'? Now Willie, why spoil a good conversation talking about such trivia… hold on… I was only joking… don't hang up!"

And so the imagined conversation went as one supreme salesman haggled with another, each having met his match. Claffey says the two got along famously from the first conversation.

"Willie was an exceptionally likeable character and I had a feeling he'd be a big hit on Midwest but I couldn't have possibly imagined the sort of impact he'd have over the next few years."

The Shoe really was about to kick local sports broadcasting into the stratosphere.

CHAPTER TWENTY-FIVE

'The phone lines are so hot I need gloves'

THE Shoe's arrival in Ballyhaunis couldn't have come at a more opportune time. Midwest's sports department had set off at a breakneck speed in the early months of 1997.

St Gerald's College retained their Connacht Colleges 'A' Championship and then went one better by reaching the Hogan Cup Final. Meanwhile, Mayo county senior football champions Knockmore reached the All-Ireland Club Final after a scintillating semi-final victory over the renowned Leinster side, Éire Óg, from Carlow. Their opponents in the final on St Patrick's Day were a then unknown quantity from Co Armagh, Crossmaglen Rangers, and it was widely believed the Knockmore men would have too much for this young, inexperienced Ulster outfit. But whatever about Knockmore or Crossmaglen, the club final in Croke Park offered The Shoe a golden opportunity to make an immediate impact in his new role as a sports reporter with Midwest.

Gerry Glennon and Michael Neary knew they were dealing with a 'live one' when The Shoe announced two days before the final that he wanted to hit the road for Dublin the next day to "soak in the atmosphere" on the eve of the big game.

"So will we record something in the team hotel then?" asked Neary.

"Not at all, Mick," declared The Shoe. "Let's do something live and raw. Let's go to a few pubs around the city and meet the fans. Sure they'll be hanging from the rafters!"

The trio duly set off for Dublin the following afternoon in The Shoe's sparkling new Ford Mondeo, which he had collected from Casey's in Castlebar earlier that morning. En route they encountered JJ O'Hara, from Foxford, who was transporting a float containing a giant goat, made from papier-maché and bedecked in the Knockmore colours of saffron and blue. JJ gave them a list of six pubs around the city where they'd be sure to meet plenty of Knockmore fans and also extracted a promise from The Shoe that he'd broadcast live from the team banquet the following night.

Back on the road, Willie put the foot to the floor and the new Mondeo readily obliged.

"Feel her go, boys," he proudly proclaimed, slapping the steering wheel. "She's a beaut, an absolute beaut."

The first pub on the list was the Portobello in Rathmines, a favoured haunt of city dwellers with rural roots. The Shoe, who was more than familiar with the streets of Dublin, tore along the Canal and pulled up outside the Portobello amid a spectacular screech of brakes.

"Let's go, boys," he shouted to Glennon and Neary as he leapt from the car. "Live and raw, live and raw."

Gerry Glennon had witnessed his share of rare characters in more than a decade of broadcasting but the performance of Willie McNeely that night left him in no doubt that Midwest had just signed a unique broadcaster. This 'Shoe' fella really was a one-off. On entering the Portobello, Willie headed straight for the microphone, grabbed it from a startled disc jockey and then leapt onto a nearby barstool.

"Rock 'n' roll gang," he shouted to the packed bar. "You're with The Shoe!"

There were only a handful of Knockmore supporters in the pub but it didn't matter. By the time The Shoe was finished it sounded as if the whole of Guiry's pub in Foxford had moved lock, stock, barrel and papier-maché goat to the Portobello.

The pub-crawl continued along Camden Street where The Shoe learned that a fundraising draw for the Knockmore team was taking place across town.

"Let's go, boys, let's go," he shouted at an already exhausted Glennon and Neary. "This is the big one! There's a draw at a quarter past ten and we gotta be there for it."

There was one problem, however. The notorious traffic in Dublin was indifferent to the arrival of Mayo's new broadcasting star. A frustrated 'Shoe' weaved in and out of cars, ignoring the cacophony of blaring horns that trailed in his wake. Eventually he gave up and just abandoned his 'beaut' of a Mondeo on the edge of a footpath outside the Bank of Ireland in College Green, the car parked at the sort of obtrusive angle guaranteed to attract the attention of every passing Garda patrol.

"Feck's sake, Willie, you can't leave her like that," exclaimed Glennon. "Sure you only just bought her!"

"Never mind Gerryeen, there's plenty more of them in the garage. Come on, let's do this!"

And with that he was off down the street, his big frame zigzagging through the crowds on College Green, shouting out to someone he knew: "How's she cuttin', auld stock, are ya up for the match?" And to someone else: "How are you me oul flower? Jaysus, it's younger lookin' you're gettin'!"

By the time the sixth pub had been ticked off the list some time after midnight, an exhausted Glennon and Neary were convinced the Knockmore team hadn't been put through a tougher training session in the previous month.

The All-Ireland Final, of course, didn't go as planned. Knockmore were defeated by a superb Crossmaglen side and the post-match banquet was, unsurprisingly, a fairly muted affair. The Shoe was in a fierce quandary. He was due to go on air at 10pm with a panel of guests but there were only a few dozen people in the room ten minutes before show-time and each was wearing a longer face than the next. Even JJ O'Hara and his papier-maché goat had decided to beat a hasty retreat west. It was time for Plan B.

"I think we might need a few oul sound effects," an unperturbed Willie told his bemused technical team.

Michael Neary sourced an audio insert of a cheering crowd just as The Shoe was taking to the stage.

"Good evening everybody," Willie yelled at the top of his voice. "It's The Shoe here live from Dublin and what a night we've got in store for you!"

He then raised his hand for Neary to cue a raucous crowd, mouthing 'Crank her up, Mick' in the direction of his technician.

The same routine continued for the next hour and by the time the live broadcast ended at 11pm, they were "going ballistic" and "givin' it washkie" at the Knockmore team banquet. In truth, there were no more than a few dozen dejected supporters and team members staring morosely into their pints as they contemplated yet another All-Ireland final defeat for a Mayo team in Croke Park. But none of that mattered to The Shoe. After all why let a few post-All-Ireland final blues get in the way of some 'rock 'n' roll' radio for the folks back home?

Glennon and Neary thought they'd seen it all with Claffey back in those madcap pirate days but their eyes were opened that St Patrick's Weekend in Dublin. This Willie McNeely dude was barely a wet week with Midwest – literally, a wet week, in fact – and already he had rewritten the entire sports broadcasting playbook. But they also found themselves swept along in the slipstream of their new colleague's infectious ebullience

"Boys, you ain't seen nothin' yet!" The Shoe cheerfully declared as the Mondeo roared down the M50 en route to Mayo the next morning. Reflecting on the eventful 48 hours just gone, Gerry and Michael were inclined to agree: they had, indeed, been living sheltered lives in the broadcasting world up to now. It was time, then, to buckle in for a white-knuckle ride because Willie 'The Shoe' McNeely was a man on a meteoric rise to the top of the West's media tree.

Gerry, Michael and the rest of the Midwest crew really had seen nothin' yet.

Willie McNeely wasn't the only new appointment in the upstairs newsroom at Abbey Street in the spring of 1997. Teresa O'Malley had spent the previous few years teaching at Dublin City University but decided to return west when the post of news editor at Midwest became vacant.

News coverage had been one of the areas of real concern for Paul and Chris when they were awarded the franchise in 1989 because journalism was simply not their forte. The requirement that 20 per cent of all Midwest's weekly output must consist of news and current affairs seemed particularly onerous for two men whose background was in music and entertainment. However, they were able to rely on the experience of Tom Courell and Terry Reilly, two vastly experienced newspaper editors, who agreed a system of sharing content that pulled Midwest through the early days.

The appointment of Kilmovee native Tom Shiel as news editor in the early 1990s was a key turning point for Midwest's newsroom, especially as it coincided with the departure of Chris Clesham who had been the lynchpin of the station's news coverage since July 1989. Shiel was a former *Irish Independent* journalist with an impeccable record of breaking exclusive stories and it wasn't long before he put his unique stamp on Midwest's news coverage. He was ably-assisted by Ballina-based Liam Molloy, a freelance journalist with a wealth of experience who covered north Mayo for the station.

In 1995, Westport native Liamy MacNally, who had worked on local radio in the United Kingdom for several years, also joined the Midwest newsroom. The station's news coverage now consisted of three main programmes – *The West Today* from 8.35 to 9am, *The Lunchtime News* from 1.30 to 2pm and *Evening Edition* from 5pm to 6pm. – and, by 1997, Midwest was setting a standard for news coverage on local radio in Ireland and was repeatedly topping MRBI polls for the highest percentage listenership in its franchise area.

Although Teresa O'Malley moved to Dublin in 1994, where she combined her teaching duties with occasional work at Dublin Weekend Radio, she also kept her hand in at Midwest and, in 1996, co-produced a documentary with Tom Shiel, entitled *Who Said Elephants Can't Fly?* The documentary, which also involved contributions from Gerry Glennon, Maria Mullarkey and Liamy MacNally, told the story of the first ten years of Knock Airport and included interviews with family and friends of the late Mgr Horan. It won an ESB National Media Award in 1997 for "outstanding work in local broadcasting", which was a real feather in the cap for Midwest's newsroom. A year later, the

Midwest team won a second ESB award for its brilliant documentary on the Big Snow of 1947, entitled *White '47*.

One of Teresa's first tasks as news editor was to organise the station's coverage of that year's general election, which saw Fianna Fáil and Bertie Ahern sweep to power as part of a coalition government involving the Progressive Democrats and some Independent TDs. However, the five-seat Mayo constituency bucked the national trend by electing three Fine Gael TDs, including Michael Ring who topped the poll with an astonishing 10,066 first preferences.

The *Mayo News* hailed Ring's unexpected success as a victory for "old-style politics", the Westport TD having held countless clinics and attended innumerable funerals across the county since his by-election victory three years earlier. But the enormous mandate for a man who had failed to take a seat in the general election in 1992 was also a ringing endorsement of the increasing power of Midwest Radio as a news and current affairs broadcaster. The shrewd Ring had recognised the potential of Midwest earlier than many of his rivals and was a frequent contributor to the station from the moment he took a seat in the Dáil. His passionate style of public speaking and his penchant for throwing in the odd memorable quote made Ring a standout radio performer at a time when many politicians were still unconvinced about the electoral influence of local radio.

The 1997 general election changed all that. In the space of five years, the Westport TD had doubled his first preference tally, and in places like Achill Island and Erris – real heartlands of Midwest Radio – he'd increased his vote in key booths by multiples of five and six. Obviously, it wasn't all down to Midwest Radio but there was general agreement at the count centre in Castlebar that Michael Ring's phenomenal vote was at least partially due to the power of local radio. From that day on, Midwest Radio would be an essential communications medium for incumbent and aspiring politicians in Co Mayo.

The dust had barely settled on the general election when Teresa was covering another major news story: the closure of the giant Asahi chemicals plant in Killala with the loss of hundreds of jobs. A few months later, North Mayo was the scene of one of the biggest tragedies to hit the west in years when a member of the local Grainne Uaile Sub

Aqua Club, Michael Heffernan lost his life while trying to rescue a family of tourists from a sea cave. One of the tourists also died.

Reporting on local tragedies was to become all-too-familiar for Teresa. A year later she found herself back in North Mayo after three local men died in a tragic accident while 'lamping' foxes.

"The one thing I have always found is that even in tragedy people will give a warm welcome to Midwest," she says. "They understand you have a job to do and will assist in any way they can."

As Midwest's chief technician in the pre-broadband days of the 1990s, Michael Neary often had to rely on the goodwill of the public and never found people wanting when it came to lending Midwest a helping hand.

"Once you said you were from Midwest you were away in a hack," he says. "There were an awful lot of great lads in the ESB and Eircom who went way beyond the call of duty to get a line for me. Midwest were seen as being part of the community and if someone could help at all they would."

But even with the best will in the world, Neary occasionally had to do it all himself. One such occasion occurred in Ballyvary when he discovered the building from where the *Mid-Morning Show* was about to be broadcast had no chimney on which to erect an aerial, leaving Neary with only one solution: stand on the flat roof and point the aerial in the direction of the mast in Kiltimagh.

"I was stuck up there for two and a half hours holding a bloody aerial in the air," he recalls with a chuckle.

Suddenly, Mass at the top of the Reek didn't seem such a bad gig after all.

In the early summer of 1997, the position of sports editor at Midwest became vacant when Stephen O'Grady swapped the microphone for the notebook and pencil by joining the *Mayo News*. There was only one credible candidate for the job: Willie 'The Shoe'.

Stephen later recalled the afternoon in May 1997 when he and Willie sat down in the studio in Abbey Street to prepare for the handover.

"When he arrived in the studio I was recording Pat Gallagher's weekly racing file. In those days, Pat used to pre-record uninterrupted for three to four minutes, outlining the main races of the weekend and offering his invaluable tips."

As a man who was partial to the occasional wager on the gee-gees, The Shoe believed Midwest could get a lot more from the talented tipster by simply tweaking his delivery. Why not converse with Gallagher instead of getting him to deliver a staid monologue?

"He was right," O'Grady recalled. "Within the next 12 months, Willie developed Pat Gallagher into a high-profile and highly-successful racing pundit. More significantly, he created a genuine radio character in Pat Gallagher as the two became an electric combination."

In his short stint at Midwest, Stephen O'Grady had earned many plaudits for his accomplished and assured presentation style but he could see, even on that first day, that Willie wanted to push the boundaries of sports broadcasting to their limits and beyond.

"Not for him were the hard facts and figures of the sporting world. He wanted more, he needed to tap into the colour and character of sport. Its personalities – even if they didn't have a personality – were there to be explored and Willie's form of exploration was unique and inimitable...

"The manner and style in which he covered sport was hardly from the media guidebook. I reckon he tossed that same guidebook out the window and into the back yard of Midwest's premises that same Saturday afternoon as I replayed Pat Gallagher's last uninterrupted file.

"Instead he injected his own personality into every broadcast from there on... Sometimes that personality appeared to overwhelm an event but it didn't matter, it really didn't. His presence, his contribution enhanced or embellished the coverage of an event like no other. It was great radio [and] it was unpredictable radio."

It was true. The Shoe would turn a coin toss into a life-or-death sporting event. There might be 40 people at a match but in Willie's mind there were 4,000. And he didn't discriminate either. An obscure Junior B Championship tie in the nether reaches of North Mayo would be given the same billing as an All-Ireland Final in Croke Park while so-called minority sports were afforded as much respect as an international soccer or rugby match. All sports and all sports people were equal as far as Willie was concerned.

But it was The Shoe's unique ability to impose his effervescent personality on every interview and commentary that made the weekend sports shows on Midwest such compelling fare.

"Pateen, I like the sound of that double, stick a fiver on there for The Shoe," he'd tell Gallagher, before declaring: "Folks, the phone lines are so hot here I need gloves!"

The 'phone lines might be colder than Siberia but The Shoe knew the best way to get the calls coming in was to tell the listeners the switchboard was already in "meltdown". One of the many yarns surrounding The Shoe relates to a broadcast from the Welcome Inn Hotel in Castlebar on a winter's night where a non-descript darts tournament was taking place.

"The place is heaving here," declared The Shoe as he went on air. "There isn't room to swing a mouse let alone a cat."

The owner of the Welcome Inn, Tony McHugh, was driving from Dublin and happened to switch on Midwest in Longford where he caught the tail end of Willie's introduction.

"Christ," he thought. "I don't have enough bar staff on."

McHugh put his foot to the floor and reached Castlebar in record time. He dashed through the hotel lobby and into the bar to discover about 30 or 40 people and half of them had no connection to the darts match at all. Not for the first time, The Shoe's enthusiasm had got the better of him and he ended up describing a scene that only existed in his mind's eye.

Teresa O'Malley was immediately taken by her colleague's limitless energy and enthusiasm.

"He'd bound up the stairs to the newsroom every morning just before 8am, enthused by sport, by life, by family and by broadcasting," she recalls. "He was never a man for half measures."

But Teresa was also impressed with The Shoe's peerless knowledge of sport and his surprising ability to focus on a job that needed to be done, showing levels of concentration that belied the excitable and boisterous caricature.

"Tereseen, when we're knittin', we're knittin'," was The Shoe's take on both work and life, and nobody could ever fault the man's dedication to either cause. He was the voice of Midwest Radio sport through the summer of 1997 as Mayo marched into another All-Ireland senior football final only to come a cropper once again; this time to a Kerry side they had easily defeated a year earlier.

But The Shoe, who openly confessed to weeping tears of joy in the Cusack Stand when Mayo ran out for the All-Ireland final in 1989, was unbowed by the latest Croke Park setback.

"Mayo men don't show the white feather," he declared in his new column in the *Western People*. "We'll be back in 1998!"

Whatever about the Mayo football team, it had been some year for Midwest's sports editor whose dramatic on-air resignation in February had turned into the smartest career move in the history of local radio. Now aged 42, The Shoe was determined to make the most of these magical, sun-drenched days. He was, by his own admission, living the dream.

CHAPTER TWENTY-SIX

Bina brews up a storm

LONG before there was ever a mention of the now infamous Mayo football curse, there was another curse that had the whole western region talking to such an extent Midwest's switchboard nearly did go into meltdown. And, yes, the phone-lines were so hot The Shoe had the gloves at the ready for Patrina McDonnell and the rest of the Midwest team.

The whole saga began fairly innocuously, as these things often do, when Paul put a call through to his old friend, Bina McLoughlin, one dreary Wednesday morning in January 1998. It was that time of the new year when the post-Christmas feelgood factor has long since dissipated, leaving people desperate for a little bit of light relief to ease those January blues. No better woman than The Queen of Connemara to lift the spirits of Midwest's listeners, Paul thought. Well, she lifted their spirits alright, but not in the way Paul anticipated.

Bina was on a mission that winter's morning. She was helping to organise a fundraising bingo session in aid of Temple Street Children's Hospital, a charity very close to her heart, and she needed the loan of a bingo machine and some bingo balls.

"Has any of our listeners got a bingo machine and some bingo balls for Bina?" Paul asked. "Give us a call here at the station and we'll get them down to Bina in plenty of time for the bingo. Where's it on again Bina?"

"It's in Maam Cross and it's for the centre here in Leenane and the children's hospital," explained The Queen.

It wasn't long before a bingo machine and balls were sourced but among the various helpful calls was one from a listener who had a bit of a gripe with Bina. Paul casually read out the comment before the show ended in the same way he would the many other messages that always came in whenever Bina took to the airwaves.

"I've a comment here from a listener who says Bina is always looking for something whenever she comes on with us here at Mid and Northwest."

That was it, the torch that lit the flame. In truth, it was little more than a passing observation, and the matter should have rested there and then, but Bina, listening abroad in her little cottage in Leenane, was less than impressed and was quick to defend her honour.

"Wasn't I doing a good thing?" she asked Paul upon returning to the airwaves the next morning.

"Well, you were," agreed Claffey. "But this listener is only offering his opinion. Is he not entitled to his opinion?"

"He had no opinion, just an evil opinion," Bina declared emphatically. "I've a good mind to put the *seacht mallacht* on him!"

"Now Bina," said Paul hurriedly. "Don't put the *seacht mallacht* on him."

"I will," said The Queen. "He deserves it!"

"Ah, Bina, not the *seacht mallacht*," said a horrified Paul.

There are curses and there are curses, and then there's the *seacht mallacht*, which translated into English is the sevenfold curse. Bina, as was her wont, had gone straight for the nuclear option and there was little Paul could do to talk her round. The unfortunate listener now had a sevenfold curse on his head and there was nothing more to it; Bina was off to tend to her sheep.

The Queen of Connemara had barely said her goodbyes when Midwest's telephone switchboard lit up. Paul and Gerry had never seen anything like it.

"Usually we'd get a fair few telephone calls during the show if something major happened but the calls that day continued long after the *Mid-Morning Show* went off the air," recalls Paul. "It was without doubt the biggest controversy that ever happened on Midwest Radio. People were up in arms over what Bina had done. They were calling from everywhere. The phone lines were literally jammed for the rest of the day."

The obvious thing to do was to invite Bina back on the show the next morning and have the curse lifted in time for the weekend. But this was the Queen of Connemara, who wasn't known to possess a reverse gear, and if she did it had been long since become wedged from lack of use. Paul put the call through the following day, more in hope than expectation.

"Bina, love, we've had a lot of callers since you were on with us yesterday," he began. "A lot of people would feel that putting a curse on this man is a bit strong."

"Well, didn't he deserve it?"

"But are you not sorry about it?"

"I'm not a bit sorry!"

"Well, a lot of people would say it's a bit harsh…"

"An eye for an eye… you can't change the Bible!"

By now, Paul was fully aware of the controversy Bina had landed herself into and was doing his best to steer her onto safer ground but the shepherdess was immune to his patient guidance. When he pointed out that around 98 per cent of the hundreds of callers were voicing strong opposition to what she had said a day earlier, Bina again reached for the nuclear button by claiming the callers were all hypocrites! A despairing Claffey could only hold his head in his hands as the switchboard lit up for the second time in a week. The controversy was set to rumble on.

"It became a serious matter because the majority of people who telephoned the station said they believed in the power of Bina's curse," recalls Gerry. "The whole region turned against her and said they didn't want to hear her on the radio again. People were really exercised about it and felt a huge amount of sympathy for the man who had made the original comment."

A week later, Paul made one last effort to extract some form of an apology or retraction from the intractable Queen of Connemara. As he dialed the number, Claffey was acutely aware that this might be the last time he spoke live on air to a woman who had been such an integral part of his show since that first conversation in the summer of 1995. He could only hope Bina, in the intervening period, had realised the error of her ways or perhaps some wiser counsel had prevailed upon her to bring the controversy to a swift and amicable conclusion.

"Bina, my dear, there's a lot of listeners who say they don't want to hear you on the radio again until you apologise and lift the curse."

In seeking an apology, Paul was being a tad optimistic but the removal of the curse was non-negotiable; listeners genuinely did not want her on again until that particular matter had been resolved. Once more Midwest Radio was making history: this was definitely the first time a broadcasting career hinged on the lifting of a *seacht mallacht!*

Bina, for all her intransigence, was a shrewd woman and must have been well aware that public opinion had turned against her. The Queen of Connemara was far too proud to go on the airwaves and prostrate herself before the listening public but she concocted a form of words that cleverly extracted her from a mess entirely of her own making.

"Lookit Bina," said Paul. "We've had thousands of callers in the last week and they are all saying that this man doesn't deserve to have a curse placed on him."

Bina saw the gap and went for it.

"Well if he didn't deserve it than it wouldn't fall on him," she said.

A mightily relieved Claffey repeated what she had just said.

"So what you're saying Bina to our listeners is that if this man didn't deserve a curse than it won't fall on him."

"That's it," The Queen added hastily. "Now good morning to you and your listeners."

And with that she was gone: the *seacht mallacht* had been lifted and everything was right in the world again.

"I'd say it was the only time in her life she ever relented," remarks Gerry Glennon.

The only pity was that nobody asked Bina whether she could also cancel the *seacht mallacht* on the poor old Mayo football team while she was in a curse-lifting mood. Admittedly, it was a long shot but it could have saved Mayo's long-suffering fans an awful lot of heartache in the next 21 years.

The furore over Bina and the Curse proved once again, if proof were needed, that truth is often stranger than fiction, but the *Mid-Morning Show* was also capable of creating a stir with telephone calls where fact and fiction became very muddled indeed.

A gifted mimic, Paul had always been a great man for a prank as his poor mother discovered all those years earlier when 'Sgt Flannelly' called to warn Mrs Claffey of an impending Garda raid on the pirate radio station operating from her garden shed. In the 1990s, Paul incorporated surprise telephone calls into the *Mid-Morning Show* and the novel feature proved tremendously popular for well over a decade.

"Practically every day listeners would write or email the programme asking Paul to catch out some unsuspecting victim on the occasion of their birthday, wedding anniversary or some special occasion in their life," explains Gerry. "From the hundreds of requests, we'd select one and a plot would be hatched to try and catch out the listener in the best way possible. These calls were live, chaotic and dangerous and we had absolutely no way of knowing how they would end up. But when they worked they were magical!"

Indeed, they were so magical Midwest put together a CD of the best surprise phone calls and released it in 2006, raising €20,000 in the process for Mayo Mental Health Association and Western Care.

Paul's strategy was simple but it worked almost every time. He'd begin with a plausible proposition and once he could see the caller was taking the bait he'd add layer upon layer of farce until it became blindingly obvious the whole thing was a set up. The Eircom broadband deal was a classic surprise 'phone call.

The victim was a housewife in Williamstown who was about to head out the door when she received a telephone call from a man by the name of Michael Timoney, who worked for Eircom Broadband Services in Longford.

Now Michael Timoney was a very well-spoken, fastidious individual who had made it his day's mission to give free Eircom broadband for three months to 14 lucky householders in Williamstown. It was "no strings attached", he insisted, and the contract could be cancelled at the end of the three months. So far, so good... the housewife was warming to the proposition.

Timoney sealed the deal when he announced that the special offer also included a free computer and printer to the value of €2,700. But would the computer need to be returned once the three months were up?

"Not at all," said the munificent Mr Timoney. "The computer and printer are all yours, no strings attached."

It was an offer the housewife couldn't refuse. She agreed there and then to sign up for the three-month contract and Timoney promised to send out the paperwork immediately.

"I'll have the workmen over to you tomorrow," he airily remarked.

"Workmen?" came the alarmed reply.

"Yes to put up the aerial in your back garden. Now it's a 50-foot tower and we'll have to put in a foundation for it too."

Timoney went on to explain that there was also a 70-foot tower but he believed the "smaller one" would be sufficient in this case. By now, the housewife was becoming extremely perturbed at the prospect that her back garden was about to become the site for a communications tower, which Timoney admitted was "a second cousin to one of those telephone masts". It was only when the lady was about to hang up that Timoney finally revealed himself to be Paul Claffey from Midwest Radio.

The surprise telephone calls originated on the *Tommy Marren Show* but when the format of that programme switched from light entertainment to current affairs, the hugely popular feature migrated onto the *Mid-Morning Show* where it took on a cult status. Paul was a master impersonator who could effortlessly morph into a concerned mother ringing Fashion Scene in Charlestown to purchase a 36DD bra for her daughter who was "fierce big on top". The daughter was home from Dublin for a wedding but the bra needed to have a fastener at the front because she found it hard to reach her back and "Seamus wouldn't be around to open it for her". When it emerged that the only 36DD bra available in the shop had to be opened from the back, the mother speculated that maybe her daughter would find someone at the wedding who might open it for her!

One of Paul's best characters for his surprise 'phone calls was Fr Barney McGrath, a softly-spoken, earnest-sounding priest who might call someone in New York on Christmas Week to extend season's greetings. During the course of the conversation, it would emerge that Fr Barney was alone in New York for Christmas and missing home terribly, especially as he would have to eat his dinner alone on Christmas Day. The unsuspecting victim would feel it rude not to invite this lovely priest over for a bit of turkey dinner at which point it would emerge that Fr Barney, having gratefully accepted the kind invitation, wasn't entirely alone and would be bringing Fr John, Fr Kevin and Sr Celia with him!

"I impersonated a priest in those early days because I knew people wouldn't curse at a priest," recalls Paul, laughing. "The big thing was to stop them swearing when they discovered it was a wind-up."

Arguably the best ever recipient of a surprise call was Ballycroy woman Bridget Heston, who had managed to lose her false teeth, not once but twice in the space of a year. On both occasions, Paul called her up pretending to have found the teeth and he caught her out each time, the second occasion pretending to be a hotel attendant from Medjugorje who had so many sets of missing false teeth he couldn't figure out which one belonged to Bridget. When it finally emerged that this foreign-sounding caller was, in fact, Paul Claffey, a highly-amused Bridget declared: "Not you again, Paul Claffey!"

But, sometimes, a serious telephone call on the *Mid-Morning Show* could take a surprising twist when it was least expected. On one occasion in the early 1990s, Paul was hosting an outside broadcast when he was approached by a man who explained that his daughter Mary had moved to Australia and was "fierce lonely".

"Would you give her a call there and let her know we're all thinking of her back home," the proud father asked, scribbling Mary's number on a scrap of paper.

Paul returned to the satellite cruiser and dialled the number live on air. A male voice answered.

"Can I speak to Mary?" said Paul, thinking the father had given him an incorrect number.

"Mary, wake up!" the man said.

It was just as well Paul wasn't pretending to be Fr Barney McGrath or the poor girl would have died of mortification altogether.

JJ O'Hara's papier-maché goat never made it home from Dublin. It was destroyed in a malicious fire while parked in a car park in Abbeylara on the night of the All-Ireland Club Final. But the indefatigable JJ was undeterred, and when the Foxford Goat Fair petered out, the charismatic supermarket owner turned his full attention to honouring the memory of the founder of the Argentine Navy, Admiral William Brown, who was a native of Foxford.

There was no better man than JJ at garnering media headlines. When England were drawn to play Argentina in World Cup '98, he saw a golden opportunity to create a bit of publicity for his new project. Foxford was a popular destination for English fishermen and JJ decided it would be a good idea to drum up a bit of friendly rivalry between Argentina-supporting locals and their tourist guests. It wasn't long before The Shoe was drafted in on the plan and an outside broadcast was arranged to coincide with the big game.

Willie McNeely turned up in Hennigan's pub in Foxford on the evening of the match to be greeted by JJ and a handful of locals decked out in the sky blue and white of Argentina alongside a few mystified English fishermen who had gone out for a quiet pint only to walk into a media circus.

JJ and The Shoe were a marriage made in heaven because one was more hyperbolic than the other when describing what was happening in Foxford that night. By the time they were finished, listeners to Midwest Radio would have been forgiven for thinking the Falklands War was being refought on the banks of the River Moy.

Nobody loved the outside broadcast more than The Shoe; out among the people was where he was at his happiest. When the legendary horse Doran's Pride, owned by Bangor Erris native, Tom Doran, contested the Cheltenham Gold Cup in March 1998, The Shoe and Teresa O'Malley set off for the North Mayo village where excitement was at fever pitch ahead of the big race. They arrived at the already-packed Talk of the Town pub at 12 noon and got ready for a live insert into the *Mid-Morning Show.*

"Within minutes of setting up, Willie was standing on the countertop, microphone in hand, and was leading the gathering in song as we linked up live to Paul back at base in Ballyhaunis," recalls Teresa. "Doran's Pride failed to make the grade on the day but the entertainment, the fun and the excitement never dwindled while The Shoe was in charge."

The following morning, The Shoe told Gerry Glennon:

"Gerryeen, if Doran's Pride runs again at Cheltenham next year, I'll be there to commentate on it, mark my words!"

It was a promise he fully intended to keep and Gerry, having watched his irrepressible colleague at close quarters for the past year, didn't doubt him. If any local broadcaster could find a way to get to the most famous horseracing festival in Europe it was The Shoe. Chris Carroll, who was now station manager, recalls Monday mornings in the late 1990s when Willie would follow him around the building in Abbey Street making a passionate case for increased hours for his weekend sports shows.

"The Shoe would have turned Midwest into a non-stop sports channel for the weekend if he could! He'd arrive in on Monday and start telling me about the unbelievable weekend of sport he had just produced and how he needed more programme time to deliver the sports coverage the people of Mayo deserved."

Bina and the Curse got 1998 off to a stormy start for Midwest but the year ended with a storm of a very different kind. On St Stephen's Day, the West of Ireland was pounded by ferocious winds, the strength of which had not been seen since Hurricane Debbie struck way back in 1961.

The hurricane left a trail of destruction in its wake. Roofs were ripped from buildings, trees were felled and thousands of homes left with neither electricity nor telephone connections.

The scale of the damage was truly breathtaking. In Castlebar, some 50 mature trees were felled at Breaffy House while an estimated 3,000 slates were torn from the old building and 30 large windows were also blown in. In the seaside resort of Enniscrone, timber-frame mobiles homes were reduced to matchsticks and caravans overturned.

There was one local fatality: 26-year-old show-jumper Michael Joyce from Ballindine was tragically killed when a tree fell on his car in Connemara shortly after the powerful winds struck.

The hurricane caught an unsuspecting public in a post-Christmas lull and brought the whole western region to a complete standstill. Entire towns were plunged into darkness and many pubs were virtually empty on St Stephen's Night, traditionally one of the busiest evenings of the year. In a pre-Internet era, the loss of electricity and telephones meant only one thing: people had to turn to their battery-operated radios for their connection with the outside world and Midwest certainly rose to the occasion.

As soon as the first trees began falling, Midwest's 'Operation Stephen' kicked into gear and the station became a vital source of information for a public struggling to come to terms with the scale of the damage caused by this devastating storm. Many of Midwest's staff were taking a well-deserved break for the Christmas and could not return to Ballyhaunis due to the countless fallen trees blocking roads around the region. Gerry Glennon, Michael Neary, Paul Claffey and Joe Freeley took it in turns to keep the station on the air for the duration of the storm. Ballyhaunis-based Joe worked in the station's accounts section and usually spent much of his week on the road visiting Midwest's clients so he knew the geography of the region better than most and was a valuable addition to the broadcasting team in this emergency situation.

"We had no idea how long we'd be able to stay on because we were convinced our transmitters would be brought down," explains Gerry. "In fact, it was a miracle our network stayed up through it all."

Normal musical requests were suspended and instead listeners were invited to telephone in reports from their areas so people could have a better idea of what was happening on the ground. Meanwhile, the ESB provided updates every half hour on its progress in restoring power to the thousands of households across Co Mayo now without power. It was a slow, painstaking process. The town of Kilkelly, for example, was in blackout mode for a full 50 hours while other, isolated places were still without power three days later.

"We stayed on for six days and six nights giving non-stop updates, firstly on the storm itself and then on the clean-up operation," recalls Gerry. "We survived on soup and went without sleep for long periods too. It was pure adrenaline that kept us going but we felt it was important to stay on the air as long as we could because we were conscious of the important service we were providing at a very difficult time for people. There was also a sense we were giving company to elderly people in isolated areas who were living alone and might be frightened without electricity."

Midwest won widespread praise – and a national media award – for its wall-to-wall coverage of Hurricane Stephen. This was public service broadcasting at its very best and a timely reminder on the eve of the station's tenth anniversary of the vital importance of local radio.

Midwest had certainly come a long way in those first ten years.

CHAPTER TWENTY-SEVEN

'I just let him talk uninterrupted'

THE dawn of 1999 unleashed a tsunami of rumination and reminiscing. Not every generation gets to be around for the end of a century, let alone a millennium, so 1999 became a year of introspection and nostalgia. Communities launched local history books and magazines; newspapers published souvenir supplements and the national broadcaster commissioned television programmes like *Reelin' in the Years* and *Seven Ages*, the latter a seven-part history of the Irish state since its foundation.

Midwest Radio had only been around for the final 15 years of the century – and very few records survived from the pirate days – so it didn't possess the sort of vast archive for a sweeping, panoramic documentary such as *Seven Ages.* However, the Ballyhaunis station was making its own valuable contribution to the preservation of Irish culture and history through the indefatigable efforts of presenters like Séamus Duffy, Joe Byrne, John Duggan and Séamus Shannon, all of whom had spent the 1990s compiling a substantial archive of Irish traditional music. In so doing, these four presenters captured much of the musical heritage of the West of Ireland, painstakingly preserving a generations-old cultural legacy that even survived those dark, wretched days of the Famine.

Writing in *Mayo in the Twentieth Century,* a supplement published by the *Mayo News* in 1999, Séamus Duffy remarked: "Irish traditional music is basically a music being of the people and by the people. It is racy of the soil of Ireland having emanated from the rural area where apart from Gaelic games little other forms of diversion were available to young and old. There was no formal musical education for traditional music – it was passed down from father to son, from mother to daughter or from one family member to another or even an interested neighbour."

In an era before the gramophone and formal music classes, traditional music depended entirely on live performances for its preservation. In 1991, Séamus decided to capture the spirit of that pre-gramophone era by recording a live show every Sunday evening, simply entitled *Fleadh Cheoil.* It was a massive undertaking but Séamus, then a mere gasúr of 61, was more than able for the task. *Fleadh Cheoil* became a much-loved staple of the Midwest schedule during the 1990s and countless up-and-coming local musicians got an opportunity to perform to a vast radio audience thanks to Séamus' determination to promote young talent. He even purchased a Marantz and went out and about recording traditional musicians in their natural settings.

"He made about 2,000 field recordings," explains Gerry Glennon. "Nobody could get the quality out of a Marantz like Seamus, whatever magic he had. He was old when he bought it and had no experience with it but he had a real gift for recording musicians live."

Chris Carroll, who was the sound engineer for many of those early *Fleadh Cheoil* programmes, says Séamus put in an enormous effort, persuading renowned musicians to travel from all over the West of Ireland to the studio in Ballyhaunis on a Sunday night. There was also an element of risk involved in hosting a live show but Séamus always had faith in the musicians to deliver.

"Radio is a special medium and while one may get away with minor lapses, the more discerning listener will quickly conclude that something is amiss if such is the case," he remarked in a newspaper article in 1997. "Timing is vital but this can be achieved through keen anticipation."

Séamus concluded that Midwest must be doing something right when he entered a pub one evening and heard two men discussing the merits of two flute-players featured a week earlier on *Fleadh Cheoil.* The popular programme marked its sixth birthday in 1997 and the inimitable Séamus celebrated in Nico's in Ballyhaunis with a cheeseburger and a pot of tea, the cheeseburger being the only concession to modern culture during the entire evening.

Fleadh Cheoil wasn't the only show on Midwest Radio that brought live traditional music into homes across the West of Ireland. John Duggan and Séamus Shannon's *Ramblin' House* was a tremendously popular programme in the 1990s, touring the western seaboard as far as Co Kerry where the great playwright John B Keane was among its guests.

The premise for *Ramblin' House* was simple: unannounced guests would drop in for a chat and a bit of music, a song, a story or even a game of cards. Duggan and Shannon were the consummate hosts, both having enjoyed great success in the Irish music scene. Elphin-born Shannon, who today presents a popular traditional music programme on Shannonside FM, is an All-Ireland champion accordionist and a respected songwriter. Together with John Duggan, Séamus established the *Ramblin' House* series as a much-loved feature in Midwest's weekly schedule and older listeners still talk fondly about it.

In that final decade of the 20th century, Midwest's *Fleadh Cheoil* and *Ramblin' House* played vital, incalculable roles in preserving a priceless musical birthright, engendering in a new generation a sense of pride and passion in the music of its forefathers. But few men have worked as tirelessly at promoting and conserving the traditional culture of the western region than the remarkable Joe Byrne, who possesses such an abundance of knowledge on Irish music and culture that an entire book would be needed to even scrape the surface of his endless research.

Joe's weekly *Ceol agus Ealaíon* took to the airwaves in the same summer that the newly-licensed Midwest was launched, but the programme's roots are as deep as a majestic, old oak tree that stands sentinel over a fertile cultural landscape.

Since 1989, Joe has used his three-hour show to bring to the fore countless performers, historians and artists; lost legends of our precious culture that would have drifted namelessly into the mists of time were it not for Joe's unstinting endeavours. He has been a cultural troubadour, even sacrificing his summer holidays on occasion to roam the highways and byways of the West of Ireland, recording the sights, sounds, stories, songs, melodies, dances and traditions of a bygone era.

"Since 1989, I've bought and used Marantz cassettes, DAT, mini-discs and digital discs." he remarks. "As the archive of recordings began to grow I decided to issue some regional collections of this material."

Joe has released over 20 CDs and more than a dozen accompanying books in his inexhaustible quest to faithfully recreate the musical milieu of our grandparents and great-grandparents.

"It is very difficult to imagine or capture what the music was like [in the late 19th century]," Joe remarked in an interview in 2008. "But to hear the sound of it we can – and we need – go no further than the very first recording of traditional music made in America by a melodeon player called John Hebburn, who was from Breaffy, near Ballina."

Forgotten musical sons of the West of Ireland like John McGrath of North Mayo have been introduced to a new generation through the research of Joe Byrne.

"McGrath was born around 1900 and it was he who composed so many of the famous reels that started coming back from the USA. His house in the Bronx was known as the Reel Factory."

As Joe talks in that soft, lyrical voice of his, a hidden history comes tumbling forth, his words weaving a rich and priceless tapestry. When Paul and Chris founded Midwest Radio, they could never have imagined that a station set up in the cloakroom of an ultra-modern Ballyhaunis nightclub, with its disco globes and flashing lights, would become a vehicle for the preservation of an Irish musical tradition spanning more than a century. Yet that is exactly what happened during the 1990s. By the end of the century, broadcasters like Joe Byrne, Séamus Duffy, John Duggan and Séamus Shannon were effectively performing a public service by capturing for posterity a musical heritage many believed was lost forever. At the same time, shows like *Fleadh Cheoil, Ramblin' House* and *Ceol agus Ealaíon* were breathing new life into traditional Irish music through the incessant promotion of emerging talent. As a turbulent century drew to a close, a century marked by sweeping change and incessant modernisation, Midwest Radio was firmly established as the standard-bearer for the cultural values and traditions of a fast-disappearing era.

It was a notable achievement, and certainly one worth celebrating, as the world stood on the cusp of a new century and a new millennium.

One young man who knew a thing or two about traditional music was Anthony Hennigan, a talented fiddle player from Foxford whose family pub was a favourite haunt of the young musicians Joe Byrne and Séamus Duffy were seeking to promote. In the spring of 1999, Anthony was attending a language school in the French Alps when he received a tip-off from home that Midwest Radio was seeking applicants for the position of deputy sports editor.

A sports fanatic, Anthony had recently completed a radio production course in Limerick and the chance of being apprentice to Willie 'The Shoe', whom he had witnessed in glorious action in the family pub the previous summer, was too good to turn down. A sample tape was required so Anthony immediately set off for the basement of the house where he was staying on the shores of Lake Annecy.

"My host family probably wondered at the sanity of their downstairs guest who was talking in strange tones to himself during the night," he recalls. "And Willie McNeely probably wondered at the sanity of his would-be apprentice when listening to my mock bulletin that described how Mayo had ended their famine and won that year's All-Ireland football final. But maybe it was that too which struck a chord... you see, Willie dreamt just like the rest of us."

The Shoe certainly did dream. MacHale Park had been Willie's playground in the 1960s and he spent endless summer's days in the old stadium, playing football on the hallowed turf during the day and watching from the stands until sundown as his heroes in green and red were put through their paces by Seamie Daly. He could recall them all. Johnny Carey, John Morley, Mick Ruane, Willie Loftus, Ray Prendergast, Joe Langan and, of course, the great 'Jinkin' Joe Corcoran who The Shoe famously described as "having sold more dummies in training than the vendors sold choc-ices on Connacht Final day".

The Shoe also grew up on fireside stories from his father, John, who recalled in mesmerising detail the great All-Ireland winning Mayo team of 1950 and 1951, and its pantheon of legends, men like Eamon

Mongey, Mick Flanagan, Padraig Carney, Sean Flanagan, Fr Peter Quinn and Henry Dixon.

So when Willie turned on this tape on a dreary February morning in 1999 and heard an enthusiastic 20-year-old breathlessly describing the end of Mayo's long famine, he promptly decided that this was the apprentice for him. It didn't matter that Anthony, by his own admission, possessed "an accent more London than Lahardane"; the only language that interested The Shoe was the language of sport and this kid clearly knew his stuff. Within weeks, Anthony had exchanged the French Alps for Abbey Street in Ballyhaunis and was The Shoe's industrious wingman, doing everything from collecting the breakfast roll to pestering Galway football boss John O'Mahony during his lunchbreaks at St Nathy's College in Ballaghaderreen. The Foxford man produced his first weekend sports shows on either side of his 21st birthday and was soon spending so much time in the boss' orbit his friends nicknamed him 'The Wellie'!

It was an exhausting job shadowing The Shoe in the spring of 1999 because he was a man constantly on the move. The day job was hectic itself but Willie also had a packed social diary that saw him attending club dinner dances and other functions the length and breadth of the county.

Typically, The Shoe delivered on his promise of a year earlier to broadcast from Cheltenham when Tom Doran gave his great horse another run in the Gold Cup. The big race was to take place on March 18, the day after Ballina Stephenites took on Crossmaglen in the All-Ireland Club Final, so The Shoe was in his element as he looked forward to this springtime sporting fiesta.

The club final delivered yet another All-Ireland defeat for a Mayo team. Ballina Stephenites kicked a litany of atrocious wides to effectively hand the title to the Northerners. Unlike two years earlier, The Shoe hadn't time to hang around for glum team banquets. As soon as the final whistle sounded, he and Jonathan Mullin headed straight for Dublin Airport to catch a flight to London ahead of the fabled Cheltenham Gold Cup for which Doran's Pride had been installed the favourite.

The next day, the Midwest team was whisked to the famous old racecourse in Tom Doran's Mercedes, The Shoe givin' her washkie over a crackling mobile 'phone as he delivered a characteristically melodramatic report for the *Mid-Morning Show* from the back seat of the Merc.

"There were two performances: one for the expectant public and another for us in the car," Jonathan later recalled.

Doran's Pride, ridden by jockey Richard Dunwoody in the green and red of Doran's native county, failed by just two lengths to claim the coveted Gold Cup. It was a disappointing end to the great adventure but The Shoe dined out for months afterwards on the unlikely tale of cruising into Cheltenham in a Merc belonging to the owner of the Gold Cup favourite.

Those were salad days for The Shoe. Mayo defeated All-Ireland champions Galway in Tuam to reclaim the Connacht senior football championship and although they eventually came a cropper to Cork in the All-Ireland semi-final, the county's minor footballers made it through to the final in late September and the senior ladies qualified for their first All-Ireland final in early October.

The Shoe had a crammed diary for September. There was the usual mix of sporting events, social functions and fundraisers. He was the kind of man who hated to say no so inevitably ended up on a merry-go-round of presentations, pitch openings, dinner dances and guest appearances. But he loved it and Paul Claffey can recall a conversation in the canteen at the Abbey Street studios in early September 1999.

"I remember him telling me how happy he was in the job; that it was the happiest he'd been professionally and personally in his entire life."

The third Sunday in September was a big one for The Shoe because he was spearheading a special fundraiser at the Curragh Racecourse in Co Kildare. Dubbed 'The Races of Castlebar', the event was being organised by Castlebar Tennis Club to raise money for a new pavilion and a special train had been laid on to take some 1,000 punters to the famous racecourse. The Shoe and Pat Gallagher enjoyed a day to remember, correctly predicting six of the winners on the seven-race card, thus ensuring the passengers on the special 'Races of Castlebar' train returned home with bulging wallets and purses.

The following Sunday was All-Ireland Final Day and there was a lot of optimism that a talented Mayo minor team could win the county's first national title at the underage grade since 1985. Nobody was more upbeat about the team's chances than The Shoe.

On the Sunday of the big match, Fr Michael Murphy was celebrating the 12.30pm Mass at the Church of the Holy Rosary in Castlebar when he glanced into the congregation and his eyes immediately rested upon the unmistakable figure of The Shoe. Fr Michael was surprised, very surprised: not because Willie wasn't a regular mass-goer but because it was so late on a Sunday. The minor final was due to commence at 2pm so something must be badly wrong if The Shoe was missing an All-Ireland final involving his beloved Mayo footballers.

Something was, indeed, badly wrong. Sadly, in the space of just a week, The Shoe's life had changed irrevocably and nothing would ever be the same again.

By the turn of the millennium, Michael Commins was hosting two late-night shows on Midwest, the first in the traditional Wednesday slot he had filled since 1988 and the second on Sunday evenings when he would interview a well-known public figure from Mayo or occasionally further afield. In 1997, Michael scored a major coup when he secured an interview with former Taoiseach Albert Reynolds who, at that time, was seeking the Fianna Fáil nomination to run for president.

Albert, of course, had a rich seam of stories from his days as a showband promoter and dancehall owner and the programme went well beyond its allotted finish time of 1am. In fact, it was nearer to 2am by the time Michael finally went off the air but the listeners stayed with him. Late-night radio has that gripping effect.

"I've always enjoyed broadcasting 'after hours' because there is an intimacy in 'Radio Land' at that time which I don't think you get during the day," Michael explains. "I never look on presenting programmes as 'work' in any sense of the word so I'd happily stay on that bit longer if it's required. The interview with Albert was one of those special nights when it was a pleasure to be in the studio. He came in for an hour and ended up waiting for two and half!"

Michael always liked to have some biscuits and a cup of tea for his guest but, on one occasion, forgot the all-important biscuits and had to make a dash for the nearest shop while the programme was in full flow.

"I put on *El Paso,* which is four minutes and 50 seconds' long!" he says. "I told the guest to just keep talking if it ran out. Thankfully, I got back from the shop in time."

Michael also made a little bit of history when he invited members of the Traveller community, Owen and Mary Kate Maughan from Claremorris, to come on his Sunday night show and share with the listeners their musical and cultural traditions. It was a programme that deservedly earned a lot of plaudits, not least because it captured a valuable part of Irish heritage, one that was in danger of being forgotten amidst the many negative portrayals of Travellers in the Irish media. The folk songs of the Travelling people had inspired many Irish balladeers, including the legendary Delia Murphy who honed her singing talents around the fires of Travellers who set up camp on her father's Mount Jennings estate in Hollymount in the 1910s.

But of all the guests who appeared on Michael Commins' Sunday night show through the 1990s and 2000s, none created a greater impression than Willie 'The Shoe' McNeely when he took to the airwaves on March 26, 2000. By then, The Shoe's illness was widely known but the true extent of his astonishing life-and-death struggle against cancer was not fully appreciated until he gave that gripping three-hour interview with Michael. The Shoe told his story in the only way he knew how: live and raw. It was no-holds-barred from the very beginning as he described in graphic detail that terrifying Monday evening the previous September when he suddenly felt unwell while faxing his weekly column to the *Western People.* An initial diagnosis of a malignant tumour unleashed a cataclysmic chain of events that ultimately left The Shoe at death's door.

"I just let him talk uninterrupted," recalls Michael. "It was his story and he was more than capable of telling it."

In typically frank language, Willie recalled how he had spent 93 days in intensive care at Mayo General Hospital, undergone six operations and suffered a deadly form of septicemia. He lost five stone alone during the month of November and only by sheer fluke had a doctor found a cure for his infection, unearthing a prescription that hadn't been used in the hospital in 38 years.

But worse was to follow in December when Willie's condition deteriorated rapidly again and he felt "a darkness descending".

"A long white tunnel appeared in the corner of my eye," he recalled. "My father, who had died earlier in the year, stood and saluted me. He told me to go back…"

It was, by any standards one of the most astonishing interviews ever broadcast on local radio in Ireland and was the talk of the province for months afterwards. In fact, an edited version of the interview, entitled *Back from the Brink*, was released on tape and CD the following June and raised a staggering £30,000 for Mayo Cancer Support. By then, The Shoe was back broadcasting. His first full commentary took place at Tuam Stadium on April 15 when Mayo took on Galway in the Connacht U21 Championship Final. In a moving gesture that reflected the esteem in which Willie McNeely was held across the province, the entire crowd rose in unison when it was announced before the game that the most popular broadcaster in the West was back behind his trusty mike.

Thirty sporting warriors were preparing to do battle out on the field but the greatest warrior of them all was above in the commentary box.

CHAPTER TWENTY-EIGHT

'Don't stand on the Taoiseach'

THE infamous millennium bug was supposed to bring the whole world to a standstill on January 1, 2000, but after all the fuss it proved a damp squip. However, the period on either side of the millennium was the catalyst for a technological revolution that is still continuing apace today.

So much had stayed relatively static in broadcasting throughout the 1980s and 1990s but everything changed with the arrival of digital technology. Suddenly, broadcasters at radio stations like Midwest were able to do things that seemed like the stuff of science-fiction movies just a few years earlier.

Siblings Paula Donnellan and Padraic Walsh were at the coalface of that rapidly changing technological environment. Paula, of course, had seen it all at Midwest, having been the first female voice on the old pirate station back in the 1980s. Like many of her contemporaries, the Castlerea native accidentally found herself behind a microphone when Chris Carroll's car got a puncture one Saturday afternoon while travelling to Ballyhaunis from Galway. Chris was due to present his *Classic Hits* show from 2 to 6pm and Paula, who was then a first-year student of Communications at Dublin City University, was on telephone duties for the day, having been offered weekend work at the station only a few weeks earlier.

"Paul and Maureen were my neighbours in Castlerea and I was their babysitter when I was in secondary school," she explains. "I'd stay over in their house every Saturday night while they were running Midas so I got to know them very well."

On completing her Leaving Certificate, Paula had no clear idea what she wanted to do at third-level apart from being certain she did not want to go down the then conventional female career paths of nursing and teaching. She choose DCU's Communications degree, then one of only two media-related courses in the country, the other being Rathmines School of Journalism. When Paul heard his former babysitter was studying communications he immediately saw an opportunity to add some female flair to Midwest's all-male team.

"He invited me over to see the station and within minutes I was recording ads for him!" recalls Paula. "I started coming in at weekends when I was home from college, just helping out around the place, mainly answering the telephone."

However, that all changed on the watershed Saturday afternoon when Chris rang the station and announced he was stuck at the side of the N17.

"You're on so, Paula," he said.

"On where?"

"On the radio!"

The teenager had no time to get nervous. She raced down to the studio, selected some records and settled in for a four-hour show. She'd never been on live radio before. When it was all over, the studio telephone rang. It was Chris again.

"Well," said Paula nervously. "What did you think?"

"You're hired!"

For the next year, Paula hitched over from Castlerea each Saturday morning with a bag of LPs on her back and presented the *Classic Hits* show. It was then back to college on Monday morning where the words 'pirate radio' weren't supposed to be even mentioned.

As luck would have it, Paula graduated from Dublin City University in the same summer that commercial radio was being legalised and found work with Shannonside FM where she presented the *Breakfast Show* among the many other duties that came with working in local broadcasting. The commercial stations might have been new but the technology was decades' old and Paula spent much of those early years perfecting the art of using a Stanley blade to cut reels of recording tape.

"You'd have bits of tape around your neck and bits of tape on the floor. It was crazy when I think back on it."

At Shannonside, Paula worked alongside Ciaran Mulooley, now RTÉ's Midlands' correspondent, and recalls walking into the newsroom one afternoon while Ciaran edited an interview with the then Taoiseach Albert Reynolds. There was so much tape around his neck he'd started to lay out strips on the floor.

"Jesus Christ, Paula," Mulooley shouted as she walked across the floor. "Don't stand on the Taoiseach!"

Paula's younger brother Padraic became a wizard in the art of reel-to-reel editing while working on Midwest's soap opera, *Glengarra*, in the mid-1990s. Launched in November 1995, *Glengarra* centred on everyday events in a typically ordinary Irish village with much of the action set in the home of fictional couple Tom and Nora Moyles. The soap opera – the first of its kind on local radio – ran once a week and was the creation of John Duggan and Margaret Niland, who wrote the scripts in consultation with Padraic.

"In those pre-Internet days we only had a limited amount of sound effects so John and Margaret would create a story around the sound effects available to us," recalls Padraic. "It was really technical for its time and was great fun to engineer."

Glengarra built up a loyal fanbase on Mid and Northwest Radio but it also proved a surprise hit in London where it was transmitted on G.S. Radio via a partnership with a broadcasting agency in the English capital.

Padraic spent the working day 'behind the scenes' during his early career with Midwest but the Castlerea man moved behind the mike in 1993 after Paul offered him the Saturday afternoon *Classic Hits* slot that had been the training ground for his older sister. In the same year, Padraic was asked to travel to Dublin to interview the winner of Ireland's Eurosong competition, Niamh Kavanagh, who was busily preparing for the Eurovision, due to be staged in Mill Street in Cork that year.

"It was my first live interview and I was a nervous wreck," Padraic recalls. "The interview was to take place in the old Point Depot as part of a media day so there were broadcasters and journalists from all over Ireland in attendance.

"I remember sitting across from Larry Gogan and his wife Florrie in the old bar in the Point and Larry could see I was nervous. He was incredibly nice to me – as was Florrie – and was just so encouraging. The interview went really well and I have always thanked Larry whenever I have met him over the years."

That first encounter with the legendary RTÉ disc jockey also planted a seed in Padraic's mind that was to bear fruit in the late 1990s when he was given his own afternoon show, *The Late Late Lunch Box.*

"He told me if I ever had a daily show to come up with a catchy quiz like the famous Just A Minute Quiz; something that you can run every day. So when Paul asked me to do the afternoon show I decided to launch the Alphabet Quiz, which has proven really popular with listeners over the years."

Today, Padraic Walsh's Alphabet Quiz is the second longest running quiz on Irish radio after the Just A Minute Quiz, which can now be heard on Larry Gogan's show on the internet channel RTÉ Gold.

Around the same time that Padraic was launching his afternoon show, Paula was vacating the early-morning slot to take up a new role alongside Teresa O'Malley in the newsroom. She arrived at a time of immense change in newsgathering as the onset of mobile telephones, email, Internet and digital technology swept away the old ways of working.

"The first day we offered listeners the opportunity to text in their requests the machine handling the texts blew up!" recalls Padraic. "Up to then, a lot of people wouldn't go to the hassle of ringing in a request and waiting on the telephone line. The convenience of the text resulted in an explosion in the number of requests."

In Midwest's newsroom, Paula went from a situation where she had been tripping over reel-to-reel tapes in Shannonside to a new world of editing content while on the road.

"In the old days, you'd be going around with a heavy Marantz on your shoulder and a big microphone in your hand. Once the interview was done you'd have to drive back to Ballyhaunis to physically edit the tapes with your Stanley blade, but once digital technology arrived, you could email everything straight back to the studio. That was a huge change."

Broadcasters like Paula had no need to worry any longer about 'standing on the Taoiseach'.

David Cawley wasn't exactly an early-morning guy before Paul Claffey offered him a trial on the *Breakfast Show* in 1998. In fact, in the mid-1990s, David's work as a nightclub disc jockey meant he was often going to bed when the summer sun was rising and his first gig with Midwest was at a very ungodly hour.

"In 1997, Midwest had a programme called *Level 2* that ran from 1 to 4am on Sunday mornings," says David. "Webster [Kevin McNeely] presented it in association with Panama Jacks in the TF Theatre in Castlebar where I was also a DJ. I stood in for him on several occasions."

Level 2 focused on the burgeoning dance music scene and was part of Mid and Northwest Radio's weekly offering for teenagers and young adults. David had yet to learn to drive so his then girlfriend Jane – now his wife – drove him to Ballyhaunis each Saturday after midnight and fell asleep in a chair outside the studio while David kept sleepless teenagers entertained with dance music classics like The Prodigy's *Firestarter* and Underworld's *Born Slippy*.

The genial Castlebar man had graduated with a Certificate in Radio Broadcasting from Dun Laoghaire College of Art and Design just a few years earlier and was now searching for his big break in radio.

"College gave you the idea you were going to be the next Gerry Ryan and it took a while to figure out that you weren't going to be the next Gerry Ryan!" he remarks, laughing. "I was pottering around doing a bit of DJ work in Panama Jacks and CRCfm in Castlebar when Brendan Redmond asked me to cover for him on the *Hot Hits Hour* for two weeks."

The short-lived *Level 2* in the wee hours of a Sunday morning hadn't offered David much of an opportunity to display his broadcasting skills to a large audience but the *Hot Hits Hour* was a different story altogether. The two-week stint went really well and Paul approached David soon afterwards to ask if he might put together some ideas for a new-sounding *Breakfast Show*.

"I came up with a few suggestions that, in hindsight, were really very city-based and I don't think Paul was convinced at all but he told me to give it a try for a week anyway," David recalls. "That was 21 years ago and I'm still on that one-week trial!"

The new show couldn't have come at a more opportune time for the then 24-year-old who had also been broadcasting a Sunday evening show on Galway Bay FM while still waiting for a proper break in radio. He quickly settled into his role as presenter of Midwest's *Breakfast Show* and also worked in the ad production department.

"Most people think that I'm back in the bed at 9.30am but the truth is that when the show finishes the real work begins," he explains. "I've been working with Padraic [Walsh] in advertising production since I joined Midwest and that's what I spend the bulk of my day doing."

The early-morning starts initially proved a challenge for a young man who had enjoyed a busy social life up to that point.

"I came from going to bed at 2am and sleeping till two in the day to getting up at 5am every morning," he remarks. "In 21 years, I've never gone to the cinema, restaurant or pub during the week because I know I cannot stay out late. In the early days, when Friday evening would come I'd be like a heifer let out in a field in the spring but that changed once the kids came along."

In the late 1990s, Midwest used to go off the air at 1am nightly so David got the idea of putting a CD of panpipe music on the turntable ahead of his own show. One day he got a telephone call from a farmer in Co Longford.

"What's that CD you put on before 7am," asked the farmer.

"It's some sort of Irish panpipes," replied David.

"Jaysus, make sure you keep playing it. My cows love it."

"What?" David asked incredulously.

"It's the truth," replied the farmer earnestly. "Whatever it is about that music when it comes on the milk flows. There's nothing up to then but once that music starts..."

Not only was David Cawley waking up the west he was also boosting the region's milk supply.

When David started on the *Breakfast Show* he was conscious many of his contemporaries wouldn't have been listening to Midwest in the early morning but as he moved into his thirties the Castlebar man was keen to develop a playlist that appealed to his friends.

"From the beginning, I wanted to play music from different genres and eras," he explains. "It wasn't the *Hot Hits Hour* but it wasn't the *Hucklebuck* either!"

As David grew older and had children of his own, he came to appreciate the importance of an early-morning routine in the lives of his listeners and to incorporate that into the *Breakfast Show.*

"The key to the *Breakfast Show* is to make it sound like it is a bit haphazard but it is, in fact, really strictly guided," he explains. "So if you are putting the lunches together for the kids and you hear me doing the Forgotten Classic you know where you should be in your life without having to look at the clock. It's all about routine and I think that is why an older listener will stick with me when I'm playing Foo Fighters or The Killers. They know that it's part of an overall routine so they will stick with it."

Even the cows in Longford got to know David Cawley's routine and liked it. By the turn of the millennium, the *Breakfast Show* was established as a firm favourite in Midwest's schedule and the Castlebar man's days as a night owl were definitely over. From now on, he'd be rising with the lark.

Angelina McHugh was only 15 when she reported on her first football match for Midwest. Her late father Frank knew Willie McNeely and Angelina recalls having several animated conversations with the broadcaster at Mayo matches in the late 1990s. The Glenisland youngster was a sports fanatic long before she hit her teens. She and her younger sister Bernie accompanied their father on trips around Ireland supporting the Mayo footballers and Angelina always had plenty of questions during the journey home.

"I'd pose 100 questions for Dad during the game and on the journey home," she recalls. "He answered them all for me and the more I learned the more I liked what I was seeing and hearing and pretty soon I was one of the roaring supporters on the sideline."

At the tender age of 15, Angelina submitted several articles to the local newspapers on sports events, prompting Willie McNeely to suggest to Frank McHugh that his daughter should consider becoming a weekend sports reporter for Midwest.

"My Dad thought it was a wonderful idea so I covered my first game between Crossmolina and Hollymount and did a match report that I agonised over for hours on end. It was recorded and broadcast and that was it – I had the bug!"

That was 1999. Angelina continued to cover sports events while a student at St Patrick's Academy in Islandeady and got a job with the station on completion of her Leaving Certificate in 2001. By then, Anthony Hennigan had been appointed sports editor at Northwest so there was a vacancy for a sports reporter in Ballyhaunis.

"In the summer of 2001, I visited Willie at his home and asked if he would possibly be able to give me a job in a full-time capacity as I was taking a year out from my studies," Angelina explains. "Willie promised me that he would not see me stuck and would come up with something."

That 'something' proved a lot more than Angelina expected. She was asked to cover Mondays and Tuesdays for Willie and was also heavily involved with the weekend sports coverage. It was typical of 'The Shoe' to find work for an aspiring young broadcaster. Angelina wasn't the only one to benefit from the sports editor's generosity. Jonathan Mullin recalls the "next-to-pointless assignments" Willie often gave him to ensure he wouldn't be short of a few bob in college.

The Shoe was in a good place in the summer of 2001. His check-ups were giving him the news he wanted to hear and his broadcasting career was going from strength to strength. In September, he launched a website for sports news, www.willietheshoe.com, and there was even speculation he might run for the Progressive Democrats in the general election in 2002.

But the bloodsport of politics would never supplant The Shoe's obsession with real sport. When Crossmolina became the first Mayo team to win the All-Ireland Senior Club Championship in 2001, Midwest's sports editor was beside himself with joy. Mike Finnerty, who was on commentary duties that day, later recalled the magical moment when it became clear Crossmolina were about to defeat the great Nemo Rangers from Cork.

"Liam Moffatt lands a big score and the Cusack Stand erupts. A giant hand crashes against the commentator's back. 'Go for it, Finno,' shouts The Shoe, his eyes dancing with delight. 'Go for it.'"

The new All-Ireland champions were afforded a hero's welcome on their return to Mayo and the first man off the team bus in Crossmolina was none other than the bould Willie 'The Shoe'!

Another source of delight for Willie was the incredible success of the Mayo senior ladies football team who claimed their third successive All-Ireland title in 2001. The Shoe had been an early promoter of ladies football and was heartbroken when his cancer diagnosis caused him to miss the team's breakthrough championship victory in 1999. But he certainly made up for it in 2000 and 2001, travelling on the team bus from Croke Park and joining in the inevitable tour of the county.

Despite his earlier illness, The Shoe kept up his hectic work schedule and even took on more responsibilities, if that were possible. He regularly called into Mayo General Hospital to visit people who were battling cancer, giving them courage and inspiration through the telling of his own remarkable story.

"I think Willie had at least 36 hours crammed into every day," recalled Seamus Kyne of 21st Century in Castlebar, the company charged with managing The Shoe's website. "[It was] 36 hours of work, play, stories and anecdotes that would have you in a spin trying to keep pace with him. When he would walk into 21st Century in the evening you just knew that the next hour would be a busy one!"

People encouraged The Shoe to slow down but it was as if he had a premonition of what was to come and wanted to cram as much into his limited time on this earth as he possibly could. Certainly, nobody could accuse Willie McNeely of not making the most of his new lease of life; he truly was a man reborn in 2001.

But, sadly, The Shoe found himself back in a hospital bed in the spring of 2002 and the life-and-death struggle began all over again.

CHAPTER TWENTY-NINE

'The mountain is sliding into the sea'

PAULA Donnellan joined a newsroom that was very different to the pirate days when she'd spend summer holidays reading out cuttings from national and local newspapers.

"There was a very relaxed attitude to news coverage on Midwest in the pirate era," she explains. "You'd have news bulletins for eight weeks when I was on holidays from college and then there'd be none at all until I came home for the Midterm or Christmas break!"

By the start of the new millennium, Midwest was well established as an important source of news and current affairs and was the first port of call for the public when a story was breaking. Sometimes the calls were scarcely believable. Teresa O'Malley returned to her desk after lunch on Holy Thursday, April 1, 1999, when the telephone rang.

"I'm ringing from Belmullet," said a male caller, breathless with excitement. "The rubber factory is on fire."

Aware of the date, Teresa was having none of it.

"Yeah right, April Fools," she remarked before hanging up.

Within seconds the telephone rang again. It was the same man.

"I knew then it must be serious," she recalls. "I didn't know the Cow Comforts plant was known locally as the 'rubber factory' so I was completely thrown when this man initially came on the telephone. But, fair play to him, he called back."

The fire turned out to be one of the biggest stories Teresa would cover as Midwest's news editor. Owned by local businessman Tom Duffy, Cow Comforts manufactured plastic mats for use on farms and exported thousands of these mats every week to the UK and elsewhere. Thankfully, nobody was killed in the blaze but the incineration of so much plastic created an enormous plume of smoke that threatened to engulf the town of Belmullet. Wary of the toxins that might be released into the atmosphere, Mayo Co Council invoked its County Emergency Plan and instructed residents of the Erris capital to remain indoors or leave the town altogether.

The St Stephen's Day storm was still fresh in the memory but already Midwest was again playing a crucial role in keeping local people informed on what was happening on the ground during a time of crisis. The story ran for rest of the day and into the following day as firefighters battled to bring the blaze under control. What initially seemed like a call from an April Fools prankster turned into the biggest story of the year. Truth, as Midwest Radio's news team would discover again and again, is often stranger than fiction.

A few months later, Teresa broadcast from the TF Royal Theatre in Castlebar for one of the most epic local election counts in Irish history when Ballycroy's Frank Leneghan defeated Mulanny's Michael Holmes by a fraction of one vote to take the last seat on Mayo Co Council. Midwest stayed with the count throughout the weekend and into the following week as the votes were parsed and analysed by a variety of political and legal experts before Holmes magnanimously conceded to his friend and neighbour. In an interview with Midwest, the Tiernaur farmer agreed that this was the ultimate example of every vote counting – and not all the votes promised to him had materialised either.

"It's not just the politicians who tell fibs on the doorsteps!" he good-humouredly remarked. Holmes, of course, went on to claim a council seat in 2004 and retained it in successive elections until his retirement in 2019.

The election count of 1999 was really just a dry run for another marathon political battle three years later when future Taoiseach Enda Kenny arrived at the count centre in the TF Royal Theatre with a concession speech in his pocket only to stage a Lazarus-like comeback in the early hours of the morning. The impending introduction of electronic voting – it was used in several Leinster constituencies that year – prompted many to describe the 2002 general election as the last of the long counts. Midwest was determined to make the most of this historic weekend and had a team of 20 reporters and presenters spread across the five count centres in Connacht. In Castlebar, Teresa and Liamy MacNally were joined by the Belmullet duo of Pat Cafferkey and Liam McAndrew, who analysed the tallies and results as they became available. There was widespread praise afterwards for the Midwest team, which broadcast non-stop for 20 hours until the final declaration of results shortly after 4am on Sunday morning, long after the music stopped in the adjacent Panama Jacks nightclub. Of course, the experiment in electronic voting failed dismally so the tradition of long counts extended beyond 2002 and continues right up to this day.

"I have discovered over the years that people listen to election counts on Midwest as they would a sport," says Teresa. "They want to know the result and they will stick with the coverage until there is a result so it is vital we stay on the air no matter how long it takes."

Apart from her day-to-day duties as news editor, Teresa has also produced a number of award-winning documentaries, including a widely acclaimed series on four Mayo natives who had a major impact globally. The four were former president of the United Nations Security Council and Foxford native Noel Dorr, Ballina-born United Nations Commissioner Mary Robinson, EU Commissioner and Castlebar man Padraig Flynn and Louisburgh-born missionary priest Fr Pádraig Ó Máille.

"The documentaries are great because you can give time to them," Teresa explains. "The *Mayo People Abroad* series was particularly satisfying. The story of somebody like Fr Pádraig Ó Máille, who was such an influential figure in Malawi, was remarkable and I think the series showed the enormous impact Mayo people have had on the world stage."

Teresa also joined forces with Liamy MacNally, who had returned to Midwest in 1999, and together they recorded several documentaries, including a critical look at Knock Airport, entitled *Knock Airport: What's The Story?*, which posed some awkward questions for one of Midwest's then shareholders. At the time, Knock Airport was in the doldrums and there were fears for its future but the appointment of Joe Kennedy as chairman and Liam Scollan as chief executive in 2002 sparked a revival in the airport's fortunes.

Midwest's daily news programmes regularly topped JNLR listenership surveys throughout the early 2000s but the living struggled to compete with the dead, as former news editor Tom Shiel wryly remarked in an article in the *Connaught Telegraph* in 1997 about the station's famous death notices.

"Even top broadcasters such as Gay Byrne and Pat Kenny take a hammering in the ratings when the death notices are read thrice daily on Mid and Northwest Radio," Shiel wrote. "At the 10am death notice slot, listenership soars to its daily peak, an astonishing 35 per cent of the potential audience."

Recalling his own time at Midwest, Tom remarked that a large proportion of telephone calls were to check on death notice details. This was, of course, in the pre-Internet era when funeral arrangements were not so readily available on Midwest's website.

Not everybody was asked to read the death notices either.

"It's a bit like the Bible," Shiel remarked, "many are called, few are chosen. It takes a special kind of voice, sympathetic yet precise, detached yet with empathy.

"Good diction is important as well as an ability to pronounce strange-sounding names like *Skeheen, Tumgesh* or *Barnalyra.*

"Even ones that look easy are difficult, like *Aughavale* Cemetery in Westport. Locals pronounce it *Uh-Wal* and occasionally ring up the station to voice their displeasure should the announcer make a mess of it."

Midwest received its share of unusual requests over the years but perhaps the most poignant came from a lady whose father recently passed away in England. She wondered if it would be possible to play Tom Jones' *The Green, Green Grass of Home* immediately after the death announcements because at roughly that time the plane carrying her father's remains would be touching down at Knock Airport. The flexibility of local radio meant the team at Midwest was only too happy to facilitate such a thoughtful tribute to a returning emigrant.

The story illustrates once again the importance of local radio over the last 30 years; national radio could not possibly provide such a personal and deeply meaningful service to its listeners.

Midwest suffered its own series of sad losses in the early 2000s as some old friends went to their eternal reward. In late 2000, Bina McLoughlin's robust health failed and she was in and out of hospital for the rest of the winter, eventually passing away at Merlin Park Hospital in Galway on February 16, 2001, at the age of 72. One of her last visitors was Éamon Ó Cuiv who presented her with his Fáinne, the emblem of those who can and want to speak the Irish language.

"She greeted him in Irish and was proud of that," the *Connacht Tribune* reported. "He presented her with his own Fáinne. It was an impromptu act. She carried it with her for no more than 12 hours in this world and died the following morning."

The crowds flocked to Leenane Church a few days later to bid a final farewell to the Queen of Connemara and the Queen of the Airwaves. The celebrants of her funeral Mass included her great friend and fellow Máméan devotee Fr Micheál MacGréil, who reflected on the proud legacy of Bina McLoughlin and the way she brought North Connemara's culture and heritage to a much wider audience through her regular radio conversations with Paul Claffey.

"Bina was much more than a colourful entertainer," Fr Micheál noted. "At times she spoke with tongue in cheek and was able to fascinate the listeners while, at the same time, she was teaching them folklore of the North Connemara community. She skillfully, with her wit and charm, was able to restore pride in our rural 'peasant' past about which we were somewhat ashamed."

Bina was afforded a send-off befitting a Queen of Connemara. Bagpiper Martin Molloy led the cortege to the graveyard overlooking Killary where Kevin Coyne and Matt Keane played a selection of Bina's favourite songs, ending inevitably with *The Queen of Connemara* as the large crowd joined together for the rousing chorus.

Oh she's neat; Oh she's sweet; She's a beauty in every line
The Queen of Connemara is that bounding barque of mine.

Later that year, Midwest released a CD of a selection of Bina's conversations with Paul – including the infamous curse – and it proved a huge hit, raising thousands of pounds for Our Lady's Hospital for Sick Children in Dublin and Máméan pilgrimage site. The latter was one of the great passions in Bina's life and she never tired of encouraging listeners to Mid and Northwest to visit the rock where St Patrick was reputed to have rested on his travels around Ireland. Bina had great faith in the healing powers of Máméan and often referred to it as *hOspidéal Conamara* or the *Connemara Man's Hospital.* The annual Máméan pilgrimage on the first Sunday of August was one of the highlights of the year for Bina; indeed, it was more important to her than the famous Bogman's Ball in Maam Cross where she was always the star attraction.

"Her Celtic Christianity was harmoniously integrated with devotion to the Mass and Sacraments, to the weekly Holy Hour and regular pilgrimages to Knock Shrine," Fr Micheál noted in his homily at Bina's funeral mass, adding that she was "never a servant to the slave mentality of today's commercialism".

Another popular contributor to the *Mid-Morning Show,* Hilda Creaby, passed away in September 2002 after battling ill health for a long number of years. She was aged 73 and had outlived her beloved husband Tom by just 18 months.

In September 2000, Hilda and Tom provided Midwest with one of its great outside broadcasts when Paul, Gerry and Seamus Moore arrived unannounced at the Creaby home in Goulboy to celebrate the popular couple's 50th wedding anniversary.

"Gerry and myself landed down to the bedroom and got Hilda and Tom out of the bed," recalls Paul, laughing. "Sure they nearly had a heart attack. Seamus Moore was out on the lawn playing the *JCB Song* and the whole family, who were all in on it, joined us. We had a mighty two-hour show and the reaction from listeners was something else."

In his weekly column in the *Western People* on September 18, 2002, Paul paid a moving tribute to Hilda, recalling Midwest's long association with the Kiltimagh woman from the pirate days.

"From the very first call I realised Hilda was a larger-than-life character and that she was going to be a great friend. Hilda said it as it was and she took no prisoners, her opinions on lots of matters were very strong but she had a huge sense of the better things in life – she loved to laugh, loved music and always saw the good in everyone. Despite her poor health, and God knows her health had been very bad over the years, she never once complained, and if I rang her six times a day she was always ready for the chat and the laugh."

The deaths of Bina and Hilda robbed the *Mid-Morning Show* of two of its liveliest characters, creating a void that could never be filled.

"They were of their time," says Paul. "Their opinions reflected the opinions of the thousands of ordinary people who never got on the radio and that's why they were so popular. The people loved them."

The people loved Willie 'The Shoe' McNeely too and his death on June 12, 2002, sparked a huge outpouring of emotion as listeners contacted Midwest in their droves to pay tribute to the charismatic broadcaster who had left such an enormous footprint on Mayo's media landscape in a relatively short period. Aged just 47, Willie's death was a devastating blow to his family, colleagues and many friends who had hoped against hope he might stage yet another miraculous recovery. But it was not to be and Willie was afforded a send-off fit for a king in his native Castlebar with thousands turning out to sympathise with his wife, young children and elderly mother Ellen. Among those to pay tribute was the president of the GAA, Seán McCague, who described The Shoe as "the voice of the GAA in Mayo".

"His unique personality, his knowledge and passion for the games and his ability to paint colorful pictures with words made him an institution that will be sorely missed by all," Mr McCague remarked.

The local newspapers published numerous tributes, including one from the *Connaught Telegraph's* sports editor John Melvin, who had chronicled Willie's meteoric rise in the media industry, having known him in his previous incarnations as shoe salesman, publican and marketing executive. Recalling the day in Tuam two years earlier when an entire stadium rose to greet the return of The Shoe, Melvin remarked: "He was the people's broadcaster."

The people's broadcaster...

It was a fitting tribute from one auld buddy to another.

It had long been an ambition of the board of Midwest to move the station from the cramped studios on Abbey Street to a purpose-built headquarters in Ballyhaunis but the financial prudence of the early years meant it would be 2003 before the dream was finally realised. A site on Clare Street – formerly Dillon's Hardware – was acquired in the late 1990s and work commenced in August 2002. The new building was opened on Friday, September 19, 2003, by the then chief executive of Special Olympics Ireland, Kiltimagh native Mary Davis.

"We built it from the ground up," explains Paul. "When it opened it was the most modern studio in the country, a new radio building fit for a new century.

"Chris, myself and the rest of the board always said we would bide our time in moving from Abbey Street because we wanted to do it right and I believe we did that with the new offices. They were worth the long wait."

Midwest was returning home to Clare Street where it had all began 18 years earlier in Midas Nightclub. But the splendid new office, with its striking glass-fronted design, spacious reception area and state-of-the art recording studios, could not have been further removed from the little cloakroom at the back of Midas with the single microphone, turntable and twin tape-decks.

"Starting out then we never imagined that in a mere 18 years we'd be in a new purpose-built, state-of-the-art building," Paul commented at the opening ceremony. "I definitely feel that part of our success story is due in no small way to the hard work and dedication of our staff. And, of course, it goes without saying that without the loyalty of our listeners and advertisers, none of this would be possible."

In many ways, the new offices were the ultimate vindication of everything Paul, Chris and the board had stood for over the past 18 years: the organic growth, the cautious financial management and the desire to stay true to Midwest's humble roots. The palatial offices might have seemed like a break with the past but the new building was merely a statement of intent: Midwest Radio was here to stay and was ready to serve the people of Mayo for another 18 years and more.

More than 300 guests attended the opening ceremony and the celebrations continued long into the evening in a nearby marquee. It was after 9pm when Gerry Glennon returned home to Granlahan and he was ready for an early night, having arrived at work more than 12 hours earlier. However, he decided to catch some of Eamon Dunphy's new chat show on TV3, which was launching that night, before hitting the hay. Gerry had barely made himself comfortable when the telephone rang. It was Gerry Coyle, the councillor from Belmullet, who had been at the opening ceremony that very afternoon. What could he want at this hour?

"Gerry, there's been a landslide down here in Pullathomas," Coyle exclaimed urgently. "Can ye get on the radio and warn people to stay indoors."

"A landslide?"

"Yes, the rain is teeming down here. I've never seen anything like it. The mountain is sliding into the sea, the roads are blocked and everything. People will be killed if we don't get on the radio and warn them."

Gerry found it hard to believe what he was hearing. It was a beautiful autumnal evening in Ballyhaunis, and while Erris sometimes had a weather system all of its own, the story seemed utterly incredible.

But he could sense the panic in Coyle's voice so he pulled on his jacket, hopped into the car and set off for Ballyhaunis where the celebrations were still continuing. Gerry immediately put a call through to Teresa O'Malley who had just arrived home to Castlebar and was settling in for a relaxing evening.

"I'd presented *Evening Edition* earlier on so I hadn't the chance really to join in the celebrations," she recalls. "I was just getting ready to sit down at home with a glass of wine when Gerry Glennon rang to tell me that calls were coming in that the top of Dooncarton Mountain had slid towards the sea, ripping a swathe of devastation through the graveyard at Pullathomas. Houses had been inundated with mud, roads were ripped up and there were fears for the safety of families in the area."

The glass of wine was immediately set to one side and Teresa headed straight for Midwest's studio in Castlebar where she spent the next two hours bringing the dramatic events in North Mayo into homes across the region.

"Gerry Coyle was brilliant because he was on the ground throughout it all and kept us up-to-date," recalls Teresa. "The following morning I drove to Pullathomas and witnessed an incredible vista. The crown of the mountain at Dooncarton was ripped away and the nearby graveyard desecrated by the brute force of nature. It was one of the saddest sights I have ever seen and must have been terribly upsetting for people who had loved ones buried in the cemetery."

Thankfully, there were no fatalities – although there were a few lucky escapes – and life gradually returned to normal in the foothills of Dooncarton Mountain. However, the extraordinary scenes are still etched in the memory of Gerry Coyle, who became Midwest's man on the ground in those first dramatic hours.

"The night of the Pullathomas landslide was one of Midwest's finest hours," he says. "As soon as I put the call through to Gerry Glennon, they were on top of the story and they stayed with it right through the night, providing valuable information to the public who were impacted by the landslides. I'd go so far as to say that Midwest saved lives that night by urging people to stay indoors and away from danger. They were there for the people of Erris when we needed them most."

The dramatic events of September 19, 2003, were a timely reminder – if one were needed – that there is no such thing as an off day in Radio Land. Gerry and Teresa would certainly never forget the day Midwest opened its new headquarters.

CHAPTER THIRTY

'I felt a great wrong had been done'

THE opening of such a magnificent new headquarters was the culmination of a long-held dream for Midwest's co-founders but the joy was tempered somewhat by the realisation that sister station Northwest was in a race against time to stay on the airwaves. Indeed, in September 2003, Paul was still coming to terms with the shock decision of the IRTC, now named the Broadcasting Commission of Ireland (BCI), to effectively revoke Northwest's licence and instead award the Sligo/South Donegal/North Leitrim radio franchise to a new consortium operating under the name Ocean FM. Even today, 16 years later, Paul shakes his head in bewilderment when he reflects on the spring of 2003 and, in particular, the fateful day of Tuesday, April 29.

"Michael O'Keeffe, the chief executive of the BAI, rang me and said that Ocean had been awarded the new 10-year licence for the northwest region," he recalls. "I was shocked, devastated… it was the toughest week in my professional career. The decision defied logic; it made absolutely no sense to me; and it still doesn't after all these years.

"I was never more disappointed in my career in broadcasting. I felt hurt, betrayed and I felt a great wrong had been done to Northwest – to the staff, the listeners, the board and everybody involved. I still feel that. Time moves on – and Midwest certainly moved on – but personally I will always feel that a great injustice was done."

The broadcasting contract for the northwest had been mired in controversy as far back as 1990 when Rosses Radio handed back its licence on the grounds that the franchise area was too small to sustain a profitable commercial radio station. When the licence was readvertised, Midwest spearheaded a consortium that made shared programming a key part of its overall strategy, thus reducing the cost base that had been such a source of concern for the Rosses Radio investors. The only other applicant – a consortium involving Highland Radio and Shannonside – had a similar business model. Midwest won the seven-year franchise and retained it in 1997. By then, JNLR surveys were consistently placing Northwest among the top three local radio stations in the country and careful financial management was delivering dividends for the shareholders, as well as a stable working environment for staff. Tommy Marren, who was station manager from 1990 to 2002, says the Northwest brand was as deep-rooted in its core area by the late 1990s as Midwest was in Mayo.

"There was great loyalty to Northwest, which was remarkable in a way because the area straddled three different counties so you hadn't the traditional county-boundary loyalty that a station like Highland in Donegal enjoyed. And then you had the Sligo town factor. People said we would never succeed with a similar formula to Midwest because Sligo was an urban centre but we had a very loyal listenership in the town.

"Everybody at Northwest worked incredibly hard throughout the 1990s to build up the brand across such a large geographical area that contained both urban and rural listeners. At times, it was physically exhausting and the job became my life for a period, there's no doubt about that. But it was also incredibly fulfilling; it was a great time to be involved in local radio.

"I was fortunate in that my wife Mary also worked at the station so she fully understood what the commitment and pressures of the job were like in those initial years."

Tommy stepped down as station manager in 2002 but continued to present his morning show. His successor, Mary Daly, seamlessly picked up the baton and Northwest maintained its place at the top of the broadcasting tree, securing a coveted nomination for Station of the Year in 2002. It won many plaudits for its programming, including its sports coverage where Anthony Hennigan was doing sterling work chronicling the fortunes of teams and sportspeople in three different counties. In GAA, Sligo's senior footballers enjoyed their most successful summer in a generation in 2002, reaching the All-Ireland quarter-finals where they lost to eventual champions Armagh in a replay.

Hennigan also secured the sports story of the year in July when he interviewed Manchester United manager Alex Ferguson who was on a flying visit to Enniscrone at the invitation of his long-time friend Joe Kennedy. Ferguson exclusively revealed that he had just broken the British transfer record by signing Rio Ferdinand from Leeds United. It was quite a coup for Northwest's young sports editor; indeed, the recently deceased Willie 'The Shoe' would have been proud of his protégé.

"There was a great team at Northwest and I was privileged to lead them for 12 years," says Tommy. "Niall Delaney was an absolutely fantastic news editor and we had a really forward-thinking production manager in Andy Matthews while there were other great guys like Austin O'Callaghan, Barry O'Neill and Anthony Hennigan."

In the summer of 2002, there was little hint of the dark clouds that were soon to engulf Northwest Radio. A year earlier, on October 27, 2001, the BCI sought expressions of interest for the Sligo/South Donegal/North Leitrim franchise and two bidders submitted applications, including the incumbent Northwest and a consortium headed by Highland Radio. The eventual winner, Ocean, did not make a submission at this stage. However, the franchise was again advertised on November 19, 2002, and this time three applications were received, including one from Ocean FM, a consortium that included high-profile sportsmen like former Irish soccer international Packie Bonner, Sligo Gaelic footballer Eamonn O'Hara and crime journalist Paul Williams, a native of Co Leitrim.

The board of Northwest was under no illusions about the challenge it now faced. Apart from the celebrity endorsements, Ocean FM also had the backing of prominent businessmen like Pat Clifford of Clifford's Electrical in Sligo, John McKeon of Donegal Creameries, Martin Reilly of Reilly Motors in Sligo, property developer Tom Daly and Tim Collins, a director with Drury Communications in Dublin.

It was astonishing really. Just 13 years earlier, the radio franchise in the northwest had been the runt of the litter, now it was the dog everybody wanted to adopt. Ocean FM's expenditure projections were simply eye-watering: the marketing budget alone was €225,000 in the first two years and a total of €646,000 in years two to five. The total investment was over €2m, including new studios in Sligo town, Donegal town and Manorhamilton in Co Leitrim, as well as outside broadcasting vehicles to be called Ocean liners and Ocean cruisers.

"We knew we faced a huge battle to retain the licence," explains Paul, "but we were making our pitch based on our track record and our track record was very strong. We'd built up a station that had a listenership figure of 70 per cent, which was the third highest in the country after Highland Radio and Midwest, and our financial position was very solid too.

"We felt we'd done a very good job during the past 13 years. Having taken the licence at a time when people said it would be impossible to make a success of a commercial radio station in Sligo, we'd proved it could be done, and while we certainly didn't feel entitled to the licence, we believed our track record spoke for itself."

The directors of Ocean FM had a different opinion of Northwest's track record. In its submission to the BCI, the high-powered consortium described Northwest's listeners as "old, lacking aspiration, conservative, retired, unemployed, and coming from a lower social class in Leitrim and [Sligo] City Centre". If this wasn't sufficiently wounding, the submission also stated: "...the education profile of listeners shows Northwest Radio meeting the needs of those who claim Junior and Leaving Cert levels. Northwest's appeal is clearly to retired, unemployed and unskilled people".

Even Donald Trump would struggle to condense as many insults into a single, late-night tweet.

It didn't take a genius to work out that Ocean FM was pinning its fortunes on the all-important under-44 demographic, which it described in its submission as "adventurous, even rebellious" and not part of the Northwest listenership. Indeed, Tim Collins went so far as to challenge the accuracy of the JNLR figures, arguing that Northwest's 70 per cent share of the market was "grossly over-estimated" and that research commissioned by Ocean put it closer to 40 per cent. It was an extraordinary claim because JNLR surveys were the bedrock of the entire radio industry and nobody had ever previously suggested the figures were inaccurate.

When the oral hearing was held in Donegal town on March 24, 2003, Midwest unveiled its own plan to capture the key under-44 demographic by proposing a new opt-out service for Sligo town called

Bay FM. In addition, it unveiled plans to build new headquarters for Northwest Radio, which would complement an earlier investment of €129,000 in a studio in Donegal town. There were a few tricky questions from the commission relating to the commercial content of outside broadcasts and sponsored programmes, but there was no sense among the members of the Northwest board that things had gone badly wrong.

"I thought we'd passed it with flying colours," says Paul. "We had a clear investment plan for the next 10 years and were committed to delivering the same quality service that had placed Northwest Radio among the top three stations in the country for the past 13 years."

The commission said it would announce the winner of the new licence on Monday, April 28, but D-Day came and went without any news from Dublin. It was on the following evening that Paul finally got a telephone call from Michael O'Keeffe informing him that the board of the BCI had voted to award the 10-year radio franchise for Sligo/South Donegal/North Leitrim to the newcomer Ocean FM. The decision was final and there was no appeal mechanism, Mr O'Keeffe explained.

Claffey was simply stunned. His sense of shock was only compounded by the fact that the BCI would not be providing an explanation for its decision for several weeks. And, to add insult to injury, on the same day it granted the licence to Ocean FM, the BCI contacted Northwest to inform station management its interim listenership results stood at an impressive 68 per cent. Little wonder, then, that Paul told the *Sligo Champion* the events of the previous 24 hours "defied logic". A week later, he was still trying to make sense of the shock decision.

"Since I got word last Tuesday evening, I have gone over the whole scenario in my mind at least a thousand times," Paul wrote in the *Western People*, "and even trying to be as impartial as I can be, I can find no sound or solid reason or basis for the decision to take the licence away from Northwest Radio."

The chief executive would spend the next year trying to figure out exactly what had happened at that BCI meeting in Dublin on April 29, 2003.

The reason the ten-member BCI had been unable to make a decision on the northwest franchise on April 28 was that it could not raise the necessary quorum. Under the Radio and Television Act 1988, five or more members had to be present to constitute a quorum so the chairman, Claremorris-born Conor Maguire, adjourned the meeting to the following day. Six of the board members attended the reconvened meeting on April 29 and there was a distinct lack of unanimity in the room on the issue of the northwest franchise. In fact, the board split 3-3, leaving the chairman to deliver the casting vote in favour of Ocean FM.

Paul Claffey was understandably aggrieved at what the BCI had done but some less partisan observers were also raising serious concerns, including the Fine Gael Senator Jim Higgins who questioned how a commercial licence could be awarded with only 60 per cent of the commission present. Senator Higgins also asked whether the commission had been influenced by the "propaganda put out by Ocean FM regarding the social status and age profile of Northwest listeners" and expressed surprise that a chairman would give his casting vote to a "new inexperienced consortium".

"Normally, a chairman in such a tied voting situation would vote for the status quo," remarked Senator Higgins.

Listeners to Northwest Radio also could not comprehend how a commission in Dublin had decided to take their local station off the airwaves. The long-time Banada correspondent for the *Western People*, Seán Owens, certainly did not fall into Ocean FM's categorisation of Northwest's listeners as "lacking education and aspiration". A retired national school principal, Owens lived by the age-old maxim that the pen is mightier than the sword and the *príomhoide* unleashed a verbal fusillade in his weekly column on May 7, 2003, railing against the "faceless clerks in Dublin" who were robbing the people of Sligo of their "favourite programmes".

"How can six people who have no interest or any loyalty to heritage or culture, or who do not even live in the region, set themselves up as judges as to what we listen to or hear?

"The people of the northwest have a right to decide in a democratic way as to what their choice is. They will let the licensing authority know as to what they wish to listen to, and when a head count is taken, it will favour Northwest Radio."

There were many more who felt like Owens and they weren't slow to make their feelings known. May Hunt, whose association with Mid and Northwest Radio went all the way back to the pirate days, told the *Western People* she was "absolutely disgusted" with the decision.

"I go down to the local nursing home a few times a week and they are out of their minds with this news. This station is one of the best in Ireland and is of great comfort to me and to all the old people. Since I heard the news, it has broken my heart. We all hope and pray this change will not go ahead."

The groundswell of support for Northwest grew throughout the early summer of 2003, culminating in a protest march in Sligo town on June 29, attended by thousands of people demanding the decision be reversed. Although there was no appeal mechanism under the legislation – that anomaly was subsequently corrected – the board of Northwest could, if it so wished, seek a judicial review in the High Court.

"I felt the odds were stacked against us in persuading the High Court to overturn the BCI decision but I also believed we owed it to the staff at Northwest and the listeners to take the judicial review," explains Paul. "The support of the listeners during that period was simply phenomenal and it made me realise the enormous impact Northwest had on people's lives in Sligo, Leitrim and South Donegal over the last 13 years. There were listeners ringing up telling us they were going to march to Dublin and camp outside Government Buildings. The turnout at the protest in Sligo was just incredible so I felt we owed it to those people to challenge the decision in the High Court."

If Claffey and the rest of the board had any lingering reservations about taking an expensive legal challenge, their minds were made up that autumn when Northwest was named Ireland's Local Radio Station of the Year. How could a station deemed the best in the country lose its licence? It was an utter farce as far as the board of Northwest was concerned.

The legal case was heard in the High Court in the spring of 2004 and much of it focused on a letter of explanation the BCI had issued to Northwest on May 26, 2003, in which it stated that the amount of shared programming between Mid and Northwest Radio had been an influential factor in its decision to award the licence to Ocean FM. In its appeal, Northwest argued that commonality between the sister stations had never been a problem in the past and Midwest had its Mayo franchise renewed a year earlier without any mention of shared programming.

Lawyers for Northwest also argued that the shredding of handwritten notes taken by a secretary at the meeting on April 29, 2003, deprived its client of evidence relevant to its legal challenge. However, the BCI contended that it had no obligation to keep the handwritten notes and the presiding judge, Mr Justice Michael Peart, ruled that the destruction of the notes was done in accordance with the secretary's normal practice after the minutes of the meeting were approved.

"I accept that this was done in a completely bona fide manner, even though with the benefit of some hindsight, it might, in my view, be wiser to maintain the existence of the notes, if for no other reason, in order to allay the sort of suggestions which a disappointed applicant may even understandably make."

Ultimately, Mr Justice Peart dismissed the Northwest legal challenge, thereby upholding the BCI's decision to award the franchise to Ocean FM. Paul and the board lodged an appeal in the Supreme Court but later withdrew it after they learned that Northwest would be forced to go off the airwaves pending the outcome of the legal action.

"The existing licence expired on October 1, 2004, so listeners would have been left without a local radio service until such time as the appeal was heard and adjudicated upon," Paul explains. "We also had to consider the massive legal costs of appealing and our chances of success. In addition, a lot of our staff had been offered work in different places and it would have been unfair to ask them to hold on indefinitely until the Supreme Court heard the case and delivered its verdict."

On Friday, October 1, Paul broadcast his *Mid-Morning Show* for the last time from the Northwest studio at Market Yard in Sligo town, and the tears flowing steadily as staff and listeners gathered to say their final farewell to a radio station that had been such an important part of life in the northwest during the preceding 14 years.

"This station is part of our lives," said Phil Cunningham from Bunninadden. "It belongs to the people. I love to hear the traditional music and Country music. I was brought up with that kind of music here in Sligo. The station has done a fine job in catering for the people of the district."

The poignancy of Northwest's final moments is forever etched in Gerry Glennon's memory.

"The last act was to turn on an oscillation tone after we had said our goodbyes to the thousands of loyal listeners who would no longer be able to hear programmes that had been such a part of their lives for so long. We then turned out the studio lights, locked the door and walked away from 14 years of service to the people of the northwest. It was heartbreaking really but there was nothing that could be done. The die had been cast and that was it."

The decision to revoke the Northwest licence and the subsequent legal action had the potential to create tension between Midwest and the BCI but long-serving chairman Michael Hughes says both sides moved on quickly.

"Our alliance with Northwest from 1990 to 2004 was mutually rewarding and highly appreciated by listeners, advertisers and industry observers and the withdrawal of this alliance by the BCI was a severe blow to Midwest. However, we managed to adapt to this challenge and continued to prosper.

"Our relationship with the BCI and its successor, the BAI, was sufficiently robust to overcome those difficult days and the board of Midwest has always found the management and staff of the BAI to be constructive, positive and unfailingly helpful in their dealings with us during the past 30 years."

Many of Northwest's former listeners in South Sligo – including May Hunt, Seán Owens and Phil Cunningham – were still able to pick up Midwest Radio so they simply switched the dial and continued listening to their favourite programmes. Indeed, the indomitable May Hunt remained one of Midwest's most loyal listeners right up to her death in December 2011 at the venerable age of 93. For people like May, Seán Owens, Phil Cunningham and countless others across South and West Sligo, there was only one radio station that mattered and no bureaucrat in faraway Dublin was going to tell them otherwise.

CHAPTER THIRTY-ONE

Rallying the troops

MIDWEST'S relationship with its listeners is special. The station's audience may be dispersed across a sprawling geographical region but there has always been an intimacy, a family-like bond that makes Midwest unique among local radio stations. The 'fireside' philosophy of John Duggan, who perfected the art of broadcasting in a relaxed, informal style, has informed much of what Midwest has done over the years. Chris Carroll says the station has been blessed in its presenters and its behind-the-scenes staff.

"We've had great presenters over the years who have struck a real chord with the listeners and that has certainly helped in making the station what it is today. But it is not just about the presenters. Everybody on the staff has had a role to play in creating that wonderful relationship with listeners. Our philosophy has been community-based from the very beginning and I think that has stood to us."

The special bond between Midwest and its listeners is best exemplified in the station's charity work with more than €2m generated for a whole variety of worthy causes since 1989. It is phenomenal really that such a large amount of money has been raised by one local radio station but then nobody can rally the troops better than the crew at Midwest.

"Whatever the cause the public will always respond," says Tommy Marren. "There's an innate generosity and decency among people and I think the instinct of our listeners is to help whenever they can. Midwest has initiated hundreds of fundraisers over the years but none of them would have succeeded without the incredible response from our listeners so they are the ones who deserve the praise. We merely facilitate people when they are fundraising for a good cause."

However, Midwest has championed its own fundraisers, too, most notably in July 2007 when the station launched the 'Seven Day Charity Challenge', an initiative that became known as 'The Magnificent 7'. Like several great Midwest ideas, the plan took shape on the back of a napkin in Val's Bistro in Ballyhaunis.

"Seven of our presenters each selected a charity and undertook individual challenges that yielded an amazing €178,666.94 in just seven days," explains Tommy. "Looking back on that frantic week I wonder how we even conceived the idea let alone pulled it off!"

The Magnificent 7 Challenge consisted of Mayo's biggest ever table quiz, the longest line-dance ever held at a racetrack (Ballinrobe), four cabaret shows in one day, the staging of a three-act play, a talent show, a mystery bus tour and the old trusty car boot sale! The presenters were Paul Claffey, Teresa O'Malley, Tommy Marren, Angelina McHugh, Viv Brennan, Chris Carroll, Padraic Walsh and David Cawley.

"That week stands out not just because of the huge amount raised but because we realised just how powerful a medium Midwest had become," explains Tommy. "The response was extraordinary and the final figure exceeded our wildest expectations."

But the Magnificent 7 Challenge wasn't the first time a Midwest Radio fundraiser had come up trumps for charity. Two years earlier, in the aftermath of the devastating tsunami in South-East Asia, the station organised a car boot sale that yielded a phenomenal €85,135.66.

"Malcolm Quigley from Castlebar was working with a non-governmental agency called VSO Ireland in the Maldives, which was one of the areas worst impacted by the tsunami during Christmas 2004," explains Tommy. "The money from Midwest listeners was used to reconstruct schools and libraries across the Maldives."

Global natural disasters have prompted some remarkable and spontaneous acts of compassion from Midwest's ever-generous 'family'. When a ruinous earthquake struck Haiti in 2010, the station's listeners rallied to a call to arms on behalf of Westport woman Gena Heraty whose orphanage on the Caribbean island had been completely destroyed.

"Gena is one of the west of Ireland's most amazing and courageous individuals and we had come to know her over the years on her visits to her native Westport," says Tommy. "When we heard what had happened to her orphanage we hastily arranged a car boot sale for Knock but to be honest we weren't sure how much we could raise because it was all done in such a hurry."

Incredibly, a total of €234,102.35 was collected in just two days, proving once again that charity really does begin at Midwest Radio.

A year earlier, the station launched its 'Fibs for Phones' initiative in association with Brendan and Julie Chambers of C&C Cellular in Castlebar. Brendan actually supplied the station with its first mobile telephones 20 years earlier and the objective of 'Fibs for Phones' was to collect as many old mobile devices as possible to fund the purchase of defibrillators for local sports clubs and voluntary organisations. The promotion yielded €164,417.98, which funded the purchase of 54 defibrillators to various groups around the region as well as substantial cash donations to 12 worthy charities.

Between the 'Fibs for Phones' and Haiti Appeal, Midwest and its family of generous listeners generated a staggering €400,000 for charity in the space of just 12 months in 2009 and 2010.

"Not even recession quenches the enthusiasm," says Gerry Glennon. "The public got behind those campaigns in difficult times and made them what they were."

Numerous charities have benefited over the years from Midwest's remarkable ability to rally the troops. The annual coffee mornings for Mayo/Roscommon Hospice, held each September in the TF Royal Theatre, generated over €75,000 during their lifetime while Pieta House reaped the rewards of yet another car boot sale when it received €42,090.32 for its first centre in the West of Ireland.

Western Alzheimer's has reaped the dividends from Radio Bingo while charities as diverse as Our Lady's Hospital for Sick Children in Dublin, Máméan Pilgrimage site in Connemara, Mayo Mental Health and Western Care Association have received money raised through the sale of CDs, namely *Paul Claffey's Conversations with Bina McLoughlin* and *Paul's Surprise Phone Calls.* In fact, the gold disc for the Bina CD takes pride of place on a wall in the reception area of the studios in Ballyhaunis.

But charity takes many forms and Midwest's willingness to lend a helping hand to anybody in need has been one of its strongest calling cards over the years. Indeed, many observers believe the bond that ties the station's listeners together comes from its humble origins as a pirate and the decision of Paul, Chris and Gerry in those early days to do things a little differently to everybody else.

"I remember we used to get fierce stick in the national press in the early days because we were putting out announcements for people looking for missing dogs," says Paul. "But you find somebody's dog and you have a friend for life. To me, that's what local radio is all about. We've had huge fundraisers over the years that have netted hundreds of thousands of euros but it is those small and seemingly insignificant acts, like finding a missing dog or warning a farmer his cattle are straying, that have made the Midwest family into what it is today."

Listeners place great store in the capacity of Midwest to locate everything from long-forgotten records to recently-disappeared pets, but some requests are a little on the optimistic side, such as the person who once called the station looking to find their cat who had been "missing for the past couple of years".

Even the magical powers of Midwest Radio have their limitations.

A few days before Willie McNeely passed away, Chris Carroll chatted with him over the telephone and they discussed his possible return to work.

"Willie wanted to come back within the next week or two but I explained to him that the main thing was to look after himself and the job would be waiting for him whenever he was well enough to resume his old role. He was worried that his job might not be there for him because he'd have known it was the busy summer season and was frustrated at having to miss so much time away from work. Nobody enjoyed his job more than Willie and he was desperate to get back and we really hoped he would make another incredible comeback."

Stephen O'Grady was drafted in to cover some of Willie's slots on the Sunday sports show while Angelina McHugh, still only 19, found herself dropped in at the deep end as she organised Midwest's sports coverage throughout the early summer of 2002. It was a steep learning curve but the teenager proved herself up to the task and was formally appointed the station's new sports editor in the spring of 2003, having served as acting sports editor in the months after the death of her mentor and colleague. Filling the shoes of The Shoe was always going to be an enormous task but Angelina was also making a little bit of history for female broadcasters when she took up her new role. The Glenisland native was only the second-ever female sports editor in the country – and the first outside Dublin.

"It was an honour but also very frustrating at times," she recalled in 2014. "It probably has taken all of my 12 years as sports editor to gain respect from some quarters of the sport world, just because I am a woman.

"Back in the early days when I would introduce myself at a game or before an interview, you sometimes would get the roll of the eyes or a little bit of a laugh as if to say 'Is this one for real?'"

"That has changed significantly over the years, which is brilliant but there still aren't enough women working in sport and much of this is to do with the barriers that have been built up and the preconceptions that surround female sports broadcasters."

Angelina quickly discovered that the world of radio involved lots of unsociable hours but it has its social perks too!

"I met my husband in Midwest so it's not all bad!" she jokes. "Well, either that or the hours are so unsociable you don't actually get to leave to meet people!"

Angelina's husband is, of course, Brendan Nugent, from Ballinalee, Co Longford, who has been Midwest's 'technie' for the past decade, having previously worked in Northwest and Shannonside. The days of importing valves from behind the Iron Curtain for temperamental transmitters may be long gone but Brendan knows only too well the many complications that come with broadcasting especially in the 21st century when technology is advancing at a rate of knots.

"The whole technical and IT face of local radio has changed dramatically in the last decade and there are even bigger changes coming down the track," he says. "Midwest has invested heavily in updating all our various systems and with social media now playing such an important role in what we do we're very much up to speed with those challenges too. The problem is that the technology is changing all the time so the trick is to stay ahead of the posse."

Brendan has been dabbling in technology for as long as he can remember, having had the best possible mentor in his father Tommy, a qualified electrician.

"As a youngster I was always fascinated about what made things work and if I couldn't figure it out then I'd start exploring," he says. "Dad was a great help when it came to electrics but I was more interested in how computers were put together and I'd spend hours just fidgeting around with developing small computer programmes and one thing would lead to another. It's a minefield and it can be a challenge but I love what I do in Midwest and there's certainly plenty of variety."

Brendan admits to being "hooked on radio" from the moment he stepped into the Shannonside studios in Co Longford at the tender age of 19. He was happy to spend his days behind the scenes but, as is often the case with local radio, he was unexpectedly pushed in front of a 'live mike' and took to it effortlessly.

"I was in the studio in Shannonside one evening when the DJ rang in sick so you know the rest! I was asked would I do the pop show in question because they knew I'd have no problem using the studio equipment. I always had an interest in music so I went for it and that led to me doing the pop programme five nights a week."

Brendan spent five years at Shannonside where he worked in transmission and technical development while also presenting the evening pop music show. However, he decided to move to Northwest when a similar technical role became available.

"Northwest was interesting because the transmission networks and technical challenges were greater and it meant I learned a lot in a short space of time – often by default! I was responsible for all outside broadcasts as well as the entire IT system and I developed computer systems that were tailor-made for the station. As a three-county franchise area, it was a real learning curve and I really enjoyed my time there."

Brendan transferred to Ballyhaunis when Northwest went off the air in 2004 and worked alongside Michael Neary in developing a "technical empire" – as Tommy Marren likes to call it – in Midwest's new headquarters. Today, Brendan is the station's technical and IT manager, a role that is so multi-faceted and unpredictable it would take a lot more than a mere chapter to describe it. Put simply, Brendan is the go-to man when the gremlins strike. His daily responsibilities involve everything from looking after transmitter sites and developing new computer systems to updating studio equipment and checking outside broadcast links. But he has also managed to keep his hand in on the broadcast side of things by fronting the *Classic Express* show every weekday from 6 to 8pm.

"Doing the radio show is often the escape valve from what can be fairly pressurised work. I've a great interest in music and I really love the '80s and '90s era, in particular. When I was offered the show I jumped at it because I really think the classic hits formula has attracted new listeners to the station over the years. No other station around us is playing that type of music at that time so it's working really well."

Brendan isn't saying whether there were sparks in the airwaves the moment he and Angelina laid eyes on each other across the studio floor but romance certainly blossomed between the colleagues and they married in Ballintubber Abbey in 2007.

"We were always great friends from the start and one thing led to another," remarks Brendan. "Angelina understands how radio works and how time-consuming the job can be so that's a recipe for a happy marriage!"

The growth of the Internet has provided challenges for so-called traditional media outlets in the first two decades of the 21st century but it has also provided many opportunities. Midwest was one of the first to embrace the potential of the worldwide web by launching its Irish Radio service in 2005, which soon reached a vast audience of Irish people across the globe.

Broadcasting to the Diaspora was familiar territory for the Ballyhaunis station and management were able to draw on their many overseas experiences from the 1990s, especially those satellite link-ups with Adrian Flannelly in New York and G.S. Radio in London when devising a strategy for the new online service.

MEP Pat 'The Cope' Gallagher joined Country music legends Foster and Allen to officially launch the new station in May 2005 and it proved an instant success.

Midwest Irish Radio broadcast 24 hours per day with a variety of live and pre-recorded programmes promoting all things Irish but with a special emphasis on Irish music categories. Amongst the presenters were Paul, Gerry, Tommy, Una Flanagan, Pam Corbett, Noel Grogan, Viv Brennan, John Kelly, Michael Fox, Brendan Mulvey, Keith Fahey and, of course, Tommy Murphy, who could now reach his friends in St Patrick, Missouri seven days a week. Indeed, Tommy continued to be associated with Midwest up to his death in 2012.

"Tommy was one of nature's gentleman," says Tommy Marren, whose association with the Ballina man went back three decades. "His talents extended beyond the microphone at Midwest. He drove the outside broadcast unit for many years and was always willing to help out in any way he could.

"He was a real professional in everything he did. His programmes were always carefully planned and brilliantly executed. He was very versatile too and presented a lot of different programmes for Midwest over the years. Tommy remained a 'true blue' to the end and is still sadly missed by his colleagues."

Midwest established its new online service in the wake of the loss of the Northwest licence and once again the Mayo radio station blazed a trail for commercial broadcasting in Ireland. Many similar services were soon being launched across the country as it quickly became apparent that there was a huge global audience for Irish radio programmes.

"The service received hundreds of emails daily from all corners of the globe with many of the listeners visiting Midwest when in Ireland," says Gerry Glennon. "It was a really important part of our commitment to the Diaspora throughout the first decade of the 2000s and it also served as a precursor to Ireland West Music TV."

Launching a television channel might seem like a radical move for a local radio station but Paul Claffey always saw it as a natural progression in the Midwest story.

"Obviously radio is our core business but the media world is evolving all the time and it's important that we keep all avenues of communication on our radar," he explains. "Satellite television is just one such opportunity and we're delighted at the reaction the TV programme has been getting since it launched at the start of the decade."

Ireland West Music TV went on air on October 3, 2011, and has proven hugely popular across Ireland, the UK and mainland Europe over the past eight years. Television is an expensive medium and management at Midwest was reluctant to invest too heavily in the enterprise until it had tested the waters. Initially, the channel's one-hour programmes, which broadcast twice weekly, were recorded at Gerald O'Donogue's Greenfield Studios in Headford, Co Galway.

"We formed a wonderful working relationship with Gerald and he gave us lots of advice and help in developing the service," says Paul. "Nothing was ever too much trouble for Gerald and his experience was invaluable.

"However, we wanted to increase the number of weekly programmes so the next step in the plan was to build our own studio."

In the spring of 2013, Ireland West Music TV opened its own studios in a building adjacent to Midwest Radio's premises on Clare Street in Ballyhaunis. Building a television studio was a significant investment but the unprecedented success of the channel in its first 18 months on the air made the decision a lot easier. Midwest also employed a number of staff to work on the television project, including Gráinne Kivlehan, John Paul Heaney, Ciaran Carty and Damien Lavin while existing personnel like Brendan Nugent, Patrina McDonnell, Sharon Behan-Woods, Angelina McHugh, David Cawley and Michael Commins were also involved either behind the scenes or presenting shows on the expanding channel, which can be found on Sky 376.

The television service operates on a similar ethos to Midwest Radio itself, promoting cultural events alongside the showcasing of new Irish music talent.

"Having our own studio has allowed us more flexibility in delivering more programmes on the service," says Paul. "Things have gone very well over the last eight years and we're hopeful the programmes will continue to entertain TV viewers across the whole of Ireland, the UK and Europe."

Interestingly, television cameras came to Midwest Radio earlier than most when Castlerea-based videographer Seán Browne shot footage in the old pirate station at Midas Nightclub on the day Midwest went off the air in December 1988. The footage came to light during the research for this book and it certainly captures a unique moment in time. Who'd have thought that three decades later Midwest Radio would own a television studio located on the same street broadcasting weekly programmes to an international audience across the continent of Europe? It's just one example of Midwest's ability to move with the times and effortlessly embrace the technology of the future.

CHAPTER THIRTY-TWO

Keeping the faith alive

GERRY Glennon and Michael Neary have undertaken thousands of outdoor broadcasts since that unforgettable July Sunday on the Reek three decades ago, but one event will always stand out in the collective memory bank of the old school-friends from Granlahan.

"Mother Teresa's visit to Knock Shrine in July 1993 would be a real highlight for me," says Gerry. "It was an unforgettable occasion and I felt privileged to be there to witness this incredible woman at close quarters and to be part of a broadcast that was listened to by tens of thousands of people right across the region because it was going out on Northwest as well as Midwest."

The pilgrimage to Knock by the world-famous nun, then aged 83 and recovering from broken ribs sustained in a fall in Rome a few weeks earlier, was the biggest event at the Shrine since Pope John Paul II famously declared he had "reached the goal of his journey to Ireland" some 14 year earlier. However, on this occasion, there was to be no rushed visit and instead Mother Teresa stayed for a full six hours, mingling among the estimated 60,000 people who flocked to the famous pilgrimage site from all over Ireland. Among them were Taoiseach Albert Reynolds and his wife Kathleen who joined Archbishop of Tuam Joseph Cassidy, Fr Colm Kilcoyne and Mgr Dominic Greally in the parochial house to await the arrival by helicopter of a woman who was, by then, a much-loved and universally admired icon of the 20th century. Gerry Glennon was invited to witness the welcoming ceremony and ended up partaking in it.

"We were all lined up to shake hands with Mother Teresa when she came into the sitting room of Mgr Greally's house," he recalls. "There were three things that struck me on greeting her. One was the strength of her handshake, which completely belied her small stature; the second was her powerful voice and the third was her piercing eyes, which she fixed on you when she shook your hand. It was an unforgettable moment for me, absolutely unforgettable, and such a privilege to be there to greet her."

Michael Neary had spent the morning hoping the broadcasting gods would shine because he had to ensure everything was in place for a live broadcast that was the most elaborate Midwest had undertaken since its launch four years earlier.

"I remember arriving in Knock and discovering that RTÉ had a team of 114 people whereas the Midwest team was Gerry, Fr Brendan, Monica Morley and myself! Mother Teresa was due to arrive at 2.30pm and we discovered at about twenty past two that the microphone on the podium where she was to speak wasn't working. This was an RTÉ mike so I couldn't do anything with it. I had to wait until they found the man responsible for that particular part of their operation. He was actually down the town eating a burger and just arrived back in time!"

Later that afternoon, Fr Brendan was afforded the distinction of a one-to-one interview with a woman who, in 1993, was the second most famous religious figure in the world after Pope John Paul II.

"It is an honour to interview you," he began.

"Oh, no," said Mother Teresa, smiling, "don't use the word honour."

Writing in the following Tuesday's *Western People*, Fr Brendan described in evocative prose the afternoon a woman destined for sainthood came to Mayo's world-famous Marian Shrine.

"It was like watching a small craft buffeted by the waves of the sea," he wrote. "In a great ocean of large, security men, the tiny Mother Teresa, in her distinctive white sari, gently moved through the great throng of people. The emotion was tangible… hands stretched towards her for a prayer, a touch, a blessing.

"The small stooped nun from the other side of the world, dwarfed by a sea of minders, turned to the voices and smiled her distinctive smile, the twinkling eyes lighting up the tanned, lined face.

"It was good to be there. Surely a day to remember."

Midwest's extensive coverage of Mother Teresa's visit won many plaudits from listeners and was another feather in the cap for the *Faith Alive* team. Fr Colm Kilcoyne had moved on from his role as head of communications for the Archdiocese of Tuam in the early 1990s, which gave greater responsibility to another 'accidental' broadcaster, Monica Morley of Knock Family Life Centre.

"Fr Colm asked me to do some training when he was co-presenter of *Faith Alive* with Fr Brendan," she recalls. "I initially thought it was more in the area of scripting and behind-the-scenes work but one thing led to another and I found myself doing a lot more on-air work at an early stage."

With a degree in psychology and vast experience from her work at the Family Life Centre, Monica's addition to the *Faith Alive* on-air team opened up new opportunities to explore themes and issues relevant to the programme's growing audience.

"I think my work in the Family Life Centre gives me a really strong handle on the issues facing people, whether as individuals, couples or communities," the Knock native explains. "I work in areas of bereavement, counselling and other supports for families and that experience is often reflected in the topics we cover on the programme week in and week out. It's real for people and that, for me, is what makes *Faith Alive* so appealing."

Fr Brendan says the weekly programme was a work in progress in those early years but a distinctive style gradually emerged.

"What we had, that other similar programmes on Midwest didn't have, was time. Just 30 minutes a week and we found ourselves with the luxury of always paring down the contents to fit the time. It worked, as radio inevitably works, when you have more time and more material than you think you need."

Striking a credible balance was always going to be a real challenge during such a turbulent time for the Irish Catholic Church but *Faith*

Alive, under the careful stewardship of Fr Brendan and Monica, has always managed to deliver a fair and unbiased assessment of the religious issues of the day.

"Fr Brendan and I work well together," says Monica. "I think what's interesting is the fact that we both come from two different perspectives and backgrounds. Fr Brendan is very much coming from the area of church reform whereas my work with families broadens the parameters of the programme at a different level."

Both presenters agree that *Faith Alive* has never been about reaching a common consensus; rather it offers an opportunity for respectful and insightful dialogue on religious affairs.

"People don't always agree with us," says Monica. "In fact, there are many issues where Brendan and I wouldn't agree on. The important thing is that we are both open to listening to what our listeners are saying and, regardless of what we think, we feel it is important that their views are articulated and reflected in what we put on air every week."

During the past 30 years, *Faith Alive* has won many awards while both the programme and an editorial feature were nominated in the Andrew Cross Awards in England in 2005. Indeed, it is a measure of the show's success that in a 30-year period when churches across the West of Ireland have emptied out, the audience for *Faith Alive* has steadily grown and the Sunday morning programme regularly features among Midwest's best performing shows in JNLR surveys.

"It seems incredible that over the span of three decades we've presented and produced over 1,500 programmes," says Fr Brendan. "I think it is true to say that in the 30 years we've established a reputation for fairness and even-handedness, for good production values and for encouraging open debate rather than for presenting formulaic answers. And people respect us for that. For radio to work, you have to trust the received wisdom. If it doesn't stand as good radio then it deserves to be dismissed as propaganda."

One of the great strengths of *Faith Alive* has been the variety of topics and themes explored from week to week.

"Apart from the big national events there have been the local good news religious stories," says Fr Brendan, "the young people who regularly reported on their trips to Lourdes to experience working with special needs children; the parishes, like Ballyconneely, who shared how they dealt with becoming one of Tuam diocese's first priestless church areas; the community of Clare Island who shared how they remembered their young curate Fr Patrick Burke who died suddenly in 2018 and the installation of bishops and archbishops for the dioceses of Tuam, Achonry and Killala.

"Of course, there were the many personal stories, too, shared by guests like Olive Foley, wife of the late rugby player Anthony Foley, who spoke of her personal journey through loss and grief; John McAreavey recalled how his life changed after the death of his wife Michaela; presidents Mary Robinson and Mary McAleese spoke of their role as leaders while Westport's Darren Cawley shared his struggles with God when living with ill health."

Apart from the change that has occurred in the attitude of Irish people towards the Catholic Church, *Faith Alive* has also broadcast during an era of enormous technological change and listeners communicate with the show in a very different way now than 30 years ago.

"By its very nature, phoning or texting comments allows an anonymity that permits the 'real' questions to be surfaced but that also acts as a kind of lightning conductor for the anger and resentment against the church so obvious in recent decades," says Fr Brendan. "However, if *Faith Alive* hadn't been part of that conversation for the past 30 years, I believe that many would feel it necessary to invent it now."

Monica says *Faith Alive* has had to change with the times by responding to the very different perspectives on the Catholic Church in Ireland today compared to 1989.

"Many of our listeners today are not regular church-goers and it's increasingly obvious that for many of them *Faith Alive* is the only time of the week when a religious dimension impinges directly on their lives. That's not to say they have no faith but, for a number of reasons, they are disengaged either casually or permanently from institutional religion. Many would describe themselves as *spiritual* but not religious."

Fr Brendan believes there is a range of religious perspectives that resonate with listeners, though many would not use the word 'religious'.

"I'm thinking of the many human and relationship issues that we try to respond to, not by preaching about them but by offering reflections on issues like forgiveness, gratitude, family, serious illness and death and so on. Many of these topics raise universal questions which reflect the hungers of the heart, hungers which Pope Francis so often acknowledges as he seeks to draw young people to the well of faith."

Apart from *Faith Alive*, Midwest has also broadcast several other religious programmes, including *Live at Ten*, a miscellany of debate and interviews that ran from 10pm to 1am on Tuesday evenings for some time and, of course, Sunday Mass. The *Faith Alive* team co-ordinated all religious broadcasts from 1989 to 2005 when Ballyhaunis parish priest Fr Joe Cooney took on the responsibility up to his retirement in 2011. Since then, an interdenominational team comprising Fr Stephen Farragher, Fr Richard Gibbons and Rev Andrea Wills of the Church of Ireland have organised religious services every Sunday morning at 10am with special broadcasts during Easter Week from St Patrick's Church in Ballyhaunis.

"I don't know of any other radio station in Ireland that commits to the same level of religious broadcasts as we do," says station manager Tommy Marren. "It's an integral part of what we do and who we are and on behalf of everyone in the station I'd like to express my appreciation to the small group who, over the years, have made sure we bring religious services to listeners both on air and online."

One of the more recent religious highlights for Midwest and the *Faith Alive* team was the special broadcast in August 2018 to mark Pope Francis' pilgrimage to Knock Shrine on a morning when the summer skies opened and 45,000 pilgrims were treated to one of those typically wet Mayo days. Although the papal visit was brief – and the numbers in attendance were a mere fraction of the 450,000 who came to see Pope John Paul II in 1979 – the significance of the occasion was not lost on the Midwest team. Paula Donnellan was at Knock Airport when the Aer Lingus plane carrying the pontiff touched down on the famous runway, thus fulfilling the original dream of the airport's founder Mgr James Horan.

"To see the plane coming out of the clouds over Barnacuige that morning was really special," Paula remarks. "Even the build up was special. I'd have been there very early in the morning – everyone had to be there hours in advance – and you could feel the excitement about the place, even among the politicians who are used to turning up at these events all the time."

As the clouds opened and the rain poured down, someone remarked that these weren't raindrops at all; they were the tears of joy of Mgr Horan, that 'old man in a hurry' who had turned a foggy, boggy Mayo hill into an international airport fit for a pope.

Faith Alive is just one example of the many shows that have stood the test of time on Midwest Radio. In an industry known for its fickleness, Paul and Chris have never believed in change for the sake of change, preferring instead to stick to a tried and trusted formula and put their faith in the instinct of presenters with a proven track record. It is not that the co-founders are afraid to experiment – far from it – but equally they don't see a need to fix something that isn't broken.

Several part-time contributors who started out with Midwest on an experimental basis have ended up enjoying long and very fruitful relationships with the station. Ballina woman Majorie Morrow-Nolan, who recently retired from her culinary advice slot on the *Mid Morning Show*, is a perfect example of someone who struck a chord with listeners after broadcasting a short pilot in 1989.

"I began with the simple recipes that I had gathered myself and the letters started piling in looking for copies of them," she recalls. "Then I'd ask listeners to send me in their favourites and the whole thing just snowballed. The whole Midwest experience has been great fun and I've met fantastic people along the way."

Through her weekly contributions to Paul's show, Marjorie became widely known across the West and Northwest and was soon writing culinary columns for provincial newspapers and *Ireland's Own* magazine, as well as making appearances on national television. She has also published several cookery books that have been widely acclaimed.

Paraic Horkan is another regular contributor to have enjoyed a long-time association with Midwest. In Paraic's case, he has been providing gardening advice to listeners since the pirate days when

Horkan's Garden Centre was located on Spencer Street in Castlebar prior to moving to its magnificent headquarters in Turlough.

"People were just starting to get really interested in gardening and when Midwest suggested a radio slot I was delighted to take it on," he explains. "It was quite incredible how many questions we got at the very start and, to be honest, it's the same ever since."

Having initially contributed to the *Tommy Marren Show*, Paraic now has his own weekly one-hour seasonal gardening show on Saturday mornings at 9am. The programme provides a wealth of information on every aspect of gardening.

"Obviously people have become a lot more knowledgeable themselves over the years but we still get a phenomenal response to the programme on Saturday mornings. We still answer all the queries but we have expanded the format. We often bring in special expert contributors on a particular aspect of gardening and even though it's radio I always bring along a few plants to the studio and talk about them. A bit like gardening itself, radio is all about variety."

The Horkan brand has come a long way since those pirate radio days when it occupied its then small premises in Castlebar. The firm now boasts garden centres in Turlough, Westport, Sligo, Galway and Dublin, and Paraic has regularly appeared on *Ireland AM* on Virgin Media Television (formerly TV3).

Midwest's rural roots meant farming was always going to be at the core of its broadcasting schedule from the moment it took to the airwaves as a legal entity. The station's association with North Connacht Farmers resulted in the co-op's former chairman, North Mayo man Billy Heffron, presenting the weekly *Farming Matters* programme in the early days before James McGrath took over later in the 1990s.

When farming became somewhat 'unfashionable' in the Celtic Tiger era, many local radio stations stopped providing regular programmes for farmers or cut back significantly on their agriculture-related output. Midwest, however, persisted with its weekly Wednesday evening show, which has been hosted for well over a decade now by Michael Neary, who grew up on a small farm on the Mayo-Roscommon border.

Michael is typical of the modern farmer in that he combines his work on the land with a 'regular' job as a freelance technician for radio stations across the West and Midlands. He believes it is increasingly difficult – if not impossible – for farmers to be full-time and profitable and worries about the dearth of young men entering a profession that has been the bedrock of rural Ireland for generations.

"When you go to a farmers' meeting, the chances of seeing lads under the age of 35 are slim to nil," he explains. "Those who do attend are fairly disillusioned and they see no incentives. The older farmers too are disheartened. For example, the policy of doing all your applications online is frustrating them. Some don't even own a computer and they just feel like packing it all in."

Michael worries that if the State does not make efforts to accommodate the traditional small farmer of the West of Ireland, the industry will simply die of neglect.

"The danger now is that farms will just be left to waste. The older generation hasn't the energy to keep going and the younger generation simply can't make a go of things. There has to be some element of balance struck to look at the long-term future of smallholdings. There needs to be a place for the smaller farmer as well as the bigger ones."

Farming Matters has had a long association with Teagasc, firstly through James McGrath and Peter Leonard and, more recently, Padraig Walsh, and Michael is very grateful to the team of experts at Teagasc who assist in putting together the weekly slots, as well as the *Farming Scene* report each weekend.

On Bank Holiday Monday, May 7, 2018, Midwest achieved another first for Irish radio when it broadcast live from a working farm, owned by Islandeady couple Padraic and Breege Joyce. The open farm event proved a huge success and the Joyce family received positive feedback from all over the world as people listened to the broadcast via the Internet.

"Kieran McGowan, Brendan Nugent and especially Gerry Glennon were a pleasure to work with, created a fantastic atmosphere and produced a thoroughly enjoyable live programme for everybody who participated as well as the large audience listening at home and abroad," says Breege. "It was such a memorable day for all of us and it is incredible to recall the memories and positive feedback we received."

Michael Neary ended his full-time association with Midwest in 2010 but hopes to continue to combine his twin loves of farming and radio for years to come.

"A bit like farming, Midwest Radio is part of my DNA," he says. "I grew up with it and it's still an important part of my life. Like farming, radio is constantly evolving but I'm delighted to be still involved on a number of levels."

Whether it's preventing bullocks from eating communications cables in Moygownagh or helping heifers to calve in Granlahan, Michael Neary has certainly had a varied career on the farm and in radio these past 30 years. Like his old schoolfriend and long-time collaborator Gerry Glennon, Michael truly is the man for all seasons.

CHAPTER THIRTY-THREE

The yin and yang of Midwest Radio

CHRIS Carroll readily agrees that he and Paul couldn't be more different in personality. "Chalk and cheese" is how he puts it. Certainly, the two former business rivals from Castlerea are the yin and yang of Midwest Radio.

Paul has always been the outgoing, effervescent public face of the station while Chris has diligently worked away in the background, serving Midwest in one vital position after another. During the past 30 years, he has held the roles of production manager, station manager and advertising manager, three positions requiring very different skill-sets but all performed with typical meticulousness and steadfastness. Chris' steady-as-she-goes style has been crucial to the success of Midwest these past 34 years and he is tremendously proud of the enormous impact the station has had on Ireland's broadcasting landscape.

"We didn't plan most of it," he confesses. "Ignorance is bliss and we certainly were very naïve when we started out. When I look back on the pirate days, if I knew back then what was ahead of us and could have foreseen some of the crazy things we were about to do, Midwest would probably never have happened at all."

When Paul Claffey pulled up in his battered Fiat during that long, wet summer in 1985 and dangled the prospect of a pirate radio station in front of Chris, the easiest thing would have been to walk away. The two men weren't even friends – in fact, they were pretty keen rivals – and Paul was in the midst of his financial woes. But Chris, wearing his pragmatist's hat, saw the potential of this unlikely partnership and the two men have worked in harmony ever since, growing the station from the little cloakroom at the back of Midas to a multi-million euro enterprise offering steady employment to dozens and dozens of people over the last three decades.

"We have never had a disagreement in 35 years," says Paul. "I'd have huge regard for Chris and for what he has done with Midwest since 1985. He has been a very loyal colleague and has worked tremendously hard to make a success of this station. Whatever the challenge has been, Chris has always risen to the task."

The mutual respect is reflected in the fact that both men have an unwritten understanding one will never sell his shareholding without the agreement of the other. That pact was put to the ultimate test in 2008 when Celtic Tiger madness reached its dizzy denouement.

"I got a call one day from a guy who explained that he was putting together a consortium to purchase a number of Irish radio stations and wondered would Midwest be interested in being included among them," recalls Paul. "He asked me to name my price and I gave him what I considered to be a crazy figure."

In keeping with the madness of the era, the man rang back a few days later and said the deal was on if the board of Midwest was of a mind to sell. Chris and Paul now had an enormous decision to make. They were being offered riches beyond their wildest dreams but, in their heart of hearts, neither man was overly keen about selling.

"I recall talking it over with my father and he would have advised caution," recalls Chris. "But equally we were both being offered a lot of money for our shareholdings and we were being given the opportunity to continue in our respective roles for another five years. It was a very good deal and we'd have been foolish not to seriously consider it."

The recent, unfortunate demise of Northwest was also at the back of both men's minds. Northwest's value had gone from €4m to €140,000 at the stroke of a pen. What if the same thing happened to Midwest and their shareholdings became worthless overnight? They would never forgive themselves for turning down this incredible offer.

Agreement was reached in principle with the prospective purchasers who were being financed by a UK-based banking institution. Five local radio stations were included in the deal and contracts were due to be signed at the end of September. The new owners visited Midwest on Monday, September 29, 2008, a day etched in Irish history books for very different reasons. This was the day when the Celtic Tiger party officially stopped, the day when the Irish government signed a multi-billion euro bailout for its crumbling banking system amid the worst global economic uncertainty since the Great Depression of the 1930s.

With the so-called international credit crunch worsening in early October, the UK bank financing the Irish radio deal got cold feet and withdrew its offer. The deal was off: Midwest Radio would not be sold after all.

Instead of being bitterly disappointed at the loss of this once-in-a-lifetime financial windfall, Paul and Chris felt curiously relieved and immediately threw themselves into the challenging task of steering the station through the subsequent Irish financial crisis.

"A lot of people might have been gutted in that situation but we never really wanted to sell in the first place," says Chris. "It was just that the offer was so good and there were also other Irish radio stations involved so we felt there probably would never be a better offer for our sector. But when it all ended the way it did we just went back to running the business as if nothing had ever happened."

Chris had taken on the role of advertising manager a few years earlier having enjoyed a very successful stint as station manager that saw Midwest reach the pinnacle by becoming the most listened to local radio station in Ireland. During his period as station manager, Chris received the Fair Play For AirPlay award in 2001 in recognition of his contribution to the Irish music industry.

"There was so much variety and opportunity within the role of station manager so it was a position I enjoyed greatly," he says. "The move to advertising happened by accident really. The position of sales representative for Galway became vacant in the run-up to Christmas and I took it up on a temporary basis. Most of the advertising space had been sold at that stage so it was a case of just getting the scripts and producing the ads."

Chris continued as station manager throughout this period but with no obvious candidate for the vacant sales representative position in Galway, he had a difficult choice to make.

"Targets had to be met so I went out on the road selling ads in January. Galway is a very important source of revenue for Midwest and it was vital we found an advertising executive. Fortunately or unfortunately, I was pretty good at the sales role so after three months I ultimately decided I could best serve the station by concentrating on sales."

Having lived in Co Galway for over a decade, Chris was on familiar ground and the new position also allowed him to spend more time with his young family.

"I'd been doing 12-hour days in Ballyhaunis up to then, leaving the house at seven in the morning and coming home at seven in the evening, so I was seeing very little of my family. Martina and I were blessed with three daughters, Jennifer, Rebekah and Rachael, so at last I could spend a lot more quality time with them and with my son Sol."

The mid-2000s was a good time to sell advertising. Existing businesses were expanding rapidly and new ones were opening everywhere. But everything came to a shuddering halt when the so-called Great Recession struck in 2008.

"The downturn happened so quickly and, like everyone else, we did not see it coming or realise the impact it would have," explains Chris. "Clients who had previously advertised with various media, including Midwest, became a lot more discerning on where they advertised and, in a lot of cases, wondered if they could afford it at all."

Advertising is the lifeblood of local radio because it is the principal – and often sole – source of revenue. Midwest's advertising team expanded throughout the 1990s under the stewardship of Harry McGowan with the likes of Margaret Jennings, Tina Mitchell, Benen Tierney and Martin McHugh all joining the team. Benen had a long history in local radio, having played an important role in former pirate station, County Sound in Galway in the 1980s, while the ever-energetic Martin McHugh was actually an advertiser on Midwest for his Castlebar-based DIY store before joining the sales team. The station had many other stalwart advertising executives over the years including Joan Connors, Bernadette McNeive, Bernie Muldowney, Edmund Barrett, Fiona McHugh, Gary Wynne, Helena Rogan-Mitchell, John Paul Steede, Kevin Sweeney, Linda Beglin, Mike Stewart, Orla Seery,

Padraig Rabbitte, Pam Finn, Mayo footballer Rob Hennelly, Susan Miller and others.

"There have been so many people over the years who have contributed to our advertising sales team and I'd like to take this opportunity to sincerely thank each and every one of them for their great efforts on behalf of Midwest Radio," says Chris. "Our current team of Audrey Duffy, Marie McGuinness, Michelle Delaney and Alan Freeman are continuing to do a fantastic job."

The downturn in late 2008 was a case of déjà vu for Paul and Chris who had cut their teeth in the brutal recession of the 1980s when the loss of a major client could spell disaster.

"When Dunnes made the decision to advertise on pirate radio that was a landmark for the industry," recalls Paul. "The cassette containing the ad would be sent down on the train from Dublin and it was a huge contract for us.

"When we went legal, Lyons Tea started sponsoring our outside broadcasts. Paddy Duggan was the chief executive at the time and he was a great supporter of Midwest. I remember remarking one day at a board meeting that if we ever lost Dunnes or Lyons we'd be in big trouble. We ended up losing the two of them in the same week. It was Armageddon!"

But Midwest navigated its way through that particular crisis and would do so again two decades later.

"My belief and confidence in Midwest as the best option in an extremely competitive media environment never wavered and I set about instilling that in the rest of the sales team," says Chris. "We recruited some new people, embarked on training programmes and got ready for the battle ahead. What doesn't break you will make you stronger and we survived the recession with little impact on our business model."

Today, Midwest is stronger than it's ever been and a demographical breakdown of its listenership suggests the station has a more cross-generational appeal now than it did 30 years ago.

"When we started we were regarded as a black pudding Country music station with a limited lifespan," says Chris. "The expectation in some quarters was that when Country music would begin to wane we'd do the same. But that hasn't happened at all. We've grown our listenership over the years by evolving seamlessly. Half the people who listened to us 30 years ago have passed on but a new generation has embraced Midwest and they have the same loyalty to the station as their parents or maybe even grandparents had back in the day."

Ironically, the very thing that was seen as Midwest's potential weak-link in 1989 – its commitment to Country music – has become a key factor in the growing popularity of the station over the last decade. Country music is now more fashionable than ever and young stars like Nathan Carter and Mike Denver are attracting a younger audience, one that is more open-minded about its choice of music than previous generations.

"*Wagon Wheel* [Carter's smash hit in the summer of 2012] was the song that changed Country music in Ireland," says Chris. "It opened a whole new generation to the power of Country music and Midwest certainly reaped the benefits from that."

Midwest's listenership is higher now than it was 30 years ago; not bad for a station many believed wouldn't make it past the 1990s.

While Chris and the other advertising sales executives have kept the wolf from the door through the worst recession in living memory, station manager Tommy Marren and the broadcasting team have ensured Midwest remains relevant in a rapidly changing media landscape. The meteoric rise of the Internet has transformed the way the public consumes news and Midwest has wholeheartedly embraced the new technology. There was a time when the station's news team structured its day around the three main bulletins – morning, noon and evening – but now news reporting is a 24-7 business.

"The immediacy is the big thing," says Teresa O'Malley. "Technology has brought its own pressures and everyone wants to be first now. As soon as I have a story completed it's on the air. The deadlines are by the second now, not the minute."

The decade began with another momentous occasion for Midwest's current affairs team when Enda Kenny was elected the country's thirteenth Taoiseach in March 2011.

"That night at the TF in Castlebar when Enda arrived as Taoiseach-elect was really memorable," says Teresa. "There was a frenzy of national and international media in the count centre but Enda took time to do an interview with Midwest before he entered."

Inevitably, in a GAA-mad county like Mayo, the fate of the senior football team has also dominated the local airwaves this past decade. Four All-Ireland finals in six years kept Angelina McHugh and the team busy through the mid-2010s and Midwest continued to expand its sports coverage despite the budgetary constraints prompted by the recession. These days the station broadcasts up to 70 live commentaries per annum, which is a far cry from 1996 when 24 was a new record. Michael D McAndrew is one of the young commentators to emerge in recent years and the Glenamoy man is proud to follow in the footsteps of men like Willie Ryan, Mike Finnerty and Rob Murphy.

Michael grew up listening to the likes of The Shoe and Angelina on Midwest and always had a keen interest in broadcasting. He studied journalism at Coláiste Dhulaigh in Dublin before completing an honours degree in broadcasting and journalism at the University of Wolverhampton that included stints with BBC Birmingham and other local stations in England.

"I got a great understanding of radio in England but there is definitely a greater appetite for radio in Ireland and Midwest has been the best learning curve of all for me. I love sport so I'm really in my comfort zone doing the sports show."

Michael D took on the additional responsibilities of GAA commentator in 2017 and has really developed into the role, striking up a fantastic partnership with co-commentator and former Mayo GAA star Martin Carney.

"Martin has a lot of experience from RTÉ over the years and he'd have commentated on All-Ireland finals with the likes of Ger Canning," says Michael D. "He was a great mentor to me when I started doing the commentaries and was always offering me constructive feedback."

Some local radio commentators wait a lifetime for the chance to describe their county's involvement in an All-Ireland final but Michael D got to do it in his debut season.

"2017 was a real heartbreaker. I had a sheet with some rough notes just to keep me from losing it altogether in those final moments if Mayo were on the cusp of winning," he recalls. "I was getting the sheet ready after Lee Keegan scored that goal into the Hill but unfortunately it wasn't to be and I ended up scrunching the piece of paper in my fist as the final whistle blew! Hopefully, I'll need to write a new one for 2020."

When Angelina took up a communications post with Mayo Roscommon Hospice in 2019, Michael D was the obvious candidate for sports editor and is looking forward to bringing Midwest's listeners some top-class sports coverage in the decade ahead.

"Our listenership for sport remains as strong as ever and one of the things that has changed in the last decade has been the number of people overseas who listen to the games via the Internet. It's great to be able to provide a service for people who'd love to be in MacHale Park or Croke Park but cannot be there for whatever reason."

These days Midwest has a vast team of freelance reporters and contributors across a range of sports. Men like Billy Fitzpatrick and Eamonn Clarke pioneered the co-commentator role in the 1990s and a new generation has picked up the baton in the 21st century. Tommy Marren is keen to pay tribute to the many people who have contributed to Midwest's sports coverage over the past 30 years. One person who is very sadly missed is Jeremy Dee from down the road in Bekan who was the station's soccer correspondent up to his tragic death in a road accident in 2012.

Michael D wasn't long at Midwest when he discovered the vagaries of live broadcasting. Mayo were playing Tyrone in a National Football League tie and Michael D, who was holding the fort back at base, stepped out of the studio to go to the toilet when some gremlins got into the works and Mass ended up being broadcast across the live commentary for a short period. One minute Aidan O'Shea was leaping for the ball and the next Fr Stephen Farragher was saying the Our Father. Bewildered listeners were left wondering whether Midwest was piloting a new method of exorcism and that the interruption was part of a cunning plan to finally rid the county of its infamous GAA curse. Meanwhile, an equally bemused Michael D had just learned the oldest broadcasting lesson of all: that when it comes to live radio, anything – absolutely anything – can happen.

Paul Claffey was inducted into Irish radio's Hall of Fame in 2014 when he received a PPI award, taking his place alongside broadcasting luminaries like Gay Byrne, Micheál Ó Muircheartaigh and Gerry Ryan. It was a humbling moment for a man who never saw himself as a broadcaster when he started out on his pirate voyage in 1985.

"I was a dancehall promoter, a band manager, a salesman, I was lots of things but I wouldn't have seen myself as a broadcaster," he says. "I only went into it because there was nobody else to do it!"

Like so many of his Midwest colleagues, Paul may have been an 'accidental' broadcaster but he took to it like the proverbial duck to water and quickly earned a reputation as the West of Ireland's answer to Gay Byrne or Gerry Ryan. Indeed, few, if any, broadcasters have succeeded in stamping their personalities on a local radio station in the way Paul has done at Midwest. Whether it is death notices, Radio Bingo or taking a bog to New York, the Castlerea man has done things that are so utterly outlandish one might be forgiven for thinking he is blessed with extraordinary good fortune. But it takes more than the rub of the green to bring a pirate station from a poky cloakroom and turn it into a multi-million euro venture. Claffey is widely respected within the media industry as somebody who is always a step or two ahead of the posse and who is never afraid to try something a little different.

"I'm always thinking outside the box. I can be driving along and suddenly I think of something that I feel would capture people's imagination. It might sound insane at first but when we think it through it actually works. It probably drives some of the staff crazy but I think they know how my brain works by now! We've done things no other radio station in the world would ever contemplate and that's what makes us so different and appealing."

Paul and Chris are quick to acknowledge the role the staff – both past and present – have played in making Midwest the successful radio station it is today.

"Our on-air team are superb but so too are those involved in administration, sales, marketing and technical," says Paul. "Running a radio station is a formidable challenge and there are so many pieces to the puzzle. We are lucky to have a team that is so passionate, making sure we deliver the full package."

In his role as managing director, Paul obviously works very closely with the accounts team and says Midwest has been blessed to have had outstanding financial controllers over the years, starting with Claremorris native Tom Monaghan in 1989 followed by Louisburgh's John O'Toole and Dubliner Enda Carberry, who is now the company secretary. The current chief financial officer is Bernie Greally who started out working with Paul in Midas back in the 1980s as a teenager when she'd make her way through the packed nightclub collecting bottles and glasses.

"Bernie went to England, got her accountancy qualifications and came back to Ireland," explains Paul. "She joined us here and now she is the chief bottle-washer! On a serious note, it is wonderful to see somebody develop like that and I have always enjoyed watching the career paths of people who started out as youngsters at Midwest or Midas and gone on to achieve great things in their careers."

While some staff move on quickly to pursue careers elsewhere others have stuck the course with Midwest, including Sharon Behan-Woods who began as Paul's PA in the summer of 1989.

"I started in the reception department and I remember at that time there was just one computer in the department," she recalls. "If ever the plug disconnected the whole system would go down and we'd have to start all over again!"

Sharon's friendly face greets visitors on arrival at Midwest's reception desk and her duties involve both administration and programming.

"The work is varied and there's always something going on around the place. A lot of people drop into reception out of curiosity just to see what a radio station looks like and we do our best to make them feel as welcome as possible."

While Sharon greets visitors in reception, Patrina McDonnell (now Cunniffe) is invariably the first voice members of the public hear when they telephone the station. Patrina plays a pivotal role in co-ordinating and directing the massive volume of calls to the station on a daily basis.

"It's a job where you find yourself in touch with the public at different levels and although the job requires lots of patience I just love the whole atmosphere around a busy switchboard and text messaging service."

Chris Carroll says the phenomenal success of Midwest can be attributed to a talented and devoted staff who will always go the extra mile for the station.

"The staff are without doubt the best people I know at what they do. Their loyalty has been unwavering throughout the last 30 years, including through some very difficult times. The dedication, professionalism and friendship they bring to each and every working day generates a pride in me that is immeasurable. I have always regarded myself as a colleague rather than a manager."

At the apex of the Midwest Radio structure is the board of directors, which meets several times each year and is always available to offer valuable advice and guidance.

"Our board has been remarkable and I'm proud to say that in the 30 years we've been on air we have never once had to take a vote at board level," says Paul. "That, in itself, is unique."

The board has seen much change over the years and the only members remaining from that first meeting in the International Hotel in Knock more than 30 years ago are Paul, Chris and chairman Michael Hughes. The two newspapers and Knock Airport are no longer shareholders but the others, namely Aurivo and the Federation of Western Churches, are still involved.

"Michael Hughes once said to me that the only constant is change and it's a comment I have never forgotten," says Chris. "Change is inevitable and it is how we embrace it that defines us. We must prepare for the future of Midwest Radio and embrace the changes on how we deliver our programmes, on the alternatives to broadcasting these programmes to a wider audience terrestrially and through the Internet and social media.

"We enjoy a considerable listenership through our online streams from around the world. This listenership is increasing daily and we are beginning to capitalise on that and through the volume of traffic to our website.

"If we don't keep abreast of what's happening locally, nationally and internationally we will fall behind. But Paul and I have always been good at adapting to whatever changes have come our way and I believe we will continue to do that."

A need to find a financial backer for the purchase of the all-important medium wave transmitter prompted Paul to slam on the brakes as he drove through Castlerea all those years ago, but such is the change happening in broadcasting in the 21st century that the managing director can envisage a day in the not-too-distant future when transmitters won't be needed at all.

"Transmitters will be obsolete in another five years because everyone will be listening on their smart-phones. The challenge now is to establish a global audience for what we do."

Midwest's willingness to embrace the Internet at an early stage has given it a healthy headstart over its contemporaries and it boasts annual online traffic that is the envy of many larger media outlets. Pages views on its website now run into the millions every year while the income from online advertising has grown enormously.

"The challenge now is to get a global audience and make money on it," says Paul. "In the old days, we struggled to get a signal to Achill Island; now we can be heard loud and clear on Staten Island! The Internet presents lots of opportunities and we hope to make the most of them in the coming years."

Both men readily acknowledge they are not getting any younger. The difficult decision on when to hand on the baton will have to be made at some point in the future, probably within the next decade. It is not something they give a great deal of thought to at the moment because they are both still as passionate about Midwest as they were 34 years ago when Chris set up his disco equipment in the Casino ballroom in Castlerea and they recorded some sample ads.

Their little pirate ship has brought them on a magical voyage they could never have imagined and they hope there's a fair few nautical miles to travel yet. Some of the current staff weren't even been born in December 1985 when Paul and Chris were erecting loudspeakers on the footpath outside Midas and playing non-stop ads for Paddy Ryan's USA biscuits, but the long-time business partners are still doing what they do best all these years later.

The yin and yang of Midwest Radio wouldn't have it any other way.

MIDWEST RADIO STAFF: OCTOBER 27, 2019

Paul Claffey
Managing Director

Paul has been Managing Director of Midwest Radio since its inception in 1989. The Castlerea-native also presents the *Mid-Morning Show* between 11am and 1pm with his unique broadcasting style where entertainment is mingled with a touch of craziness and fun. He has received numerous radio awards over the past 25 years culminating in the Hall of Fame award by the PPI in 2014 for his outstanding contribution to radio broadcasting in Ireland. Since 2011 Paul has co-presented a very popular twice-weekly TV programme on Ireland West Music TV.

Chris Carroll
Sales Manager

Chris hails from Castlerea and is a Director of Midwest Radio. He has many roles within the organisation that encompasses both on-air and off-air duties. His broadcasting career extends across a range of music programmes and he currently presents the popular *Country Classics Show* daily from 1.30 to 3.00. As Sales Manager he co-ordinates the entire Sales team within the company

Tommy Marren
Station Manager

Tommy is a native of Tourlestrane in Co Sligo. After a short stint in the banking industry he joined Midwest Radio as a sports presenter in 1989. The following year he became Station Manager of Northwest Radio which covered the Sligo/North Leitrim/South Donegal region. He was appointed Station Manager of Midwest Radio in 2007 and presents the popular morning current affairs show between 9 and 11 am.

Gerry Glennon
Producer/Presenter

Since joining Midwest Radio at the tender age of 18 during the pirate radio era Gerry has presented, produced and being involved in a wide range of programming on both radio and TV. He comes from Granlahan, County Roscommon and currently co-presents the *Mid-Morning Show* and a twice-weekly show on Ireland West Music TV.

David Cawley

Production Manager/Presenter

David is Midwest Radio's earliest riser! The Castlebar man has presented the highly popular breakfast show on Midwest Radio for 20 years and his chirpy presentation style has woken up more than one generation. He is also Midwest Radio's Production Manager and is passionate about making sure that Midwest delivers an authentic sound that is very much the hallmark of the station's success

Teresa O'Malley

Head of News

Although born in Boston, Teresa is very much a Mayo woman. Having moved to Foxford at early age she trained as a National School teacher. However, the broadcast bug took hold and in 1989 she joined the current-affairs department and presented the weely *Wednesday Report* programme. She has been Midwest Radio's Head of News since 1997 and during that time has won seven national and one international broadcasting award.

Michael D. McAndrew

Head of Sport

Michael D. comes from Glenamoy in north Mayo. His career with Midwest includes music, sport and news broadcasting. He trained in journalism at the University of Wolverhampton which included broadcasting stints with the BBC itself! As Head of Sport and a passionate sports enthusiast he can now mix business with pleasure.

Paula Donnellan

News Journalist

Paula studied communications in DCU before taking up a role with Shannonside Radio. However, three years later she joined Midwest Radio and anchored the breakfast show before moving into the News department. She is the recipient of a number of awards during her broadcasting career and although she hails from Castlerea she now resides in Ballyhaunis.

John Morley

News Journalist

John joined the Midwest Radio news team in July 2019. He is a native of Ballyglass, Claremorris. He has a BA in Journalism from DCU and has worked for a number of media outlets including the *Mayo News* and Newstalk's *Off The Ball*.

Padraic Walsh
Head of Music/Presenter

Padraic is the man behind the *Late Late Lunchbox* – a lively mix of afternoon music and competitions every weekday from 3 to 5.30pm. He is also Head of Music and is heavily involved in the Production Department of Midwest Radio. He comes from Castlerea and apart from the microphone he loves having a golf club in his hands.

Brendan Nugent
IT Manager/Presenter

Brendan was born in Longford but now lives in Ballaghaderreen. He started his career in Shannonside Radio at the tender age of 19 before joining Northwest Radio in the mid-1990s. He was appointed to the technical team in Midwest Radio in 2004. As well as responsibility for IT, transmission and outside broadcasts he also presents *Classic Express* every Monday to Friday from 6 to 8pm,

Enda Carberry
Company Secretary

Having joined Midwest Radio as Chief Financial Officer in 2001, the Dublin native quickly made Mayo his home – immersing himself in ladies GAA both at underage and senior level for a number of years. However, in 2018 he decided to pursue new opportunities in Australia where he now resides.

Bernie Greally
Financial Controller

After leaving Ballyhaunis Community School, Bernie moved to London to start a career in the accounting sector. When she returned to Ireland in 1990 she joined the accounts department and was appointed Financial Controller in 2018. Bernie is a proud Rossie and was born in the parish of Gortaganny.

Mary Raftery
Credit Controller

One of Midwest Radio's 'originals', Mary has been with the station since 1989. She began working as a receptionist before moving on to the accounts and credit control department. Along the way Mary presented various programmes – including the much loved sponsored programmes. Her abiding memory will always be the very first request she took on July 24, 1989.

Erika Ryan
Accounts Assistant

Erika joined Midwest Radio's account department in 2017. She studied Commerce at NUI, Galway. The Knock native is a passionate athlete and is a member of the Mayo Athletic Club and Claremorris Cycling Club.

Audrey Duffy
Sales Executive

Audrey is from Knockmore in north Mayo and is based at the Midwest Radio studios in Ballina. She has a degree in Economics and Social Policy and has been a staff member for the past ten years. Her family is steeped in the world of show jumping.

Marie McGuinness
Sales Executive

A beauty therapist by profession, Marie always had an interest in marketing and sales and so it was no surprise when she opted to join the Midwest Radio sales team in 2012. She is a native of Kiltimagh but now lives in Knock.

Michelle Delaney
Advertising Executive

Michelle lives in Tulrahan, Claremorris but is equally proud of her Bekan connection. She has spent all of her working career in Sales and Marketing roles. Apart from work, Michelle considers traditional music a big part of her life – particularly playing the fiddle.

Alan Freeman
Sales Executive

Alan Freeman is a native of Castlerea and joined the sales team in 2019. Prior to that he worked for a number of agencies including CPM. He is an avid Glasgow Celtic supporter and would also count the GAA as one of his other great sporting passions.

Sharon Behan-Woods
Office Administrator

Sharon joined Midwest Radio just weeks after the station went on air in 1989. She carries out a series of duties within both programming and administration for Midwest Radio and Ireland West Music TV. Born in Manchester ,Sharon moved to Kilkelly at the age of 11 and away from work she is deeply involved in the Eire Og GAA club.

Patrina Cunniffe
Head On-Air Receptionist

Patrina – a native of Swinford – joined Midwest Radio in 1995. She plays an active role in the day-to-day running of the station. She co-ordinates her responsibilities between both administration and programming duties to keep both listeners and presenters happy.

Cathy Regan
Receptionist

Cathy joined the Midwest Radio receptionist department in 1999. She was born in London where she worked in a number of administrative roles including a term at the BBC. She moved to Ireland in 1996 and now regards Ireland as very much her home.

Patsy Browne
Receptionist

Patsy is a native of Cloonfad and has had a long career in various administrative roles. She worked in England for ten years before returning to Dublin where she spent a further eleven years in various administrative roles.

Teresa Cunningham
Receptionist

Teresa was born in Ballinlough, Co Roscommon. After second-level education she joined the Civil Service where she spent a total of 15 years. In 1999, she joined the Midwest Radio receptionist department and works predominantly at weekends and is currently employed as an interviewer with the ERSI.

Kieran McGowan
Maintenance Manager

Kieran was born in London and at the tender age of six moved to Castlerea. After finishing school he returned to the UK to work in the construction sector. Music has been a huge part of his life having been involved in the family band for many years. As well as looking after the maintenance of the Midwest studios in Ballyhaunis, Castlebar and Ballina, he also drives the Midwest Radio Satellite Cruiser.

Eileen Sloyan
Caretaker

Eileen is from Castlerea and spent the first ten years of her working in Elphin, Co Roscommon. For the past 15 years, Eileen has been responsible for keeping the Midwest Radio broadcast centre spick and span.

Jacinta Moyles
Receptionist

Jacinta first came to Midwest Radio in 2001 and has worked in our News Room, Traffic and Reception, as well as other administrative roles. She's from Foxford and now lives in Kilfian.

CURRENT PRESENTERS

Eamon Kelly
Michael Goulding
Joe Byrne
Michael Commins
Michael Neary
Tim Norton
Brendan Roache
Philip Costello
Deirdre Kelly
Fineinn Quinn
Eunice Moran
Noel Grogan
Eamon McPhilomey
Beverley Stafford
Brendan Hoban
Monica Morley
Laurita Blewitt
Brendan Magee
Viv Brennan
Seamus Duffy
Mildred Byrne

AUTHOR'S NOTE

My year of 'Magic & Madness'

ON Christmas Week 2018, I took part in a book promotion at the Castle Bookshop in Castlebar from where Tommy Marren was doing an outside broadcast. I had just completed a mammoth publication for Aurivo Co-operative Society and was looking forward to a long sabbatical from the pressure-filled world of book publishing. Tommy wasn't convinced, however.

"You'll be writing a book again next year, mark my words," he proclaimed as we exited the Castle Bookshop.

I stopped in my tracks.

"Tommy, read my lips, there won't be a book in 2019."

Later that afternoon, I was back in the office in Ballina when the telephone rang. It was Tommy.

"I know you said earlier you weren't going to do another book for a while but I was just chatting to Paul and we had a bit of an oul idea..."

So, ten months later, here I am.

It was impossible to say no to the Midwest Radio project because I knew the material would be so good the book would write itself. And it certainly has. Researching and writing this book has been a hugely enjoyable experience and one that has reinforced my respect for what Midwest has achieved over the past 30 years.

My earliest memories of Midwest are of those anarchic *Sunday Night Live* broadcasts from Midas back in the late 1980s and that unforgettable Connacht Final commentary from Liam Horan on the week the newly-licensed station went live in July 1989.

Like anyone who grew up in Mayo in the 1990s, Midwest is part of the soundtrack of my youth and as a journalist I have come to know and greatly respect the station's staff who do such sterling work week in and week out, be it in news, sport or entertainment. It has been a privilege, therefore, to chronicle their efforts in these pages and I hope *Magic & Madness* does them justice.

Writing a book is a bit like climbing a mountain. The writer sets off with unbridled enthusiasm before reaching that dreaded, energy-sapping midway stage where the summit seems a long, long way off but returning to base is no longer an option. A good guide is always helpful and my 'Sherpa' during this expedition was that wonderful stalwart of local radio, Gerry Glennon, a man possessed of an encyclopaedic knowledge of Midwest Radio. Anyone who knows Gerry will agree that he is a broadcaster of immense talent and versatility and I came to rely greatly on his expertise and judgement during this project. However, any missteps are entirely my own; after all, the Sherpa can only do so much!

I have drawn heavily on newspaper archives for a lot of material in this book, including many interviews with Midwest's current, former and deceased staff and presenters. In particular, I want to credit the station's 25th-anniversary publication, researched and edited by Tommy Marren, which was a fantastic resource. Similarly, local newspaper supplements published in the *Western People* and *Connaught Telegraph* at the time of the launch in 1989 proved invaluable.

Old pictures always evoke a rich tapestry of memories and I am particularly grateful to my old friend from Westport, Frank Dolan, for supplying material from his extensive photographic collection and to Aidan Connaughton, Shrule, for delving into the archives of his father, Michael.

Sincere thanks to everybody who provided interviews, shared memories or assisted in any way with this project. In particular, I wish to thank Paul Claffey, Chris Carroll and Michael Hughes for their invaluable inputs throughout the past year and to all of the team at Midwest who have made me feel so welcome on my frequent visits in 2019; my sincere appreciation also to Seán Lynch for his wonderful design skills… and his patience.

Finally, thanks to Tommy Marren for landing me with this project! On a serious note, Tommy has been a great media colleague and friend for well over a decade and I really appreciate this opportunity to record the history of my local radio station. Once-off projects like this don't come along too often and it is lovely to be part of them when they do.

I'm also conscious of Midwest's long-standing relationship with the *Western People* since 1989 and am delighted to continue the tradition of co-operation between our two media organisations.

Gerry, Tommy and myself spent October Bank Holiday Saturday in Midwest's offices in Ballyhaunis pouring over the final proofs. When everything was completed and I was preparing to leave, Gerry – with tongue firmly planted in cheek – remarked: "So, Laffey, what's the next project?"

"Read my lips…" I began.

"But I think I've found a *really* good one for you…"

Don't go there, Gerry, don't go there!

I hope you have all enjoyed reading this book as much as I have enjoyed my year of 'Magic & Madness'.

Here's to the next 30 years of Midwest Radio.

James Laffey
October 28, 2019